CIVILIZATION AND THE CAESARS

The Intellectual Revolution in the Roman Empire

CHESTER G. STARR is Professor of History at the University of Illinois. He was Visiting Professor at the University of Michigan in the summer of 1950 and at the University of Washington for the 1963-64 academic year. A graduate of the University of Missouri, Professor Starr took his Ph.D. at Cornell in 1938. During the Second World War he became Chief of the Historical Section of HQ Fifth Army in Italy, where in 1944 and 1945 he directed the writing and publication of the nine-volume *Fifth Army History*. He was a Fellow of the American Academy in Rome from 1938 to 1940, a Guggenheim Fellow in 1950-51 and in 1958-59, and became a Member of the Center for Advanced Study at the University of Illinois in 1963. His publications include: *Roman Imperial Navy* (1941, 1960); *From Salerno to the Alps* (1954); *Emergence of Rome as Ruler of the Western World* (1950, 1953); *Civilization and the Caesars* (1954); *Intellectual Heritage of the Early Middle Ages,* editor (1957); *History of the World,* 2 vols., with others (1960); *Origins of Greek Civilization, 1100-650 B. C.* (1962); *History of the Ancient World* (1965); and many articles and reviews.

Augustus Caesar (from Prima Porta), in the Vatican Museum, Rome.
Photograph from Brunn-Bruckmann,
Griechische und römische Porträts 703.

CIVILIZATION
and the CAESARS
The Intellectual Revolution
in the Roman Empire

CHESTER G. STARR

Professor of History, University of Illinois

The Norton Library
W · W · NORTON & COMPANY · INC ·
NEW YORK

Books That Live
The Norton imprint on a book means that in the publisher's
estimation it is a book not for a single season but for the years.
W. W. Norton & Company, Inc.

ISBN 0 393 00322 1

PRINTED IN THE UNITED STATES OF AMERICA

67890

In Memoriam
M. L. W. LAISTNER
1890-1959

Preface

THE purpose of this work is an interpretive survey of a crucial period in the development of civilization, the four centuries from Cicero to Augustine. In this era classical civilization collapsed, and the bases for the modern view of man and the world emerged in pagan and Christian circles alike.

Rather than heaping up catalogues of names, I have concentrated upon typical or significant thinkers who must be considered at proper length. Always, moreover, my aim has been to search for the inter-relations and roots of the major developments. Since the political evolution of the Early Empire is taken up early, in order that cultural changes may be set in a proper light, let me make clear that the fundamental forces were not political in character. The reader who wishes to have in mind from the outset the very different elements which I consider primary may find a brief summation in Chapter XII, but the proof in any historical study must lie in its extended description of the course of civilization in the Empire.

The longer I have pondered the nature of history, the more clearly I have felt that the source of its enduring strength and appeal has been the fact that its generalizations arise out of concrete events which have definite location in time and space. Although the following pages con-sider some of the major problems of human development, my discussion has been cast always in historical, not in philosophical, terms; yet I hope that the same factors may be found to account alike for the

decline of classical civilization and also for the appearance in the same centuries of a new outlook.

The large scope of the study has forced me to forego detailed docu-mentation; full references to ancient and modern literature would require a large volume in themselves. My debt, conscious and unconscious, to modern scholarship is nevertheless a great one; the bibliography is intended to suggest that debt in some detail.

Ancient sources I have usually cited in the translations of the Loeb Classical Library, by the courtesy of the Harvard University Press. For the major works of Tacitus I have used the translations of G. G. Ramsay, published by John Murray of London. Passages from Virgil's *Georgics* are in the fine version by C. Day Lewis (copyright 1940, 1947, by Oxford University Press), and passages from the *Aeneid* in the translation by Rolfe Humphries (copyright 1951 by Charles Scribner's Sons), each with permission of the publisher. The use of other translations is indicated by the addition of the translator's name in parentheses. I am indebted for further permission to quote as follows: *Cambridge Ancient History*, Cambridge University Press; M. L. W. Laistner, *Christianity and Pagan Culture*, Cornell University Press; G. H. Sabine and B. S. Smith, *Cicero on the Commonwealth*, Ohio State University Press; and Herbert Box's translation of *In Flaccum*, Oxford University Press.

The argument of this book is based on artistic as well as on literary evidence. For permission to reproduce some important examples I am obligated to F. Bruckmann KG (Brunn-Bruckmann; Ernst Pfuhl, *Malerei und Zeichnung der Griechen*); W. de Gruyter & Co. (*Die Antike; Antike Denkmäler; Jahrbuch des Deutschen Archäologischen Instituts;* L'Orange-Gerkan, *Der Spätantike Bildschmuck des Konstantinsbogens*); Archaeological Institute of America (*American Journal of Archaeology*); La Libreria dello Stato (Moretti, *Ara Pacis Augustae*); and Phaidon Press, Ltd. (Thassilo von Scheffer, *Die Kultur der Griechen*).

In this edition typographical and factual errors have been corrected, as far as I am aware of their existence; but the text has not seemed to need alteration either in substance or in line of argument. Subsequent investigations, indeed, of the other extreme of classical civilization — its origins in Greece from 1100 to 650 B.C. — have sharpened my feeling that the picture drawn in these pages reflects some of the basic qualities and innate weaknesses of the ancient structure of civilization.

CHESTER G. STARR

Champaign, Illinois
March, 1965

Contents

List of Plates

xiii

Part One

THE END OF THE
ROMAN REPUBLIC

The End of the Roman Republic

THE development of Rome spans a full millennium of human history, which historians are accustomed to divide into two parts, the Republic and the Empire. The point of division lies shortly before the birth of Christ, when the young Caesar Octavian seized the Roman political machinery. A convenient year to mark the change is 27 B.C., in which Octavian received the honorific title of Augustus. Thenceforth the Mediterranean world was subject to that famous series of rulers now called the Roman emperors or Caesars. The Roman Empire has often been eulogized as an era of lasting peace, but to gain that peace the subjects of the emperors surrendered their destinies to the arbitrary whims of absolutism.

Before coming to the implications of this situation, we must consider briefly the Roman Republic, for men of the Empire long continued to be influenced by ideas and customs which had developed before the days of Augustus. The Republic, in turn, had borrowed heavily from the great treasury of Greek civilization, which had been heaping up its riches while Rome was still winning domination of the Italian peninsula.

Especially in the last century of the Republic came a great cultural efflorescence, rising to its peak in the figure of Cicero, whose alert mind swept widely over the field of knowledge of his day. The true nature of the Greco-Roman synthesis of the last century before Christ has not always been appreciated. Those who are blinded by the glories of Greece are inclined to deny any originality to Greco-Roman culture, but to take

3

this stand is to lose a main key to the understanding of the development of imperial civilization. While the forms and techniques employed in the arts and letters of the Late Republic were very largely Greek, the spirit expressed therein was a new one.

Our main concern, however, must be the Roman Empire. This structure was an autocracy which swallowed up with ever-more-ravenous appetite the political powers of the aristocracy, of the cities within the Empire, and of the individual humans; a remarkable aspect of the process is the fact that the subjects, for the most part, voluntarily sacrificed their political freedom to the ideal of the father-emperor. A modern observer, perplexed and alarmed by the frightening rise of autocracies today, may well speculate on the effects of ancient Caesarism, especially when he notes that classical civilization collapsed while the Caesars ruled Rome. The problem is a significant one, which must be examined carefully; the conclusion must yet be that the decline of ancient culture cannot be attributed primarily to the effects of the political system. The experience of the Roman Empire, in other words, suggests that the human mind can never be permanently crushed by autocracy.

If political repression did not produce the decline, then what were its causes? The main area in which the historian must always search for his answers lies within the human being himself, and here may be found the answer to our question.

The individual in Greece and Rome was limited in his freedom to think for himself and to express his thoughts; ancient man did not enjoy the measure of individuality which is taken for granted in the modern Western world. Civilization was still too precarious and hard-won an achievement to be imperiled by the free play of individuals. An occasional hero or tyrant might fill a stage with his swelling personality, but men as a mass might express themselves only within very definite limits. In ancient times the rational world under human control was separated merely by a thin barrier from the vast world of nature, where untamed forces roamed up and down, beating at the boundary. The state, again, might demand body and soul, fortune and life, from its citizens.

Accordingly, liberty of thought never developed into an ideal virtue in ancient civilization; or, in more general terms, the human was not viewed as a cosmically significant individual. As civilization advanced, however, the prescriptive demands of the society and political groups enfolding man lost their potency, and the mind found ever greater range for its exercise. The counterpart was the rise of autocrats of one or another type, to whom men surrendered their political capacities.

In the Empire the release of the individual from his old ties reached its completion. In this fact must be found the basic cause at once for the inexorable decline of the old structure of Greco-Roman thought and also for the rise of a new order of thought; a major aspect of the argument of the following pages is its insistence that these two factors, too often disjoined in modern analyses, are intimately connected in their essential causes. The new order of thought is best demonstrated in Christianity, but it was not originated by Christian thinkers. The intellectual revolution in the Roman Empire was an internal, general movement of ancient society independent of creed or of class.

Since modern civilization rests squarely upon the new view of the nature of man and the world hammered out in the four centuries from Cicero to Augustine, we may justly term the era of the Caesars one of the great turning points in human intellectual development, worthy to be placed beside the formative years of Greek civilization. To prove this statement and to illumine in detail the causes of sterility and fertility in imperial thought is the function of the last part of this work.

I

The Horizon of Republican Culture

DURING the last century before Christ the Republic was dying, but Roman culture was thriving. To appreciate both aspects of the era there can be no better guide than Cicero (106–43 B.C.). In his political activities Cicero was a patriot who tried to save the Republic and lost his life as a result. Intellectually he was the most gifted luminary of the extraordinarily productive last generation of the Republic.

Cicero's World and Its Sources

The world of Cicero was an advanced system, and behind it lay centuries of political and cultural development. Geographically the center was the Mediterranean Sea, on or close to whose shores lay the major cities and seats of learning. Only in the East could a man travel away from the sea and still expect to find marks of civilization. To the south was the Sahara, to the west the ocean, to the north the uncivilized stretches of Europe, into which Roman arms had thus far penetrated only a brief distance.

Politically all the Mediterranean shores were directly or indirectly under Roman sway. The western half of the basin had been conquered as Rome moved out of the Italian peninsula during the later part of the third century B.C.; Roman rule of the eastern Mediterranean had been established in the century before Cicero's birth. This part of the world was the home of Hellenistic culture, as we term the civilization resulting from Alexander's conquest of the Orient (334–323 B.C.).

Many of the ideas imparted to Cicero in his years of education under Greek philosophers and rhetoricians had been created in the Hellenistic Age by men who wrestled with the problems of humanity in the great world of that era and who were fired by the expansion of the horizon which followed the conquest of Alexander. The original impetus to Greek civilization, however, lay far behind the Hellenistic world in the Greek city-states about the Aegean Sea, which had come into existence in the dim centuries of the Homeric period. To this originally simple development more than to any other event Western civilization owes its genesis.

Not all of Cicero's views could be traced to Hellenistic and Greek thinkers. His speech was Latin, and he prided himself a Roman; he had frequented the houses of great nobles, had watched the processes of Roman government and law, had even served briefly in the army. In family customs, in views on government, and less obviously in his concepts of man's place in life, this polished, civilized man of the first century B.C. had inherited a great deal from the pattern of Roman thought which had been formed before the Roman conquest of the Mediterranean.

The ancient world, in sum, was a far simpler structure than modern society, but the influences which beat upon Cicero were of greatly diverse origin and character. By the time of the Late Republic these influences had been partly amalgamated and outwardly unified by two centuries of conscious cultural adjustment between Greece and Rome; behind the horizon of Cicero's age lay a significant liberation of man in both Greek and Roman spheres. This process deserves at least brief attention, for it is an underlying development of great significance in intellectual history.

Greek Limits on the Individual

In his *Republic* Cicero contrasted the Roman and Greek spirits. The latter he visualized as one of rampant individualism; the former, as one of submergence of the individual in the good of the group. This was a favorite contrast for the proud Roman of the Late Republic. When one compares the enduring cohesion of Roman society and the individualistic, often politically indifferent Greeks of his day, it has some justification, but in the root of the matter it is an extraordinary reversal of the truth.

Although not all Greeks were organized into city-states, that was the vital form of political structure in Greek history; and the city-state was by virtue of its very smallness a jealous claimant for its citizens' loyalties. The aim of the "good life" to which these Greek states were dedicated was a communal, not an individual, matter. True enough, the citizens enjoyed within and through these states liberty of person and property and at times the right of voice in the government. It is also true that in these hothouses men's energies burgeoned in an amazing economic, political, and intellectual growth. Nevertheless, sober reflection will quickly disclose that the extraordinary development of Greek civilization rested very largely upon the mutual connection of thinker and society.

This connection fructified the individual, but it limited the freedom with which he could see or speak on matters of group interest. Apart from the occasional hero or tyrant, who lies partially outside the rules, the individual in the great days of the city-state was nowhere entirely free to act or speak as he desired. Either by law or more often by custom the personal behavior of the individual was restricted for the benefit of the group in all Greek states for which evidence is available. Even in Periclean Athens, long famous for its freedom of speech which Cicero calls "license," the citizen was expected to yield to the needs of society, and opposition to the introduction of new ideas was obvious in the plays of the conservative Aristophanes. At a few points this opposition had led to the suppression of thought.

To some degree the limitations on thought in the Greek world arose also from basic aspects of the Greek view of the world. Greek philosophy was stamped with an idealist view which could never establish the individual as an independent object justified in independent thought. Greek religion on its aristocratic plane imposed few bars on men's thought; yet when scientific advance led thinkers to the concept that the happenings of the world might be explained naturally and when they denied ideas firmly held by the masses, at times they encountered disapproval or worse. "Men say," admitted Plato, "that we ought not to enquire into the supreme God and the nature of the universe, nor busy ourselves in searching out the causes of things, and that such enquiries are impious." [1] That the Greek thinkers could proceed as far as they did was due largely to the aristocratic control of society, but there were always limits to the acceptance of their ideas and so indirectly to the range, or survival, of their thought.

[1] *Laws* 7.821A (Jowett).

By the fourth century B.C. the power of the city-state to absorb the energies and devotion of its citizens began to wane. The horizon of the Greek world was broadening out both intellectually and geographically, and no efforts by the conservatives could withstand the criticism of old ways which the rational movement of the sophists in the fifth century unleashed. The greatest philosopher Greece ever produced, Plato, tried to erect dams and dikes against the freeing of the individual from ancestral custom, but the very intensity with which this frightened thinker felt it necessary to censor the music, art, literature, religion, and education of the ideal citizens of his *Republic* is a reflection of the strength of the currents which he opposed.

The fourth century B.C. was marked by a bitter warfare among the Greek states, which left them an easy prey for the rising monarchy of Macedonia to the north. The greatest of the Macedonian kings, Alexander, then went on to conquer the Orient as far as India; after his death in 323 B.C. his generals carved up the Greek world and the Near East into large monarchies. So began the Hellenistic Age, into which the Roman Republic was to enter and from which it was to borrow heavily in many fields.

Development from the fourth century into the Hellenistic Age was along two outwardly opposed but actually complementary lines, one leading toward repression of liberty of thought and the other encouraging individual autonomy. On the one hand, the individual citizen became less significant politically. The city-states of the Aegean lost their independence of action to the monarchies; settlers in the new Greek cities of the Orient displayed a remarkable local patriotism but were still subject to absolute kings and their bureaucratic aides. In the interaction of the Greeks and the Orientals which formed the Hellenistic Age, Greek ideas of freedom on the political level were subordinated to Oriental autocracy. In return for the sacrifice of their ideal of political freedom, the Greeks clutched the material reward of temporal prosperity.

For a time the arts and letters flourished in the glittering new world of the great monarchies. The kings created new cities or beautified those already in existence; they subsidized artists and authors; at both Alexandria and Pergamum great libraries arose. From the Museum at Alexandria flowed great discoveries in medicine, astronomy, and other sciences; even more significant was the scholarly activity in the standardization of texts of the classical authors. Artists and men of letters, to be sure, were expected to celebrate the virtues and deeds of their patrons, and in relief and ode alike a great variety of modes of adulation was worked out, to serve as models for the Roman world. The bluntness of Euclid, who told the first Ptolemy that there was no royal road to geometry, was rare; undue independence of mind could bring suspension of support, imprisonment, or even worse. The rulers might subsidize the Museum munificently, but as one contemporary put it, the Museum was after all a "bird cage." [2]

On the other hand, men were no longer tied so intimately to the city-state. A Greek of Athens who settled abroad could not carry with him all the power of the gods and religious rites associated with a specific spot in his homeland; nor could he transplant the bonds of family, clan, and other social units, which weakened even at home as culture became cosmopolitan. In the later years of the Hellenistic Age, at least, the human became far more an individual as he walked the streets of the great cities, "lost in the crowd, become a simple number in the midst of an infinity of human beings like himself, who knew nothing of him, of whom he knew nothing; a man who stood alone in bearing the weight of life, without friend, without reason for existence, who revolved like a beast until he died—and all was ended." [3]

In Hellenistic art and literature man's interest in man is more apparent and more self-conscious. Less bound by old social and religious customs—though not entirely free—he might hold and voice opinions in fields where previously uniformity was almost automatic; and actual modes of life varied widely thenceforth until a new code of morality began to emerge in the third and fourth centuries after Christ. To support themselves, some men fashioned new philosophies of personal conduct, such as the Stoic and Epicurean, which emphasized internal independence; others turned to astrology and magic.

It is unfortunate that the Hellenistic Age is so scantily illumined; for the more one considers any aspect of this era the more one finds precedents for policies which the Republic and then the Empire followed—one must never forget that the Romans had no direct contacts with Greece in the Periclean Age.

[2] Timon of Phlius, in Athenaeus, *Sophists at Dinner* (*Deipnosophistae*) 22D.
[3] A. J. Festugière, *Liberté et civilisation chez les Grecs* (Paris, 1947), 57–58.

Roman Limits on the Individual

The Hellenistic stream formed one of the main influences on Cicero and the horizon of his age. Although Cicero had read Plato, his philosophic thought was far more influenced by the Hellenistic polymath Posidonius; his contemporaries who were poets drew heavily from the erudite, polished, Alexandrian techniques; the artists and architects who framed Roman public and private life in the Forum and noble mansions and villas found the models of Pergamum and Alexandria more congenial than those of the Acropolis. And yet the intrusion of Rome into the eastern Mediterranean interrupted the logical pattern of development of ancient civilization; Cicero's thought was not simply a direct continuation of Hellenistic attitudes, despite an outward similarity which has often misled students of the Late Republic.

As Cicero looked back to the heroic days of the past, he felt that Rome had been less individualistic than Greece. The great historian of the Republic, Livy, painted a glorious picture of the early Romans as a patriotic people who were above all else obedient to established, legal authority—the family, the state, and the gods. In a sense this picture was true. When Rome entered on the broad stage of the ancient world about 200 B.C., its mode of thought and its social organization were restrictive much as had been those of an early Greek city-state.

In other equally important respects, however, the Roman tradition was one of greater freedom for the individual or, more properly, for the family, if it belonged to the upper classes. Although the political organization of the state in terms of clans and families had early been broken at Rome, the noble families continued essentially to dominate the social, political, and economic structure of the city; the political history of the last two centuries of the Republic must be written largely in terms of the conflicts and alliances of these blood groups operating through the Senate and magistracies. In the existence of the aristocratic families lies a solution to the puzzling fact that restraint of the individual by the customs of society had distinct limits at Rome; thence springs the tendency of Roman law to elaborate the rights and duties of the individual, i.e., essentially of the *pater familias,* whose power over his offspring, slaves, and retainers was almost unlimited.

Thence too arises the sharp distinction between the upper and lower classes, the upper being relatively free and the lower quite closely checked. Since the early third century Rome had accepted the concept that the will of the people was sovereign, but the people had extraordinarily little voice in their government. Social theory, as outlined by Cicero, emphasized the need to judge one's actions by their effect on the common, rather than the individual, good; in actual practice the restrictions on freedom of expression and action at Rome in the last two centuries before Christ, were designed chiefly to protect the position of the dominant classes, who were given ample opportunity for contention and self-expression. In the main the aristocracy preferred, down to the last century before Christ, to fight its internecine battles on its own level, and it did not look with favor upon appeals to the common people which might result in the loss of dignity to individual nobles.

Nowhere in the Roman Republic will one find Romans asserting, as some Athenians had done, that freedom of speech is a vital part of *libertas*. The right to speak one's mind was considered as an aspect of the dignity and authority of a noble's position rather than as an inherent principle of the entire political system; to exponents of the senatorial views in the first century, such as Cicero in some statements (though he did not entirely agree with his fellow senators), liberty in its political sense denoted the power of the aristocracy to run the state without interference and the unchecked ability of the senators to express opinions.

The lower classes, in this view, were free in the sense that they voluntarily accepted the authority (*auctoritas*) of the wiser part of society. Associations of the lower classes were tolerated so long as they did not cause public unrest; but when Bacchanalian groups in 186 or clubs in 64 threatened the peace, the Senate struck harshly at them. The playwright Naevius, who claimed the right of free speech and attacked a noble faction from the stage, was jailed until he recanted, then was exiled. Ennius summed up the situation in a pregnant line: "It is dangerous for a plebeian to mutter aloud." [4] Not until the nobles themselves had lost their freedom of speech in the Empire did men begin to see the need for a general principle of such a freedom.

The theoretical and practical influences at work in Roman thought are most easily detected in the field of religion. The Romans long remained proud of their devotion to the gods who protected the rise of the state and felt that the tie between these guardian spirits and the pious people of Rome was a peculiarly intimate one. Such a connection between gods and humans was a mark of the city-state everywhere; the political success of Rome, however, ensured the endurance of the state cult as a vital

[4] Festus, *On the Meaning of Words* (ed. by Lindsay), p. 128.

force far longer than was elsewhere the case. What distinguished particularly the Roman form of religion were the lack of dogma and of
native mythology and the complete control of all public religious activities by the state machinery. The magistrates, assisted by the religious
experts, carried out the worship on behalf of all; on religious days the
private citizen needed only to keep quiet.

The Romans might be expected a priori to display a marked intolerance to all divagations by citizens from the established religious pattern,
whether they fell to worshiping foreign gods or neglected the great
gods of the Capitoline Hill. But actually Roman religion in the Late
Republic was an official cult more than an internal belief, and as long
as the cult was maintained individuals were relatively free to believe
what they desired. The religious policy of the Republic, which laid the
basis for imperial treatment of Christianity, is an argued point, but it
may, in my opinion, be summed up as one of theoretical intolerance of
deviation which very rarely led to positive steps—unless the aristocracy
considered the deviation one likely to rouse the common folk to immorality or disobedience. The fact that punishments could then be
levied certainly demonstrates the absence of any concept of complete
religious liberty at Rome; at the same time the motives behind these
punishments show the reluctance of the state to dictate to individuals on
purely religious matters.

By the Late Republic the old idea that a citizen's outward expression
of religion could and should be controlled appeared chiefly in the theory
of such men as Cicero and Varro. Generally, actual limitations on expression had decreased markedly in the chaos of the first century B.C.;
and even in the field of theory Cicero felt much less keenly than Plato
that censorship of the arts and letters was necessary for the benefit of the
state. The drama was to be checked in Cicero's ideal Rome insofar as it
attacked the dignity of the nobles, but Cicero does not in the preserved
part of his *Republic* directly urge censorship on the grounds of morality
—the Roman state actually paid little attention to the effect of the stage
on morals. Again, though Cicero laid down a rule that music was to be
regulated by law, he explicitly affirmed his belief that Plato overempha-
sized the relationship of new types of music and the growth of effemi-
nacy; quite possibly men were already corrupted by other vices when
they took up the more seductive, emotional music of the day.

These concessions are not simply a mark of the less doctrinaire spirit
of Cicero. During the three centuries since Plato the Mediterranean

world had moved toward a greater factual liberty of the individual, and by the age of Cicero Rome itself was far advanced along the common path.

Greco-Roman Synthesis

To go farther in tracing this path would carry us into the Empire, so we must turn back to consider briefly the general intellectual development of the Late Republic. This development is one of the most fascinating stories of cultural transfer in human history.

Arts and letters in Rome before 300 B.C. had existed on a very low level. With the conquest of south Italy and then of Sicily in the third century, Hellenistic influences began to seep into Rome, but the onrush of Eastern culture did not reach full flood until the second or even the first century, when Roman generals and soldiers came into direct contact with the main centers of the Hellenistic world and brought back booty, slaves, and hangers-on to Rome.

These rather naïve and simple conquerors looked the more favorably upon the luxuries and arts of the cosmopolitan, graceful inhabitants of the East for their own lack of a native tradition of learning and philosophy; moreover, insofar as any outside civilization had influenced Rome since its foundation, it had been primarily that of the Greeks. Nevertheless, the degree to which the conqueror bent culturally before the conquered and humbly admitted his own inferiority in thought and tongue was extraordinary. Not only were the Greeks permitted a wide latitude of cultural freedom, but also the Romans accepted—and preserved for posterity—a great deal of Greek culture even while looking with a certain scorn upon the contemporary bearers of that culture.

Yet it will not do simply to say that the Romans took over Hellenistic civilization lock, stock, and barrel. Their general cast of mind, and direct state activity as well, combined to place definite restrictions on the type of borrowings from the general frame of Greek culture. The Romans accepted from Hellenistic science mainly practical discoveries. Then, too, Hellenistic philosophy disassociated man from the state too much to have widespread effect at Rome until the eminent Stoic Panaetius in the middle of the second century mitigated the severity of Stoic doctrine; thereafter it was more palatable to the Roman taste. Even so, philosophy in Rome always remained practical and eclectic. A commonsensical Roman praetor once called together the philosophers at Athens and urged them to make a composition of their differences: "He said, if they really desired not to waste their lives in argument, that the matter might be settled; and at the same time he promised his own best efforts to aid them in coming to some agreement." [5]

More important than this qualification is a just appreciation of the general relationship of Roman to Hellenistic thought. The influence of Hellenistic civilization is obvious wherever one turns in the Late Republic, so obvious that it has often led men to call Roman culture in root merely Greek civilization under a Latin veneer. With so narrow a view I must register my fundamental disagreement; to hold it is to lose all capability for understanding the course of intellectual developments in the Empire. A cardinal premise of the following pages is my firm opinion that the Late Republic bequeathed to the Empire the beginnings of an essentially unified Greco-Roman or Mediterranean civilization politically centered on Rome. The ideas in Cicero's mind were not all Greek, and those which did derive from Hellenic culture had undergone a significant sea-change in their transplantation to the Roman environment.

This synthesis was not the work of a moment, nor was it complete by the end of the Republic. In Roman arts and letters alike the third and second centuries were prone to absorb and copy Greek models directly and simply, but the men of the first century had passed beyond this in architecture, painting, sculpture, and literature alike. In the arts there appears a changing view of the interrelationships of man and the world which we must examine later; in literature the feeling that one is dealing with Romans, not Greeks, overpowers the reader who progresses through Lucretius and Catullus to Horace and Virgil.

The civilization of the Late Republic rested thus on an amalgam of Greek and Roman elements. Greece contributed from its long experience a great stock of techniques, motifs, and polished concepts; Rome brought primarily a sense of fresh enthusiasm, practical hard-headedness, and optimistic belief that new triumphs could be won. Formed by the Greek concept of culture (*paideia*), which had been elaborated in the fourth century B.C., Republican civilization displayed itself in the ideal of the perfect orator, as exemplified by Cicero, at home in the classical literature of the past, capable of intellectual analysis and skillful composition, and powerful above all in swaying the minds of Senate and Roman people in debate and oration. Cicero had a broad view of man as a civilized, humane being which was rarely to be attained again.

[5] Cicero, *Laws* 1.53.

Although the culture of the Late Republic possessed great potentialities, it suffered from ominous limitations. The Greek inheritance which such a man as Cicero faced was no longer the essentially simple, unified structure which Periclean Athens had known. In art, in literature, in political thought, in almost any field, a Roman of the first century B.C. faced a host of subtleties and complexities which had evolved in the classic and Hellenistic ages and of which he had to take account if he wished to be an expert. True innovations had become ever more difficult, and men's minds were molded by points of view long canonized by precedent. Basically this structure of thought rested upon a stock of ideas formed in the city-state period of Greek development.

The great question was whether Roman vigor of mind could master the weight of past experience and push on to draw new conclusions. In this effort the Roman suspicion of theory had a double edge: while it limited the depth of thought, the general reluctance of the Romans to be engaged in fine-spun theorization and subtle but shallow dialectic might allow them to see with new vision, to break out of the classical system of ideas.

Cicero, for example, poured out works on a great variety of subjects. In these works the concepts were Greek, but the influence of Roman tradition brought significant changes in their formulation. The poet Lucretius, who opposed the competition for money and power which upset his world, displayed a terrific vigor in proffering the "quiet citadel" of Epicurean beliefs, from which men might gaze down serenely on the aimless wanderings of humanity. The intellectual substance in his work *On the Nature of the World* was Greek; the missionary zeal came from other roots.

The advance, however, was not too great. The doctrine of Lucretius led toward political inactivity and sketched a hopeless picture of a decaying world, where all is the same and death ends all, where the gods pay no attention to man. Cicero retained an underlying optimism in the quality of mankind and in the possibility of intellectual advance; but still, when confronted with the jarring philosophic arguments of the Greeks, he was driven to skepticism concerning man's possibility of determining ultimate truth. So he joined the Academic school of suspended judgment. Other Romans, in becoming skeptical both politically and intellectually, lost their power of action or slid into Neopythagorean mysticism, which had an extraordinary, significant revival in Cicero's day.

Another, crucial problem: Could Roman thinkers take the great step of evolving a new view of man in the universe which would root him as citizen and thinker in a universal Mediterranean state? The Stoic philosophers of the Hellenistic world had made tentative efforts in this direction but had necessarily concentrated on the individual, in a cosmopolitan world, to be sure, but in an essentially unpolitical one. As inheritors of the Greek tradition, they could not work seriously toward a justification of the absolute Hellenistic monarchies, all too Oriental in practice, which loomed above them. The Romans likewise shared traditions of loyalty within a city-state framework. In fact they were building a world-state, but in theory their thinkers clung to the past. Both the *Republic* and the *Laws* of Cicero were couched in terms of a Roman city-state, not of the empire which lay about him. His contemporary, Caesar, had more cosmopolitan ideas.

Most of Cicero's fellow aristocrats were interested primarily in the heaping up of wealth, in living luxuriously, and in gaining political power. Serious attention to the problems of empire is rarely to be found, and the nobles were more attracted by the amenities of life than by the essentials of civilization. Even more dangerous was the fact that the unity of the upper classes was rapidly dissolving. Roman nobles had long been proud of their individual dignity and had fiercely vied for the outward marks of dignity, which in their eyes were the great offices of state. Nevertheless a sense of corporate unity had tended to confine the jockeying within their own group and to mitigate its extreme expression; the religious and social sanctions of group unity and family spirit had had a powerful influence in keeping men up to their duty. Upon this happy balance of contrasting qualities had depended the tenacious yet supple drive of the Romans to mastery of the Mediterranean.

As the nobles grew richer and as they learned to act as individual monarchs in their provincial commands, the cleavages grew deeper, and they could not discover in Hellenistic philosophy any spring of moral action which was as imperative as the old traditions. Family life tended to dissolve, the prosecution of noble feuds became ever more vicious, and for their own selfish ends the nobles began to utilize support from the lower classes to an alarming degree.

It became increasingly doubtful whether the weak Roman form of government could preserve individual initiative in the political sense and also continue to govern the Mediterranean world. The ruthless effort of each Roman noble to rise by pushing down his peers had historically to lead to the destruction of the state and so to the catastrophic collapse of Mediterranean civilization—a present threat to men of the dying Republic—or to result in the domination of Rome by one man and in the destruction of political liberty for all. In either event the Roman Republic could not lead on into a Mediterranean state in which all men could be active citizens and from which they could draw the lifeblood of thought.

II

The Political Collapse
of the Republic

THROUGHOUT the century before Cicero's birth social and economic tensions mounted in Rome as the contrasts between rich and poor, free and slave, Roman and non-Roman became sharper. In Italy the reaction of Rome's allies to their dependent, less privileged position quickened and led to revolt. The provinces suffered from inadequate government by yearly changing governors; Rome had not yet really accepted the thesis that ethical responsibility accompanied political mastery, and the narrow group of senatorial aristocrats refused to copy the elaborate state organizations of the Hellenistic monarchs.

Since the Senate could not maintain its control over the large armies required to uphold Roman domination, the way was paved for the military supermen, who held together the empire, expanded its frontiers, and all too often wrested control of the central government. The last century before Christ was one of chaos and civil war, as one man after another tried in vain to furnish a solution which could harness the unleashed forces.

The result was, at least for a time, to unlock the gates of free expression of opinion in all fields to all elements of society. It became ever more difficult to control the social behavior of a citizen body made up increasingly of foreigners to whom "Italy was a stepmother," as one aristocrat contemptuously told an assembly.[1] Each phase of the political struggle

[1] Scipio Aemilianus, in Velleius Paterculus 2.4 and elsewhere.

19

was waged in a blazing light of propaganda, to which may be attributed in part our greater knowledge of the period, even though we must see the era largely through the eyes of senatorial adherents. Yet the victory of one faction brought with it factual or legal suppression of freedom of speech for the defeated side. Varying in degree with the intensity of the strife or the personality of the victors, this suppression tended to grow over the decades.

Another consequence of the almost incessant unrest was the tendency of men to withdraw from political activity and to seek peace by any means. This had a serious effect on the quality and scope of political thought and was eventually a significant factor in bringing the end of the revolutionary period. Prominent even among the nobles, the cry for peace rose ever louder among the middle classes and the lower classes. Though neither the masses at Rome itself nor the Italians initiated much action, one may not overlook their influence in throwing up the successive individual masters of Rome in the first century B.C. As the rich and poor drew farther apart, the lower classes lent an attentive ear to demagogues who promised to elevate them or at least to destroy the ever-more-vicious mastery of the wrangling senatorial order. Liberty in the Ciceronian sense was a dim ideal of little value to the bulk of the Roman citizenry if it were accomplished by noble factionalism at the expense of corporate unity, by civil war, and by unrest which kept the bellies of the masses empty. All over Italy the well-to-do elements, which had risen rapidly in the second century, disliked disorder and at the same time were not themselves able directly to take part in the Roman government.

Dictatorship of Caesar

In the years 48–45 B.C. Julius Caesar gained mastery at Rome by his victories first over Pompey and then over other dissident elements. While darting about the empire in these wars, and in the year of relative peace before his murder, he moved steadily toward the creation of a world state with a cosmopolitan citizenry under his own suzerainty. The basic outlines of his dream are clear, though fierce debate has raged among modern scholars as to the final position which he planned to assign to himself and the manner in which he would have governed. As a presage of the future, these brief years of Caesar's dictatorship compel attention.

Caesar's mastery promised the restoration of stability, the prevention of the clearly threatened dissolution of the Roman hegemony and so of

Mediterranean civilization. As such, many men were willing to accept it. Even Cicero, though proud of the Roman unification of the world, had his fears for its fall as well as his hopes for its eternity. In an oration which he delivered before Caesar, Cicero could assert that on Caesar's life "depend the lives of his fellow citizens"—and in that phrase there swing suddenly open before us the gates to the noble, empty halls of imperial theory. Cicero is worth hearing further:

It is for you and you alone, Gaius Caesar, to reanimate all that you see lying shattered, as was inevitable, by the shock of the war itself; courts of law must be set on foot, licentiousness must be checked, and the growth of population fostered . . . it is all these wounds of war's infliction which you are called upon to heal, and which none but you can treat.[2]

Yet the period of Caesar's dictatorship was a mighty blow to the freedom of political thought in Rome. The state was clearly subject to the whim of one man, and toward that individual all men and all open political activity began to turn as to a magnet. Worse still, he manipulated the Roman political machinery at his will and paid only scant respect to the Senate or to old tradition, whether the question at hand was a rational reform of the creaking calendar or the reorganization of the Roman constitution.

This very rationality was at once his strength and his weakness. Though he had come to power on the culminating wave of a revolution against oligarchic control, he did not try to appeal to men's ideals, and he proclaimed that revolution now at an end. Though the aristocracy had by and large opposed him, he thought it should accept the award of the battlefield. He quickly suppressed the military aspect of his rule and dissolved his own bodyguard; former opponents like Brutus and Cassius he put into office in an effort to unite all parts of the senatorial aristocracy behind his program; for by respecting the personal position of the individual senators he hoped to mollify their opposition to his destruction of their political control through the Senate. Conspiracies and nocturnal meetings against him were merely stigmatized by public proclamation. The resulting clash between his outward show of tolerance and the essential logic of his autocratic position was insoluble; it led directly to his murder.

Caesar, to be sure, attempted to win men's minds mainly by positive means. In the days of his early political apprenticeship he had learned

[2] *For Marcellus* 23–24.

how to appeal to the Roman masses. In his wars he had won over his army to the point where it followed without question and against any odds, and he had shown remarkable skill in shaking the confidence of enemy forces in their leaders by a variety of means of propaganda. Both in the field and at Rome Caesar was a master of psychological warfare, the like of which had not been seen. In that warfare he built up a machine of rumormongering; we know only little about it, but it was apparently inherited by his grandnephew Octavian.

To the masses he made practical promises of money, peace, and security; to the nobles he proceeded on a different plane, as a craftsman of both the spoken and the written word. The powers of Caesar in personal blandishment must have been extraordinary; he won over Catullus and other poets who had attacked him, and he reconciled himself outwardly with Cicero. As dictator he himself wrote a defense of his civil wars; he encouraged friendly authors and the teachers of the liberal arts; he planned a state library of Greek and Latin literature at Rome, to be directed by the scholar Varro (though this mark of Roman intellectual maturity was not to be completed until the next generation). Cicero, Brutus, and others wrote tracts on the life and suicide of Cato the Younger, who had steadfastly opposed Caesar and supported the Senate, and thereby began to canonize him as a noble exponent of republican spirit. To check these outwardly insignificant, yet irritating, steps, Caesar and his aides only composed Anticatos. Men seemed to be free to write or speak as they would; we are informed that Caesar merely warned those speaking ill of him not to continue their offense.

Still, Caesar was dictator. Rational though he might be, tolerant and forgiving through deliberate choice, he could not avoid exerting a pressure toward conformity, the diverse aspects of which may be illustrated first from the cases of Laberius, Caecina, and Cicero and then from his obvious limitations on opposition.

Laberius was a noted producer and actor of the popular skits called mimes; he had pointedly retired from his profession on the rise of Caesar. The dictator, however, virtually ordered him to emerge and adorn the stage on the occasion of the celebration of Caesar's victories. This the doughty Laberius dared not refuse, but in his prologue he complained of the compulsion; later in his mime he appeared as a beaten slave with the line: "Henceforth, O citizens, we have lost our liberty!" Another allusion quoted by later writers was the statement that "he must fear many, whom many fear," whereon all eyes swiveled to the spectator Caesar.[3] At the conclusion of the performances Caesar gave the palm of victory to Laberius' rival Publilius Syrus but attempted to mollify Laberius by restoring him to equestrian status. The dictator's geniality and toleration scarcely mask his powers of compulsion and the significance of his approval, both of which must have weighed heavily on less valiant souls than Laberius.

The second figure, Aulus Caecina, had pamphleteered against Caesar during the civil war. So exceedingly had he irritated the dictator that Caesar refused to extend to him the general clemency proclaimed after the end of the fighting. From his exile in Sicily Caecina composed a work of apology, which he sent to Cicero to correct and presumably to present to the master of the Roman world. Knowing the foibles of his friend, the exile carefully explained in his covering letter that he could praise Cicero only sparingly in his book if he were not to offend Caesar, and went on gloomily: "If in his literary efforts a man is not only bound down but crippled by so many cruel restrictions, what can he produce worth listening to, or likely to win approval?" When he comes to Caesar's name, Caecina continued, he trembles; does this word sound suspicious? shall I change it? will the change make it worse? whom shall I praise, whom reproach? "When most of what one writes is adapted to what one guesses to be the feelings of another, and not to the expression of one's own judgment, you may be sure that I appreciate the difficulty of emerging unscathed." [4] The very awkwardness of Caecina's phrases reveals the problems of a writer out of favor in a new era, when freedom of speech has vanished. Whether Caecina won pardon is uncertain; at Caesar's death there were still exiles.

Cicero and Caesar

Even more significant is the history of Cicero's inner reaction to autocracy, as preserved in his works and letters. Though Cicero was not of the highest aristocracy, his ambition had gained its goal of the consulship in 63 B.C. There he had quelled a dangerous plot against the state; he had even, so he dreamed, secured the endurance of the Republic by uniting the agricultural and commercial wealthy, the senatorial and equestrian groups. But alas! within two years his carefully knit union fell apart, and by 59 Cicero had been forced to witness

---

[3] Macrobius, *Saturnalia* 2.7; also in Seneca, *On Anger* 2.11.3.
[4] Cicero, *To His Friends* 6.7 (December 46).

the First Triumvirate and the consulship of Caesar, which launched the latter on his way to greatness. More immediately the use of illegal force in Caesar's consulship had clamped a considerable limitation on the political speech of men such as Cicero.

Worse than retirement, however, befell Cicero, for in 58 he was driven into exile. Though Pompey shortly recalled him, Cicero could not play a truly independent role during the contentions of the 50's. His general attitude toward political events is summed up in a sad letter to Atticus: If he said what he ought about the state, he would be taken as a lunatic; if he said what he should, as a slave; if he were quiet, he was no more than a coward and a helpless bondsman. When Pompey and Caesar finally split, Cicero reluctantly joined Pompey as the lesser of evils, but after Pompey's defeat he secured swift pardon from Caesar. Sorrowing for the destruction of the Republic, he could yet detect a few saving aspects of the mastery of Caesar: "Perhaps you are not at liberty to say what you think, but you are quite at liberty to say nothing." [5]

Cicero was incapable of being entirely quiet. In part he turned to nonpolitical subjects, though even here he felt himself serving the state in philosophy, if not in politics. During the last years of Caesar's life Cicero poured forth dialogues and discussions of philosophy, oratory, and other subjects in which he passed on to the West a great amount of Greek speculation and essentially invented a philosophical vocabulary for the Latin language. Ostensibly these works are free from Caesar's influence, but the dictator's sway goes far to explain their emergence. It is not accidental that Cicero reiterates the Stoic ideal, born under Hellenistic autocracy, that liberty is an internal, moral quality: "For what is freedom? The power of living as you wish. Who then lives as he wishes save the man who lives rightly?" [6]

Cicero continued also to write political essays and could not break off his flow of oratory. In the orations of the period of Caesar's dictatorship a sadly changed political climate is apparent. No longer did Cicero address the Senate and the people, for Caesar was the ultimate judge. At least one of these later speeches, from which we have already seen passages, was delivered in Caesar's own house; those which had the Forum as background were on trifling cases. When one man became

[5] *To His Friends* 4.9.2 (before mid-September 46).
[6] *Paradoxes of the Stoics* 34.

sovereign in Rome and decided matters within his own heart, the significance of political debate waned swiftly.

In a work specifically on political theory, the *Laws,* Cicero looked back to the golden days of the Republic in the second century B.C., when the state had been undivided. Here he tried, as he had earlier in the *Republic,* to fire the aristocracy of his day to active, just political life, the fruit of which would be the tranquillity of the state and the possibility of dignified repose for the individual noble after his years of activity. Even in addressing his son Marcus on the duties of the individual (*On Duties*) he placed first the claims of society and emphasized the higher aristocratic ideal of the state as embodying justice.

The perfect state of which Cicero dreamed thus had few points in common with the Caesarian model, for in the last analysis Cicero considered political activity the highest expression of human strivings. Liberty under the confines of obedience to law was an essential attribute of that political organism in which men found their unity.

In these views Cicero thought mainly of his fellow aristocrats; only to this circle did his concept of liberty, though genuine, actually extend the rights of free speech and thought. Cicero still could dream of a higher humanity united in mutual sympathy and the cultivation of learning. He was, in fine, a man of ideals. Although he failed to offer a truly practicable solution to the problems of the world-state under Roman domination, he could not remain silent on political problems even under Caesar, and his effort was a truly republican one. In essential fiber of thought Cicero refused to yield to Caesar.

Limitations on Opposition

Men scarcely needed the examples of Laberius or Caecina or the implicit criticism of Cicero's *Laws*—not published before his death— to realize that under Caesar they were not free to speak the truth. Caesar could not muffle the logic of his position; an opponent even quoted him as asserting "that the state was nothing, a mere name without body or form . . . that men ought to regard his word as law." [7] Inexorably Caesar destroyed the means of open political opposition.

In the chaotic 50's ruffians had formed gangs, which coursed through the streets in their warfare, setting fire to opponents' houses and slaying foe and bystander alike. Thus far the Romans had had little cause to

[7] Suetonius, *Caesar* 77.

limit freedom of association save through social custom or the exercise of magisterial power; the nobles themselves made use of clubs and the like in swaying the elections, and had their own groups, *circuli,* from which emanated much of the rumor and pamphleteering of the age. A senatorial decree of 64 which imposed some limitations on associations was revoked six years later by a rabble-rouser who rammed through a law forbidding any hindrance to the right of association of citizens. Shortly thereafter new restrictions of more limited scope were required; Caesar then placed on the clubs and gilds (*collegia*) an almost total ban, which Augustus was soon to make a permanent part of autocratic control.

Already in 59 as consul Caesar had ordered the debates of the Senate taken down and published as a check upon its expression of aristocratic feeling; now he had the right to speak his opinion first, and in other ways curtailed the freedom of discussion in that body. The magistrates, whom he essentially picked, swore oaths on their installation not to oppose any of his decrees. As overseer of morals from February 44, he issued edicts against luxury and might have proceeded to more stringent supervision of men and morals if he had lived.

In 63 he had been elected chief priest of the Roman religious structure, *pontifex maximus;* in his dictatorship he began to make efforts to restore that structure, disrupted by the civil strife of the past half-century, as an integral part of the Roman state, and to interweave therein his own figure. Every five years the priests and vestal virgins were to offer public prayers for his safety. Through the sanction of religion Caesar may even have been moving to regularize his position as a Hellenistic king. This "god manifest, descended from Ares and Aphrodite and public savior of human life," as he is hailed in an inscription from Ephesus, was a true colossus bestriding the world.[8]

To oppose their lord, who blocked the outlets of public expression, malcontents resorted to rumormongering, to anonymous pamphleteering, to the scrawling of brief epigrams on the walls and statues of Rome. Within the political structure, however, there still seemed in early 44 to be some room for display of discreet opposition, at least to the abhorrent idea that Caesar become king, and certain tribunes manifested this opposition. When Caesar openly frowned on their independence, they boldly issued an edict asserting that they could not

[8] *Corpus Inscriptionum Graecarum* 2957 (48/47).

speak their minds "freely and safely on behalf of the public good"; [9] in the upshot the dictator removed them from office and Senate with the concurrence of that outwardly pliable body. This direct challenge to the freedom of the tribunate, one of the most hallowed institutions of the Republic, was a crisis in the drama of Caesar's end; thenceforth the plot against his life moved swiftly to its denouement on the Ides of March.

Last Battles for the Republic

"Liberty! Freedom! Tyranny is dead," cried Shakespeare's Cinna as he, Brutus, Cassius, and the other assassins ran out of the meeting of the Senate where they had murdered Caesar. They sought to rouse the people to regain their republican rights, but the few bystanders in the Forum greeted them with scant, puzzled cheers—this had been an aristocratic plot rather than a popular uprising. By the end of the day the conspirators had withdrawn for safety to the Capitol, where a band of gladiators protected their persons.

Modern historians have usually regarded this group as contemptible. It had laid no plans for the conduct of the state and had naïvely believed that the removal of the dictator would automatically restore the Republic. Yet it is true that Caesar, in establishing a cosmopolitan autocracy, had underestimated the significance of contemporary aristocratic feelings. The subsequent solution of Augustus was to placate the Roman aristocracy to a much greater degree, perhaps even too much, but the Augustan system endured for centuries.

Whether Caesar's structure could so have endured and whether it would have allowed greater or less freedom of thought can scarcely be guessed. Certainly Caesar had paved the way for the control of public thought, both by his positive propaganda and by his suppression or discouragement of opposition; and though Caesar may have dreamed of a state where individual liberty might be retained under a master who needed no armed force to protect his rule, that dream was assuredly impossible of realization. Succeeding Caesars, from Augustus on, were to be essentially military monarchs.

To contemporaries such as Cicero the death of Caesar seemed to give one last opportunity to restore and consolidate liberty. Brutus and Cassius talked much of freedom. They struck a coin bearing the words "Ides of March," with a liberty cap between two daggers, a clear argument that by their murder of Caesar on that date they had liberated the fatherland. Athens, in erecting bronze images of the two, deliberately placed the statues beside the group of the famous Athenian tyrannicides Harmodius and Aristogeiton. Cicero might have been dubious because the conspirators had not really restored the powers of the Senate and seemed as bent on personal glory as had any other nobles, but he himself, after brief hesitation, entered the great debate which sprang up on the future disposition of the state. Both in its course and in its bloody end this debate was as vehement as any Rome had seen, and in its consequences it was to be decisive.

The principal figure in Rome, once Caesar lay dead, was his burly, jovial, self-seeking lieutenant, Mark Antony, who immediately seized Caesar's papers and wealth. Another figure, apparently of little significance, was Caesar's nearest male relative, a grandnephew on his sister's side, who had been adopted and made heir by Caesar's will; this youth of eighteen we call Octavian. A third was the venerable Cicero, who led complicated maneuvers to raise the Senate against Antony. Cicero rose to the greatest heights of his career as orator and patriotic defender of ancestral liberty in hurling his *Philippics* against Antony during the winter of 44–43 B.C., but all too soon his efforts, which began successfully, turned to complete failure.

From the upper classes of the Republic Cicero's support was neither complete nor wholehearted. Men tended to support individuals rather than abstract ideas; and many would pay for peace and security at any cost in ideals. Octavian had met with little favor from Antony and so had joined the Senate with a privately raised force of Caesar's veterans, but he was well aware that the Senate planned only, in Cicero's words, "to elevate and then eliminate" him. After collaborating with the senatorial troops in driving Antony out of Italy, Octavian marched on Rome in July–August 43. For himself he extorted the position of consul and the legalization of his adoption; on the assassins of Caesar, who had begun to build up their own forces in the Eastern provinces, a sentence of outlawry was imposed. Then he secured a reconciliation with the chastened Antony, and together with Lepidus, a third but minor leader of the Caesarian party, Octavian and Antony formed the Second Triumvirate.

Late in 43 the joint leaders came down to the city and forced the passage of a law by which they were named triumvirs for the reorganization of the state for five years. On the next day the first proscription list was posted, and murderers began to range the streets of Rome and paths of Italy. Before the purge was over, three hundred senators and two thousand equestrians had been executed.

High upon the list stood the name of Cicero, for Antony's hatred of his opponent was implacable. The soldiers dispatched to carry out the sentence found the weary, indecisive Cicero in his litter near Formiae; Cicero forbade his slaves to oppose them and met his end nobly. His head was brought back to Rome and placed on the Rostra, the speaker's stand (now in the Forum) from which his golden voice had often swayed the people; there Antony's wife Fulvia mockingly pierced the tongue with her bodkin.

Three years separate the theatrical suicide of Cato at Utica from the pitiful slaughter of Cicero by the side of the Appian Way. Of the two events the death of Cicero far more properly signals the end of the Republic and of that political liberty which Cicero had praised in his *Republic* and had exemplified in his orations. Freedom of thought had never in the Roman Republic been considered a necessary characteristic of the ideal state as a whole; rather, it had been an incidental possession of a privileged aristocracy. There at least *libertas* had existed; but it will not be found under the Caesars. After the death of Cicero Rome never again had a true respite from the rule of individuals, nor could one find a more apt if gruesome symbol of the end of free speech than the horrible treatment of Cicero's tongue.

To be sure, the rulers were now three, and the assassins of Caesar still had their military force; but in the course of the next twelve years the party of the assassins was to be eliminated, and the three were to be reduced by civil war to one, Octavian, eventually called Augustus. With that change in name the Roman Empire had begun.

Any consideration of the Empire, however, must often refer back to the broadening of the Roman horizon in the Republic. Under the direction of its aristocracy Rome had united the Mediterranean, an immense political achievement which it handed on to later generations. The intellectual accomplishments of the age which Cicero's work dominated had been truly extraordinary. It was not yet clear that Roman vigor could push the Greco-Roman synthesis beyond the frame of Hellenistic inheritance or that Roman practical genius could fashion an enduring political structure within which civilization could search out sources of strength. In these respects the experience of the dying Republic, more particularly of Caesar's brief dictatorship, seemed ominous. While Rome rose, the individual had been severely limited by ties of group custom; in being liberated therefrom he was also losing his political independence of action.

a. Realistic expression of individuality ("Cato and Portia"), in the Vatican Museum, Rome. Photograph from Brunn-Bruckmann, *Griechische und römische Porträts* 267.

b. Search for internal space (painting in second style), from villa at Boscoreale. Photograph from Ernst Pfuhl, *Malerei und Zeichnung der Griechen* 3 (Munich, 1923), Fig. 707.

I. The Roman Synthesis

a. Procession on south side. Photograph from Giuseppe Moretti, *Ara Pacis Augustae* (Rome, 1948), Fig. 2.

b. Mother Earth (Tellus). Photograph from Moretti, Pl. 22.

II. Altar of Augustan Peace, in Rome

a. The Conquered (silver cup from Boscoreale), in the Collection of Edmond de Rothschild, Paris. Photograph from Ant. Héron de Villefosse, "Le Trésor de Boscoreale," *Monuments Piot* 5 (1899), Pl. 31.

b. The Majesty of Victory (Gemma Augustea), in the Kunsthistorisches Museum, Vienna. Photograph from A. Furtwängler, *Die Antike Gemmen* 1 (Berlin, 1900), Pl. 56.

III. Propaganda of Empire

IV. Imperial Censorship

Photograph from Brunn-Bruckmann, *Griechische und römische Porträts* 221.

V. Marcus Aurelius, in the Piazza del Campidoglio, Rome

VI. The Second Century

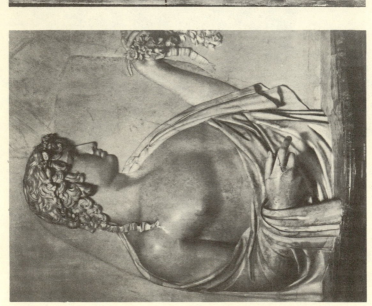

a. Antinous, favorite of Hadrian, in the Villa Albani, Rome. Photograph from Brunn-Bruckmann, *Griechische und römische Porträts* 368.

b. The merciful Marcus Aurelius, in the Palazzo dei Conservatori, Rome. Photograph from Brunn-Bruckmann 268.

a. Greek Temple of Poseidon, in Paestum. Photograph from Thassilo von Scheffer, *Die Kultur der Griechen* (London, 1938), Fig. 149.

b. Interior of the Pantheon (drawing, by Antonio Sarti), in Rome. Photograph from Ludwig Curtius, *Das Antike Rom* (2d ed.; Vienna, 1944), Fig. 147.

VII. Development of Architecture I

a. Minerva Medica, in Rome. Photograph from G. T. Rivoira, *Roman Architecture* (Oxford, 1925), Fig. 225.

b. Arch of Constantine (north side), in Rome. Photograph from H. P. L'Orange with A. von Gerkan, *Der Spätantike Bildschmuck des Konstantinsbogens* (Berlin, 1939), Pl. 1*a*.

VIII. Development of Architecture II

IX. Revolution in Sculpture I

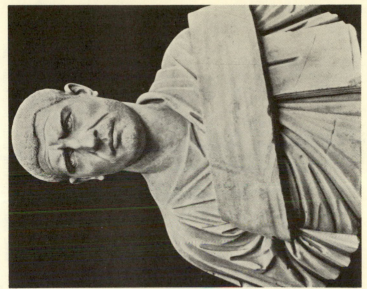

a. Commodus (180–192), in the Terme Museum, Rome. Photograph from Brunn-Bruckmann, *Griechische und römische Porträts* 230.

b. Philip the Arab (244–249), in the Vatican Museum, Rome. Photograph from Fritz Wirth, *Römische Wandmalerei vom Untergang Pompeiis bis ans Ende des dritten Jahrhunderts* (Berlin, 1934), Fig. 82.

X. Revolution in Sculpture II

a. Constantine (306–337), in the Palazzo dei Conservatori, Rome. Photograph from Brunn-Bruckmann, *Griechische und römische Porträts* 891.

b. "Valentinian" (probably Marcian, 450–457), in Barletta. Photograph from Brunn-Bruckmann 896.

a. Ludovisi Sarcophagus, in the Terme Museum, Rome. Photograph from *Antike Denkmäler* IV, Pl. 41.

b. Philosopher Sarcophagus, in the Lateran Museum, Rome. Photograph from G. Rodenwaldt, "Zur Kunstgeschichte der Jahre 220 bis 270," *Jahrbuch des Deutschen Archäologischen Instituts* 51 (1936), Pl. 6.

XI. Third-Century Relief

a. Arch of Constantine, Donation Scene (detail of left side), in Rome. Photograph from H. P. L'Orange with A. von Gerkan, *Der Spätantike Bildschmuck des Konstantinsbogens* (Berlin, 1939), Pl. 16.

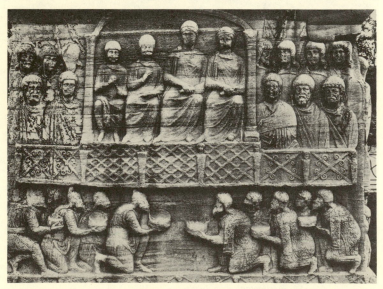

b. Obelisk of Theodosius, barbarian tribute, in Constantinople. Photograph from Gerda Bruns, *Der Obelisk und seine Basis auf dem Hippodrom zu Konstantinopel* (Istanbul, 1936), Fig. 37.

XII. Fourth-Century Relief

Part Two

THE UNFOLDING

OF ABSOLUTISM

The Unfolding of Absolutism

TO THE reflective student of history the age of Augustus is one of the most fascinating in all human development. Its peculiar mark is the restoration of order after a century of turmoil, the halting of a revolution which appeared unending. Other men, such as Napoleon Bonaparte, have dammed the outward courses of revolutions, but only by deflecting the unleashed forces into foreign conquests which eventually brought their own downfall. Augustus too had to drain off Roman energies in a series of conquests on the northern frontier, but these wars were peripheral in every sense; in his main task of establishing a new system of government which would assure lasting peace for the Mediterranean he was remarkably successful. His own reign extended forty-five years after his defeat of Antony, and the system he created lasted in essence for another two centuries, the great period of the "Roman peace." Augustus has not captured the world's imagination as did the meteoric Caesar, but in lasting effect on human history his role has been much the greater.

Augustus died on August 19, A.D. 14, at the Campanian town of Nola. As he lay dying, he begged his entourage for their approval of his life's acts; later the Senate placed the official stamp of acceptance on his rule by formally proclaiming him a god. Yet much was still latent, even undecided, in the new system of government which he had established, the Principate, and no man then living could have prophesied surely the changes in its character which were to ensue. The workings out of the trends of the Augustan Principate cover immediately a period which runs roughly from the death of Cicero to the accession of Hadrian (43 B.C.–A.D. 117).

The first six decades of this era were dominated by Augustus himself. Then a series of individuals connected with him by birth or adoption—the Julio-Claudian Caesars—ruled for another five decades to the death of Nero (A.D. 68). After a brief fever of civil wars, which covered a year, a new family sprung from Italian stock, the Flavian, held imperial power down to 96, when it was supplanted by the amiable Nerva (96–98); his adopted son, Trajan, opened the golden second century of the Empire. The first century itself has always had a dread fascination for mankind, for our ancient literary sources present a lurid picture of its luxuriant vice, its incredible monster-rulers who seem beyond the limits of ordinary humans, its fantastic incidents and displays—the milk baths of Poppaea, the mirrored rooms of the lecherers, and a host of other tales. Of the twelve rulers from Augustus down to Trajan, seven met violent ends, and an eighth (Nerva) escaped only because he adopted the strongest general he could find as his heir.

However autocratic an emperor might be, he was always living on top of a maelstrom of hidden tensions and conflicts reaching out from his own family through the aristocracy of Rome to the territorial, social, and cultural cleavages in the provinces. In the Golden Age which Hadrian proclaimed on one of his coins, the emperors had at last managed to consolidate their world into a reasonably tidy scheme, grouped in concentric circles about the rulers. By his time it is possible to estimate the price which had been paid for the success of these rulers, as measured in the loss of local autonomy by the cities, which were the fountainhead of civilization, and in the decay of initiative of the aristocracy.

To a surprising degree this price was voluntarily paid. In rising to the foreground as a single, unique figure, Augustus had concentrated upon himself the yearnings of his contemporaries (which one may call almost messianic) for a deliverer, a savior, and a benefactor. To this man, more as symbol than as living creature, men everywhere had tended to turn for assurance of peace and prosperity in the material world, for a sense of security and purpose on the spiritual level. Quite apart from any imperial effort to influence men's minds, the subjects persistently thrust up the rulers on a high pinnacle and revered from afar the giver of earthly blessings. The flattery, even worship, of the ruler ever grew as a threat to independent thought and action by the subjects.

Men yielded their own minds. In return they received, or hoped to receive, a symbol on which they might rely for mental security and material prosperity—in a word, stability.

III

Augustus:

The Winning of Men's Minds

THE cry for peace which welled up from the Mediterranean in the last days of the Roman Republic echoes in our hearts today with much of the force it must then have possessed, for these troubled days have deepened our historical sensitivities. Yet we can understand too the perverse influence of old attitudes. Crystallized into institutions, they impeded the bringing of peace to the ancient world until decades of violence had shattered their sway and had removed their main adherents, such as Cicero and Cato.

Secretly Octavian may already have envisioned himself as an eventual pacifier, but this role would not have been apparent to the Romans who read the proscription lists in the last fall days of 43. As they gazed on the bloody head of Cicero, the young Caesar must have appeared as another of those evil spirits of murder and vengeance of which the world lately had seen far too many.

The next years were not much better. Antony and Octavian moved east in 42 to destroy the armies of Brutus and Cassius at Philippi in Macedonia. They then split the Roman world between themselves: Lepidus got a small share, Antony stamped out the last embers of opposition in the East and raised money, Octavian pacified Gaul and settled the veterans of the joint armies on the Italian countryside. This policy provoked against Octavian a civil war by those dispossessed; there followed a long, costly naval war against the semipirate Sextus

Pompey, who controlled the Tyrrhenian Sea to the west of Italy. Finally Octavian skillfully engineered a break with Mark Antony, defeated him at Actium in 31, and pursued him to Egypt, where Antony and Cleopatra committed suicide in 30.

Octavian was now master of the Roman world. At this point he was one year younger than Alexander had been on his fevered death in Babylon; unlike Alexander, who was hailed as king by his father's army at the age of twenty, Octavian had commenced with only the potential resources embraced in the inherited name of Caesar. His native cold intelligence and perhaps a certain appeal of his youthful, yet sickly nature had done the rest.

Shift in Octavian's Policy

In particular, Octavian had begun to win men's minds. From about 40 B.C. it becomes apparent that he had tacked from his ruthless policy and set his sails on a more suitable course for a long voyage. Now that he had avenged Caesar, he paraded a policy of reconstruction of Italy; that is, he shifted from a negative program which could inspire only fear to a positive plan which might, and did, gain true support. Sundry personally unpleasant and frightening experiences during the war against Sextus Pompey (40–36 B.C.) may also have had their effect. Quite early in the struggle the Roman mob, which was being starved through Pompey's control of the Tyrrhenian Sea, informed Octavian of its displeasure by stoning him in the Forum; Octavian was snatched from death only by the intervention of Mark Antony. The mob could not be permanently put down by force, and Octavian's position tottered until Mark Antony patched up a truce at Misenum (39 B.C.) between Octavian and Sextus which allowed the inhabitants of Rome once more to get food.

Even more alarming perhaps to Octavian in these years was the revelation of his essential dependence on the good pleasure of Mark Antony. It was Antony who had really won at Philippi while the sick Octavian dragged about the field. The civil war in Italy had ended in Octavian's victory only because Antony held back his zealous lieutenants Asinius Pollio and Plancus from supporting his brother Lucius and his wife Fulvia, the leaders of the rebels. Once more, later, Antony had saved Octavian by revealing to him the treachery of one of his trusted friends, his deputy in Gaul. If Octavian were to remain a permanent figure on the political scene, he needed to create a firm body of support;

and it was now quite clear that such support could not be dragooned by force.

General policy and his insecure position alike led Octavian to adopt a more moderate attitude in the early 30's and ever more clearly to take the stand of a supporter of the old Roman way of life, in which he had to a considerable extent been reared by his mother. The victory of 36 was utilized as an opportunity for a formal, full expression of his program. In speeches to the Senate and the people he recounted his exploits and attempted to justify his acts from the beginning. These speeches were circulated in pamphlet form; at the same time he burned all the propaganda of hate which he had issued during the war against Sextus Pompey. Either in these speeches or at the same period he promised a full restoration of the constitution when Antony returned from the Parthian war he was then waging. The civil wars, averred Octavian, were at an end; peace and good will had returned— and with them, we may add, internal security and safety of the seas. The spirit of 36 was duly immortalized in a gilded image of Octavian erected in the Forum on a column and bearing the inscription, "peace, long disturbed, he re-established on land and sea."

From this point forward Octavian's policy was built around the principles of moderation, peace, outwardly constitutional conduct, and the domination of a conjoined Italy and Rome in the Mediterranean world. His conversion had as consequence the conversion of others to his support, for his program thenceforth appealed to very important Roman and Italian elements. Many of the senators began to support him; although no public opinion polls exist to measure Octavian's popularity in Italy, his backing there certainly increased rapidly from 36. The poets Virgil and Horace give us actual examples of this shift, for both abandoned doubt or hostility to support Octavian's program in the 30's.

A more general indication of Octavian's success is the fact that the young man dared to turn against his former buttress Antony and pressed on to the complete destruction of his erstwhile partner. In a skillful campaign of vicious propaganda Octavian assailed his opponent as falling away from things Roman for the fleshpots of the Orient, embodied in the siren Cleopatra. The success of this attack is marked not only by the extraordinary view which later generations have had of the beautiful Queen of the Nile, but also by the unanimity of ancient sources in accepting Octavian's argument that Antony had been bewitched by this creature "plotting ruin 'gainst the Capitol and destruction to the empire, with her polluted crew of creatures foul with lust." [1]

To modern eyes the conflict of the two was merely another round in the struggle for personal pre-eminence which characterized the Late Republic. To his contemporaries Octavian lifted his preparations almost to the level of a crusade and rose from the role of factional leader to that of a champion of Roman ways. Italy paid to him heavy, extraordinary taxes, and its inhabitants in 32 swore "of their own will" an oath to support Octavian. Relying on this evidence of loyalty, Octavian gave up his despotic power as triumvir and posed for the next few years as leader by universal desire, a position which was to underly his later reconstruction of the Roman government.

From every point of view the result of the battle of Actium on September 2, 31, was foreordained. Morally, Octavian had won so complete a victory that many of Antony's leaders had deserted to him before the battle; militarily, his admiral Agrippa had employed the same navy which had defeated Sextus against Antony's communications, in as masterly an attack as the world has ever seen, and so had hemmed in Antony on the barren east coast of the Adriatic. When the sun set on the day of the battle, a sullen Antony was brooding in silence on the poop of Cleopatra's fleeing ship; his halfhearted, puzzled forces were preparing to surrender to the victor.

Constitutional Reorganization

Three years later, after annexing Egypt with its treasure and reorganizing the Eastern provinces, Octavian returned to Rome and celebrated a triumph over Cleopatra and various barbarians, but not over Antony—Roman did not triumph over fellow Roman. When the great procession had made its way up the Capitoline Hill to the temple of Jupiter Optimus Maximus, and life began to slip back into the more humdrum ways of peace, the time had come for Octavian to make a decision on his position in the Roman state. Caesar had been avenged, the forces which caused unrest in Italy had been exterminated, all serious sources of opposition in the Mediterranean had been suppressed —but the spirit of *res novae*, of unrest in men's minds, had not yet been exorcised. If the Roman revolution were to end, two things were neces-

[1] Horace, *Odes* 1.37.7–10.

sary: a safe diversion for the urge to action, which must have showed itself particularly in the army, and a great gesture of final settlement of the Roman constitution.

The diversion was furnished by turning Roman arms against such internal dissidents as the tribes of northwestern Spain, in making the great series of conquests on the northern frontier which secured the Rhine and Danube as the imperial boundaries, and in extorting from the Parthians a favorable settlement of the Eastern question. To the subjects the word "peace" had much the meaning it does today, and Augustus gave the interior of the Empire that peace. Thrice he closed the gates of the arches of Janus to symbolize the fact—in all previous Roman history they had been closed only twice. To the Roman nobles *pax* was also a dynamic concept involving the constant expansion and pacification of the Roman domain; peace was gained by war, which was a natural part of life (see Pl. III). The armies and fleets of the Empire were busy throughout most of Augustus' reign on the frontiers. Each war, however, was carefully calculated to bring profit without loss. In Augustus' words, gambling on war was like fishing with a gold fishhook, the loss of which could not be made good by any catch.

Not all Octavian's contemporaries were entirely satisfied with his nebulous constitutional position. His opponents in the wars had raised the cry of liberty against him; the inhabitants of a north Italian town, Nursia, had buried their dead in the civil war of 41–40 under the inscription, "they died for liberty"; the neutral historian Asinius Pollio seems to have asserted that the battles of Philippi marked the end of liberty and that in later wars, as between Octavian and Antony, the Roman people merely determined who was to be their master. When Pollio talked of *libertas,* indeed, his concept of the term was that of the senatorial aristocracy, but even in this sense no one could honestly feel that the laws were supreme or that Octavian's annual re-election to the consulship suited the republican spirit.

Octavian, however, could not easily admit that he did not follow the republican tradition. He fined the Nursians heavily, but against such a man as Asinius Pollio the use of force would merely prove to the Roman aristocracy the very point he wished to deny. To convince this group that he was really an adherent of the republican constitution was not simple, yet it was essential. Octavian could look back to the fate of his greatuncle Caesar, who had openly accepted a position of autocracy at the eventual cost of his life. Caesar, a relentlessly logical person, had quite ignored the power of tradition; Octavian realized more clearly the intense, if intangible, belief of Rome that it was the seat of liberty. To the aristocracy and Italian upper classes, the groups which he particularly wished to use to help him carry the burden of government, he must appeal by other arguments than those of the restoration of peace and the reassertion of Roman might, however important these steps might be in preparing the way for his acceptance.

The result was that Octavian first made a careful series of gestures throughout 28 to gain general favor; then he dramatically met the Senate on January 13, 27 B.C., when he returned his power to that body and so "restored" the Republic. The Senate in turn handed back to him some of this power in legal form and on January 16 gave him the title of Augustus, superhuman in its religious connotations.

The speech which the historian Dio Cassius manufactured for Octavian on this great occasion reflects at least the nub of the situation: he had promised to restore constitutional government in 36, and now he was carrying out his promise as far as the Senate was concerned. The people might remain the titular font of power henceforth, but Octavian definitely quashed any remote possibility that the Roman revolution might end in a true rule of the people. The stability of the Roman state was to rest on the co-operation between the upper classes of Rome and Italy and the "first citizen" (*princeps*) whose authority was voluntarily accepted by all.

As regards the powers conferred on Augustus the decisions of the year 27 B.C. were not final. Augustus was not sufficiently clairvoyant to foresee the centuries of the Empire or even the remaining decades of his life; there was in consequence a process of change and development in the position of the *princeps* which was far from completed by his death. Nevertheless the essential distribution of functions was clearly accomplished in 27 and had been foreshadowed by the previous decade. Augustus received control of all the major armed forces, which he reorganized as permanent institutions. He governed through deputies most of the provinces likely to require military operations against either external or internal foes. The rest of the republican machinery was reinstituted, but Augustus had a sufficient accumulation of powers to check or impel any part which malfunctioned and to curb the unrestrained rivalry of nobles for "dignity" which had cursed the Late Republic; by law he had really full liberty of action. No student of practical politics can doubt that Augustus was the master in this system and that his hegemony would continue so long as he retained the support of the armed forces. For the present, absolutism lay veiled, but that it was implicit in this structure later Caesars were to show.

Augustus himself recognized the old mastery of law and safeguarded the rights of his fellow citizens. Much of mankind does not wish to think beyond outward forms, and in this era many people were glad to have any system which gave peace so long as it paid lip service to old precedent. Men from the East, indeed, were content simply to take Augustus as a Hellenistic king, the deputy of a god or a god himself, but the Principate refused to accept these ideas. A consolidation of the necessary changes in the past century, the new system was a masterpiece of delicate adaptation of old machinery to new needs. Its greatest tribute perhaps is the fact that modern analysts seem more confused and discordant about its true nature than the people ruled by it.

Augustan Program

More important in the present connection than analysis of his specific powers is a consideration of his program to rally support behind his new form of government. Its main outlines were in gestation during the 30's, but after 27 they deepened and widened considerably. At this point a word of warning is necessary. In dealing with the Augustan structure, historians have all too commonly assumed that Augustus originated its policies and have failed to note his subtle adaptation of ideas already current.

An extraordinary example of the extent to which Augustus was willing to go in meeting the opinions of his contemporaries can be seen in his later treatment of Caesar. In effect, Augustus jettisoned Caesar, the idol of his youth and the source of his first claim to power. In the early days the young Octavian had played heavily on his relationship to Caesar and had trumpeted his intention of avenging his murder. Once triumphant and acclaimed Augustus, he did his utmost to disassociate himself from the aura of autocracy, radicalism, and cosmopolitanism connected with Caesar, which had made him an object of hatred to the upper classes of Rome. In Augustan sculpture there was no widespread effort to portray Caesar, and on coins the star of the deified Julius and the claim of Augustus to be *divi filius* waned after 27 B.C. Men were free to speak as they pleased about Julius Caesar and so built up a picture of the civil wars in which he appeared to be the villain. Augustan poets tended to pass lightly over Caesar, apart from evoking him as a star looking down from Heaven on Augustus or using his divinity to prove that of his adopted son Augustus; the difference between Virgil's treatment of Caesar at the end of the First Georgic, which depicts the sun hiding his head on the Ides of March, and the poet's neglect of Caesar in the *Aeneid* is notable.

Not only did Augustus sacrifice his greatuncle on the altar of senatorial approval; he even unblushingly went so far as to link himself with the republican hero Cato the Younger, as a model of rectitude and civic justice and as a supporter of due order in the state. Thus he drew the sting of the Catonic opposition which had vexed Caesar. In fine, Augustus tended to dismiss Caesar as an unfortunate interruption to Roman development, a view in which he could secure wide support; his own policy was portrayed as a direct continuation of that of the Late Republic. In blotting out Caesar, Augustus was ungrateful as a "son," but he was most certainly being practical in tailoring his views to those of the aristocracy.

Augustus' aim was to build a political system to secure stability for the world:

May it be my privilege [he announced by edict] to establish the State in a firm and secure position, and enjoy therefrom the rewards of which I am ambitious, that of being called the author of the best possible government, and of carrying with me when I die the hope that the foundations which I have laid for the State will remain unshaken.[2]

From the provinces he expected acceptance of Roman rule, as marked by proper payment of taxes and recruits and the end of rebellion or civil disorder. In return he admitted that obligation to protect the subjects which republican thought had begun to couple with imperial position and which Virgil was soon to enunciate in majestic terms. Augustus improved the practice, if not the form, of provincial government, established a permanent, efficient army and navy, maintained the autonomy of the local oligarchies, and tolerated local customs. He did his utmost to guarantee prosperity, not by state control and planning save in the field of grain supply for Rome, but by eliminating causes of disorder, furnishing a sound currency, and otherwise reducing governmental interference.

From the upper classes of Rome and Italy Augustus expected acceptance of his regime, as marked by active assistance in the governance of

[2] Suetonius, *Augustus* 28.2.

the Empire. He made great efforts to pass around public offices in the right quarters, allowed such old marks of distinction as triumphs and public funerals, and permitted a considerable latitude in speech. Although class distinctions were sharpened under Augustus, it became possible to move more easily from one class to another. The old fight between the exclusive republican nobility and "new men" such as Cicero finally ended in the opening of senatorial ranks to merit and in the regularization of equestrian careers—all this, of course, depending upon winning the good will of the ruler.

Prosperity and order—the "care for the common life of all men" in the phrase of Vitruvius' preface—could win many men; honors could entice others. Augustus sensed also the need for an ideal about which to rally the Roman spirit, and that ideal he strove incessantly to provide throughout his reign. To put it briefly, in the terms of Eduard Norden, this ideal was a mystic rejuvenation of the Roman race along traditional lines, under the leadership of Augustus as an embodiment of the old Roman spirit.

Augustus was a conservative. In politics he turned to the right; so too religious and moral regeneration to his mind would arise from the resuscitation of the old institutions and from the unification and protection of the Romano-Italian stock, the virtues of which were so clearly sung by Virgil. Upon this solid core he hoped to build his "best possible government." The sense of romanticism, of looking back, had been strong in art and literature since the middle of the first century; as men became more conscious of the revolution which had been occurring in political and intellectual fields alike, they sought more eagerly to attach themselves to earlier, more tranquil days.

Augustus, like Caesar, harnessed the tendency to his political aims, but in doing so he was exploiting an attitude in which he himself participated. The initiation of Augustus into the venerable Eleusinian mysteries, the style and language of his *Res Gestae*, the solemn mummery of his Secular festival—all are part of a spirit which communed with an ideal past; but perhaps the most astounding illustration of his nature is the fact that he desired to be called Romulus after the founder of Rome. Regretfully he had to give up this idea for fear of its kingly associations, but he honored Romulus in every possible way. The acts of great political leaders are likely to be a bizarre combination of the shrewd and the simple, of conscious exploitation of current attitudes and intuitive superstition; and conservatives, who look to the past, are not thereby less likely to believe in fantasy than are radicals.

Modes of Propaganda

The depth and character of the Augustan program had far-reaching effects on Augustus' attitude toward the thought of his age. All physical defiance of his sway had failed, and Augustus kept under arms a sufficient force to make any subsequent opposition of this nature a most foolhardy gamble. For his system of government to succeed—especially for his program of rejuvenation to bear ripe fruit—he had permanently to gain not men's bodies but men's minds. The efforts which Augustus made to this end show that he drew the proper conclusions and that he realized the difficulty of his task.

Genuine success rested primarily upon untiring attention to the details of government. His acts, however, might be reinforced in two complementary directions: he could implant his program in public opinion, and he could prevent the vocal or physical expression of discontent. Augustus shrewdly utilized a host of means to bend the thought of his contemporaries and of posterity—for always he had in mind the judgment which later generations would pass on his work. Upon the Augustan foundations his successors built a mighty structure of propaganda and control, the development of which is a mark of the unfolding of their absolutism.

Augustus thus shaped a great appeal to public opinion and extended it far beyond the mere security of his personal position, though that aspect was never forgotten. His message was addressed to all levels of society, from slaves, freedmen, and provincials to the upper classes of Rome and Italy, but was aimed particularly at the latter. To present his ideas to these groups Augustus utilized physical objects—coins, sculpture, inscriptions, and architecture—and words, both his own in edict and speech and those of the authors of the era. Beyond these vehicles lay also his personal example, his deft interweaving of himself into the patriotic and religious institutions of Rome and the Empire, and other subtle devices.

In the Roman world coins were a means of exchange and payment, particularly of the troops; by the Late Republic they had also become a potent vehicle for the explanation of state policy to the public. In the Empire the legends and types of coins came to change as frequently as those of modern stamps, as varying aspects of state policy came to the fore or dropped back. Coins could be charged with great symbolic value by combinations of very simple motifs such as the representation of Concord, Peace, and other virtues, Greco-Roman deities (each aiding man in a special sphere), military standards, harvest tools, and the like. Though much of this significance is undoubtedly lost to us, the essential messages had to be put very directly, and so we can detect at least the main lines of official policy as reflected on the coins.

The republican coinage had been theoretically carried out by junior officials under the control of the Senate. In the late second and the first century B.C. the types had been chosen largely by the mintmasters to celebrate current events or the glorious deeds of their own ancestors. This coinage, ever more factional, led on to nearly independent issues by the great warlords in the provinces; Caesar, the greatest of these, gained mastery of Rome and was the first to place the head of a living person (himself) on Roman coins in his last years when he was claiming divine honors. In the civil wars after his death the triumvirs, as well as Brutus and Cassius, struck with their own heads, but Augustus proceeded even further in bending the state coinage to his own purposes.

In his reign imperial coins of gold and silver were struck at one or more mints in the East, in Spain for a brief while, and from about 8 B.C. at Lyons, which became the other great mint (beside Rome) for the Empire. The mint of Rome, which was restored to operation about 20 B.C., was likewise under imperial control, though the mintmasters continued to refer to their own family history, at least sporadically, down to 12 B.C., when gold and silver issues at Rome halted for the rest of the reign. Most coins even before this date are purely imperial in character, and the formal current description of the copper issues of the Roman mint as "senatorial" is only nominally correct. Augustus and his successors really dictated the contents of all coinage and so put their achievements and their promises in direct, yet subtle, fashion before the eyes of the imperial audience in Rome and in the provinces.

The types represented on the coins of the Augustan mints do not furnish as complete a statement of policy as do those of later rulers, but they do indicate the general road down which Augustus tried to steer public opinion. The military and diplomatic triumphs of the reign are quite frankly emphasized—Actium, the conquest of Egypt, the recovery of the Roman standards lost to Parthia in the defeat of Crassus and two later generals, the domination of Armenia, and to a lesser extent the victories on the northern frontier. Augustan peace is clearly not a craven matter; Augustus was directing the bulk of his coinage not at the provinces but at the citizen body of Rome and Italy.

More important than peace, according to the coins, was internal security, and this arose from the moderation of Augustus; a common motif is the shield of virtue, often held by a flying Victory, which had been given him by the Senate in 27 B.C. His salvation of the Roman citizen body by ending the civil wars is also emphasized. The Senate presented to him, likewise in 27, an oak crown, the usual trophy for a soldier who had saved a fellow soldier, and this wreath appears frequently on the coins, encircling the words *ob civis servatos*. The type, which emphasized clearly to the subjects that their security depended on their rulers, became standard under later emperors.

Even the briefest examination of the Augustan coinage reveals both the pride which Augustus felt in his achievements and also his effort to convince the Roman world that he was all-important to its continuation. Vows taken by the Senate and the people for his safe return to Rome after his various trips or for his health in time of sickness are carefully commemorated. Except for the few republican-type coins before 12 B.C., his head always appears on the obverse of gold and silver coins and on the copper *as,* which was used particularly in paying troops. The legend conveys his legal powers in considerable detail. Frequently the reverse is given over to such types as a globe (for universal domination), the rudder of Fortune, the cornucopiae of prosperity, the Capricorn of his birthday, statues and arches erected to him, and the like.

The mystic undertones of his program rose closest to the surface in the celebration of the Secular festival of 17 B.C., which was designed to mark the end of an old era (*saeculum*) and to herald the beginning of a new, more fortunate age. This event was noted by the Roman and Spanish mints and was commemorated for years after the actual celebration. Augustus' policy of reconstruction otherwise was not easily subject to portrayal on coins. Although some reference might be expected to the reconstruction of temples and honors to the gods, the divine powers which guarded Rome turn up on Augustan coins usually in very close connection with Augustus himself. For example, the legend "Apollo of Actium" is frequent; a coin of 16 B.C. attests vows to Jupiter Optimus Maximus by the Senate and the Roman people "for the health of Imperator Caesar because the state has been increased and made tranquil by him." [3] Such vows were a standard practice throughout imperial history and were taken yearly in the normal course of events.

In the later years of his reign the variety of Augustan coinage decreased. The Lyons mint emphasized year after year a few major themes, first Augustus the victorious and then, from 2 B.C., the continuation of his dynasty. A long series celebrates his grandsons Gaius and Lucius even after their death; then another belatedly notes the final selection of his stepson Tiberius as his heir. The monotonous repetition of these themes is in a sense a testimony to Augustus' security of position; in another respect it may also serve as evidence of his weariness, of the fact that he and his world no longer felt the fresh appeal of his program.

The imperial coinage reflects most directly the ideas of Augustus, but the ordinary subject in the provinces saw chiefly the copper or, in some cases, silver issues of his local city or province. The tone of these countless issues followed, though at considerable distance, the Augustan picture of the reformed constitution and the security of the new system, and alluded discreetly to the local bearing of the new order.

An outstanding example is the Alexandrian mint, which coined for all Egypt. This mint began its coinage as an affiliate of the Roman mint by repeating some symbols of sovereignty of the previous kings as well as types appealing to native and Greek religious feelings (throne of Isis, Athena, and so on). Yet the Alexandrian mint was not permitted to follow a totally independent course. In values, in style of dating, and to some extent in types, it linked onto its Ptolemaic predecessor, but as J. Vogt has pointed out, Roman types also were introduced; the coins of Alexandria, like those of Rome, fitted into a general imperial pattern of emphasis on Augustus' achievements and his dynastic plans. Other coins present the argument that the fertility of Egypt was due to Augustus. Since the days of the Pharaohs it had always been necessary to strengthen the inherited trust of the fellahin in the divine powers of their rulers to control the forces of nature; now that conquered Egypt was to pour its surplus grain into the mouths of the Roman populace such reassurance was doubly necessary. In 2 B.C. Augustus was officially given the significant title *pater patriae,* which he had already held in popular inscriptions. The senator Messalla Corvinus, in offering the token of reverence, had argued that the felicity of the state was connected with that of Augustus and his house; the mint of Alexandria took up this truly

[3] British Museum, *Coins of the Roman Empire* 1 (London, 1923), 17, n. 91.

autocratic concept and coupled the bestowal of the title with the prosperity of the age.

To sum up the program of the Augustan coinage generally, the *princeps* was not reluctant to emphasize his own military accomplishments or his virtues, which were evidently to be taken as a guarantee and source of felicity to the Roman world. The appeal of the imperial coinage was primarily to Roman and Italian circles; to find any great emphasis on the themes of peace and prosperity or local sentiments one must turn to local coinages, especially of the Eastern cities.

The tone of the coinage is a positive one. Augustus might roam his palace begging Varus to return the legions destroyed in the German disaster of A.D. 9, but the coins of Alexandria in 10 and 11 tell the subjects only of the "victory" secured by Tiberius on the Rhenish frontier during those two years.

These small pieces of metal spoke directly from the ruler to his subject, but they could convey complicated ideas and programs only to a limited extent. A fuller plastic representation of these ideas comes in the architecture and sculpture of the Augustan era. Both literary references and the surviving fragments attest the great wave of construction all over the Empire. Old centers were embellished; new cities were founded. The latter were frequently named after Augustus or members of his family, and much of the public building everywhere was connected with Augustus. Throughout the world, says Philo, he was honored with temples, porticoes, sacred precincts, groves, and colonnades; both at Alexandria and at Caesarea in Palestine his temple looked down on the harbor as a "hope and beacon of safety to those sailing in or out." [4] The extent to which men went in linking their building to the name of Augustus is displayed in the great palace of Herod at Jerusalem, which consisted of two main structures named respectively Caesareion and Agrippeion—upon the support of Augustus Herod's rule stood or fell.

The building in the provinces was not carried out by the ruler, though it honored him and often imitated monuments erected by him in Rome. To find a direct reflection in architecture of his ideas one must travel to the city of Rome and especially to the Campus Martius, a section transformed under Augustus into a splendid complex of marble buildings. The eighty-two temples which he restored or rebuilt, the porticoes, the theaters, and the other buildings added by him and his associates—all

[4] Philo, *Legation* 151.

marked a beginning of the process by which republican Rome vanished beneath the imperial city; the boast of Augustus that he found Rome in brick and left it in marble was intended allegorically, but has its architectural truth. Physically as well as spiritually Rome was to be made the center of the Mediterranean world. Vitruvius, who dedicated his work on architecture to Augustus, rightly asserts in his preface, "With respect to the future, you have such regard to public and private buildings, that they will correspond to the grandeur of our history, and will be a memorial to future ages." On the esthetic attitudes manifested in this work it will suffice to observe here that Augustan building differed from the Greco-Roman pattern already established in its greater size, opulence, and sureness of taste. In all the arts Augustus encouraged a return to the past and more specifically to the classic Greek era.

The colossal Augustan building program was carried out mainly at the expense of the ruler. So he manifested his glory to Rome, and so he supported many of its citizens. His name did not appear on all of the edifices, no great palace rose on the Palatine in his reign, and there were no temples to Augustus in Rome itself during his life. Nonetheless one comes away from his buildings with a clear feeling that everything he erected was in a sense a lasting exemplification of his policy of interlacing past and present, and of weaving his own figure inextricably into the general pattern for future contemplation.

One of the more subtle examples is the arch in the Forum on which he engraved in public view those long lists of consuls and triumphators which are still preserved in large part; to the latter list he added Romulus, and he did not fail to include his own victories. A more obvious illustration is the great Forum of Augustus. Its focus was the new temple of Mars the Avenger, whose statue was placed between those of Venus the Begetter (as ancestress of the Julian line) and of the deified Caesar. Here, where three divine forces symbolized both the superhuman protection of Rome and the exalted position of Augustus, sprung from Venus and Caesar, the Senate met thenceforth to vote military honors; here standards recaptured from the enemy were dedicated.

In front of the temple were two great hemicycles on north and south for the display of statues. Augustus placed in this Valhalla effigies of the "leaders who had raised the estate of the Roman people from obscurity to greatness" and by edict announced that they were to be held as an example to himself and succeeding *principes*.[5] His insertion among these

[5] Suetonius, *Augustus* 31.5.

worthies of the statues of his mythical ancestor Aeneas and of four historical relatives, only one of whom was truly distinguished, was a skillful argument that his ancestors were among the founding fathers of Roman greatness; both here and in his funeral procession there was an unwritten assertion that Augustus was the heir to all the great men of the Roman past. Though the spirit of its builder was everywhere present in this great Forum, Augustus carefully avoided his own representation until 2 B.C., when the Senate voted to erect in its center a statue of the ruler in a chariot with the new title *pater patriae*. Later the temple of Mars served as center of worship for the deified Augustus until his own temple could be built.

Of the Forum of Augustus only scraps remain today. The most perfectly preserved monument of the period is the Altar of Augustan Peace in the Campus Martius close to the great northern road. Decreed by the Senate in 13 B.C. after the pacification of Spain and Gaul, the structure was dedicated in 9 B.C. Although its preservation is accidental and Augustus built many other noble monuments in Rome, he probably would have been willing for the modern world to judge of him by this altar alone; for he emphasizes it in his *Res Gestae,* and the workmanship is of the highest quality throughout. The reconstruction of this jewel is a product of the Fascist commercialization of Romanitas, for which we may be grateful, despite the garish edifice in which it is now housed on the banks of the Tiber.

Essentially the Altar of Augustan Peace is a simple altar surrounded by a curtain wall on all four sides, a perfect embodiment of ancient architecture, which attempted to delimit and set off its spaces sharply from the outside world. The floral decoration filling the lower half of the curtain wall is a most elegant illustration of the Greco-Roman style. Derived from nature, the luxuriant pattern yet reveals, as Morey says in general terms of ancient art, "axial symmetry, the ordering of subordinate and lateral units about a central dominating stem, so that the resultant figure is self-sufficient and needs no suggested continuation to complete it." [6]

Even in marveling at the free handling and fanciful detail of the delicate floral decoration one realizes that the altar is not a Greek but a truly Roman monument. This impression becomes even more overpowering as one raises one's eyes to the frieze above. On either side wall the frieze is given over to a stately, solemn procession of Romans in

[6] C. R. Morey, *Medieval Art* (New York, 1942), 8.

their togas advancing to a sacrifice, either that with which the altar was dedicated or that attending the public thanksgiving for the safe return of Augustus from the Western provinces (see Pl. II *a*). The religious spirit of these men, women, and children is as intense as that of the horsemen and maidens on the Parthenon, but it is of a different order. The movement is slower, almost halted; the figures, sometimes a trifle harsh, do not stand out individually but gather strength from submergence in the group; the children, who symbolize the eternity of the Augustan world, are not to be found on the Parthenon. Above all, this frieze mirrors the Roman emphasis on the historical fact as opposed to the idealization of the Parthenon figures, which are free in space and in time. Though the altar owes so much to Greek techniques that it may well be the product of men Greek in speech, even the synthesis in technique "is so complete that the work cannot be pulled apart into Greek and Roman elements." [7]

To be more precise, the Altar of Augustan Peace is not only ancient, not only Roman, but also—and most directly—Augustan, both in style and in subject. The serenity and certainty of the figures, the religious spirit, the scrupulous rendering of Roman dress and ornament—all these are a reflection of Augustus himself; but especially in the subjects depicted is it apparent that one is looking at a work planned by Augustus to make visible his policy of order and restoration.

On the front and rear curtain walls, to either side of the two entrances, are single sculptured panels. Of those on the front, that on the left apparently represented the suckling of Romulus and Remus by the wolf, but only a majestic, helmeted head of the spectator Mars has been well preserved. The other frontal panel, which is in much better condition, depicts Aeneas at the site of Rome, solemnly sacrificing to the Penates, the family gods of Troy, whom he has brought to be guardians of Rome. Since the *Aeneid* was already published by the date of the dedication of the altar, the literate Roman could have construed in this scene of *pius Aeneas* the presage of majesty of the future Rome, and the identification of the Julian house with its rise, which Virgil wove into his epic.

On the back, the two panels rise from the pseudohistoric to the symbolic. The right side apparently was given over to a representation of Rome, seated on a pile of armor and holding a Victory in her hand, a composition found on a derivative altar at Carthage. Peace to the Romans was the product of victory in war; but men had also another

[7] Gerhart Rodenwaldt, *Kunst um Augustus* (Berlin, 1943), 51.

view of peace, which is illustrated on the left side. Here is Terra Mater (less probably Italia), a truly Roman matron seated on a rock, holding on her lap two children and fruits of the earth and surrounded by other emblems of fertility, much as she appears in Horace's *Secular Hymn* (see Pl. II *b*). Heavily restored and so more appealing to the modern eye, this lovely figure is a superb realization of the idea that the peace of Augustus brought prosperity. The Terra Mater panel suggests what we have lost in the damage or destruction of the other three; an ancient spectator must have read in the figures of all four an almost complete exposition of the Augustan program.

The two long sides of the curtain wall are given over to the frieze already noted, in which Roman dignitaries advance in two columns toward the front side of the altar to carry out their sacrifice. On the one side are the Senate and the Roman people with wives and children, both groups reformed and stabilized by the ruler. On the other appear the major figures of the Augustan family including Augustus himself, who is preceded by twelve lictors and followed by the consuls Tiberius and Quinctilius Varus and the four flamens.

After the flamens come Agrippa, probably, and the rest of the Augustan circle, male and female, child and adult. While the assertion by Augustus of his own pre-eminent authority and of his dynastic plans is apparent, his figure, shown in three-quarters view, is only subtly marked off from the others by a slight emphasis on height and prominence and by the deference of the lictors. The old officers and trappings of state and the new emphasis on an individual are joined on this frieze and sublimated by the hieratic pose of religious devotion. The religious note appears once again on the frieze running about the altar proper, but this apparently generalized portrayal of the consecration rites in 9 B.C. has not been well preserved.

The Altar of Augustan Peace and the *Aeneid* of Virgil are, each in its own field, the most perfect artistic reflections of the Augustan program. Both are the products of artists who accepted that program, enriched its esthetic content, and gave it by their work a wider currency; but the essential similarity of idea in both indicates clearly the uniformity of the underlying policy. Who the architect and sculptors of the altar were, and exactly how Augustus infused his view of himself into their receptive minds we do not know; illumination on the relationship of ruler, craftsmen, and end product may be gained more clearly from the career of Virgil.

Apart from reliefs there was a great deal of attention to the figure of the ruler in sculpture in the round. Unlike Caesar, of whom no absolutely certain bust or statue survives, the features of Augustus are preserved in numerous statues. In age and attributes they vary considerably, but at Rome itself there is in general an underlying similarity which cannot be accidental; it must, that is, go back to the conscious desires of the ruler himself to be portrayed in an attitude of calm security. Real variation may be found only in provincial examples, and even here local styles often worked subtly within the general convention of simplification and "purification" required to make the ruler's face a symbol of universal significance. The serious political role of his statues must have discouraged free invention on the part of the sculptors who carved these representations of the savior of the world.

The ubiquity, even more the significance, of statuary in the ancient world is difficult to understand today. In our busy city streets statues are inconveniences, doomed to decay in the acid-laden air, and photographic reproductions of our heroes are both cheaper and easier to handle. In general attitude also there is a tremendous difference, for the ancient world conceived a mystic relationship between a man such as Augustus and his replica in stone or bronze.

Just as a cult image of a god was in some sense the god, so the statue of a man was felt in a way to be the man himself, or at least to be filled with a divine spirit, especially if it were dedicated in a religious precinct. Plutarch, in talking of the statues of humans, shields, pillars, and other objects in the temple close at Delphi, says that they seem to "have movement and significance in sympathy with the god's foreknowledge, and no part of them is void or insensible, but all are filled with the divine spirit." [8] The same was felt to be true of statues of men of such semidivine character as Augustus and his successors, wherever these images were placed. Both Augustus and Tiberius insisted sharply that their statues were to be not cult statues (*simulacrum*) but simple portraits (*statua* or *imago-effigies*), but the imperial subjects must have found it difficult to disentangle the human from the divine. Though the Epicureans and later the Christians might scoff at the idea that bits of marble could possess spirit, an abundance of evidence shows that the great majority of the Empire felt quite otherwise.

The results of this view were of far-reaching consequence. In the first place, a statue could foretell what was to happen to the person it

[8] *Moralia* 398A.

represented or to the community generally. Ancient literature is full of stories of statues turning about on their pedestal, or falling, or growing grasses and vines, and so on. Each type of miraculous event had its meaning; when statues sweat or weep, a late author tells us, a civil war is in the offing.

Then again, expression of men's opinions found easy vents in the statues always at hand. Not only their erection or destruction but also lesser acts of garlanding or defiling statues had a mystic meaning of great import, and the statues of the emperor were asylums to which one could appeal from unjust treatment. The worship of the emperor's statues, at first spontaneous under Augustus, became ever more common and later compulsory as a public duty of reverence, at least to that superhuman force or *genius* embodied in the ruler's person through which he assured divine blessings and temporal felicity.

By their very erection in such profusion, then, statues of Augustus had a great significance. Much might also be conveyed by their attitude or embellishment. The most famous portrait of Augustus is his imperious representation in military cuirass, holding out his hand in address to his troops; the statue was found in the villa of his wife Livia outside Rome (see Frontispiece). This Prima Porta statue, probably though not certainly carved in a later generation, shows Augustus in the prime of life, and in its Vatican niche today it still expects of the spectator the silent obedience due the pacifier of the world. At the side of the statue is a cupid on a dolphin (in allusion to the divine origin of the Julian clan from Venus); the breastplate is so laden down with symbolism that one almost loses sight of the powerful head, which expresses better than any other in its idealized realism the will and certainty of Augustus. The subject of the cuirass is an elaborate allegory of empire, revolving about the peaceful surrender of the Roman standards by a Parthian to the god Mars. On either side of this central scene is a conquered province; above are Dawn and the Sun, bringing a new order, and over all Heaven draws a mantle of protection; beneath the central group are Terra Mater with the patron divinities of Augustus' battles, Apollo and Diana, who bulk large on the later coinage of the reign. In discussion of this statue or the reliefs of the Altar of Augustan Peace, scholars have discerned subtleties of interpretation which bind all the products of the Augustan Age in an immensely complicated yet firmly interwoven pattern. Though the subtleties may at times reach far beyond what the artist or Augustus himself intended, the Augustan program was assuredly urged upon many different levels of understanding.

While statues of the complexity of the Prima Porta example are rare, representations of Augustus did abound in imperial Rome and also in the Empire, both in his lifetime and long afterward. As a result the features of Augustus must have been more familiar to his subjects than had ever before been the case with a Greco-Roman ruler in his lifetime. Either through Augustus' own contriving or at the direction of provincial governors, client kings, and wealthy subjects, the architects and sculptors of the Empire had to work in the imperial spirit if they were to attain success. At least one architect dared to disagree with a later emperor, but there is no evidence of any opposition or refusal to be a tool of imperial policy in the Augustan period. The numerous commissions must have been extremely tempting, and in such cases as the Altar of Augustan Peace some artists at least seem to have assented to the Augustan program with their hearts. The same assent may be found in several authors of the age, but Augustan literature must be reserved for the following part.

Augustus as a Symbol

Of few persons do plastic representations so well reflect the man as do those of Augustus. Unlike the usual political leader, who has a chance to develop a flesh-and-blood personality during his rise from obscurity, Augustus leaped onto the center of the Roman political stage in his late 'teens and never again left it. His character, his entire way of life, had essentially to develop before the intense gaze of the public. Like Alexander, the youth Octavian had little more privacy than a growing amoeba under a microscope; and Alexander at least had had two more years of life than Octavian when he took over public responsibility.

To fend off prying minds, the spirit of Augustus had to retreat far behind an outward shell of studied behavior—so far that to us, and to many even of his contemporaries, the shell becomes the impenetrable marble of the statue, as in Prima Porta, where the eyes look far in the distance (see Frontispiece). The inevitability of this outward process of ossification must have been accentuated by Augustus' realization that the great bulk of his subjects wanted in him a symbol— a symbol of certainty, calmness, justice tempered with mercy, a mixture of the divine and the paternal. Driven by these outward and inward pressures, Augustus adopted a formal pattern of appearance which was rather reinforced than destroyed by his pleasure in simple games and his occasionally reported quips; after the first impetuosity of youth had been damped, we hear of few events in his life which cracked his shell.

Augustus, in other words, was in one sense his own most potent means of spreading his program, for his life and acts were a studied embodiment of that program both in its aspects of general restoration and in its emphasis on his own personal place in the general plan. In viewing the married life of Augustus and Livia, which began in an unconventional way but quickly became a symbol of simple virtue, an American may well think of George and Martha Custis Washington; of all modern historical characters the Father of Our Country perhaps approaches most clearly the symbolic, statuesque dignity and respectability of the *pater patriae*. Once Augustus proffered his marriage to his fellow senators as an example of the proper subordination of wife to husband, though on this occasion the senators backed him into the corner by professing intense interest in the exact means by which he kept Livia, well known as an imperious lady, under control.

At other times the example of simplicity, morality, and moderation given by Augustus may well have had greater effect on the upper classes of Rome. A slave of Vedius Pollio dropped and broke a costly cup of myrrh at a banquet offered by his master to Augustus; when Vedius ordered the slave thrown to man-eating carp, Augustus countermanded the order, called for all Vedius' precious cups, and calmly broke them one after another. The treatment of slaves, one suspects, improved thereafter whenever the *princeps* was visible. Although Augustus was not entirely successful in reforming the morals or the manners of the senatorial order, the significance and weight of his own way of life may not be entirely overlooked. "When in Rome, do as the Romans do" meant to many people in this era to do as Augustus did.

The character of Augustus as a symbol of general virtue was given official approval on numerous occasions, the most outstanding of which was the senatorial dedication in its meeting place of a golden shield commemorating his bravery, clemency, justice, and sense of duty (*virtus, clementia, iustitia, pietas*). Augustus himself was not backward in advertising his own sterling worth. The emphasis of the coins on his virtues has already been noted. His speeches and letters, which must have circulated widely, were not overmodest; and the two more formal assessments of his life which he composed were surely designed not only to justify his political career and state its noble aim of restoring

Roman virtue but also to notice properly his rectitude. One, an auto-biography, covered his first four decades and has not been preserved intact. The other, the *Res Gestae*, was set up by his explicit order before the great mausoleum he had constructed for himself in Rome; his survey might almost have been dictated by a statue in its terse, impersonal appreciation of Augustus' achievements and universal acceptance.

Beneath the statue, however, lay a shrewd political spirit; and beyond the creation of a symbol of virtue we can easily detect in Augustus' writings and acts that same intention of wedding his own position to the most vital forces of Roman tradition which is apparent in the Altar of Augustan Peace. This effort led Augustus to skillful maneuvering, which modern scholars have pointed out in detailed analyses of Roman attitudes and of Augustan literature and art. To summarize, it may be said that he subtly inserted himself into the traditions of Roman history, partly by bringing them back to popular notice, partly by quoting appropriate sentiments from worthies of the past. At his funeral the spirit already noted in his Forum appeared once more in striking form, for behind his body marched men clad in the masks of his ancestors—and also in those of distinguished Romans from Romulus to Pompey. So the past of Rome gave forced tribute to Augustus as its worthy descendant.

Similarly Augustus, in reinvigorating and extending Roman cults, linked himself thereto. Apollo, for instance, was a god who received widespread attention from the generation of Augustus, which was attracted particularly perhaps by his classic Greek position as a force promoting balance and order and by his capacity as a healing god. Augustus' adopted clan, the Julii, had long worshiped a more earth-bound Italian form of this deity, Veiovis; Augustus made his connection with Apollo as close as possible. After his house on the Palatine had been struck by lightning in 36, he dedicated the site to Apollo and built a great temple to the god, who also aided him at Actium. The transfer of the Sibylline Books to this temple, which lay by his new home, gave him control of the chief oracle of Roman religion and also the prestige of being in a sense its custodian. Augustan literature and religious rites, such as the Secular festival, emphasize both the Sibylline Books and the cult of Apollo, in part as a chthonic spirit destroying evil, but also as the sun, the patron of the arts; poetry and art often identify Augustus with Apollo.

The household gods of Rome, the Penates—which loom large in

Virgil's *Aeneid*—and Vesta, the guardian spirit of Rome, were likewise pressed into Augustan service by the construction of a new temple in their honor on the Palatine after Augustus became *pontifex maximus*. The major priestly colleges also admitted the ruler as a member and celebrated in their rites his important anniversaries. On a lower but more extensive level came the addition by 7 B.C. of the *genius* of Augustus to the popular worship of the neighborhood Lares in the various districts of Rome. Some of the altars of this cult have survived and show now Augustus with Livia and members of his family, now his Victory or oak wreath for saving the citizen body, now the legendary Aeneas, as well as the Lares themselves. And over all is the more-than-human connotation of the very term Augustus, "the venerable," which had usually before been applied to the gods of Rome.

In the provinces men went even further in consecrating Augustus. The great bulk of epigraphic and other evidence from the Empire attests that the world had been waiting for a savior, and that in Augustus its appeal had been answered—at least for a time.

To the East, indeed, the Roman Republic must have long appeared not only destructive but also drab, when the glamorous kings were replaced by annually changing, practical, and businesslike Roman governors who were so often uninterested in local culture; though Roma had been deified, this was too abstract a figure to gain much real devotion. Now, however, the figure of Augustus rose high. Some of the messianic feeling crept into the work of Horace and Virgil, but its full intensity appears in such places as the decree by the province of Asia about A.D. 15, which begins:

Whereas eternal and deathless Nature has vouchsafed to men, as the greatest good and bringer of overwhelming benefaction, the emperor Augustus; the father who gives us happy life; the savior of all mankind in common whose provident care has not only fulfilled but even surpassed the hopes of all: for both land and sea are at peace, the cities are teeming with the blessings of concord, plenty, and respect for the law, and the culmination and harvest of all good things bring fair hopes for the future and contentment with the present.[9]

A similar decree of about 9 B.C. makes the year commence with the birthday of this god, the beginning of life for all men. The dignitaries who adopted these decrees had little interest in the complexities of

---

[9] *Ancient Greek Inscriptions in the British Museum* 4.1, ed. by Gustav Hirschfeld (Oxford, 1893), no. 894; the translation in part by David Magie, *Roman Rule in Asia Minor* 1 (Princeton, 1950), 490.

the legal position of the Roman *princeps* or in the rejuvenation of Roman ways, and Augustus did not particularly desire that they should. To them he emphasized his benevolence and careful guard over their good government.

Against this background the deification of Augustus in his own lifetime by the provinces is more properly understood. Modern men may reverence their heroes to an extraordinary pitch of self-abnegation, but they cannot quite raise their idols to the status of the divine. The ancient world could and did take this last step with humans to whom it felt deep gratitude. Gods were essentially embodiments of protective or destructive forces of nature. What more natural, then, than to worship a human ruler who had visibly protected mankind by his acts? In those days, again, the gods stood closer to man and operated at times through human beings; and the human had, on some theories, a spark of the divine within him. So ancient men could, in worshiping a ruler, feel that they were worshiping the god who had chosen this "benefactor" or "savior" as his vehicle and had imparted to him some of his divine force. Deification as a form of homage had been known in the classic Greek period, became more usual in the Hellenistic Age, and was easily transferred by Greeks to a few Roman conquerors or governors of the Republic.

Worship of Augustus, yoked usually with the personified Roma, was begun voluntarily in the Eastern provinces; of their own will Eastern traders erected his temple at a port in far-off India. The new departure was the seizure of the idea by Augustus and its wide extension by imperial directives. It was Drusus, stepson of the emperor, who dedicated in 12 B.C. the great altar at Lyons to Augustus; the presumably final pacification of the conquered Rhenish districts was marked by the erection of another altar to Augustus at ara Ubiorum, the modern Cologne.

Within Italy itself an official cult of the living ruler was not encouraged either by Augustus or by any of his successors who eschewed open autocracy, but voluntary worship of Octavian, the son of the deified Caesar, can be found from the year 36 B.C. In this year the Italian cities gave thanks for his restoration of peace by honoring him in their temples; after Actium his birthday became a public holiday, and his name was coupled with that of the gods in hymns. The final step, however, was not taken until Augustus' death, when he was officially deified and worshiped everywhere.

The institution of emperor worship was a mighty means for expressing loyalty to the emperors. For this very reason undoubtedly its provincial forms were fostered by Augustus. Though such reverence must in the end remain puzzling to modern men, we may not scoff at its effectiveness—nor overestimate its religious import. Constitutionally the ruler remained a human, and neither Rome nor the Western provinces took up the cult save as a demonstration of loyalty; but to the bulk of his Eastern subjects, he appeared an earthly Redeemer. Down past the adoption of Christianity by Constantine the worship of the Caesars was a potent force in securing political loyalty, and a motif of great influence in the arts and letters of the Empire.

Success of Augustus

In his efforts to gain general support Augustus pursued a subtle policy of toleration and encouragement of the arts and very deftly tailored his program to accord generally with the ideas of the Roman aristocracy. Thus he reduced outward friction. He sacrificed Caesar to the opinion of this group and attempted to link himself to the steadily more sanctified figure of Cato; he even went so far as to permit the display of images of Brutus and Cassius and the praise of these republicans in his own presence. He himself emphasized his legal powers, behind which his control of the army was carefully hidden, and lived a simple, approachable life as "first citizen." Before the provincials he upheld the majesty of the Roman state and reasserted the control of the Empire by its Roman and Italian elements, yet he also consciously shouldered the burden of justifying the Empire by guaranteeing its good government and public order.

His success in winning men's minds needs little proof beyond that which has already been given in passing. Senators and slaves alike, it quickly appeared, wanted an end to unrest. The more recalcitrant nobles had been removed by civil war and proscriptions, and the others had no doubt learned by the lesson; but one must speak more of relief than of fear in explaining the acceptance of Augustus by the bulk of the senatorial order, especially when his intention of upholding its position became patent.

This acceptance is particularly clear and significant in the case of the middle classes of Italy, which had risen into an economically and socially powerful position during the previous two centuries. This group had rallied to Octavian in the 30's during his wars against Sextus

Pompey and Antony—Virgil and Horace may serve as its vocal repre-sentatives—and it seems to have stood squarely behind him on most issues thereafter. Augustus, after all, had been born in the Italian town of Lanuvium, and his closest advisers, Maecenas and Agrippa, came from Italian stock; his age, moreover, may have represented the peak of Italian prosperity in the ancient world.

This element was willing to give up a political liberty it had never really enjoyed, if forms were observed, if economic liberty and a resulting prosperity were safeguarded, and if Augustus would admit "new men" from this class into the senatorial aristocracy. The most enthusiastic Latin praise of Augustus after his death was penned by Velleius Paterculus, a man of Italian equestrian origin who rose to the Senate under Augustus. To match it elsewhere one would have to turn to provincial opinion.

IV

Augustus:
The Reverse of the Medal

A SURVEY of Augustus' attempt to mold public opinion will justly give precedence to its positive aspects and should underline his general popularity. Nevertheless our minds must not yield entirely to his blandishments, nor our voices join the modern and ancient chorus which hails him as a benign father.

Augustus actually believed as little in complete freedom of speech as any other autocrat, and perhaps less than some. Not only did he dislike downright opposition; he was also touchy with respect to his own dignity, for this was one of the main bases of his position and so had its political character. A man who engaged in jests and tossed off obscene verses about others, he did not appreciate retaliation; and though he liked eulogy, he "took offence at being made the subject of any composition except in serious earnest and by the most eminent writers, often charging the praetors not to let his name be cheapened in prize declamations." [1] Even Horace refused to write of the deeds of Augustus until he was in proper form, lest the ruler kick if stroked the wrong way, and the poet was always careful to have his poems put before Augustus when the latter was in a good mood.

It is, indeed, unlikely that Augustus looked with favor upon any outright advocacy of un-Roman ideas in religion or morality or upon the encouragement of luxury. In his middle years he seems to have re-

[1] Suetonius, *Augustus* 89.3.

acted openly only when confronted by improper acts; he thus limited public banquets, gave Vedius Pollio a rude lesson on the proper treatment of slaves, and curtailed the mimes' disrespect to nobles. Nevertheless, one suspects that even in the prime of life he could not disguise a dislike for improper words. Later Ovid was to suffer therefor; at all times the slightest frown or twitch of the ruler's face must have had an effect in damping free expression of thought as far as the ordinary writer or speaker was concerned.

Augustus was the ruler of the Roman world, not an ordinary citizen. On his favor hung the acceptance of society, financial reward, and in the case of nobles public advancement. His displeasure, if aroused sufficiently, might bring down on the hapless culprit a mighty machine of force which could not be entirely disguised. What Asinius Pollio had said in the days of the triumvirate, when Octavian had attacked him in verse, was still true: "I shall keep quiet, for it is not easy to scribble against a man who can proscribe me." [2]

Not all men, however, could be trusted to keep quiet. Like Napoleon and Stalin, Augustus devised an armory of potent, dangerous weapons with which to attack any expression of thought distasteful to him; these weapons were to be kept well polished by his successors. The arsenal included the control of political expression, the concentration of all significant political powers in Augustus, the secret police, various laws against the employment of force and against treason, and the perfection of necessary punishments. Since modern students of the Empire quite commonly prefer not to see its seamy side, the existence of these weapons must be stressed.

Restraints on the People

Of the two major elements in the Roman structure, the Senate remained relatively free under Augustus, but the people lost in practice their scanty constitutional powers. In the provinces Augustus supported the upper classes and even suspended the assemblies in the Eastern cities which had backed Antony. At Rome itself the entire weight of the Augustan system of government was heavily against democratic ideas and toward the general policy of the senatorial aristocracy. Augustus did not venture to abolish the annual election of magistrates in popular assembly, and he did his part in soliciting votes for the candidates he favored; but by the process of commending cer-

[2] Macrobius, *Saturnalia* 2.4.21.

tain candidates he made these elections more and more of a formality. While organizing the people in wards and *vici,* Augustus did not permit this new organization to have more than religious functions.

His relations, however, with the people as a political force were never easy. On the one hand he was intensely suspicious of any person who really tried to win the favor of the people. M. Egnatius Rufus, who established a fire brigade in his term as praetor, was eventually crushed because of his popularity, and Augustus even rebuked Tiberius as well as the people for praising his grandson Gaius at the games of 13 B.C. On the other hand, Augustus ran into the old republican contradiction, which could not be solved in his day: the very people who were to be bought by money and food were yet the sovereign font of power in the Roman constitution. The citizen body might have been a rabble in the eyes of Augustus and his friends, but they had to be kept up to the old standards of religion, dress, and customs. Admission to citizen ranks was carefully safeguarded by laws limiting the number of slaves freed at one time, and regulating informal manumission; for the quality of the Roman people had to be maintained if it were to remain master in the Mediterranean world.

The people do not seem to have objected to their loss of power. The same savior complex might be found in the masses of Rome itself as in the provinces, and for much the same reasons; the little men of this world must always be most concerned over their daily bread, and this Augustus attempted to provide. He emphasized his care of the people through his tribunician power; all men could see that he had replaced the restless rivalry of the republican aristocrats by internal peace; he even permitted or encouraged a vent for popular adoration through the worship of his *genius* at the local shrines of the Lares. The products of his government, as summed up by one ancient author, were "public works, largesses, games, festivals, amnesty, food in abundance, and safety, not only from the enemy and from evildoers, but even from the acts of Heaven, both those that befall by day and those also that befall by night."[3] Something over 200,000 residents of the city were partially fed by the state; his gifts of cash on special occasions were munificent.

Augustus himself really seems to have enjoyed the games, which he gave in profusion; they were perhaps a compensation for his sickly nature as well as a means of relaxation. Yet the praetors were directed

[3] Dio Cassius 56.41.4 (funeral oration of Tiberius).

to keep due order, and though Augustus allowed athletes and actors greater privileges than ever before he watched them closely. Overly presumptuous players were punished or exiled. The story is told of one, a certain Pylades, who retorted on being reprimanded, "It is to your advantage, Caesar, that the people should devote their spare time to us."[4] From such a remark the path leads straight to the criticism of the later Juvenal: the Roman people, who had once conducted affairs of state, now cared only for bread and circuses.

This famous quip, the spawn of aristocratic contempt, has misled too many critics. The people had never had an active part in government and had not in the Republic dared to speak freely. Now they were no longer able to group themselves in the *collegia*, which had taken an active part in the unrest of the civil wars, for all except "ancient and legitimate" associations were abolished by Augustus. The formation of new *collegia* thereafter required specific authorization based theoretically on their public utility, though relaxations were to come in practice under later rulers.

Still the people could shout, and they could whisper. From the days of the Gracchi, even perhaps in the earlier Republic, mob action had swirled through the streets of Rome, and the vilest of innuendoes had been circulated in the partisan battles of the Late Republic or had been yelled at the games. The police system inaugurated by Augustus may have reduced the intensity of the demonstrations; still, in 22 B.C. there arose a great popular outcry that Augustus become dictator for life. The populace, indifferent to the subtleties of his compromise with the Senate, knew with simple insight that the "first citizen" was really their Lord and saw no reason for hiding their knowledge. This outbreak Augustus could stop only by a public appeal in which he tore open his toga and threatened to commit suicide. In A.D. 7, again, the people were wrought up because of frontier wars and a shortage of food, and some woman practiced divination which excited them yet more. To quiet them, Augustus made a solemn, open vow with regard to the Megalensian festival "and proceeded to do anything that would make the crowd cheerful."[5]

The other outlet for popular agitation was rumor. To invent stories calls for at least a little acquaintance with what is happening, and the rumors which survive in our literary sources seem to have been generated in the close-knit governing body of Roman society; the historical

[4] Dio Cassius 54.17.5.   [5] Dio Cassius 55.31.3.

tradition of the Empire embodies a tremendous mass of this impalpable whisper. To some extent the "chilling rumor which spreads from the Forum through the streets" concerned the actual course of events on the frontiers and in the Empire,[6] but other tales were veiled attacks either on the person of the ruler or on the character of his system. Anonymous critics spread the story that Drusus the Elder, Augustus' stepson, had wished to restore the true Republic and had been poisoned by Augustus in retribution. His relations with his possible successors were all subject to attack: the ambitions of Marcellus were said to have aroused his suspicions; Agrippa's last trip to the East was called exile; the deaths of Lucius and Gaius Caesar were laid to his account; and the relations with Tiberius were the subject of countless tales. His friends and wife too were attacked. Livia suffered gross slurs; the low birth of Agrippa was the subject of jests; and a certain coolness between Augustus and Maecenas seems to have been exaggerated by the rumormongers into an open break.

Virgil has given a canonical description of Fama in his *Aeneid* in terms which remind one of Rossini's swift sketch of Calumny in the *Barber of Seville:*

> Rumor
> Than whom no other evil was ever swifter.
> She thrives on motion and her own momentum;
> Tiny at first in fear, she swells, colossal
> In no time, walks on earth, but her head is hidden
> Among the clouds . . .
> She heralds truth, and clings to lie and falsehood,
> It is all the same to her.[7]

Virgil's view of Rumor as an essentially evil agency stemmed partly from Hellenistic conventions, but the vigor of his language strongly suggests a reflection of what he heard and saw in Rome of his day.

To fight such canards Augustus probably relied largely upon counter-rumor. Manipulation of public opinion, especially at elections, had long been carried out by nobles through their agents. As a youth Octavian had quickly built up an extensive, deft machine to assist him in spreading his own rumors and pamphlets and had scored by this means remarkable victories against Antony and Lepidus. The extent to which this highly successful vehicle for propaganda was continued after

[6] Horace, *Satires* 2.6.50 (Wells).   [7] *Aeneid* 4.174 ff.

27 B.C. cannot be ascertained, but that it did continue we may consider likely. Apart from fighting fire with fire, Augustus recognized the impossibility of suppressing rumor; to his heir Tiberius he wrote, "Do not be indignant if anyone speaks ill of us; it is enough if no one can do ill to us." [8] At the most he issued statements of his own in rebuttal to particularly irritating canards; it was perhaps for this reason that he himself composed a life of Drusus.

Among the aristocrats, rumors sometimes took the more tangible form of anonymous pamphlets, and opposition could even be voiced through the Roman custom of making comments about persons and the world in general in one's will. At these points Augustus might take more positive steps if he so desired, but for long he refused thus to limit aristocratic freedom or to permit the Senate to curb its own critics. Once he vetoed a senatorial resolution to limit the license of wills. When insulting pamphlets were spread in the Senate House against him, probably in connection with the mysterious efforts of Plautius Rufus to stir up the masses in A.D. 6, he urged only that the authors of pamphlets published under fictitious names be prosecuted thenceforth; a search, however, was made for the people stirring up the mob. His steps in his last years will appear shortly.

Difficulties with the Aristocracy

From the purely practical point of view it is difficult to criticize Augustus' endeavors to meet the material needs of the people; but he, more than any other individual, was responsible for the loss of such political capacity as the Roman citizen body had had. That the aristocracy fretted over this development may be doubted, for its organ, the Senate, continued to be favored under Augustus. The public statements and debates on policy (*contiones*) which had occasionally taken place seem now to have disappeared, and elections were hampered both by a Julian law restraining electioneering and by Augustus' practical control of the election results, but within the walls of its House the Senate enjoyed relative freedom of speech on political matters. Modern scholars cannot enter this charmed circle and hear its debates, nor could the people of Rome; for Augustus suppressed publication of the *acta senatus* (though later historians of senatorial rank seem to have been able to consult old files).

Even within the Senate walls the senators did not in reality have the

8 Suetonius, *Augustus* 51.3.

necessary foundations for true freedom of speech. Beside them sat the
"first citizen," who politely played his part as their peer and genuinely
tried to bring his policies into general accord with those of the aristocracy. The *princeps,* however, was also independent of the Senate as
the master of the armies and the savior of the world, exalted in popular
reverence. He had, moreover, the legal power of speaking first in the
Senate and could veto through the tribunes its actions. Once he bolted
from the floor in irritation at senatorial opposition; the senators shouted
after him that they ought to be able to speak concerning the state, but
their claim betrayed the hidden pressure against the Senate's freedom
of speech.

Their master, again, knew far more than did they, for the regime had
begun to wrap a veil of secrecy about its acts. The daily official bulletin,
the *acta diurna,* continued to be published, but its items seem to have
referred to court events, prodigies, and unusual events and accidents—
the type of material which still fills most of our newspaper columns—
together with religious announcements and the like. Cicero had emphasized the obvious necessity that a senator must be familiar with the
affairs of the state, but after the example of Agrippa in 14 B.C. the subordinates of Augustus tended to send their dispatches solely to the ruler,
who relayed them to the Senate at his pleasure.

Both Tacitus and Dio Cassius comment explicitly on the difficulty of
writing histories under this veil of imperial secrecy. The verse of Horace
shows that men under Augustus still tried to gain and pass to absent
friends information about the general course of events, but the effort
of the good citizen to remain enlightened met an iron curtain all too
often. The results were the noising of rumor, disbelief even in the truth,
and, worst of all, political passivity.

Augustus himself can scarcely have failed to notice these unfortunate
results with respect to the aristocracy. The Roman nobles were a most
maddening group, who posed for the ruler an insoluble dilemma. He
attempted, as Cicero had done in his political treatises, to spur them
to political life and to utilize their vigor. So he found himself forced
to interfere with their dissipations by a great series of laws designed to
encourage simplicity of table, childbearing, and sanctity of married
life. These laws, which he backed by impassioned speeches and his own
example, form one of the most notable examples of attempted social
reform in the ancient world. Yet all was of little avail for the moment,
though such measures as the public trial and punishment of adultery

and the public proclamation of divorce were a root of the steadily greater control of the family by imperial legislation. Throughout his reign Augustus met determined resistance to his efforts at social reform. These "gentlemen of the fishponds" were too deeply impregnated with the vices of luxury and the concomitant pursuit of the necessary wealth to support their way of life to be won back by Augustan blandishments to the dull path of virtue. No turns and twists of positive propaganda could end their resistance; from it eventually sprang one aspect of the repression of his later years.

Although the aristocracy wished to sin and scoff with impunity, it opposed the Augustan reform of the constitution far less stubbornly. Here Augustus met little active resistance, but as little real co-operation. He genuinely desired to share the burdens of government with the Roman aristocrats, but he found them most reluctant to take up their tasks. Young nobles attempted to avoid military service—one equestrian even cut off his son's thumbs. Senators avoided attendance at meetings of the Senate; almost as much through their indifference as through Augustus' overriding power their real independence rapidly waned in practice.

Men, in fine, were tending to become unpolitical in the Augustan system, to retire from a political stage where the limelight followed the pacing of their lord. Their refuge most often was the pursuit of money. Another outlet was a life of idle luxury, which was mitigated at times by a delicate devotion to poetry or to declamation or by a more stern dedication to philosophy. Maecenas himself, in Augustus' own circle, displayed this tendency, and it may be that the ruler's tutor, the Stoic Athenodorus, surrendered "to the times"—too quickly, in Seneca's view —by urging retirement from public life.[9] The very prosperity of the era led toward hedonism, the rise of the Italian middle classes into the aristocracy may have reinforced the trend, but the main forces impelling men to desert the service of the state were embodied in the position of Augustus himself.

Some aristocrats, however, remained ambitious and strove egotistically for political fame. If Augustus were out of the city, senators fell back into the old habit of rioting over the election of magistrates; when sent out to the provinces as governors, they had still the engrained tendency to exploit the provincials or to create an overly high position for themselves.

[9] Seneca, *On Tranquillity* 4.1.

One man who went too far was C. Cornelius Gallus, the first governor of Egypt. Presumably carried away by the honors shown him in that supple province, he gossiped disrespectfully about Augustus, set up images of himself all over Egypt, and had his achievements inscribed on the Pyramids. In 26 B.C. one of his associates apparently accused him of treason. Though Augustus only banned him from his own provinces, "because of his ungrateful and envious spirit," [10] the Senate unanimously voted to punish Gallus by exile and the loss of his estates; subsequently Gallus committed suicide. His friend Virgil struck his praise from the Fourth Georgic, and the Egyptians erased his name from the inscriptions they had carved. Would men in court have continued to read and quote his elegies?

Another individual, M. Egnatius Rufus, curried favor with the people as aedile and so became praetor immediately, contrary to law. In this post he acted independently and then tried to run for consul. He had, however, gone too far in defying the system; the consul of 19 B.C. in charge of elections refused to accept his candidacy on the grounds of his improper acts and his debts. In despair Egnatius may have connived to assassinate the ruler; a plot at least was reported, and he was arrested and killed in prison. So Augustus taught him—and others—"not to exalt his mind above the mass of mankind." [11]

The support of the ruler by the Senate is significant in both of these instances. In the punishment of Gallus, the Senate was willing to go even further than the ruler in upholding his honor; against Egnatius Rufus the aristocracy probably reacted because of his demagoguery and perhaps in suspicion of his ambition. The distressing eagerness of the Senate to sacrifice freedom of action for individuals it disliked so that it might protect its own interests will recur in the cases of T. Labienus and Cassius Severus.

An even more ominous foreshadowing of senatorial decline was the lack of respect for the bounds which Augustus had set for his own position. Much of the simplicity of public life which Augustus adopted must have been directed to discourage the ceaseless offers of honors and the flattery by the senators. To give only one example—and there are many more—the Senate appealed to him in 19 B.C. to enact whatever laws he desired, and promised to take an oath beforehand to accept them. This offer he refused, for it was clearly contrary to the spirit of the Augustan system that the law was supreme; moreover, as

[10] Suetonius, *Augustus* 66.2.   [11] Dio Cassius 53.24.6.

he observed, the senators would actually obey only the laws they agreed with, and the others they would ignore despite ten thousand guarantees. Both foes and friends tried to push him toward open absolutism, but Augustus deftly balanced himself among these pressures. For forty-one long years to his death in A.D. 14 he clung to his general line of policy, and so established a pattern which heavily influenced the events of the next two centuries.

Controls and Punishments

Of outright plots at revolution Augustus encountered at least five after 31 B.C., in addition to unrest within his own family and isolated attacks. Every effort was caught in time, for Augustus had divers means of uncovering focuses of opposition.

All parts of the imperial and local government checked each other and passed information up to the ruler. Within any one province the imperial financial officials, the procurators, and the governor might often be at loggerheads, and each, as well as major military commanders, reported directly to their master. The local upper classes, who were often at odds with the imperial officials, also had means of getting around their superiors to make reports directly to the emperor.

At Rome itself volunteer informing against suspected offenders was extensive. The weakness of the state system of prosecution in ancient law made private accusers—the famous delators—and informers (*mandatores*) almost necessary, as Tiberius once told the Senate; and the financial reward which delators gained from the property of any man they accused and convicted tempted men exceedingly. This destruction of the upper classes from within cast a lurid light over later reigns, but its first glimmers shot up in the lifetime of Augustus. Seneca relates a story of a senator in his cups who expressed the hope that Augustus would not return from the journey he was about to make. Some fellow guests carefully noted the utterance—Seneca does not need to say why! —and on the following morning the contrite culprit rushed to the Forum to beg Augustus' pardon. Seneca, who tells the story for the point that Augustus had to prove his forgiveness by granting the senator a large gift of money, comments that "it was not yet true that a man's utterances endangered his life, but they did cause him trouble." [12]

Apart from the not-always-trustworthy group of scoundrels ready to

[12] *On Benefits* 3.27.1.

act as informers, there seems to have existed a web of imperial agents under Augustus. As Octavian he had had men who dispatched undesirable persons with a minimum of fuss. The tribune Offilius, who stirred up the soldiers after the victory of Mylae (36 B.C.), disappeared the next day, and "it was never known what became of him." [13] Another opponent, the praetor Q. Gallius, disappeared in 43 B.C., ostensibly on his way to Antony, but a hostile rumor asserted that he had never lived to be put on board ship.

The extent to which this machine continued after 27 B.C. is quite obscure, for Augustus was so generally popular that he did not need to spy in the uneasy fashion of Herod of Judea. Nevertheless, the emperor himself was so well protected by his praetorian guard that only persons familiar with court procedure had any chance to deliver an attack, and there are hints of secret agents scattered abroad. Maecenas, as prefect of the city, probably used agents of this type to ferret out the plot of Lepidus the Younger, "quietly and carefully concealing his activity" so that he could crush it without any disturbance.[14]

Under any ruler, to make a general observation on the Empire, politically significant persons—of wealth, family, or culture—had always to watch what they said. Dio Cassius two centuries later quite correctly judged that Rome never again had complete freedom of speech after Philippi. Even more graphic is an observation made by Philostratus; meant for Rome a century later, it is applicable in essence to the Rome of Augustus as well:

To live in a city, where there are so many eyes to see and so many ears to hear things which are and which are not, is a serious handicap for anyone who desires to play at revolution, unless he be wholly intent upon his own death. On the contrary it prompts prudent and sensible people to walk slowly even when engaged in wholly permissible pursuits.[15]

Augustus possessed the ultimate sanction of force, but his view of his position required him to cast a cloak of legality about that force. Under neither ancient nor modern dictatorships do men like to feel that arbitrary might has replaced the sanction of law. The legal structure by which he, and later rulers, could control the subjects was a mass of custom, republican laws running back to the Twelve Tables, magisterial privileges, and the extensive series of Julian laws on various subjects, all

---

[13] Appian, *Civil Wars* 5.128.   [14] Velleius Paterculus 2.88.3.
[15] *Life of Apollonius* 8.7 (Kayser ed., p. 321).

consolidated and expanded as time progressed by *senatus consulta,* imperial constitutions, and judicial interpretations.

Custom played its part in the restrictions on travel in the Empire. Every man had a place where he belonged, his *idia* or *origo,* and though he might leave it he could usually be forced to return to it or otherwise be limited in movement; from 29 B.C. Augustus thus forbade senators to leave Italy without his permission. Restraints on libel went back to the Twelve Tables and the republican concept of *iniuria* as involving injury to one's dignity as well as to one's body; but in the case of anonymous works a *senatus consultum,* perhaps of Augustan vintage, laid down methods of investigation and fitting punishments.

Augustus also gathered up the major powers and privileges of the magistracies and united them into an overriding set of powers. As *pontifex maximus* he controlled the state religion; as holder of the sacrosanct tribunician power he could check the magistrates, and attacks on him by word or deed immediately put the guilty party beyond the protection of the laws; as virtual censor he controlled membership in the Senate and equestrian order, which were purged on several occasions in his reign.

Upon both the courts and the sources of law Augustus laid a weighty hand. He himself had all the republican power of issuing edicts, and he gave directions to his subordinates, replies to petitions, and judicial decisions which passed practically as law. The technical source of legislation, the popular assemblies, was ever more superseded by the Senate, which passed *senatus consulta;* through his privy council, which examined all business to be laid before the Senate, the ruler had essential mastery over its acts. In keeping with republican practice, and still more consonant with the virtual absolutism which rose from his *auctoritas,* the emperor might conduct extraordinary judicial investigations (*cognitiones*) and lay arbitrary penalties (*coercitiones*), unchecked now by the tribunes. Thence possibly arose one of the great high courts in the Empire for appeals or the trial of important cases; the other was the Senate, which began under the presidency of the consuls to try a variety of cases in Augustus' later years. The regular Roman system of justice continued to be directed by the praetors, who were really chosen by the ruler, but a beginning may have been made in seizing control over the legal profession itself if jurisconsults were licensed, as seems probable, to back their opinions with the emperor's *auctoritas.*

Among the numerous formal pieces of legislation called the *leges*

Iuliae it is not always possible to distinguish accurately the share of Caesar and Augustus. Those regulating electioneering have already been noted. One, or more probably two, Julian laws on public and private violence forbade public and private holdings of arms beyond a normal amount, the incitement of slaves or free men to armed action, or the use of such force to disturb the processes of justice and the due enjoyment of private property.

These laws protected the upper classes against the social unrest unleashed in the civil wars, when armed bands had roamed the countryside, but they also prohibited official misuse of *imperium* or *potestas*. As enforced, they effectively cut off the possibility that political opposition might proceed beyond words to action outside the military sphere proper. Ideas may be much more fatal things than guns, but at least the aristocracy was left only one type of armed force, the private schools of gladiators, which were themselves taken under imperial control by the Flavian emperors.

The civil wars had also witnessed a great deal of treasonable collusion with such enemies of Rome as the Parthians, the desertion of duly appointed leaders, and the like. To correct this a Julian law on *maiestas* was drafted.

The republican concept of treason was commonly in the last century before Christ called *laesa maiestas*. Any damage to the reputation or honor of the Roman people could be "diminution of its majesty"; in the words of Cicero "*laesa maiestas* is a lessening of the dignity or high estate or authority of the people or of those to whom the people have given authority." [16] The term virtually supplanted earlier concepts of the crime and appears ever more frequently in legislation of the first century B.C., especially in a not-very-well-known law of Sulla.

The fragments of the Julian law on treason which have survived show fairly clearly that it was, like the Julian laws on public and private violence and on electioneering, a part of the general effort to restore the order of the Roman state. Offenses which it specifically covered were the raising of a force against the state, the killing of a magistrate or of a person holding *imperium* or *potestas*, the support of public enemies, the encouragement of unrest in the army, desertion, flight, and a great many other such matters.

The law was couched in terms of offenses against the Roman people. Augustus, however, was the representative of the people and was en-

[16] *On Invention* 2.17.53.

dowed by it with various public powers, especially those of the sacro-sanct tribunes. Did the concept of *maiestas* also protect his personal position? On this critical point various men, as we know from Seneca the Elder, argued forcefully, but their effort to secure the limitation of *maiestas* to clear offenses against the state was foredoomed to failure. Both in scope and in means of punishment, the concept of *maiestas* was rapidly expanded under Augustus, for here was the necessary, all-inclusive tool whereby he could suppress any type of criticism of his essentially autocratic system. *Maiestas* was to be a mighty weapon in the arsenal of absolutism throughout the history of the Empire.

At least one plotter was charged with *laesa maiestas,* and the same charge was probably directed against the other efforts to overthrow Augustus. The drunken senator who openly hoped for Augustus' death was presumably liable on the same score. He was pardoned; a plebeian who threatened the ruler was exiled. Before the ruler's death his *maiestas* had been extended so far as to cover the unfortunate cases of adultery within the imperial house, for the guilty in these cases were killed or exiled on the grounds of *laesa maiestas.* As Tacitus comments, this action was clearly beyond the law, but such an extension was only the beginning.

That the care of Augustus for his safety and honor extended even to the provinces is attested by an incidental reference in the famous Cyrene inscriptions, which deal mainly with unrest between Romans and Greeks in the North African province. At one point three provincials approached the governor and told him they knew something affecting the safety of the ruler. As was customary thenceforth in such dangerous business, the governor immediately sent the men under guard to Rome to inform Augustus himself; lawyers later in the Empire had to warn governors not to let culprits slip out of local trial by fabricating news of danger to Caesar.

Here too it turned out that the story was pure invention, and two of the three were released. The third was held, for Cyrenean envoys accused him of having taken a statue of Augustus from a public place in the city of Cyrene. What happened to the unfortunate Stlaccius on further investigation we do not know, but the case, however trifling, seems to corroborate the statement of a later legal writer that under Augustus any act against a statue of the ruler was considered an attack on his *maiestas.* Dio Cassius comments that many suits on this score had arisen before the accession of Tiberius.

To sum up the general use of the concept, not only under Augustus but also in its developed form, attacks on the august, sacrosanct ruler which could be punished on this score extended beyond physical attacks or threat of attack to verbal slurs, insults to the ruler's statue or other representations, the use of imperial insignia or rights—including the imperial purple and the striking of coins or medallions with a private individual's head—and the consultation of the supernatural to determine the future. The concept, it may be noted, was primarily political, not religious, even though the Greek term for *laesa maiestas* was *asebeia* (impiety). When later historians essayed to cast the blame for its expansion upon Tiberius, they went too far; Augustus must be considered responsible for extending the concept into the major fields where it was later employed.

Since republican scruples had made imposition of the death penalty difficult, the punishment for those convicted of *laesa maiestas* was for long no more than simple exile from Italy. Contemporaries of Augustus, however, beheld a rapid intensification and differentiation of punishment for those who fell afoul of the regime on any grounds.

For the most severe cases thenceforth, death was coupled with confiscation of property and *abolitio memoriae,* that is, the destruction of the condemned person's statues and honors, the wiping out of his name in literature and inscriptions, and the denial of honorable burial—though the clement Augustus did permit relatives to bury the deceased. Both the rewriting of history and the changing of monuments to eliminate the memory of unsatisfactory passages were characteristic of the Empire (see Pl. IV), and each had begun before Augustus' death. Much of this work was done by private individuals without explicit directives from above.

Apart from death, ban from office, and fines, men could be exiled. In the reign of Augustus this punishment took on numerous, graduated forms, all evolving essentially from the republican power of the magistrates to expel or incarcerate individuals.

Persons could be barred temporarily or permanently from a particular place or places, usually Rome and Italy or their native province, but they could live anywhere else they chose. Or they could be exiled to a specific spot without suffering further penalty; Ovid thus was "relegated" to Tomis. Or they might suffer the most serious form of exile, "deportation," which brought not only internment in a designated spot, fixed as an island in A.D. 12, but also the loss of one's property (or the greater part thereof), limits on the number of servants, and so on. For all practical purposes, and perhaps theoretically too, men who were deported lost their Roman citizenship, and they suffered *abolitio memoriae* at least in theory. The small islands off Italy held such members of the imperial house as Augustus' ne'er-do-well grandson Agrippa Postumus whom the ruler wished to keep under close control; for general exile the islands of the Aegean were frequently used.

Two modes by which thought might have been subjugated, it may be noted, were not actually employed to any significant degree by Augustus. One was library censorship. Ovid, who was exiled in A.D. 9, pictured his later work as seeking its earlier brothers in vain at the great Palatine library; mournfully he visualized its rebuff first at the two libraries founded by Augustus, the Palatine and the Porticoes of Octavia, and then at the library of the Atrium Libertatis, founded by Asinius Pollio. Ovid seems even to have feared that all his works might be placed on an index. "Exile was decreed to me," he argued in a poem addressed to Augustus' librarian, "exile was not decreed to my books; they did not deserve their master's punishment." [17]

Some modern scholars have lent their ears too much to Ovid's fears and assume that the creation of imperial libraries by Augustus was a skillful stroke to control literature. That Augustus' librarian, like Napoleon's, carefully analyzed books and pamphlets for his master may be doubted; that library censorship meant the complete destruction of a disapproved work is most unlikely. We do not know that such a ban was coupled with a general prohibition of circulation; Ovid goes on to hope that his poems may at last find a resting place in private hands, and even the products of his exile (the *Tristia* and *Letters from the Pontus*) have survived.

Once a volume had been published, its preservation or loss depended far more on private ownership and reproduction than on copies in the imperial libraries, which had a bad habit of burning down every few generations. To prohibit circulation in private hands apparently required a *senatus consultum,* as in the cases of Titus Labienus, Cassius Severus, and Cremutius Cordus. Since the works so punished survived into later generations, their eventual loss is due to other reasons than imperial censorship. On the whole an official removal or addition of

17 *Tristia* 3.14.9–10.

works to the libraries, of which examples will appear later, had its effect only in indicating the emperor's opinion to court circles—and to the dejected or triumphant author.

The domination of education by the upper classes was likewise subject to little challenge by Augustus. He chose one teacher, M. Verrius Flaccus, for the children of his household and forbade him to take other pupils. His organization of citizen youth into bands of *iuvenes* and the official celebration of the Trojan equestrian exercises did serve as means of regimenting the youth along certain ideas favored by the first *princeps,* but neither can be called a serious effort to seize control over education.

Further Augustus did not go, nor were his successors to deal hardly with the schools during the Early Empire. In view of the importance of education in passing on the traditions and attitudes of a civilization, the lack of imperial supervision may appear surprising. Still, Augustus and most of his successors felt themselves to be socially members of the aristocracy, and the schools cannot be shown to have engaged in any serious subversive activity.

Last Years of Augustus

Although not all aspects of the punitive structure of the Empire were fully developed by Augustus, his was the hand which traced the pattern, and in his old age that pattern fell black-barred across the sunny squares of Rome. By this time the early friends and advisers of Augustus were dead, his beloved grandsons were gone. As he moved into the lengthening shadows of senility, his only companions were his wife Livia and his gloomy stepson Tiberius. Augustus, too, cannot have been entirely happy with the results of his earlier work. His curbs on luxury and vice at Rome had been completely unsuccessful. His efforts to recall the aristocracy to the duties of family and state were mocked in practice. His control of his family to secure a dynastic succession had brought grief to all concerned. As the defeat of Varus by the Germans in A.D. 9 showed all too clearly, the military structure of the Empire was barely adequate to its needs. Increasing conservativism, slackness of rein, decreasing deftness are all apparent in these last years.

Below Augustus stood the aristocracy, now in a younger generation which had not experienced the unrest of the civil wars or the sigh of relief in the Roman world at the restoration of order. These men might revere, but they could hardly understand, their aged ruler. Flattery is more often to be found than reverence; opposition too is unmistakable in the social sphere and on various political planes.

The senatorial aristocracy struggled particularly to regain from the weary ruler that freedom of mutual attack and struggle for pre-eminence which had characterized the Late Republic. In three *causes célèbres*— those of Ovid, Cassius Severus, and Titus Labienus—and in several smaller incidents, this unhealthy situation bubbles up into our view; the precedents there created for arbitrary control of speech were to be powerful in the next century.

The exact course of the battle over the Augustan social legislation cannot be followed, but the evidence is enough to show that Augustus obdurately essayed to improve the birthrate and to safeguard the sanctity of marriage, and that the aristocracy, particularly its equestrian wing, was as determined in its recalcitrance. Not until A.D. 9 did Augustus confess partial failure in the *lex Papia Poppaea*, and even then he refused to give up entirely. It is not perhaps accidental that the case of Ovid, which is directly connected with the social battle, is the one where the ruler most clearly bears full responsibility for open suppression of thought.

Ovid has been termed the first "court poet" of the Empire. The expression is not entirely accurate, for Ovid embodies the major aspects both of adulation and of rebellion which became apparent in the post-Actian generation. Born in 43 B.C., Ovid was only twelve when the battle of Actium was fought. He did not begin to gain fame until about 20 B.C., when he abandoned a public career for his verse. For the next two decades, while Augustus was pressing his social legislation, Ovid was writing those marvelously facile, erotic works which pleased the aristocracy but can scarcely have delighted the emperor. The gay, light poet disapproved of childbearing as making women ugly; he wrote a manual on seduction and scoffed at marriage; he appealed to Apollo, the divine guardian of Augustus, as patron of the art of love; and his praise of Augustus was incongruously inserted in such places as a discussion of the games given by the ruler—where lovers might meet their mistresses.

In his forties Ovid turned from the physical aspects of love to the rhetorical, almost-frivolous reworking of mythology (the *Metamorphoses*) and to the superficial celebration of great days in the Julian calendar (the *Fasti*). Though the flattery of the ruler and the celebration of Rome's mission grew more prominent, there is no evidence that Augustus suggested the composition of these works. It is impossible to guess whether the poet's natural instincts, the backward gaze of the age, or a sense that he should write on more respectable themes turned him to the new subjects.

Suddenly, while Ovid was vacationing in Elba, Augustus struck and relegated Ovid to the bleak Black Sea city of Tomis. In January, probably in A.D. 8, Ovid saw his beloved Rome for the last time; he died at Tomis in 18.

Ancient authors did not care to discuss this exile or its reasons. Ovid himself, though he wrote many a mournful poem about his life on the frontier of the Empire, never directly indicated the causes of his exile. Hoping for pardon, he says, he refused to renew the wounds of Augustus. This curious expression, when coupled with his allusions to his having seen a crime he should not have seen, has led most scholars to believe that he was connected with the adultery of Augustus' granddaughter Julia, as an agent of liaison with her paramour Silanus or in some other way, for this sordid affair broke into the open in A.D. 8.

His "stupidity" in the crime, whatever it was, may have been the immediate cause of his relegation, but the poet makes quite clear the existence of another reason as well. "Two crimes, a poem and a blunder, have brought me ruin . . . the charge that by an obscene poem I have taught foul adultery." Again he imagines someone rejecting his new book on seeing its author's name and tells him to look at the title: "I am not the teacher of love; that work has already paid its deserved penalty." [18]

Ovid clearly felt that Augustus struck at him at least in part because of the success of his erotic verse and its inconsistency with the imperial program of social reform. That Augustus would eventually have banished him simply because of this is unlikely; but the significant point is that Ovid was punished, and that everyone in Rome knew his pen helped to bring on him that punishment. The effect on other authors, then and later, must have been considerable. The ramifications, moreover, of the relegation of Ovid were extensive as far as the reception of his own work was concerned. The passage quoted at the end of the previous paragraph and his failure generally to name the addressees of the *Tristia* sug-

[18] *Tristia* 2.207–212; 1.1.65–68.

gest that the reading public was loath, at least in the first years of his exile, to handle the work of a man who had met the emperor's displeasure.

In the rebellion against Augustus' social reforms the aristocracy secured the privilege of destroying itself during the following century. The opposition to these reforms was paralleled by a less successful effort to throw off Augustan limits on the freedom of political action. Here two quite distinct groups are apparent: one attacked the Principate in the discreet and muffled field of political theory; the other, far more important, asserting the old senatorial privileges, tried to raise their personal fortunes by knocking down the less powerful.

Not everyone accepted Augustus' contention that he had restored the Republic, but safe vents for theoretical opposition were not easy to find. One man, M. Antistius Labeo, who was the greatest jurist of the age, was "mindful of the liberty in which he had been born" and stalked about Rome in grim defiance of the new system.[19] Labeo refused the consulship offered by Augustus; insistent upon the spirit and not the form in law, he pointedly refused to accept the subtle alterations in the Roman constitution which Augustus had carried out while maintaining the old republican frame. Against such a doughty figure Augustus could only venture to promote his rival jurist, Ateius Capito, a leader of the proimperial party.

Others dared not be so bold, yet could not silence their tongues or pens. The careers of those men who turned to write history will be discussed with Augustan literature in Part Three. Oratory attracted a wider circle. Though both the Senate and courts long remained available for a man bent on making a speech, the height to which rhetoric might ascend in these arenas was restricted, and speakers came to devote their talents in part to declamations, i.e., speeches on imaginary subjects designed primarily for the instruction of beginners but also much used in the Empire to show an orator's ability to his fellow nobles.

The material thus handled is illustrated in a work on the rhetorical displays of Augustan and Tiberian orators by Seneca the Elder. Immediately apparent in themes preserved by Seneca is the lack of allusion to the Augustan system or to any contemporary events. Some declamations deal with tyrants or the murder of tyrants, but sober judgment can scarcely find any direct connection between tyrant and *princeps*. The

[19] Porphyry on Horace, *Satires* 1.3.82.

tyrants are quite unreal shadows drawn on Greek lines, evil figures like pirates who appear merely to explain the mishaps of characters. Like the preacher who was against sin, the declaimers were all opposed to tyrants, but only in later reigns can remarks on tyranny be proved, and then rarely, to have a reference to contemporary conditions.

Beneath the surface, however, veiled attacks were delivered on aspects of Augustus' rule; in one case, for example, an orator hit at his adoption of the sons of Agrippa. A vein of "literary republicanism" can also be detected, as in the oratorical treatment of Cicero's career. Of the muted criticism Augustus could scarcely take notice without damaging his picture of the restored Republic; rather, he frequently attended these display declamations, perhaps because he considered them a safety-valve for the energies of the aristocracy. So he tacitly permitted declamation to become an integral part of the aristocratic system of life.

As one reads the pages of Seneca, one feels oneself in a world essentially false, where imagination and fantasy are dominant, plagiarism is rampant, and fact has become unimportant, where the intellect displays itself not in connected probing of the nature of the world but in sparkling little bits. For students such exercises had their value within limits; for adults the practice of declamation seems rather absurd. Yet to dismiss it as meaningless is to make a grave error, for it remained popular for centuries. Here, moreover, may be found manifest some of the roots of later literary style, as well as of the development of the law toward equity and humanitarianism.

Rather than attacking the ruler, senators probably assailed their fellow senators in declamations just as they did in lawsuits, pamphlets, and the spread of rumor. Mutual rivalry and jealousy of honor remained viciously strong in the aristocracy. Horace had devoted two satires to preaching tolerance toward personal criticism in a city "where envy is keen and slanders rife"; [20] and in another satire he showed where his greatest fear of censorship lay—not in the possibility that he might offend the ruler but in the danger that some noble might take his general criticism personally and so charge him with a suit for libel under the Twelve Tables. Worse was actually to befall two of the most outspoken senatorial critics in the last decade of the weary Augustus.

According to Seneca the Elder, Titus Labienus pushed liberty of speech to such an extent that he attacked the upper classes at random, thereby gaining the nickname of Rabienus, the Raving. Seneca adds also

[20] *Satires* 1.3.60–61 (Wells).

that he was still a Pompeian even in the present peace—in other words, he opposed the pretense of the Augustan system to be the Republic. His rise despite his initial poverty and the fact that he was detested by the majority of the senators suggests that his stand appealed to elements in Augustan Rome.

Labienus also wrote a contemporary history which he read in public, omitting certain sections as too dangerous for general consumption in his lifetime. His enemies secured his trial for an unknown pretext, and his books were all burned by senatorial order; Labienus himself was apparently not punished but committed suicide. The date of the trial is unknown, but it must have taken place not long before the affair of Cassius Severus.

Cassius seems to have had an equally sharp, censorious tongue and is known to have assailed several of Augustus' friends in the courts as well as to have composed saucy attacks on the aristocracy. One of the Vitellian family, quaestor under Augustus, tried to make it appear through a pamphlet of a supporter that he was descended from the god Faunus; Cassius described the family as rather descended from a freedman, a cobbler by trade and an informer, whose son by a harlot became a Roman knight. This dispenser of vitriol eventually was accused before the Senate for *laesa maiestas* because of "slanderous pamphlets"; his works were burned, and he himself was exiled to Crete. The trial is placed in A.D. 7 by Jerome, though modern scholars have tried to bring it down to A.D. 12. Despite the punishment, the works of Cassius survived to be read by Suetonius a century later.

In both of these affairs appear senatorial animosities, only partially disguised under the cloak of protecting the emperor's dignity. In other aspects too a resurgence of senatorial virulence mars the last, dimly lit decade of Augustus' life, and helps to explain an otherwise puzzling pattern of appeasement and severity on his part. After the defeat of Varus in 9 Augustus allowed knights to fight as gladiators and accepted all sixteen candidates for the praetorship in 11. In the latter year foretellers of the future were forbidden to prophesy to any person alone or to make predictions about forthcoming deaths even to groups—men were fishing in the troubled waters of succession to the aging ruler. Restrictions on the abode and way of life of exiles were promulgated in 12, a year in which Augustus discovered pamphlets attacking various senators. Six years earlier the author of a pamphlet against Augustus, circulated under the name of his exiled grandson Agrippa Postumus, was fined;

now, to appease the nobles, an official search was conducted by the aediles in Rome and by the local authorities in the other cities. The pamphlets were burned; some of the authors were punished.

Augustus and Freedom of Thought

In their blindness the senators who thus pushed Augustus on to open suppression of thought may appear incredible, but their attitude cannot be misunderstood. Augustus had the support of the aristocracy in curtailing the political action of the masses; whether dealing with plotters or with independent-minded officials he had the Senate overwhelmingly on his side. If the Julian laws on public and private violence, as well as the Julian law on *maiestas*, are a product of the Augustan period, the Senate probably approved them wholeheartedly. In all these measures, and particularly in the repression of such critics as Cassius and Labienus, the more stupid among the senators may have felt that they were winning an ever-stronger position. The expansion of the Senate's power to act as a judicial body, particularly for the trial of its own members, which is notable in the last years of Augustus' reign, may have been a product of its own desires rather than of imperial policy.

Although the emperor did not have to take the initiative in punishing the froward either in Rome or elsewhere in Italy, the men who fell had attacked Augustus as well as the Senate. The opponents of Labienus and Cassius could not have ventured to assail these critics had not Augustus permitted it, and the burning of the works of the two by the aediles at Rome and the duumvirs in other towns must have required his tacit approval.

The two cases were a landmark which impressed the Empire far more than the relegation of Ovid, for in the sentences passed on Cassius and Labienus the repression of free thought advanced a decisive step beyond the punishment of the poet. Whereas Ovid's person had been punished and his works suffered only secondarily in the official disapproval of the author, the accusation and punishment of the later pair lay primarily against the works themselves, and the authors suffered in secondary degree.

Later generations forgot the complicity of the Senate and singled out the ruler as the culprit, for they had learned that the extension of *maiestas*, the book-burning, the exile of dissidents could be directed against the aristocracy itself. Even at the time far-seeing senators may have realized that the emperor was not entirely dependent upon aristocratic support. Buttressed by his control of the armies, reverence among the city masses, and general adherence of the Italian middle classes, he might venture to suppress elements within the Senate. If such senators existed, they failed to convince their fellows of the dangers of the policy of censorship they were jointly helping to establish. Nobles of the Augustan period were too eager to secure their own position, threatened in the last century of the Republic, to be overfussy about the means employed—conservative groups often make these dangerous bargains with the Devil.

This age, one must always remember, did not attach the modern importance to the untrammeled expression of ideas. Horace is the only contemporary of Augustus who directly refers to the subject, and he repeats the assertion of Cicero that Athenian license (*parrhesia*) would not do in Rome. As far as our evidence extends, no one in the reign of Augustus advanced a claim to complete freedom of thought, unless perhaps Cassius and Labienus did so in their desire to assail their fellows and the ruler. These rabid assailants were pulled down by the majority of the senatorial order, conservative in essaying to maintain their individual places and for that very reason proimperial.

Senatorial opinion generally, as these cases suggest, did not support freedom of expression as an abstract concept. Ateius Capito contended that the recalcitrant Antistius Labeo was driven by "an excessive and mad love of freedom," and Seneca the Elder, while praising the toleration of Augustus, wasted scant sympathy on "those who prefer to lose their heads rather than a *bon mot*." [21]

Men of the following centuries were those who paid for the bargain, as emperors turned against them the precedents created in the reign of Augustus. When these men looked back at Augustus, they tended to have mixed emotions. His memory among common folk of later times stood high, and the bureaucracy long continued to celebrate the great events in his reign by coins, calendars, and both public and court rites and festivals. The writers of the aristocratic tinge, from Seneca the Elder on, accepted him as inevitable and necessary to stop the Roman revolution. In their effort to show succeeding Caesars that he had truly upheld freedom of thought, especially for the Senate but also for literary men, they praised to exaggeration his benevolence. This effort maltreated the facts badly, but it could not quite get around them; Tacitus, while wishing to lay the blame for the extension of *maiestas* on Tiberius,

[21] Aulus Gellius, *Attic Nights* 13.12.2; Seneca the Elder, *Controversies* 2.4.13.

had to admit that his charge was not really true. Yet these writers who praised Augustus rejected almost unanimously his claim that he had restored the Republic. To them the Empire was an autocratic system, and Augustus was the first autocrat—Dio Cassius considers the constitutional changes of 27 B.C. as sheer hypocrisy.

The argument was common that Augustus was outstanding in fortune, not in virtue, and a current of thought denying even his general benevolence came into the open by the middle of the first century after Christ. In the play *Octavia*, ascribed to Seneca (the Younger), the emperor Nero is made to argue that Augustus secured the preservation of his rule by fear. Tacitus calls Augustus both deceitful and bloodthirsty. Much later the emperor Septimius Severus on one occasion sent shudders down the backs of his senatorial audience by dilating on the desirable cruelty of Augustus, which he compared with that of the republican warlords Sulla and Marius. If Augustus had seen the yet-unborn spirits of the future as he lay on his deathbed, begging for the applause of the bystanders, he might not have been entirely happy.

Historians of aftertimes may agree that the aristocracy was no longer able to bear its task, and that Augustus had been remarkably successful in halting a revolution long in process. Beginning in repression and force, he quickly advanced to a positive line of action and brought the world back to stability. Thereafter he reformed the government so as to assure his own position while yet conciliating the spirit of tradition. In these endeavors his actual achievements were reinforced by the deft use of every means of expression to convey his own attitude.

Nevertheless the Augustan period marks a great stage in the breakdown of the old basis of the Roman state, that close-knit, self-denying aristocracy which had acted as a group in the building of Roman dominion. For well over a century the unity of that group had been dissolving in the absence of serious foreign foes. This dissolution had been impelled by native family pride, and was abetted by the pressure of the individualistic character of Hellenistic civilization. Now, when one individual emerged as the master about whom all others must revolve, the cohesion of the aristocracy suffered another, shattering blow. Nowhere did Tacitus see more deeply than in the passages where he described this development under Augustus:

But when he had won the soldiery by bounties, the populace by cheap corn, and all classes alike by the sweets of peace, he rose higher and higher by degrees, and drew into his own hands all the functions of the Senate, the magistrates and the laws. And there was no one to oppose; for the most ardent patriots had fallen on the field, or in the proscriptions; and the rest of the nobles, advanced in wealth and place in proportion to their servility, and drawing profit out of the new order of affairs, preferred the security of the present to the hazards of the past . . . Thus a revolution had been accomplished. The old order had passed away; everything had suffered change. The days of equality were gone: men looked to the Prince for his commands.[22]

The history of the Principate is in one sense the working out of the antithesis between the shoring-up of the outward structure of the Empire and the internal dissolution of the fundamental ideas of the Roman state. In another it is the story of the capitulation by the Caesars to the pressure of their subjects, who desired to idealize and lift beyond the mortal sphere the embodiment and symbol of their hopes of peace and prosperity, the guarantor of the eternity of the Empire by his foresight. Before this father-emperor they offered up in voluntary adulation their freedom of thought.

Panegyrists often compared the ruler to Jupiter or Zeus, but they might better have drawn their similes from the brazen, fiery Moloch to whom men fed their dearest, first-born offspring. The cities of the Empire yielded their autonomy; the aristocracy, its independence—and paralleling the decline of political freedom was a decline of thought which is already visible in the last years of Augustus.

[22] *Annals* 1.2.1, 1.4.1.

V

The Loss of Local Freedom

ABOUT its capital the great world-state stretched in every direction to the uttermost ends of the Mediterranean. Within the Roman sway were enfolded alike the barbarians of Europe and those Eastern seats of civilization which were old when Rome had been young, whence the Mediterranean civilization had taken its impetus and still derived its motive power. In moving away from Rome to view the concentration of local power in the hands of the upper classes and the slow transference of that power to the imperial government, there is no need to halt at the provinces themselves, for these were for the most part merely arbitrary units of imperial administration. Nor, again, can one talk easily with the great mass of the rural population of the Empire, inhabiting the silent countryside. The ancient world consisted of an inarticulate substratum of toiling farmers who upheld a vocal upper crust; these landlords, traders, and administrators lived, in more civilized districts, in the cities and enjoyed the fruits of the world.

City life is the life reflected in almost all our sources, and it was the cities which bore the cultural tradition of the Mediterranean world. This tradition became ever more uniform in the Empire; but behind the common mold there lay a tremendous variation from area to area among the simple peasants, speaking native tongues, worshiping native gods, and having ideas and emotions not necessarily akin to or even consistent with the culture of the cities. Only in the third century did the country begin to rise into greater prominence, as the cities decayed and as city life ceased to be the ideal of the upper classes.

The flavor of ancient municipal life was quite different from that of modern urban existence. Today the dweller in a city owes allegiance to many other units, and the mobility of our life gives to city ties an ephemeral nature. In the ancient world the ordinary man lived and died within the city where his ancestors had lived. Almost all cities controlled a wide expanse of countryside, which extended in more recently urbanized areas as far as fifty miles or more from the city walls; they thus resembled an American or English county more than our purely urban units of government. Commerce and industry might have some significance within this complex but did not need to do so, for its unity rested primarily on administrative, agricultural, and psychological bonds.

Within each city the ties of fellow citizenship, marked by a common divine patron, festivals, and customs, were very powerful. Many cities of the Mediterranean world had originally been independent states, and even those which had never existed independently took over much of the character of their models. The intensity of ancient city life was of an order not to be found today; Greco-Roman civilization had been born in these little, exclusive units and had derived its vigor from their very parochialism.

Not all areas were municipally organized at the outset of the Empire, nor indeed was all its territory ever so grouped. City life, however, represented generally the highest form of local organization. The material ruins of the cities attain an impressive completeness in places like Pompeii, Ostia, and many others and so enable us to visualize the backdrop against which their citizens operated; the countless tombstones go far toward illuminating the life and problems of the individual humans who walked their streets. There is, nevertheless, a serious gap which no amount of archeological work quite fills. Physical remains will not illustrate the vivid life, the swirling rumor, or the interplay of the viciously sharp economic and social contrasts within the city walls, and the ken of the ancient historians of the Empire did not often extend beyond the armies and the capital. We know, that is, far more of the theory of municipal government than of its practice.

Since most of the Western provinces yield little but the low murmur of inscriptions, actual developments must be seen largely through the eyes of Easterners. Particularly helpful are the essays of the famous biographer Plutarch, a native of Chaeronea in central Greece, and the orations of Dio Chrysostom, the Golden-mouthed, a native of Prusa in northwestern Asia Minor; both flourished at the turn of the first century under Domitian and Trajan. Although one must allow for certain inevitable diversity, the life they describe is representative of the rest of the Empire.

Urban Oligarchies

As a modern man enters the cities of the Empire, it is the bustling, pompous men of wealth who first draw his attention, whether he stands in assembly, market square, or inner halls of decision. Distinct in dress, seated prominently at the festivals, commemorated by statues (often erected at their own expense), the wealthy men in the towns of the Roman Empire who gained the local magistracies and sat in the councils could swell with pride in life. By their gifts of buildings and endowments, which are attested in laudatory inscriptions, they might also feverishly hope to have achieved the only kind of immortality most of them knew, for it was "marble graven with public records, whereby breath and life return to goodly heroes after death." [1]

Position in the cities, as in Rome, tended to correspond closely to wealth, so long as a man was freeborn. The escalator of imperial society operated particularly in the new cities of the West, where families rose rapidly and then often simply disappeared as they lost their wealth again or died out. In older areas the agricultural possessions on which wealth usually was based tended to remain in the same hands. Members of the same family can be traced in Asia Minor for generation after generation in the magistracies, priesthoods, and other honors of a city; here the local aristocracy by the second century at least was a well-nigh closed corporation whose members could boast that their fathers and forefathers had been councilors. An amalgamation, varying by locality, of pre-Roman nobles, priests, and other eminent families together with former centurions, Roman colonists, and so on, the aristocracy had a pride of origin which may have been fictitious but was nonetheless significant.

By and large only the well-to-do had an effective opportunity to speak their minds on local political matters. In the West the town council, normally of one hundred men, was chosen for life and was composed chiefly of ex-magistrates; members as a rule had to be freeborn and possess a certain amount of wealth in addition to paying an ad-

[1] Horace, *Odes* 4.8.13–15.

mission fee. Magistrates had to meet approximately the same requirements and were expected to contribute lavishly to public works of
various sorts. The election appeals on the walls of Pompeii still attest
the vigor of local elections, but the people had little other positive
function in their government. In the second century they lost even the
power of election, which was shifted to the council.

In the East the assembly retained greater powers of legislation in
some cities. At many others the magistrates alone introduced legislation, as agents of the council, and only candidates approved by the
council were submitted to the voters. The council in the East may have
been elected, though the evidence is not clear on either this point or
its term of office; in some cities of Asia Minor censors seem to have
controlled the list of councilors. Here too magistrates were unpaid and
had to pour out their wealth generously to help balance the local budget.

Quite generally the ordinary farmers of the countryside were unable,
practically or legally, to take any important part in urban government
or to have much share in urban culture. Living in villages scattered
through the city's territory, the farmers had some form of local organization in which they might legislate on social, religious, and administrative matters; but often the city sent out prefects or other officials
to administer the villages. The city also collected the imperial taxes and
its own rents and controlled the major markets to which the farmers had
to resort.

To keep order among the lower classes of both city and country and
to control movement, the cities and provincial governors usually collaborated. The uncertainty of life and property in the Roman Empire
was far greater than in any advanced state today, but the most important
cities of the Empire had an established police. As the oppressed peasantry and proletariat grew more surly and unreliable in the economic
decline of the late second and third centuries, many cities, especially in
Asia Minor, expanded a form of rural police, however inefficient it may
have been, which caught not only robbers but also Christian martyrs.
In Africa the governor's staff, according to Tertullian, kept lists of such
malefactors as prostitutes, tavernkeepers, thieves in the baths, and
Christians.

To back up the local police in some of the major cities or to take its
place in many rural areas there were available a great number of army
detachments (*stationes*). Especially prominent in the third century,
as the disorder of the Empire increased, these detachments helped to

collect supplies for the army, at times co-operated with tariff collectors or the postal system, and also inspected travelers and perhaps even mail. Runaway slaves were often caught as they drifted by these check points. Androcles hid in the deserts of Africa for a time after his flight, but within three days after he left the cave where he befriended the lion he was "seen and caught by some soldiers," and sent to his master in Rome.[2]

In addition to such controls over men's bodies the local aristocracies had also powerful means of regulating men's minds. Massilia banned mimes entirely at one point, and the stage was generally an official institution. The Greco-Roman system of education catered necessarily to those who supported it by their private contributions, and public schoolmasters were chosen by the same elements operating through the city government; the advice on ethics and daily life offered by the orators and philosophers smacks much of an aristocratic tinge and is cast in a common mold everywhere. The men of the cities looked down on the farmers, off whom they largely lived but to whom they made almost no attempt to extend the schools, gymnasia, and other urban modes of civilization. Insofar as literature appeals to municipal elements, it addresses itself to the aristocracy; only once, for instance, is the powerful freedman organization of the Augustales mentioned in extant works.

The well-to-do man also manipulated the powerful lever of religion. That Church and Change worked together is neatly attested by the shop insignia at Pompeii and by inscriptions elsewhere which show the interconnection of religion and business. The priesthoods of the imperial and local cults were filled by the men of wealth, who could afford the handsome sums required from holders of such offices. Men might consult the pagan oracles about their personal problems, including even such questions as flight to avoid payment of taxes; but any sensible oracle-giver carefully avoided encouraging men to oppose the established order of things. The notorious charlatan Alexander of Abonoteichos did not answer, but kept, questions of a compromising nature for purposes of blackmail. In at least one case (Tanith at Carthage) prophecies of a local cult were used deliberately by the Roman governor to repress seditions in the late second century.

In the unofficial Oriental cults the well-to-do members, though not always directly a part of the local aristocracy itself, frequently had a

[2] Aulus Gellius, *Attic Nights* 5.14.26.

great influence. The pages of Josephus show again and again the efforts of the wealthy Jews to damp down the fanaticism of their poorer co-religionists; even in the young Christian Church the usual meek submission to temporal power was not entirely the product of Christian ethics. Though the rise of Christianity was at times a reaction of the lower classes against their limitations in the political and cultural life of the cities, only in rare cases—as in Revelation—does their possible hostility to the upper classes or to Rome find expression.

By a diversity of means the urban aristocracies could, within the limits of custom, direct the general pattern of life on the local level and impose upon that life the ever-more-uniform polish of Greco-Roman culture which marks the remains and literature of the Empire. Even politically, however, the aristocratic grasp on urban life had certain limitations, both from above and from below, and also from within itself.

To speak of these oligarchies as closed, coherent groups is misleading. During the rule of Nerva, for instance, Dio Chrysostom returned to his native Prusa and tried to benefit his city both by his influence with the emperors and by an ambitious building program. He soon discovered an irritating vein of discontent with his activities. Though he carefully secured the approval of his plans by the governor and the local assembly and had the support of many of his fellow citizens, others grumbled about so-and-so's old smithy, torn down to make way for his new colonnade and library, as if the smithy had been the Parthenon; ten years later the malice of his enemies was still hindering the transfer of the edifice to the city. In this bitter warfare rumors and false stories were broadcast: one element even tried to lodge a complaint of *laesa maiestas* with Pliny the Younger, then governor of Bithynia, because Dio buried his wife and son in the courtyard of a building containing a statue of the ruler.

Plutarch gives a more succinct, but impressive, account of factional rivalry at another place, which began in quarrels over dancers and harp players, proceeded to squabbles over places and positions, and went on to the cutting off of aqueducts. Finally the rivals lost everything through exile (by Domitian) except their hatred, which persisted in exile and poverty. Such factionalism was not peculiar to the Greek East; a decree of Italian Pisa on the death of a grandson of Augustus comments on the disruption of civic business due to the contentions of the candidates for municipal office.

In part the rivalries were the outcome of the race for local honors; but in part they must have arisen from cleavages of economic interest, though we have little information on this. Most well-to-do men of the cities seem to have rested their wealth on their landed possessions, but the trade of the Empire was sufficiently extensive to create in some favored places a commercial middle class. In times of famine the urban classes proper occasionally found the landed proprietors reluctant to disgorge their grain. After a famine Cicero had to appeal to the land-owners of Cilicia to release their supplies, and from the rule of Domitian we have a governor's edict to Pisidian Antioch which was designed to aid the local government in equalizing the food supply and in keeping down the price of grain. Cities also tended to create municipal monop-olies of banking and exchange, of ferrying, and so on; when these monopolies were challenged by those outside the "ring," there resulted dissension which required extensive imperial interference and regula-tion.

Occasional social differences within the cities cannot be overlooked. A distinction between colonists and original inhabitants must have oc-curred frequently in the West. At points in Asia Minor the great priestly families, which generally dominated their environment, had to reckon with the descendants of invading Gauls, Macedonian settlers, and others within the city framework. Quite independent of the urban government, yet within the same walls, congregations of Jews or resident Roman traders might in early days have their own independent government as a *politeuma* or *conventus civium Romanorum*.

Urban Mobs

More vocal than the peasants were the lower middle classes and the poor who lived in the urban centers but had—the latter at least—an appallingly small share in the political and cultural life of the cities. This element the oligarchies bribed in a sense by fixing prices or by providing those festivals, baths, granaries, and cheap grain of which their inscriptions boast so frequently. The food supply in particular was always a difficult problem in an era of poor land communications and ever-present danger of crop failure; but the people felt the state had a duty to underwrite the provision of the essentials. Having bought their people, as did the emperors in Rome, the oligarchs then might run the cities with relative freedom, though with due circumspection. Meetings of the assembly were doubtless often "rigged"; Plutarch

calmly advised his fellow aristocrats to arrange for a little polite opposition on important matters to deceive the people before shoving their
measures through.

So much the people got, yet they could not be kept entirely quiet.
Rumor ran through the streets of the great Eastern cities as freely as
at Rome, and the populace spoke out its mind rather sharply, at times in
idle chatter about the affairs of the emperor or the community, at times
in the laughter, anger, hissing, and rough jokes of the festivals and
the assembly—"the means by which you terrify all men and always
dominate men everywhere, both private citizens and princes," as Dio
said to the Alexandrians.[3]

Both Alexandria and Syrian Antioch, populated by hundreds of thousands, had especially unruly city mobs. Marcus Aurelius once forbade
Antioch to hold games, public gatherings, and any sort of public assembly; its witticisms against rulers from his coemperor Verus on to Julian
in the fourth century were both cutting and widely quoted. First prize
for intensity and persistence in outcries, popular songs, and epigrams
must nonetheless be awarded to the great port of Egypt. Its common
reputation throughout the Empire as a city of unstable men, blown by
every rumor, talkative, deceitful, and prone to rioting, is a platitude
which the Romans inherited from the Hellenistic world, but there is
adequate proof that the Alexandrian reputation had a considerable
basis in fact.

Popular expression of opinion was not limited to catcalls or to that
scratching of opinions on walls which we find at Pompeii, nor was it
entirely haphazard. The riots which flared up in Eastern bazaars and
then quickly died away may to some extent have been self-generated,
but true popular discontent took deeper, less conscious channels of
action. Mob action more commonly, I suspect, was set afoot by the
incitement of the gilds and clubs and claques.

The rulers since the days of Augustus firmly discouraged any organization of their subjects which might focus unrest, but the social
instincts of mankind could not be entirely eradicated. In general the
Caesars permitted and gave exemptions from public services to truly
cultural organizations, and such professions as the theatrical artists of
the East might group themselves on a provincial or wider basis. The
assembly of young men for education and athletic purposes (*iuvenes,*

[3] *Oration* 32.22.

neoi) and, in the East, the federation of the older, well-to-do men into a *gerusia* were likewise sanctioned; the latter often became the virtual dictator over town policy. For the purposes of common worship or burial the poor everywhere could form *collegia* from the reign of Claudius; for the same purposes persons in a particular trade came together frequently in outwardly religious groups or gilds.

Such gilds were probably under the control of, or were even restricted in membership to, the more conservative shopowners, but the experience of Paul with the silversmiths of Ephesus shows that even so they might start riots. In Italy itself an altercation between the neighboring towns of Nuceria and Pompeii over a set of gladiatorial games was expanded into regular war through the action of the gilds of the two towns. When such legal organizations upset the peace, it is small wonder that the drinking and purely social societies, like those jestingly called the "little thieves" or the "late drinkers" at Pompeii, had a bad name as being the focuses of disturbances.

These clubs in turn were quite generally pawns which aristocratic factions marshaled against each other—or at times against the imperial government, for the local oligarchies, though supported by the Romans, did not always respond with the proper submissive affection. In the Republic there had been a great deal of agitation against the inadequate, uncontrolled, often rapacious, and sometimes contemptuous government of the Roman aristocracy. Cities of the Greek East had for a time in the 80's supported the invading Mithridates of Pontus, but they found Roman might too great and turned aside to war on the safer plane of the intellect.

Greek writers, for instance, seized upon the old story that Alexander had planned to conquer Italy and speculated on the results if this hero of Hellenistic culture had attacked Rome. Hostile historians investigated the rise of Rome and consoled themselves that this spectacular emergence of "robbers and thieves" had been due not to Roman virtues but to Chance or Tyche, a powerful idea in the Hellenistic world, "which inconsiderately showers her greatest favors upon the most undeserving." [4] Others circulated, usually with discreet anonymity, oracles which predicted the early fall of Rome before an Asiatic avenger and promised retribution for its enslavement and looting. Even in the Empire the East threw up pseudo Neros, and the Christians were to picture a return

[4] Dionysius of Halicarnassus, *Roman Antiquities* 1.4.2.

of Nero as the forerunner of the Antichrist. In more subtle fashion Hellenistic scholars waged battles over mythological and Homeric points which had still a practical connection, such as the story of Aeneas.

In the Empire this hostile propaganda sank below the surface save among the Jews and the nobles of Alexandria. As the Greeks, however, moved into a cultural and economic renaissance in the late first century after Christ, their leaders were not always satisfied with the extent and speed of their admission to Roman citizenship and offices, and they chafed, now at the blunter forms of Roman suzerainty, now at the infiltration of Roman ways into the eastern Mediterranean. Greek thinkers thus became at times overbold in opposing their cultural superiority to the barbarism of the uncouth Romans; a good example is the essay *Nigrinus,* in which the second-century Lucian assailed Roman pride and lack of culture and depicted Rome itself as the home of flattery and subservient minds.

More open and more persistent trouble rose in Alexandria. Here neither Augustus nor his successors dared rest their control on the local aristocracy of the conquered, once-proud capital of the Ptolemies. The turbulent city had no council and no elected officials apart from the gymnasiarchs and a few other directors of the cultural and religious life of the Greek community. The disgruntled aristocrats reacted against the Empire. In papyrus tracts on imperial persecution of the Alexandrian patriots, miscalled the Acta of the Heathen Martyrs, the gymnasiarchs turn up frequently from the days of Gaius down into the third century as leaders of anti-Semitic—really anti-Roman—activities. At other times the aristocracy operated by inflaming the mob; of this process Philo furnishes a clear description.

One of the main anti-Semitic leaders in Philo's story was the gymnasiarch Isidorus, a turbulent fellow and a demagogue—

a past master in creating disorder and confusion, a foe to peace and stability, a genius at manufacturing commotions and disorders when they did not exist and at cementing and inflaming them after they had come into being, who made it his aim to have about him a disorderly and turbulent mob composed of a promiscuous flotsam which he distributed into sections after the fashion of committees.

On the numerous drinking societies in Alexandria this Isidorus had a powerful influence; Philo asserts that whenever Isidorus wished a demonstration these groups came together at one signal and did as they were ordered. On one occasion before A.D. 37 Isidorus fell out with the governor Flaccus and proceeded to hire "the touts and bawlers who sell their shouts as though in the market to those who are disposed to buy them." Through their cries he filled the gymnasium with a crowd which began to yell against Flaccus. Since Tiberius was still alive and Flaccus felt his position secure, he crushed the riot by arresting and questioning a few of the mob, who confessed the amount of pay they were to receive (part down and the rest afterward), the disbursing agents, and all the rest of the mechanism. Flaccus disclosed the whole setup to others of the aristocracy, who apparently were not on Isidorus' side at this juncture, and was able to force Isidorus to retire from the city.[5]

Although in this instance Flaccus did not dare to punish further the aristocratic promoter of a riot, rousing the mob was a device not lightly to be undertaken. Men who tried to stir up Greek cities to imitate their ancestors, i.e., professional Hellenists in the political sphere, were playing with fire, Plutarch warned, for "what is done to them is no laughing matter, unless they are merely treated with utter contempt."[6] Talk of the ancient Greek victories of Marathon and Plataea should be left to the schools of the rhetoricians.

In his view of the relations of the emperors and the cities Dio Chrysostom agreed very closely with Plutarch. Both stood squarely for the preservation of Hellenic culture, and in this sense Dio was the more professional Hellenist of the two. He praised Rhodes for its calm pattern of life which forced even the rushing Romans to walk sedately, for its gentle clucking in applause at the festivals. Elsewhere he condemned the strong tendency to import gladiatorial games and to ape Roman customs; yet he admonished his readers and auditors against treading too independent a political path. He warned Prusa not to be riotous in its assemblies when the imperial procurator was near. To Tarsus he urged social reform and threatened that if the city complained too much of the officials it might lose its freedom of speech entirely. In addressing the Alexandrians he bluntly reprimanded the people for their unruly behavior and pointed out that God had given them guardians and guides to improve their conduct, i.e., Roman troops. Plutarch put the matter more succinctly in warning his compatriots always to remember that above their heads were Roman boots, and "the dread chastiser, ax that cleaves the neck."[7]

[5] Philo, *Against Flaccus* 135–145 (Box).
[6] *Moralia* 813F–814C.   [7] *Moralia* 813F.

Empire and the Cities

The upper classes, in fact, steered the machinery of local government in the Empire only so far as the Caesars permitted them to do so. The loss of local freedom was but partly the result of the increasing concentration of powers within the cities in the hands of the few, for aristocratic political and social domination had always been marked in city life, even in democratic Athens of the Periclean Age. In the Empire, it is true, popular participation in government reached a nadir, and the sense of unity among the citizens tended to diminish before the obvious fact of aristocratic omnipotence. In this respect the vital forces of ancient civilization suffered a serious blow.

Even more significant, however, was the loss of local initiative and power to the central government. The loss did not take place all in a day, and its reasons are manifold; to explore them as fully as they deserve one must wander down many twisting lanes of city life.

In brief, the policy of the imperial government with respect to the cities was ambivalent. While granting autonomy and relying upon the upper classes to keep the masses quiet, the emperors put distinct restrictions on the freedom of local government. More ominously yet, they tended slowly to increase their interference so as to counter intercity and internal unrest and to put some limit on the exploitation of the poor by the rich.

From Augustus on, the Empire generally sustained the "flower of the colonies and municipalities, to wit, the good and rich men." [8] Not only was it easier to deal with the few, who alone were accustomed to rule in many areas, but also the few, who were rich, were more inclined to support the Roman efforts to maintain order, particularly if they were given authority locally. In this grant of self-government to the upper classes the Empire followed the policy of the Late Republic, which frequently reversed the policy of its predecessors in the East, the Hellenistic monarchs. The latter rulers tended to superimpose a centralized system of government and sent out royal governors as a rein on local actions; such despots as those of Egypt or of various states in Asia Minor had even limited the formation of cities in the interests of centralized control. The Republic, on the other hand, tended to leave the great bulk of government in the hands of the basic political units.

In its conquest of Italy, Rome had fashioned a policy of tolerating, even of protecting, local forms of political organization and customs to

[8] *Corpus Inscriptionum Latinarum* XIII 1668 (the emperor Claudius).

a degree unusual among conquering powers. This policy was continued thereafter, though more so in the East than in the West, where Rome sometimes laid a heavy hand on its less civilized provinces. Toward the Hellenized areas of the eastern Mediterranean, however, Roman aristocrats tended to be polite politically and even humble intellectually. By their own interest, their financial support, and their general attitude of toleration they helped to protect Greek civilization and, at least in the first century B.C., to assure its upper classes a freer scope than they had enjoyed under Hellenistic monarchs.

Eventually the Empire itself was to swing back to Hellenistic centralization, but only after it had built up the necessary central bureaucracy; in the simple system of Augustus the realm was too large to be so ruled. The discontent of Alexandria and the occasional diatribes of professional Hellenists cannot disguise the fact that for many decades the upper classes of the cities were essentially satisfied with their paramount local position. The emperors, indeed, felt sure enough of the cities to utilize their framework for the control of the less civilized elements, both in town and in the countryside, and to expand the structure of urban organization widely over the Empire.

Self-rule was a gift rather than an inalienable right. The traditional belief of the city-state that it must be an entirely free sovereign unit had been opposed by the Hellenistic kings; to Rome neither *autonomia* nor the technical grant of "independence" (*libertas*) to certain favored cities meant much more than the right to use local law and conduct local courts without undue interference by the central government. *Libertas* theoretically conveyed the idea of freedom from meddling by the provincial governors but was a privilege which could be given or taken away at the desire of the ruler or could be circumvented indirectly. All depended on the emperor's calculation of his own interests. Under Domitian the technically free cities of Caria put the matter succinctly in a dedication describing themselves as "free and autonomous from the beginning by grace of the Augusti." [9]

To control the lower classes the emperors and the local oligarchies thus entered into a partnership, but one of most unequal character, for the central government was chary in granting parochial leaders— as such—any serious voice in imperial affairs.

From the end of the first century the Empire as a whole was more

[9] *Numismatische Zeitschrift* 52 (1919), 117, nn. 3–4 (Magie, *Roman Rule in Asia Minor*, 2, 1450, n. 2).

stressed in imperial propaganda and thinking. Hadrian marked the shift by spending half his reign away from Rome and, in a great coin series, depicted the armies and the major ethnic blocks or "provinces." The provinces also rose steadily in economic strength in contrast to Italy, which lost ground; and their most wealthy and influential men were gradually admitted to Roman citizenship, then into the Senate and magistracies as the old limitations were broken down. By the second century a great imperial aristocracy had emerged in place of the old senatorial group of the Republic. Neither this development, however, nor the official emphasis on the Empire led to the creation of extensive machinery for the expression of local opinion.

The best vehicles for expressing this opinion were three in number. Embassies were always streaming up and down the great roads of the Empire, bearing honorary decrees for every event in the emperor's career, announcing complaints, or merely informing the ruler that a Triton had been heard and seen playing a shell in a near-by cave. These embassies kept Rome in touch with local problems and interests and probably served as a sounding board for general imperial opinion, at least as regarded the upper classes. More economical, and at times more efficacious, was a written appeal to a senator of local origin, a hereditary patron from the senatorial or equestrian order, even a client king, or in the case of oppressed farmers of the third century to a soldier of the army or praetorian guard.

Finally the cities in many areas had available their provincial assembly (*concilium, koinon*), which supervised the imperial cult and also debated matters of common interest. From this discussion might grow either a decree in honor of the governor or a decision to prosecute him before the emperor or the Senate or to send an embassy. One man thus went from Asia to Rome to convey provincial congratulations to Augustus' elder grandson on his reaching manhood and also "honestly and carefully watched over the interests of Asia, neglecting no opportunity but displaying all zeal for the advantage of the Hellenes." [10] The development of these assemblies, however, was hampered by the particularism of the cities, the disinclination of the Caesars to foster potentially dangerous rallying points, and the influence of the provincial governors.

Through embassies, patrons, and provincial assemblies the cities

[10] *Sardis, VII: Greek and Latin Inscriptions,* ed. by W. H. Buckler and David M. Robinson (Leyden, 1932), no. 8. ix (Koinon of Asia, 3–2 B.C.).

conveyed as best they could their opinion on imperial policy. That the subjects, and especially the armies, kept their eyes on general imperial developments insofar as communications and imperial secrecy permitted is clear, and an important influence was certainly exerted upward beneath the surface. The provinces in the second century felt that the imperial government hearkened to their needs. As strong an influence, however, was exerted in the other direction.

Modern panegyrics of the "Augustan peace" do not always recognize that the peace of the Empire in many respects resembled that of death. Both to preserve order and to maintain their own position the Caesars tended instinctively to oppose any change, to drive underground symptoms of tension and discontent which might upset the *status quo*. To this motive must be assigned the disarmament of the Empire, for the strict limitations on the possession of arms in the Julian laws on public and private violence were rather rigidly enforced. Suspicion of the unruly natives led the governor Flaccus to disarm the Egyptian countryside in 34–35 and to publish an order against the bearing of arms; a similar disarmament may have taken place in Gaul a decade later as a prelude to a minor revolt. Though provision was occasionally made for calling out local militia, as in the Caesarian charter of Urso in Spain, or for the training of youth, the emperors did not encourage strong local military bodies. In Asia Minor even the police were only half-armed.

Revolts, which are the last means of venting dissatisfaction, did occur sporadically in the Empire, even breaking out in Greece under Antoninus Pius; but these affairs, which are discreetly hidden in our sources, were not numerous. Not only was the Empire reasonably well satisfied but also, as Agrippa unavailingly pointed out to the Jews before their great upheaval of 66, the Roman army appeared irresistible. Centuries later, when that army proved not to be invincible, the pacification of the Empire by imperial will proved to have been too thorough, for its inhabitants were unable to protect themselves against the barbarians; yet the emperors who presided over the breakup of the Empire were still to prove loath to allow the military training of local bodies.

To maintain their majestic peace the emperors also suppressed two innate forces of the ancient city, its rivalry with its fellow cities and its internal dissensions. Intercity jealousy and hostility were inherited from the days of Greek independence and continued far down into the Empire in frequent altercations of neighboring cities over frontiers, tolls, relative ranks of honor, and so on. Even in a tribally organized area like Gaul these antagonisms existed, and the neighboring rural units in Egypt, the nomes, frequently attacked each other with staves and other weapons when their taboos had been violated.

During times of imperial disorder this hostility bubbled more freely to the surface. In 68–69, for instance, the emperor Galba honored Vienne and confiscated the revenues of its great Gallic rival Lyons. When Vitellius revolted, the Lyonnais urged his army to wipe out Vienne altogether and painted its riches in glowing terms—it after all was originally a Gallic city, while Lyons was a Roman colony! Only by abject submission did the Viennois escape the doom plotted by their neighbors' machination.

The burning of the amphitheater at Piacenza during the same period was laid by the local populace to men of the neighboring colonies, moved by envy and jealousy. Their charge may have been correct, for the rivalry of ancient cities in their public buildings was of an order which we no longer know in our general indifference to the appearance and beauty of public structures. Only rarely, as in Africa, could the leading city of a province gain the support of the other cities in shifting its political allegiance; and even here a fierce local quarrel over agricultural plundering led to Oea's calling in the barbarians to lay waste the territory of its rival Lepcis. One of the most pressing problems after Vespasian's final victory was generally recognized to be the need of damping down this internal turmoil, but the feuds did not disappear. Once again in the civil war of 193 Nicomedia and Nicaea, Laodicea and Antioch, Tyre and Berytus took opposite sides purely out of rivalry and mutual hatred.

To repress this contention of city with city the emperors could always employ force or threaten its use, but they made serious efforts to remove the causes of conflict by arbitration either through their officials or through provincial assemblies. They also permitted the creation of those commercial ties which are marked in numerous instances by joint civil coinage of two or three cities commemorating Concord (*Homonoia*), but they stood squarely against combinations or conquests which might upset the proper order and balance. Local particularism had its defects, but it also made united revolt difficult.

Another safety vent lay in diverting the rivalry to the establishment of competing festivals or in increasing the number of honorary urban titles. This competition for vain honors—called "Greek failings" in Rome —dismayed men such as Dio Chrysostom, who everywhere tried to discourage the intercity rivalries. When Smyrna and Ephesus quarreled, he pointed out that they were squabbling over an ass's shadow, for "the right to lead and wield authority belongs to others." [11] The strength of feeling in this rivalry was not thus to be halted; a letter still survives in which Antoninus Pius tried to soothe the anguished Ephesians' complaint that their old rival was not using in letters Ephesus' due title of First and Greatest Metropolis in Asia.

The ancient city was an institution which swallowed up much of its citizens' hearts. The emperors were undoubtedly right in feeling that the Roman world could not endure outright war among its constituent units, but the necessary alternative was deplorable: the race for titles was miserable stuff to fire civic loyalty and to promote urban thinking. The blessings of a state, said Plutarch, are (external) peace, liberty, plenty, abundance of men, and concord; but now local statesmanship had no effect on peace, and "of liberty the peoples have as great a share as our rulers grant them, and perhaps more would not be better for them." [12] The tone seems wistful.

In the great days of Greek independence, the city-state had suffered almost as much from internal dissension (*stasis*) as from external war; both were inherent parts of the intensity of city-state life. Bad enough in the fifth century as pictured in the vivid pages of Thucydides on the war of oligarchs and democrats at Corcyra, this tendency to *stasis* grew worse in the fourth. By the time of the Roman intervention in the Greek world about 200 B.C. great external wars tended inevitably to be the signal for internal conflicts.

In the Republic the Romans had sometimes made use of this local unrest; but once they had gained mastery in Greece, they turned conservative and tended to repress revolutionary movements harshly. In thus reaching over the city walls, the Romans in part protected minorities, while at the same time they ensured the advantage to the party which favored the Roman side. When a democratic riot at the city of Dyme, for instance, led to the burning of the record office late in the second century B.C., the pro-Roman party appealed to the governor of Macedonia, who placed it in control again and condemned the main conspirators to death or exile; in his extant letter he spoke his mind

[11] *Orations* 34.48, 38.38.   [12] *Moralia* 824C.

harshly about such men who upset the freedom which the Romans had restored in Greece. A generation before, a leader in Demetrias had said, "Under the guise of freedom all things happen at Rome's pleasure," and had been exiled for his "untrue" statement.[13]

The imposition of a relatively uniform, and certainly powerful, system of provincial government under Augustus greatly reduced the possibility of *stasis,* and the resurgence of prosperity soothed considerably the friction which could lead to internal disturbances. Yet disturbances there were from time to time over the supply of grain, the oppression of the poor by the rich, and other problems; and in many cases we hear of the difficulties precisely because the central government was called in to curb the outbreaks. In A.D. 58 both the decurions and the people of Puteoli appealed to the Senate, the one complaining of the violence of the masses, the other assailing the avarice of the magistrates. The upshots were first a riot and then repression by a praetorian cohort, which extended to a few executions. Though Tacitus is terse in his report, one suspects the commoners provided the victims.

When matters came to a showdown, the imperial government inevitably took its stand beside the upper classes of the city, but Augustus and his successors discovered that for a variety of reasons they simply could not turn the populace of the Empire over to the rich without any check. At times the upper classes proved either unwilling or unable to keep the rest of the populace under control when questions of religious and social conduct abhorrent to the majority arose; the silversmiths of Ephesus led the outbreak against Paul, and only the warning of the town secretary of imperial intervention quelled the trouble. The fury of the mobs against Jews and Christians, or even against the imperial government, was often the product of aristocratic incitement, and, contrariwise, the aristocrats must often have limited persecution or unrest in fear that the emperors would have reasons to throw their troops within the city.

Imperial interference was also required to prevent local injustice. It is difficult to overemphasize the amount of extortion and the degree of ruthless inhumanity which many of the wealthy, the officials, and the members of the armed forces displayed toward their inferiors. The papyri of Egypt are one long outcry of complaint against the avoidance of state burdens by the rich and against the robbery of the peasants, both of which the governors vainly tried to check. If the evidence for

13 Livy 35.31.12 ff.

the rest of the Empire is not as specific, it is largely because there the paper has vanished and the stones chanting the glories of the upper classes have survived.

The great despot of Sparta, C. Iulius Eurycles, was thus honored by Roman merchants and Greek cities in his lifetime and was lauded by his descendants; literary sources show that the victims of his actions all through Greece secured his temporary exile after two appeals to Augustus. The famous Herodes Atticus of the second century, who beautified Athens and lavished his money on the major cities of Greece, seems to have been another rapacious robber. Even Athens complained formally against its great son, who corrupted the Roman governors with his honeyed eloquence and escaped punishment; his freedmen agents, however, were condemned by the emperor Marcus Aurelius.

When the occasional brief and pitiful tales from stones are added to such scraps one can sense the oppression which was all too endemic in the Empire. The apparent eagerness of the rich for high office and expensive public duties in the first century was not always due to patriotism and civic pride. More often than our records reveal, disbursements out of private pockets for grain supplies or the like must have been a reluctant effort to assuage the populace bilked in other ways; both in extraordinary and in regular magistracies men often sniffed out means to enrich themselves at the cost of the community. "Had we the full records of municipal history from the standpoint of the common people, we should undoubtedly find that many a record of brilliant service carved on enduring marble was amply repaid by the emoluments of office." [14]

Growth of Imperial Bureaucracy

Increasingly, though reluctantly, the Caesars had to interfere to protect the economically underprivileged and to correct misgovernment by the local oligarchies. The ruler could not|deny his position as a powerful savior, to whom the minorities and the oppressed, whether poor or wealthy men at odds with their neighbors, might turn as a "secure refuge against the power of their local rulers." [15] In imperial theory all good things came from the emperor, and to secure these good things the imperial government felt no constitutional scruples at med-

[14] F. F. Abbott and A. C. Johnson, *Municipal Administration in the Roman Empire* (Princeton, 1926), 187.
[15] Aelius Aristides, *On Rome* 65.

dling in urban affairs. All that was necessary was a clear realization of the problems and the erection of an appropriate bureaucracy.

The issuance of orders to the provincial governors was the obvious vehicle for imperial interference, but this channel proved unsatisfactory. At times the governors and the local aristocracies were at loggerheads over matters from taxes to the governor's failure to observe urban holidays. Then the governor might play the oligarchies on a short line, but he might also mulct the rich and stir up the people. More often the governors and men of wealth engaged in collusion, the governors striving to prevent complaints to the ruler which might ruin their future careers and also to make a profit out of their posts, the local leaders seeking to protect their fortunes against the envy of others. It was charged, observed Philostratus, that rich men could not afford to be good subjects.[16]

Two examples of the mischief which could result will suffice. One, under the emperor Gaius, is the anti-Semitic outburst at Alexandria, which the governor Flaccus condoned in an effort to gain the support of the aristocratic leaders. The second, under Nero, is the trial of the Cretan Claudius Timarchus before the Senate on the usual charges "against provincials whose wealth and importance enable them to lord it over their inferiors." [17] In the trial it was hinted that Timarchus secured the acquiescence of the governor by holding the provincial assembly in his pocket. "Once," exploded the doughty Thrasea Paetus at this point, "Roman citizens controlled the provinces; now they paid court to them to gain votes of thanks; and whereas the governors did well at the beginning, they fell away quickly in the search of favor." From the days of Sulla the Roman government tried to protect the cities from being forced to pass honorary decrees or set up statues to their governors, but prohibitions by Augustus, Tiberius, and Nero were of no avail. The provincial assemblies and cities continued to vote such honors to "good" governors, and the governors in turn continued to truckle to the local oligarchies.

In the first century imperial interference in the cities by other means was spasmodic and of doubtful efficacy; in the next century it became more direct and pressing. Even more than the rulers their hosts of bureaucratic assistants had a natural penchant for uniformity. In the West urban organization had followed almost everywhere a standard

[16] *Life of Apollonius* 7.23 (Kayser ed., p. 278).
[17] Tacitus, *Annals* 15.20.1.

pattern; in the East local diversity was the product of the long centuries of the urbanizing process and was not outwardly attacked in this period. Nevertheless the practice of government was subtly brought into conformity with imperial ideas, and new cities tended to be stamped out in the same mold. Regulations such as those of the fiscus applied to all, and the tendency was ever for the imperial bureaucracy to promulgate general rules for one aspect after another of municipal life— though most of this activity falls after the reign of Hadrian.

From Trajan, or possibly Domitian, the rulers also occasionally appointed curators for individual towns, especially in senatorial provinces and in Italy. These officials stepped in temporarily and exercised control over municipal finances and property, while special governors like Pliny the Younger were set over an entire province where the accounts of the cities were in a state of disorder. In this policy the emperors were motivated largely by their fears for the transmission of direct imperial taxes, which were collected by the cities on imperial account, for a cardinal point in Roman government, preceding all others, was the prompt payment of the tribute. "Once they obtain this," observed Josephus, "they grant you everything else, the freedom of your families, the enjoyment of your possessions and the protection of your sacred laws." [18] At this time, however, the amateur conduct of local government conjoined with a hidden decay of urban resources to impair the financial stability of the cities. When some parts of the Empire built overlavishly and others suffered from corruption, the emperors and their ever-more-efficient central bureaucracy felt compelled to intervene.

The correspondence of Pliny, however, shows that the imperial government was also concerned over factional disorders in the cities and local injustice. Apart from the curators and special governors, the regular provincial governors clearly gained a greater control over the suits of the subjects in the second century. Appeal from local decisions became ever more common, though limited in the second century, at least at some places, to serious cases; the tendency to try matters first in the provincial court steadily grew. Though it has long been clear that Roman law did not entirely supplant local law, the most prized aspect of *autonomia*—the right of the community "to use its own laws"— tended to decrease in the actual administration of justice—and largely through the effort to preserve justice to *all* local elements.

[18] *Jewish War* 5.406.

Even after a considerable discount of the propaganda of the coins and edicts and the flattery of second-century authors who saw in the Caesars social justice personified, there can be no doubt that these rulèrs tried very seriously to ameliorate the social and economic condition of the lower classes, while maintaining social distinctions. They improved the legal rights of slaves, widows, and orphans; protected the small proprietors and renters; and safeguarded even in minute details the ability of the city masses to buy their food at reasonable prices. A decree, probably Hadrianic, ordains that fish at Athens must be sold by the importer or first purchaser, "for third buyers increase the price." [19] Other inscriptions, more certainly of the Hadrianic period, attest imperial efforts to secure a supply of oil to Athens at fair prices, or again to protect the fish dealers at Pergamum. The scanty records of labor troubles in Asia Minor suggest that the imperial government did not direct open compulsion against men who quit work unless there was also a riot.

If, in pursuing such noble ends, the rulers broke down local autonomy yet further, few men protested at this time. The prosperity of the period permitted the rich to acquiesce in policies which were later to be the source of tension when the economic well-being of the Empire decreased. The curators, who were only temporary officials down through the second century, may at times have been requested by the local government; the provincial Aelius Aristides even praised the dispatch of imperial agents to cities which had lost their ability to behave themselves. Early in the third century Dio Cassius advised in his history (through the mouth of Maecenas) not only that the meeting of the people in assemblies be forbidden, since they caused riots, but also that cities be strictly watched to prevent the wasting of funds or the financial coercion of individuāls.

The heaviest weight of this imperial interference was not to come until the financial collapse of the third century; but as imperial supervision brought a limitation on the independence of action of—and exploitation by—the local magistrates and converted honorific, unpaid posts into expensive obligations, the interest of the urban aristocracies in public office waned rapidly. Even under Trajan men were forced to become town councilors in Bithynia against their will; by the third century men had everywhere to be dragooned into public posts and then carefully checked lest they shift their burdens onto the poor.

[19] *Inscriptiones Graecae* II and III² 1103.

Bloom and Decay of the Cities

Externally the cities appeared to bloom well down into the second century. Those cities already in existence expanded and beautified themselves with all manner of public buildings, and their inhabitants generally benefited from the prosperity of the period. In almost all the provinces new cities arose on standard Greek or Roman models and spread the outward aspects of Greco-Roman civilization, now to the frontiers of Rhine and Danube, now to the desert wastes of Africa and Transjordan.

Local elements tried to expunge their peculiarities and appear as Greek or Roman as possible; essentially the Caesars could rely upon the upper classes to keep down civil strife and undue political activity of the less civilized elements. By the second century the Empire had the fair appearance of a union of self-governing cities, supervised by a benevolent series of rulers who aimed at promoting social justice everywhere. In the East, at least, civilization seemed to be rising anew in the Hellenic renaissance.

Men in this renaissance, such as Dio Chrysostom or Plutarch, were enthusiastic for the benefits of the Empire. They, as well as the Roman Tacitus, could see that if the Empire were in one sense servitude it was also security, and that upon its maintenance depended Mediterranean civilization; the decree of a Phrygian town which established a public celebration announced that its endurance was guaranteed "by the eternity of the Roman Empire." [20] Yet the hosts of imperial statues and inscriptions, the games and the festivals, and all the other marks of local respects to the emperors were not necessarily results of a sincere appreciation for imperial blessings by all elements of the urban population. Far more directly they attested recognition by the governing classes that their rule depended on imperial support, regardless of the character of the individual ruler; that their only hope to gain the coveted Roman citizenship, which was more and more open to them, lay in unquestioning loyalty to the imperial system.

The propaganda of the Caesars found a willing mouthpiece in town councils, and any discontent must have been rather well stifled on the local level. Apart from the Jews and the professional Hellenists of the late first and second centuries little of such criticism appears in the urbanized sections of the Empire. In his apostrophe to Rome the soph-

[20] *Inscriptiones Graecae ad Res Romanas Pertinentes* 4.661.

ist Aristides bluntly stated that "the greatest and most powerful men in each city guard it for you"; thus the Empire had a double hold on the cities, through its own machinery and through the Roman citizens scattered abroad.[21] The contradiction between imperial absolutism and local democracy was ever more clearly resolved by the elimination of the latter and the factual delimitation of the classes.

When these Greeks turned to discuss their homelands, a note of depression and sterility crept in. This feeling, they clearly show, was due not to local suppression and unrest but rather to an interconnected set of quite different causes: the search for material prosperity, the triumph of the commonplace and trivial, the irresponsibility and factionalism of the upper classes, and imperial interference with local autonomy.

In two essays specifically directed to political life in the Greek cities, Plutarch repeats the old Greek view that public activity was not a special service, "but is a way of life of a tamed social animal living in an organized society, intended by nature to live throughout its allotted time the life of a citizen and in a manner devoted to honour and the welfare of mankind." [22] Yet all our evidence shows that the lower classes had less and less part in the political life of the city, and these very essays demonstrate the pettiness of the politics in which a man could engage— Plutarch even pictures himself as standing and watching the count of tiles or the delivery of concrete and stone for the public works of his native city. The great problems of peace, of war, of liberty no longer lay in local hands. Let the magistrates, warns Plutarch, imitate actors, "who, while putting into the performance their own passion, character, and reputation, yet listen to the prompter and do not go beyond the degree of liberty in rhythms and metres permitted by those in authority over them." [23]

The cities had not only completely lost control over very important spheres of action but also were tending throughout this period to abdicate their autonomy in the other fields of action which remained to them. On the one hand their leaders were not always able to maintain financial, political, and social order pleasing to the emperor, and on the other they tended to appeal to the central government on local matters for every conceivable reason, including vanity. The clear-sighted Plutarch urged the local statesman, while being obedient to Rome, not to humble his city and subject his neck to the yoke

[21] *On Rome* 64.   [22] *Moralia* 791C.   [23] *Moralia* 813F.

as some do who, by referring everything, great or small, to the sovereigns, bring the reproach of slavery upon their country, or rather wholly destroy its constitutional government, making it dazed, timid, and powerless in everything. . . . Those who invite the sovereign's decision in every decree, meeting of a council, granting of a privilege, or administrative measure, force their sovereign to be their master more than he desires.[24]

Far better to be defeated on a measure than to call in the Roman outsiders! So he preached, while the inscriptions of the Greek East are a running proof that the cities turned to the emperors on every conceivable occasion.

Between the paternal benevolence of the central administration and the servility of the oligarchies the vigor of local politics waned; the cities were not granted, as a substitute, a really significant, inspiriting influence on the imperial government. In all this the Empire was wiping out not merely freedom of thought in the political sphere but the very possibility of serious political action for the bulk of its subjects. So it was destroying a very important focus for the forces which had led to the expansion and remarkable vitality of Mediterranean civilization up to this point. The upper classes and the Caesars both delivered devastating blows at the sense of local attachment, the solidarity of the city, from which the thinkers of the past had drawn their strength.

[24] *Moralia* 814F–815A.

VI

Autocracy in Rome
A.D. 14–69

IN RETURNING from the provinces to Rome one emerges, as it were, from dingy, twisting lanes into a densely thronged open square where villains and saints pass through the murmuring crowds. This lurid stage too often enthralls the modern spectator, for events at Rome were warped by that dominant position which the city inherited from the Republic and maintained through the presence of the emperor. Roman developments were not necessarily as important as the Romans themselves took them to be. The feuds among the senatorial factions, the struggle between them and their ruler, the riots of the Roman people— these often had little repercussion out in the provinces. In root, moreover, the cities of the Empire as a whole, and not Rome, were the major sources of intellectual strength in the ancient world.

Within these limitations a significant battle for freedom of thought on the political, and also on the intellectual, level was waged and lost in Rome during the first century after Christ. Here were the political elements of traditional importance in Roman history; here alone lay a possibility of concerting important political opposition to the Caesars. Fought often in subterranean passages which escape our view, the battle now and then comes into open sight in the pages of Tacitus, Suetonius, and other extant works.

Neronian Autocracy (*in the* Octavia)

The first century after Christ may be divided into two parts. After the civil wars of 68–69 comes the Flavian family; before, the Julio-Claudians drop one by one off the family tree of Augustus and Livia: first Tiberius (14–37), then Gaius (37–41), Claudius (41–54), and Nero (54–68). The swift changes of the civil wars elevated Galba, Otho, Vitellius, and finally Vespasian within a year. In considering the manifestations of absolutism down to 69 it may be best to begin with the reign of the last of the Julio-Claudians, Nero, and sort out the threads which led to the autocracy of that despot, so far removed from the benign moderation of Augustus.

More specifically, let us commence with a sad event of the year 62, the exile of Nero's ex-wife Octavia to the island of Pandateria. Octavia was a woman to be pitied. Her mother, Messallina, was taken in open adultery and executed. Her father, the emperor Claudius, was murdered by her mother-in-law Agrippina, who had married Octavia to her own son Nero. Nero killed her brother and his own mother and loathed Octavia herself. After an open break in 62 she was exiled to Campania, but was still harshly attacked by Nero's new love, the notorious Poppaea; before the end of the year the unfortunate girl was removed to Pandateria, as a prelude to the execution which swiftly followed.

As a victim of personal emotions within the imperial court Octavia is a sad figure; but her tribulations gain special significance from the fact that an account survives of the events just before her exile. The play *Octavia*, the only surviving Roman historical drama, concentrates not so much on the character of the heroine as on her helplessness. In structure it is a simple work. Octavia and her nurse, Nero and Seneca, Poppaea and her nurse, the prefect of the guard, a chorus now of the people, now of the court—these elements move on and off the stage and explore aspects of the situation. Action is scant, the clash of personalities is refined to intellectual terms, and the tone is one of unrelieved gloom from the opening appearance of Octavia, moaning the arrival of a new day, to the final chorus lamenting her exile and fore-shadowed death. Even the triumphant Poppaea appears only to retail a fearful dream and then rushes off to propitiate the gods by sacrifice. Withal the play casts a vivid light on current conditions and contains a superb criticism of Neronian autocracy; more than inveighing against

Nero its author was musing on the eternal clash of justice and tyranny.

The authorship of the play is a debatable point. Since this impassioned attack was not meant to be performed, it could have been penned in secret at any time after the event or, better, after the fire of Rome (64) but before the suicide of Nero; for in my judgment the author was certainly a contemporary of Nero who knew a great deal of the inner workings of the court. The manuscripts ascribe the play to Seneca, who wrote a number of extant tragedies on Greek models, but this ascription has often been questioned, principally because the ghost of Agrippina rises to prophesy the desertion, flight, and execution of her son Nero, which took place three years after the death of Seneca. This prophecy, however, is couched in the general terms of tragedy and does not contain any specific reference to the events of 68 or the dawning of a better world thereafter. A secondary argument against Senecan authorship on the grounds of meter is as dubious as any such argument from internal evidence, and is not supported by any peculiarities of vocabulary or dramatic construction.

The author was assuredly a man with real dramatic ability, he was deeply conversant with Seneca's line of thought and earlier writings, he shared Seneca's general view of the Principate as inevitable and also his lack of sympathy with the extreme senatorial position, and above all he had an independence of judgment and pen which can be found in undoubtedly genuine works of Seneca such as the *Apocolocyntosis* or the essay *On Clemency*. To imagine two people of such similar nature living at the same time seems unnecessary, and I shall thenceforth proceed on the assumption that the *Octavia* is a genuine work of Seneca, completed in his last bitter days after the fire of Rome in 64. In the present conjunction the play itself is the important thing, and the name of the author means little.

To return now to the plot of the drama, Octavia is in a threatened position under a ruler who, unlike Augustus, wished to be absolute. The question is, To whom shall she turn for aid?

The possible answers are the gods, the people of Rome, the Senate, and the emperor with his servants. To each the play gives its attention, and incisively suggests whence came this absolutism, and what part each of these elements played in its creation.

In her opening lament Octavia appeals to her mother Messallina "if any consciousness remains among the shades." Later the old nanny, appropriately to her character, tries to soothe the anguished girl by promising that the divine force will bring better days. Octavia, too, notes the appearance of a comet as a celestial sign suggesting ills for the subjects of Nero but then slides off into a bitter complaint against Jupiter for hurling his darts so aimlessly. As she goes into exile, she loses hope:

Now Piety no longer has divinity, nor are there any gods; grim Fury reigns throughout the universe [ll. 911–913].

To men of the modern world, who know the Roman gods to be powerless fictions, the failure of divine aid is inevitable. For its own era this play grimly displays a pessimistic doubt of life after death and the general inability of pagan aristocrats to find a support outside the material world encircling them. Though the shade of Agrippina rises with flaming torch from Tartarus to threaten the punishment of Nero by the Fury, of what avail was such an artifice upon an emperor who ruled the official cults? or even bluntly asserted that he made gods (in allusion to his deification of Claudius)? More generally the work of Euhemerus, of the Stoics and other philosophers—let alone that of Homer and other ancient poets—had stripped from the great pagan gods their scant ethical force; the advanced elements of society now operated on a rational plane marred only by lapses into magic and astrology. They may often have desired to believe in the old gods and certainly felt that the world, itself divine, was under a divine control, but from that abstract thought they could draw no tangible aid.

Populus Romanus

A woman in distress must rather turn to forces of this world, and much of the plan revolves about the sympathy manifested for Octavia by the Roman people. Indignantly the populace rises to overthrow the images of Poppaea and attacks the palace itself. The very riot, nonetheless, makes the exile of Octavia more certain. Haughtily Nero rejects the disgrace of yielding to the masses whom he suspects—and probably rightly to judge from Tacitus' parallel account—of being stirred up by clients and slaves of Octavia. When Seneca argues that the best support of a ruler lies in the love of his subjects, Nero spurns the idea and rests his power on the sword:

The huge mob grows riotous, distempered by the blessings of my age, nor hath it understanding of my mercy in its thanklessness nor can it suffer peace; but here 'tis swept along by restless insolence and there by its own recklessness is headlong borne. By suffering must it be held in check, be ever pressed beneath the heavy yoke, that it may never dare the like again, and against my wife's sacred countenance lift its eyes; crushed by the fear of punishment, it shall be taught to obey its emperor's nod [ll. 834–843].

In their lack of distinction and very numbers the people are really safe, though the emperor raves on about burning all the city—a sidelong repetition of the charge that Nero set the famous fire of 64—threatens to reduce the mob to hunger, and grows wroth with the prefect who refuses to kill the people wholesale. Yet everywhere in the play the conclusion is the same: the citizenry may riot and cause trouble, but it cannot successfully oppose the emperor.

Such was the famous *populus Romanus* in the days of Nero. When the chorus asks, Where now is the manhood of the Roman people which had once conquered illustrious foes and had given the symbols of office to their elected leaders? any reader could give the answer. The same process which stripped the assemblies of provincial cities of their power had been at work in imperial Rome with even greater intensity; as an organized political force, the body of citizens had essentially ceased to exist by the reign of Nero.

Augustus, it will be remembered, had limited the organization of clubs, had severely restricted the active participation of the people in government, and had looked with suspicion on any aristocrat currying favor with the masses. Tiberius went further by shifting the election of magistrates to the Senate, where it remained thereafter apart from a brief reversion to the people under Gaius. Tiberius and subsequent Caesars received their legal powers for life; and even though the legal theory of the Principate always based the ruler's constitutional position on a grant by the sovereign people, it is not clear that a popular assembly, rather than the Senate acting in lieu thereof, actually voted this grant.

The people did not thereby give up all modes of expression, for as the mob of a great city which was the capital of the Empire and the usual residence of the ruler it continued to speak, no longer in the imperative of election, but in the optative of riots, demonstrations, and rumor.

Some rioting was self-generated by the pressure of sales taxes, the temporary scarcity of food, and the like; the emperor Claudius once found himself pelted in the Forum by a hungry crowd and had to run for his palace. A considerable part of the populace was also willing to lend itself to demonstrations through boredom and discontent or for pay. Operating via the four circus factions, social clubs, and other means, the upper classes or members of the imperial circle could utilize clients and freedmen to start the masses rioting in Rome. Such manufactured unrest occurred under all the Julio-Claudians.

Rioting provided an exciting break in the humdrum of urban life, but it had its dangers. Less risky and more frequent was the wagging of tongues in rumor, as in the days of Augustus. The rumors continued usually to smack of aristocratic origin; and the emperors, by and large, recognized the impossibility of fighting intangible whispers. "Nailed to a pinnacle," as Seneca puts it,[1] the Caesars bore the pitiless attention of the people to their every act.

Tacitus comments that in Rome everything was known, talked about, and believed if only it were bad news; and Juvenal sketches a lively picture of wives gadding about the city and clacking boldly with the generals. Such women knew what the Thracians and Chinese were doing, who loved whom, who had got the widow with child and when. As bad as the women and itinerant dinner gossips (the ancient columnists) were the slaves, who revealed their masters' secrets for malice or retribution. Nearly everything which took place inside the palace made its way out to the aristocracy and to the people. When it did not, the malicious invented evil stories to account for puzzling imperial actions. The death of any member of the imperial house—from the heir of Tiberius, Germanicus, to Lucius Verus, coemperor with Marcus Aurelius—was sure to bring whispers of poisoning or worse, and a constant rumor of immorality surrounded almost every woman of the imperial house. The most extreme example is perhaps the nauseous canard of Faustina's love for a gladiator, who was killed by the command of her husband Marcus Aurelius so that she might bathe in his blood—the result being the conception of the hated Commodus. "Does that Roman tongue," jibed Tertullian, "spare any one of its Caesars?"[2]

This rumor was at times reflected in the Atellan farces, as their writers and actors played the dangerous game of innuendo in their search for public favor; or the public might of its own accord seize upon an old, outwardly innocent line about, say, an old goat and twist it to mock some imperial lechery. Another deposit of the vocal feeling of the day was the charcoal scribbling on the plastered walls of Rome. The jurists solemnly pronounced that anything put on public monuments for the sake of defaming another was to be erased, but the ordinary man continued anonymously thus to express his views. As papal Rome had its Madama Lu-

---

[1] *On Clemency* 1.8.3.　　　　　　[2] *Apology* 35.6.

crezia and the Pasquino for the posting of popular jests, so the ancient city had its imperial statues by the score; some bold wag thus veiled a head of Nero in a bag to indicate this murderer of his mother deserved the'parricide's punishment of being thrown alive into the sea in a bag.

The Caesars might suffer in spirit, but they realized in the main that this grumbling was merely a complement to the essential acceptance of their rule. Under Augustus the people had been quite willing in the main to surrender constitutional rights of little value for the security of life which the Principate brought.

Therewith the masses had had to take some few curbs upon their mode of life. Numerous edicts restricted the sale of cooked meats or of wine before certain hours and essayed to check other incitements to luxury and depravity which might corrupt what was still in theory the sovereign fount of power. Some futile effort was made by the emperors to limit the access of citizens in Rome to non-Roman gods like Jehovah and Isis and Sarapis. The most popular form of entertainment, the mimes, was occasionally censored because of its license or the riots over its popular actors; Nero, after first withdrawing in 55 the troops which kept order at all public affairs, found the result was rioting between the claques and so banned the Atellan farces for four years.

Despite fitful discontent with these shackles the people felt almost any ruler to be far better than the Senate had been in the Republic. An imperial bureau supervised the grain supply of Rome and even supported the poor by free allowances; entertainments were furnished on an ever-more-extensive scale; imperial building projects provided an important source of employment. Vespasian rewarded the inventor of a machine for moving columns but refused to use it lest "the poor commons" lack work. The masses were in truth bought by bread and circuses, and any political potentialities they may have had were stifled; but a humanitarian judge must also admit that their poverty needed support (see Pl. XII). That their spiritual lacks could also be met by the Principate one may doubt.

Distrusting the Senate from of old, the people showed little concern over senatorial battles for limiting the emperor's prerogative. This fact is one of the principal reasons why the multitudes are so scorned in imperial literature, which was mainly written by or for the aristocracy. The populace, rather, enjoyed seeing the mighty topple and were always ready to drag down the statues of a man such as Sejanus and maltreat his

corpse. Octavia, to return to our hapless heroine, might arouse a sentimental sympathy and popular outcry, but the results would be worse
than useless. In sum, if Nero were an autocrat, the people did not greatly
object so long as they were secure; and on the whole the ordinary citizen
would support the ruler against the other elements of the state.

Decline of the Senate

Neither the gods nor the people could give effective aid to Octavia, a
helpless individual before the machine of autocracy. Better might perhaps be expected of the venerable Senate. Augustus had made it a partner in his government; the emperor Otho was soon to praise it, according
to Tacitus, as the ancestral balance wheel of Rome. When we turn to the
Octavia, however, we find almost no reference to the Senate. A nurse
tells Poppaea that the Senate is amazed at her beauty, and that is nearly
all.

The reason for this silence is simple: under Nero no victim could hope
for any outward marks of sympathy from the Senate. To such an abject
state had the senatorial aristocracy decayed under the Julio-Claudian
rulers.

When the aged Augustus breathed his last in A.D. 14, Tiberius was
already regent, and the grant of various legal powers had clearly
marked him out as the next ruler. At Rome, says Tacitus, "All—consuls,
senators, and equestrians—were plunging into servitude," by taking an
oath of allegiance to the new *princeps,* but this bitter phrase, which is
characteristic of Tacitus' misrepresentation of the reign of Tiberius,
throws the attitude of the new ruler entirely in the wrong light of
hypocrisy and veiled drive for absolutism. Tiberius desired nothing so
little as that the Senate should be his slave.

After the funeral of Augustus, his weary stepson, fifty-four years of
age, displayed a real reluctance to take up the burdens of state. Though
at last the pressure of inevitability forced him to accept the "slavery"
of the imperial position, he made clear from the outset that he expected
the Senate to help him, and went far beyond the practice of Augustus'
last years in respecting senatorial autonomy. By the transfer of the election of magistrates to the Senate it became a co-opting body entirely independent of the people. Tiberius upheld the authority of the Senate; he
lifted the veil of secrecy over imperial administration to a considerable
degree; a yearly oath of allegiance to his acts by the Senate, which was

later customary, Tiberius rejected; and he fostered freedom of debate in the Senate House to an extent which the historian Tacitus could not comprehend.

Tiberius perhaps brought down his later troubles upon himself by failing to note how far the hands of the clock had already moved. On the one hand the imperial bureaucracy was accustomed to look only to the ruler and made frightened protests when Tiberius tried, for instance, to have the executioner of Augustus' grandson, Agrippa Postumus, report to the Senate. The "secrets of empire" must not be divulged, nor the powers of the ruler weakened, by his referring everything to the Senate. And indeed, if the Empire were to continue to enjoy the better administration it had under Augustus, its affairs could not again be subjected in every detail to the wrangling delays and personal factionalism of the Senate.

On the other hand, and more significant, stood this very factionalism of the Senate. The luxurious aristocracy of Rome, still split by its family quarrels and rampant individualism, had, now that its responsibility diminished, even less cohesion than in the Late Republic. In part it grouped itself about Livia; or Agrippina the Elder, the widow of Germanicus; or the chief minister Sejanus; or the ruler and others in vicious personal cliques. Throughout the twenty-three years of Tiberius' long reign the Senate also kept up its internecine, even intrafamily, rivalries. L. Piso, an independent man, might announce his decision to retire in his disgust at "the favouritism of the courts, the corruption of the tribunals, and the savage eagerness of orators in threatening prosecutions," [3] but Tiberius, chained to his post, could only look on in dismay and do his utmost to moderate the attacks.

In this struggle Tiberius perhaps committed his gravest mistake, for when a praetor inquired about cases of *maiestas,* he announced that "the laws must be enforced." [4] Thus he gave to the senators an open field in which those attempting a rival's ruin might boldly experiment. Modern surveys of the trials for *laesa maiestas* under Tiberius generally tend to support the conclusion that he actually tried to mitigate the application of the concept. Trials were duly carried out by normal, open process and not in the emperor's privacy; deliberately false accusations were rigorously punished, and charges involving misuse of the emperor's statue or casual remarks were almost always dismissed.

[3] Tacitus, *Annals* 2.34.1.
[4] Tacitus, *Annals* 1.72.4; also in Suetonius, *Tiberius* 58.

The reign of Tiberius makes crystal clear what was already suggested in the Augustan period: a substantial part of the Senate was not interested in maintaining the independence of that body but preferred to concentrate powers upon the *princeps*. Repeatedly the Senate refused to take the initiative or even to make decisions, despite the warning of Tiberius that "every increase in prerogative was a weakening of the law." A Roman knight summed up the attitude of many in arguing that "to you the Gods have given the supreme direction of affairs; to us has been left the glory of obedience." [5] This thesis led directly to the absolutism of Nero and eventually—I may note here—to the accepted constitutional theory of the next century.

Still, Tiberius tried to allow the Senate to operate as it would. "A well-disposed and helpful prince," Suetonius quotes him as saying, "ought to be the servant of the Senate. . . . I have looked upon you as kind, just, and indulgent masters, and still so regard you." [6] The compulsion which drove him now and then to break with his policy was not any secret yearning for absolutism, but rather the conduct of the senators themselves.

To secure the emperor's favor almost all the Senate engaged in the most outrageous flattery, a nauseating proceeding which is better left undescribed but which was intensified by the very forthrightness of the ruler in attempting to reject it. According to tradition Tiberius summed up the adulation in his bitter cry, "O men ready for slavery!" [7] Even his servants were subject to the incessant ripple of compliments, honorary statues, and the like. His chief minister Sejanus received honors both from his master and from the Senate the like of which no other non-imperial character was ever to obtain. Under this incitement he decided to strike for the supreme power but failed; the Senate scarcely redeemed its dignity by its quick abandonment and violent denunciation of Sejanus on his fall in 31. The counterpart of flattery was a vicious undercurrent of oral and pamphleteering attacks on the stiff, unbending ruler, which helped to blast his posthumous reputation and at the time aided in leading the Elder Agrippina into open opposition to Tiberius.

The tragedy of the reign of Tiberius rises largely from the interplay of senatorial animosities and the diffident hesitation of the aging, disappointed ruler, who had an almost archaic respect for the old forms of the constitution. In trying to restore the Senate's independence, he

[5] Tacitus, *Annals* 3.69.6, 6.8.7.   [6] Suetonius, *Tiberius* 29.
[7] Tacitus, *Annals* 3.65.3.

made its lack of true power, its servility, only the more apparent; those senators who urged frank acceptance of imperial control may have been the more realistic. Nor by his own example could Tiberius check the senatorial spendthrifts, who still flayed the provinces to gain money or crawled shamelessly to the ruler, begging for support. Though invited by the Senate to resume the effort of Augustus at moral reforms, the emperor refused to engage his energies in the hopeless task.

Under Tiberius the Senate had one last chance to exercise free speech and assume an independent part in the government of the Empire. The fruits were the plot of the bloated Sejanus, mutual charges of *maiestas*, and sons haling back their fathers from exile for yet further accusations. If a contemporary could later assert that there was "a common and almost universal frenzy for bringing charges of treason," [8] it must be said to have stemmed as much from the Senate's factionalism and the ambitions of the Elder Agrippina as from Tiberius' sense of the necessity of executing the laws and his fear for his position after the plot of Sejanus. The next ruler, Gaius (Caligula), was to open the path to true terror.

The accession in 37 of this young son of the Elder Agrippina and Germanicus seemed to his panegyrists to bring back the sun. A decree of Cyzicus hailed him as the "new sun," who had "wished to illumine with his rays the kingdoms that are the bodyguards of his Empire, to the end that the greatness of his immortality might be the more august," [9] and the Alexandrian mint celebrates Gaius as Helios steadily after his first year. At the outset Gaius virtually dropped *laesa maiestas* and prated much of deferring to the Senate's authority, though that body flattered him outrageously. In deference to senatorial hatred of Tiberius he even abandoned his intention of deifying him.

This attitude lasted scarcely a year. Poorly educated in the court of his gloomy predecessor, corroded by flatterers, and perhaps not entirely sound of mind, Gaius soon marched toward outright autocracy. In this endeavor he proceeded logically. His whole policy seems to reflect the actual power of a Caesar; he would make plain what was latent in the position of the master of the armies, the object of unbounded flattery by the Senate, the god on earth to many of his subjects. To Gaius autoc-

[8] Seneca, *On Benefits* 3.26.1.

[9] *Inscriptiones Graecae ad Res Romanas Pertinentes* 4.145; Magie, *Roman Rule in Asia Minor* 1, 511; cf. *Bulletin de Correspondence Hellénique* 12 (1888), 307, l. 60.

racy was not an opportunity to benefit his people as shepherd and protector; it was rather the necessary condition for the exercise of caprice, and in this his reputed madness may lie.

Despotism in the Empire always brought the amputation of senators' heads. Under Gaius actual condemnations seem to have been limited to suspected governors and to a few others—including one poor senator who bluntly said that the Senate thought one way and voted another. Nevertheless the senators lived thenceforth in uneasy suspicion of each other and their ruler, for not even the proimperial party could ever feel sure of striking the tone which would suit their ruler's whim. At one banquet, for instance, where Gaius broke out laughing, he blandly explained to the near-by consuls his amusement at the idea that he could have their throats cut by one nod of his head.

In 40 Gaius went on to express his hostility to the Senate more forcibly; to stir up the Jews; to alienate the people of Rome, whom he had earlier favored, through his taxes; and finally to lose the support of his own administrators. Teetering unsteadily, trying everything in his desperation, Gaius even came back to the Senate and pretended a reconciliation, which the Senate solemnly celebrated; his rule, however, became ever more autocratic, and he intensified his effort to deify himself or to equate himself with the gods.

No resource could restore the security of a youth who roved the palace at night and cried out for day to come. One conspiracy failed; then on January 24, 41, Gaius fell to the dagger of a tribune of his own guard, Cassius Chaerea, and other conspirators who struck to re-establish liberty. Only the half-barbarian German troops and, to a lesser degree, the people tried to avenge him.

In his intentional exploration of the autocratic possibilities latent in the Principate Gaius served as forerunner of Nero and Domitian. He also opened, if only briefly, the eyes of the Senate to the frightful consequences of pushing its ruler toward absolutism. The reaction was violent. The sudden death of Gaius left the Empire without a designated successor for the first time, and the Senate dared to hope it might abolish the whole system.

The day following the murder of Gaius was one of great significance, for these twenty-four hours witnessed a serious effort by some elements to restore the Republic. The consuls immediately convened the Senate on the Capitol and by edict ordered the people and garrison of Rome to return home. Already, unfortunately for the Senate, the praetorians had discovered the uncle of Gaius, Claudius the "fool," quaking behind a palace curtain and had dragged him off to their camp to hail him as new *princeps;* but the consuls went ahead on the project of reanimating the Republic.

One consul, Cn. Sentius Saturninus, made an eloquent speech, the outlines of which are preserved by Josephus. Sentius himself could not remember the former time of liberty, but he knew well the mischiefs of tyranny, that teacher of flattery and slavish fear. Now all might freely voice their opinions without fear of punishment, and let them do so— nothing had so contributed to the increase of tyranny of late as sloth and timorous refusal to contradict the emperor's will. "Men had an over-great inclination to the sweetness of peace, and had learned to live like slaves." [10] Here, in the mouth of a senator himself, loom the main reasons why the Senate had lost its freedom of speech; to make the picture complete, a ring bearing the visage of Gaius flashed on Sentius' gesturing hand. Another senator snatched and broke it, the consuls gave the watchword of *libertas* to the four urban cohorts which supported the Senate, and this body settled down to deal with Claudius.

Within the following night and day the bold attitude of the Senate collapsed completely. The Senate itself spent its precious moments of liberty arguing whether to restore the Republic or to elect a new *princeps,* and on the latter question all the old rivalries sprang to the fore. Worst of all was the Senate's failure to gain support outside its ranks. The people, Josephus reveals, first rejoiced over the death of Gaius, but when face to face with the possibility of senatorial rule they quickly rallied behind Claudius in fear both of civil war and of the *pleonexia* (greediness, arrogance) of the senators. The praetorian soldiers likewise reflected on the senatorial vices and the inability of the Senate to govern the vast Empire; and it was not to their personal advantage to have a new Caesar chosen without their help. The clever outsider Agrippa, who happened to be in Rome, quickly cast his lot with Claudius.

A nocturnal meeting of the Senate was called to consider Claudius' refusal to abdicate, but many senators were missing. They had hidden in the city or had fled out of town—"better for them to be slaves without danger to themselves, and to lead a lazy and inactive life, than by claiming the dignity of their forefathers, to run the hazard of their own

[10] Josephus, *Antiquities* 19.181 (Whiston).

safety." [11] Throughout the day of January 25 the senators seem to have drifted to the praetorian camp to make their peace with the new Caesar and his soldiers. By evening Claudius was in the palace, the murderers of Gaius were executed, and the next day Claudius received the formal plaudits of the Senate.

In this sad sequence of events men discovered that killing a ruler did not bring "liberty." The political opposition of the aristocracy to the Principate as an institution came to a whimpering end. The Senate could command no armed force of consequence, either in Rome or in the provinces; it could not rely on the people; it was split within itself; many of its members were either bound to the system through the honors they had received or lacked the strength of mind to face the prospect of danger and personal exertion. On the suicide of Nero twenty-seven years later no one seriously raised the battlecry of the Republic; if the events of 68–69 have claimed more modern attention than the fiasco of 41, it must be attributed to their greater bloodshed and to the masterly description of the later unrest by Tacitus.

The main problems under the later Julio-Claudians and Flavians were two: Who was to be the king? and, To what extent would he voluntarily limit his autocracy so as to be a "good" ruler, particularly as regarded the Senate? Skirmishes on these points thenceforth took place as much on the theoretical as on the political plane; of especial interest are *l'affaire* Thrasea Paetus under Nero and the character of the civil wars of 68–69.

The reign of Claudius, which came before these events, prefigured in many respects the eventual solution of the relations between the ruler and the aristocracy. Claudius treated the Senate with outward consideration. He abolished the charge of *laesa maiestas,* proclaimed a general amnesty, and attempted to maintain the dignity of the Senate by eliminating unfit members in his censorship and by enforcing attendance at its meetings. In one speech, preserved on papyrus, he sounds a note familiar alike under Tiberius and Trajan, for he recalls the slothful senators to a sober execution of their duty:

If these proposals are approved by you, show your assent at once plainly and sincerely. If, however, you do not approve them then find some other remedies. . . . It is extremely unfitting, Conscript Fathers, to the high dignity of this order that at this meeting one man only, the consul designate, should make a speech (and that copied exactly from the proposal of the

[11] Josephus, *Antiquities* 19.248 (Whiston).

consuls), while the rest utter one word only, "Agreed," and then after leaving the House remark "There, we've given our opinion." [12]

Whereupon, one suspects, the senators thanked Claudius for his encouragement to freedom of speech and then voted unanimously as they felt he desired.

The collapse of republican ideas and the codification of the Principate as an institution stand explicit on the Claudian coins with the legend Imperial Liberty (*libertas augusta*) and the figure of the goddess of liberty, last seen on the issues of the tyrannicide Brutus. This type may be taken as a promise that the ruler would maintain for the Empire a liberty every whit as good as that proclaimed briefly by the Senate. The exact connotation of that liberty is perhaps suggested in a notable statement of the governor of Asia which foreshadows the imperial theory of the next century: Claudius, "having received the whole human race under his own protection, has granted among his foremost benefits, dearest to all men, that each should enjoy his own." [13] Autocracy, public service, outward respect toward the aristocracy—these are the hallmarks of the future.

Actually Claudius wielded a firm mastery over the Senate. Soldiers were forbidden to have social relationships with senators. The ruler took control of senatorial travel outside Italy so as to bind the senators in "golden fetters." Equestrians were used in minor provincial commands and in other posts to an unprecedented degree; even in Italy the ruler encroached on senatorial functions. Above all, Claudius sought advice principally from his notorious freedmen aides, who regularized and expanded considerably the central bureaucracy. To them and to his ambitious wives were due in large part the numerous victims, senatorial and equestrian, and the secret trials of his reign.

When Claudius finally fell, it was to internal family intrigue, in which courtiers and bureaucrats jockeyed on either side behind the façade of ceremonial. His last wife, Agrippina (the Younger), murdered him with a dish of poisoned mushrooms in 54, so that her son Nero might hold the imperial power.

The youthful Nero began well. In a speech to the Senate, written by his adviser Seneca, he promised to abolish the closed courts of Claudius

---

[12] *Berliner Griechische Urkunden* 611 (trans. by M. P. Charlesworth, *Cambridge Ancient History* 10 [Cambridge, 1934], 697–698).

[13] Magie, *Roman Rule in Asia Minor* 1, 546.

and to respect senatorial authority; the senators enthusiastically voted to have the speech inscribed on a silver tablet and read anew by the incoming consuls each year. Then they settled down, in the phrase of Dio Cassius, as if to enjoy a good reign.

Their influence remained powerful for only five years. First came the murder of Claudius' own son Britannicus, then Nero removed his mother Agrippina; after the death of the praetorian prefect Burrus and the retirement of Seneca in 62 the steadily more despotic, egotistical character of Nero's rule became obvious. Outwardly the senators masked their resignation by adulation; many retired from public life. Their inner bitterness broke out in the only possible form it could have taken, the feckless plot of Piso in 65, which failed miserably and dragged to destruction many of the senatorial leaders as well as Seneca, Lucan, and other glories of Neronian culture. Not until the armies had lost their confidence in the lyre-strumming ruler could the governors and generals of senatorial stock lead a successful revolt in the provinces.

The truly new departure of Nero's absolutism consisted in this: not only opposition but also neutrality and retirement were no longer to be possible. Men were not at liberty to say nothing, as Cicero had asserted of Caesar; everyone had to support the autocrat actively. Culturally the aristocracy was under heavy pressure to applaud Nero's virtuosity, as we shall see later, and to participate in the Neronian festivals from the Juvenalia of 59 onward. At these affairs a Roman knight mounted an elephant and slid down a rope; worse yet, a noblewoman eighty years of age danced in a pantomime. These puerilities of later scandal need not weight the scales of reprobation against Nero, for fools always are seeking notoriety; the ban on political neutrality is a different matter.

This ban first becomes evident in the trial of Thrasea Paetus in 66. Though P. Clodius Thrasea Paetus, consul in 56, was a member of the ever-increasing section of the aristocracy which had risen through imperial favor since the days of Augustus, he attempted to maintain the independence of the Senate. As long as it was feasible, he took an active part in senatorial debates, even weighing gravely such minor matters as the number of gladiators to be allowed at Syracuse. As Nero's autocracy became more violent, Thrasea more obviously expressed his discontent; in 63 he retired, and for three years his face was not seen in the Senate House.

Previous emperors had not viewed kindly such retirements or the suicides of senators in their discontent with the burdens or boredom of life, but none had gone beyond exhortation in essaying to discourage these steps. Even under Nero various senators withdrew to far-off estates without punishment. Thrasea's disassociation from the regime, however, apparently had a flaunting air, and the regime decided in 66 to strike at his tacit opposition; though our main informant, Tacitus, may have sharpened the issue at stake, the general lines of Thrasea's trial seem clear.

In the year after the Pisonian conspiracy Thrasea and a number of others were formally accused of *laesa maiestas*. The prosecutor of Thrasea was Capito Cossutianus, a personal enemy whom Thrasea had once helped to convict of extortion; rare was the senator against whom his rivals were not eager to move! One of his codefendants, Barea Soranus, was accused of currying provincial favor with treasonable intent; the daughter of Soranus was likewise a defendant on the charge of consulting astrologers against Nero. The indictments against Thrasea as preserved by Dio Cassius and Tacitus do not entirely agree, but among the specifications were his absence from the Senate; his refusal to take part in the sacred festivals founded by Nero, though he was willing to do so in his native Padua; and even his failure to listen to the emperor's singing and lyre playing or to sacrifice to Nero's divine voice.

The speeches of Cossutianus and his coadjutor, the notorious informer Eprius Marcellus, before and during the trial are given to us by Tacitus; however embellished they may be, they seem to form a fine expression of the proimperial point of view. Incessantly they revolve about the point that if Thrasea were not with the government he must be against it. By withdrawing he was not fulfilling the duties of a senator, of a priest, even of a citizen; his specific failures to act in each capacity, as itemized, show how deeply bound a senator was to the imperial system. "Let him be cut off from a country which he has long ceased to love, and which he now refuses to behold." [14] Nor might Nero permit such examples of open defiance to be cited at large. Even at that very time the armies and provinces were reading the *acta diurna* to see what Thrasea had not done, and his example might lead to wider secessions among his disciples, "whose unbending and gloomy faces are intended as a rebuke to your [Nero's] frivolity." [15]

Another line of attack is of great significance despite its obscure expression. Eprius argued that the Senate was inferior to the ruler;

[14] Tacitus, *Annals* 16.28.6 (Eprius Marcellus).
[15] Tacitus, *Annals* 16.22.3 (Capito Cossutianus).

Cossutianus goes on to affirm that the efforts of Thrasea to overturn the Empire by asserting senatorial liberty would actually destroy liberty itself. Though we may doubt the basic premise that Thrasea actually wished to restore the Republic, this argument by a henchman of Nero contains the theme which the panegyrists of the second century were to emphasize, that the freedom of the ordinary citizen depended on his acceptance of the rule of the Caesars. Freedom in this sense refers to economic and social well-being rather than to freedom of thought; Eprius accordingly pictures Thrasea as mourning the current prosperity.

The senators who were to vote on these charges approached the Senate House through throngs of the populace and military formations in dense, threatening array. There they listened dejectedly to a violent letter from Nero in reproof of their neglect of their duty and then hearkened to the bellowed accusations. Thrasea, naturally, was convicted but was permitted to choose his manner of suicide; the other defendants were similarly punished or were given lesser penalties.

Thrasea talked in his last moments of the fitting path to take in public life under the Caesars, and lets us infer that his martyrdom cast a light upon that path. Our historian of the trial, Tacitus, did not exactly know what the path should be, and Thrasea himself had no very clear ideal in his martyrdom other than the sense of his own dignity as a Roman senator. "Nero," he used to say in Stoic fashion, "can kill me, but he cannot harm me." [16]

Yet it is significant that by this time autocracy had pushed its claims to the farthermost point; under Nero men of the upper classes who thought otherwise than did the autocrat were to deny their inner heart by outward, positive support of what they detested. One further point is notable. Against Thrasea, who asserted his inner independence, the people, the administrative aides, and great parts of the Senate itself were willing to accept, and even to foster, the position of the ruler as uniquely powerful.

Can one marvel that Octavia, dying four years before Thrasea, could hope for no aid from the Senate? On her death this body of frightened men voted new honors to their tyrant; Seneca could do no more than surreptitiously compose his tragedy, wherein he underlined the tyranny and bloodthirstiness of an irresponsible autocrat. The Nero of this play boasts, "My fortune doth allow all things to me," and proclaims the sword and fear his best protection: "Whatever is high exalted, let it fall."

[16] Dio Cassius 61.15.4.

Such absolutism could be countered only by the stealthy knife of the assassin or the violent expression of military opinion in outright revolt.

Civil War

Nero, indeed, lost control of the armies in 68 and so fell himself from his high exaltation, but his inattention to the business of the Empire and his pose as a master of verse and lyre brought that fall more surely than did his numerous executions. Thereupon the Empire discovered anew, as in the days of Octavian, that the man with the superior army could claim its mastery. Since the various provincial armies threw up different candidates, the issue of military superiority could be settled only by a series of swift but bloody civil wars in which the armies were set in motion by their senatorial leaders, but thereafter they moved almost of their own accord as fiercely destructive agencies.

Accompanied by revolt and intercity feuds, these wars shed vivid light on the inner tensions of the Empire. It is small wonder that rulers in more peaceful times, conscious of these underlying tensions, tended to grow ruthless when they came up against troublesome senators, or that moderation increased as the Empire became more unified. The wars may also have imposed a check, but only a temporary one, on the increasing centralization and absolutism of the imperial system. Still, no one seriously proposed the restoration of the Republic—the field of debate had narrowed considerably since the days of Brutus and Cassius or even the fall of Gaius.

Nor did the Senate play any independent part. Though the rival leaders showed it outward respect, it only accepted with hidden resentment anyone presented to it who had a preponderance of force at Rome. Each emperor in turn received the usual flattery, which fell in scarcely lesser rain upon his agents and adherents. The factionalism of the Senate continued unabated, even grew greater in the dance of the emperors, for men rose and fell rapidly in the year 68–69. On the whole the wars may have shown more clearly to thinking aristocrats that the Empire needed its Caesars.

In a brief analysis Josephus sketched neatly, and with essential truth, the attitude of the major elements in Rome as they awaited the arrival from the East of the final victor, Vespasian. The Senate desired nothing more than to gain again a ruler who was of age and who had military force, and the bulk of the senators were willing to accept his exaltation over their heads. The people, still more eager for their new master, expected a release from their miseries and hoped for security and prosperity. The army, i.e., the praetorian guard, demanded a ruler whose military prowess it could respect; though Josephus does not make the point explicit and modern scholars often forget it, winning the army permanently required more than the lavishing of money.

So all poured out with garlands and incense as Vespasian finally approached the capital in the fall of 70, to greet him as benefactor and savior and then to hold feasts by tribes, families, and neighborhoods. The framework of empire, which had appeared to totter, was again upright. The bond of the commonwealth, as Seneca had described the ruler, had been restored.

VII

The Opposition of the Philosophers
A.D. 69–96

VESPASIAN did not belie men's hopes. During his reign (69–79) he brought back into order the army and navy, the provinces, and the frontier districts; restored imperial finances; and repaired the rents in the appearance of constitutional government so that men could again for a century forget the powers of the military. Vespasian deliberately opposed himself to the policies of Nero by modeling his outward conduct upon that of Augustus. His elder son and first heir, Titus (79–81), was likewise mild; absolutism of the Neronian type did not return until the accession of his second son Domitian in 81. In 96 Domitian was murdered, and the Senate elected one of its own group, the elderly Nerva, as *princeps*.

The Flavian dynasty repeated the Julio-Claudian shift from the moderation of Tiberius to the despotism of Nero, but the reprise is in diminuendo. The republican aristocracy and its traditions were disappearing. No serious elements in the Senate thought now of abolishing the Principate, and only a diehard group continued to claim equality for the Senate. The utmost demanded by the vast majority was that senators be free to speak their advice and that the ruler respect outward forms. When their own choice, Nerva, could master neither the imperial bureaucracy nor the praetorian guard, the senators were glad to huddle under the firm hand of the emperor Trajan; by his reign (98–117) the

Empire had clearly slipped into an established groove, on which it was to run for about a century.

Grounds of Philosophic Opposition

The acceptance of absolutism had as prelude the battle of the Flavian emperors with the philosophers, for this was the last effort of the aristocracy to retain political freedom of thought. The happier era of the second-century Empire is in a sense a monument to the battle; another significant testimonial is the philosophic proclamation of liberty by Epictetus, even though this latter was to be stated purely in nonpolitical terms.

The precise points at which the state pressed on philosophic consciences are not easily defined. The references to the *causes célèbres* are very incomplete, and we do not have the works of the heretic philosophers—philosophic opposition remained a dangerous subject in later times. To begin, however, with philosophic doctrines is to put the cart before the horse, for the root of the troubles was not philosophic but political. In 41 the last and only serious senatorial effort to restore the Republic fizzled out in twenty-four hours. Open political opposition thereafter was hopeless, but elements of the Senate continued to attack the absolutist characteristics of the Principate and utilized as battleground the realm of ethical and political theory.

Very rarely can the recalcitrants be shown to have had true republican feelings, for this hopeless anachronism is scarcely to be discovered in any thinker after 41. The one example is the poet Lucan, who was fired to oppose the Principate as a system by Nero's esthetic dictation. It is in my judgment highly doubtful that Thrasea Paetus desired more than freedom of speech for the Senate, though his opponents cast republican charges at him. While the views of the great Stoic Musonius Rufus are not entirely clear, he seems not to have chafed at monarchy, provided the ruler were a just, self-controlled benefactor. So little the opposition wanted, but under Nero and Domitian could it feel secure even in so narrow a claim?

It is notable but understandable that aristocratic malcontents did not turn first to the prominent field of rhetoric. The rhetoricians, after all, had a tradition of accommodation to political life as it actually existed at any point of time. When the judicious Quintilian wrote on rhetorical training during the reign of Domitian, he asserted that the orator must be wise in a Roman style, i.e., not in abstract study but in the active life of the citizen. Under Gaius one rhetorician had been executed for overly bold remarks on tyrannicide, under Nero one teacher of rhetoric was exiled for stirring up the youth, but other examples of a cleavage between the supple rhetoricians and the state can hardly be found. State support of higher education began, indeed, in the institution of chairs of rhetoric at Rome at the time of Vespasian, and we shall shortly see one rhetorician attacking the philosophers for their resistance to the rulers.

Philosophers, on the other hand, had for centuries been charged with withdrawing themselves afar from the market place to bury themselves in abstruse, unprofitable studies. Worse still, philosophers formulated theoretical standards, quite independent of practical life and politics, and applied these standards in arrogant criticism of the earthly, imperfect city. This suspicion of philosophy was widespread in the Empire. Trimalchio, the gross freedman of the *Satyricon,* planned to have inscribed on his tombstone, "He never listened to a philosopher." [1] More significantly, both the emperor Nero and the senator Agricola were diverted by their mothers from overly deep study of philosophy. If a practical Roman learned the lessons of ethics, that was enough; it was unsuitable for aristocrats to devote themselves to Greek sophistries or the more recondite questions of the nature of the world and of the absolute standards which underlay ethical practice.

Philosophy, then, was an apt subject to attract the politically discontented and to arouse imperial suspicion. Some schools of philosophy were more suitable than others for the grumblers. The Epicureans considered the state merely a social and economic expedient and preached retirement and acceptance of life without struggle; professed Epicureans displayed political feelings only in the days of Caesar and Antony. The Stoic and Cynic schools had a much more positive view of ethics and the conduct of man, on both the social and the political level; in the resulting ambivalence of their political theory must in the end lie their attractiveness to men who were occasionally inclined to clash with the state. The Cynics opposed most forms of political organization as limiting the freedom of the individual in the cosmos and were given to snapping loudly at the heels of the great from Alexander on. The Stoic tradition, eclectic by the time of the Empire, could point either to opposition or to support of monarchy. Though the latter aspect was prevalent in the later Stoics, even they drew a distinction between true kingship, directed toward the benefit of the subjects, and tyranny—a

[1] Petronius, *Satyricon* 71.

distinction which could be explosive in conjunction with the Stoic feeling that a man must do his public duty.

In sum, the key to the philosophic unrest and to its suppression in the half-century from Gaius to Domitian must surely be its connection with the political struggle of the era. Aristocrats who were politically dissatisfied tended to explore the potentialities of philosophic theories. The very pattern of martyrs accords with this conclusion, for the men who suffered death were almost always senators prominent for their disagreement with the Caesars. When they fell, professional philosophers might be exiled for being their abettors and friends, for daring "to bark against the emperors," as the Christian Tertullian later put it, but their punishment went no further. Vespasian, for example, is quoted as saying to the Cynic Demetrius, who persistently attacked him, "You are doing everything to force me to kill you, but I do not slay a barking dog." [2]

Persecution of the Philosophers

Brutus and Cato had been members of the Stoic school, and the accommodation of Stoic theory to republican tradition had been marked since the days of Panaetius. Augustus nevertheless managed to avoid trouble with the Stoics, more because the senatorial aristocracy generally accepted him than because he professed considerable interest in philosophic doctrines. Philosophic debate, however, began to be opposed by force in the next reign. The minister Sejanus then collided somehow with the Stoic Attalus, who had to withdraw because of the rift. Gaius executed, again for unknown reasons, the Stoics Julius Canus and Rectus.

Nero went much further. Attachment to Stoicism now became outward grounds for the attack on several dangerous senators, including Thrasea Paetus and Soranus. The Stoics were termed "breeders of meddlesome and seditious citizens." One of their leading lights, Musonius Rufus, was exiled after the Pisonian plot to desolate Gyara for teaching philosophy and arousing the spirits of the youth—"for the crime of being a sage," quipped Philostratus.[3] The most famous Cynic for generations, Demetrius, was apparently banished; another, Isidorus, was exiled for openly baiting Nero as a good singer but a poor ruler.

[2] Tertullian, *Apology* 46.4; Dio Cassius 66.13.3.
[3] Tacitus, *Annals* 14.57.5; Philostratus, *Life of Apollonius* 4.35 (Kayser ed., p. 153).

Philostratus exaggerates when he asserts that Nero banned philosophy, but the contemporary Seneca shows something of the mutual hostility of ruler and thinker. In his Seventy-third Moral Epistle Seneca addressed himself directly to those who thought that adherents of philosophy must necessarily be stubborn or rebellious against public authority; in rebuttal he tried to prove that philosophers really were grateful for the peace and security which permitted them to retire and think, undisturbed by political duties or turmoils.

Against Nero's policy of political and esthetic autocracy aristocrats, Cynics, and Stoics could join, whatever their theoretical bases of argument. Even more prominent in philosophical circles appears to have been their ethical reproof, arising ostensibly from their concern for virtue and the nature of society and often marked, no doubt, merely by severity of countenance. Some Roman aristocrats did grieve over the moral decay of their order, and may well have tried to fix the blame on their luxurious ruler; as for the professional moralists, Lucian later jested that philosophers at a drinking party were as bad as a dog in the baths. When Vespasian came to the throne, the philosophers could no longer employ the arguments from ethical theory, for the first of the Flavians was a tolerant man of simple life, patient toward "the veiled attacks of lawyers and the stubbornness of philosophers." [4]

At first sight the existence of this stubbornness is extraordinary; the new Augustus, indeed, felt himself in the end compelled to go even further than the despot Nero in muzzling the Stoics. The explanation, however, is not far to seek. The autocracy of Nero had shown bluntly the weakness of the Senate; the civil wars had shaken the authority of the Caesars. Although Vespasian essayed the role of Augustus redivivus, although the miracles which he performed at Alexandria under the protection of the god Sarapis were paraded before the provinces to show his powers, he could not at once hope to enjoy that *auctoritas* which Augustus had gained. Despite Vespasian's scrupulous politeness toward the aristocracy, the Senate could not be restored to the position which it had held under the first *princeps* and then had lost, largely through its own stupidity. Still, an element in the Senate continued to hope for the impossible and stubbornly, tactlessly expressed its hopes. This group is represented for us by Helvidius Priscus, the son-in-law of Thrasea Paetus.

The strife between Vespasian and the dissidents revolved primarily

[4] Suetonius, *Vespasian* 13.

about the independence of the Senate. Outwardly it was expressed in other terms. First came the question of punishing the informers of Nero's reign. To complicate this problem, men such as Eprius Marcellus, who had helped to drag down Thrasea Paetus, were also the leaders of the senatorial party favoring imperial supremacy.

As soon as Helvidius had been restored from exile by the ephemeral emperor Galba, he moved to prosecute Eprius and tried generally to lead the Senate into a more independent path. Galba sacrificed some of the minor informers to this assault; others were yielded by Vespasian's aides, who directed affairs in Rome for almost a year before the ruler's arrival; but the new regime could not afford to abandon its major senatorial adherents. After numerous skirmishes the baying pack lost its zeal by 70, and Eprius became governor of Asia. Several years later he joined, for unknown reasons, a plot against Vespasian, which was nipped in the bud by Titus.

Long before Eprius committed suicide, rancor had led Helvidius to his own destruction. As praetor in 70 he passed over the ruler in his edicts and engaged in open attacks. Later historians assert that he and his group were essaying a revolution; the truth seems rather that they were reviving a line of attack which may have been tried under Claudius, i.e., a discussion of the problem of imperial succession in an effort to rouse the Senate to independent action. In emphasizing the theory that the "best man" should be adopted by the ruler, they may have hoped to gain a wide backing, partly on the theoretical level of the Stoic argument that virtue is not inherited, partly on the practical level, for Titus, as praetorian prefect, was harsh in ferreting out plots and Domitian appeared incapable.

The veiled attacks on his sons touched Vespasian on a tender point. He first exiled the arrogant, intransigent Helvidius, then ordered his execution, and in probably the same year (71) expelled the philosophers from Rome. Though our ancient sources describe the banishment as a sweeping one, probably only some of the Stoics and Cynics were affected. Philosophers were still in Rome in 75 to object to the impending marriage of Titus and the Oriental princess Berenice; at this time Musonius Rufus may have been banished.

The coolness of both contemporaries and later historians toward the circle of Helvidius Priscus is interesting. The young Dio Chrysostom, who practiced rhetoric in Vespasianic Rome, vigorously attacked the recusant philosophers, though he himself moved in philosophic circles.

After suffering spiritually in the era of Domitian, Tacitus praised Helvidius with some reserve but comments that others judged him too greedy of fame, "that last infirmity of even philosophic minds"; [5] Eprius apparently called his opponent a fanatic. Tacitus, moreover, has given us a dignified defense of the proimperial party from the lips of Eprius himself (in one of the debates with Helvidius):

He [Eprius] was not unmindful of the times in which he had been born, nor of the form of polity which their fathers and grandfathers had set up. He admired the past, but he accepted the present; he prayed for good Emperors, but he put up with them of whatever kind they were. It was not his own speech, so much as the judgment of the Senate, that had brought about Thrasea's condemnation . . . Helvidius might have all the firmness and the fortitude of a Cato or a Brutus, but he had been a member of the same slavish Senate as himself. Let him be advised not to set himself above the Emperor, nor attempt to lecture a man of Vespasian's age . . . for as the worst of Emperors loved unlimited domination, so even the best of them approved of some check on liberty.[6]

Helvidius and his associates may have been the last senatorial elements to assert any real equality with the Caesars, but in that event they certainly gained little support from the "slavish Senate." In another thirty years the acceptance of imperial primacy was to be well-nigh universal; but first Domitian had to reign and die.

Those philosophers who had opposed the inheritance of the imperial purple must have felt their argument justified in 81, for then the gloomy, poorly trained Domitian came to power after the jovial Titus. Ere long the emperor was traversing the old road toward autocracy; he also permitted the intensification of the imperial cult to an extraordinary degree even in Rome. Though he himself never officially took the step of proclaiming himself a god in the capital, his subordinates frankly called him Master and God in their edicts from 85–86. Gold and silver statues of the ruler were set up in profusion on the Capitoline, and arches were erected everywhere. The names of two of the months were changed in his honor; the poets Martial and Statius scraped the ground before this present divinity.

The inevitable result was serious discontent among the senators, which Domitian met head-on with calculated cruelty. The most violent phases of the terror followed the unsuccessful revolt of the governor of Upper Germany, L. Antonius Saturninus, early in 89; by then, too, Domitian

[5] *Histories* 4.6.　　　　　　　　　[6] Tacitus, *Histories* 4.8.

was in serious need of money to maintain his army during the Danubian wars. Thereafter heads of the politically prominent—and rich—began to roll in Rome at a rate which rivaled or perhaps even exceeded that of the last days of Nero. The emperor had only to open up the charge of *laesa maiestas,* and the ambitious rushed to take up the trade of informer and begin their "traffic in hatred and feud."

The most famous victims among the philosophers were those who were also members of the Senate. In and after 93 Junius Arulenus Rusticus and Herennius Senecio were charged with writing the praises of the Stoic saints Thrasea and the Elder Helvidius; Helvidius Priscus the Younger, who tried in vain to bury himself in retirement, was perhaps accused of censuring the emperor's divorce in a theatrical piece but presumably suffered because of his paternity. At the same time his mother Fannia, the widow of Thrasea (Arria), and others who may have been connected with the circle of Thrasea and Helvidius were relegated. The secret police preyed even on ordinary people, if we may trust Epictetus' revelation:

A soldier, dressed like a civilian, sits down by your side, and begins to speak ill of Caesar, and then you too, just as though you had received from him some guarantee of good faith in the fact he began the abuse, tell likewise everything you think, and the next thing is—you are led off to prison in chains.[7]

While senators died, the professional philosophers suffered exile. Shortly after 82 the rising young sophist Dio Chrysostom was barred from Rome and his native Bithynia, in part because he was a friend of a condemned senator, in part because he would not truckle to the tyrant "at a time when many were glad to save their lives by any deed or word at all."[8] A more general banishment of philosophers and astrologers from Rome is reported for 88–89, and in 95 Domitian expelled all philosophers not only from Rome but also from Italy. This is the most sweeping ban on philosophers in the Empire of which we are aware.

Epictetus liked to assert that the philosopher was "the stripe of red that stands out from the toga." Philosophers were nevertheless not the only men to suffer from Domitian's capricious mastery, for the emperor was also driven by a stern view of morality and religious practice. Censor for life (probably from 85), he instituted a number of laws

[7] *Discourses* 4.13.5.   [8] *Oration* 50.8.

against castration, child prostitution, and other sinful acts; and he even buried a vestal virgin alive for immorality. The poet Martial cast worried glances at this all-powerful censor, whose acts were incalculable, and carefully excused his filthy jests as innocent entertainment which did not reflect the true quality of his own moral life.

Christians and Jews also remembered Domitian as a despot who was on the point of attacking them in his last years; against the Jews, indeed, open hostilities had already begun. Charges of Judaism were leveled at numerous people to enforce payment of the special tax on Jews or to seize the property of those who had failed so to register. The ruler's innocuous cousin Flavius Clemens and his wife Domitilla, as well as Acilius Glabrio, were condemned to death on the pretext at least of atheism—"a charge," says Dio Cassius, "on which many others who drifted into Jewish ways were condemned." [9] These persons have long been considered to have been Christians, but on dubious grounds. Within the framework of established religion Domitian preferred the cult of one deity, Minerva (or Athena), and emphasized publicly this preference to an extent unparalleled in the first two centuries of the Empire. A literary competition was instituted in honor of the patroness of learning and war, and the gold and silver coinage monotonously bore Minerva in numerous poses year after year from 81.

End of the Struggle

In 96 Domitian fell victim to a plot concocted by his administrators and his empress. When the news of his murder filled the streets of Rome, the senators hastily brought ladders and tore down the shields and images of their erstwhile master in the Senate House. His statues were overthrown; official order brought the erasure of his name from monuments in Rome and provinces alike; his memory, formally accursed, was eternally blasted by historians and philosophers. This hostility, however, was felt within very narrow limits, for neither army, people, nor provinces seem to have shared the anger of the senators.

So ended one of the most serious efforts in the Early Empire to force general acceptance of imperial standards in politics, morals, and religion. The upper classes now hoped to put back the clock under the amiable Nerva, whom the plotters chose and the Senate confirmed as the new *princeps*. Although all at first seemed rosy, Nerva found it necessary to validate the general run of Domitian's acts and to stop

[9] Dio Cassius 67.14.1–2.

senatorial attacks on the informers. The praetorian guard forced him to punish the murderers of Domitian, while wide parts of the army seem to have been disaffected. Between the Senate and the army his rule tottered ever more until he adopted a strong general, Trajan, as his heir and then promptly died.

Now began the famous golden age of the second century. The provinces appeared content with Roman rule and enjoyed a remarkable degree of prosperity. The army defended the Roman peace, even expanded the frontiers skillfully; it obeyed its new ruler without question. At Rome Trajan and the aristocracy lived on the best of terms, and the ruler directed the Senate "to resume its liberty, to take up the cares of, as it were, a common Empire, to watch over public needs." [10]

A new era was opening. Trajan marked it in his great series of coins, which commemorated the leaders of the Republic as well as the more respectable Caesars of the past century; Republic and Empire were thus drawing together into one vast historical process. In the "rare happiness of these times, when one may think what he pleases, and may say what he thinks," [11] the subjects turned backward to ponder over the bonfires and tortured groans of the first century.

The judgment of Trajan's age was twofold; the aristocracy accepted absolutism but rejected outright autocracy. In the rejection the bitter experience of the first century was distilled.

Men vented their wrath on Domitian in part in satire, biography, and history. Freedom of thought and speech, if one may believe the ecstatic utterances of Pliny and Tacitus, seemed almost untrammeled, once the vengeful hands of Domitian and the feeble grasp of Nerva had yielded to the firm hold of Trajan.

In his first published essay, the life of his father-in-law Agricola, Tacitus announced his purpose of "recording the servitude we once suffered." [12] In his major subsequent works he took up first the civil wars of 68–69 and the Flavian dynasty (*Histories*) and then went back to treat of the corruption of ruler and ruled during the Julio-Claudian line from Tiberius to Nero (*Annals*). A masterful psychologist above all, Tacitus concentrated on the depreciation of human dignity and freedom which inevitably accompanied the mastery of the Caesars.

Beside his mournful pessimism must be placed also the philosophic thought of his generation. Philosophers were now free to live where they

[10] Pliny, *Panegyric* 66.2–3.   [11] Tacitus, *Histories* 1.1.
[12] *Agricola* 3 (Mattingly).

would and to speak with relative freedom; Trajan's wife Plotina even favored them. The greatest philosopher of the age, Epictetus, neglected political theory for ethics, but his ethical theory arose out of past politics to a greater degree than is commonly observed. In his statement of a human dignity which is independent of the state, Epictetus' work is even more surely a summation of the first century than is the moan of Tacitus' bitter pen.

In his school at Nicopolis in Epirus, Epictetus taught the scions of the nobility in plain, simple terms how to live in their world. A primary motive in that teaching was to free men from the fear of force, or of Caesar, in the Epictetian phraseology. The personal characteristics of Domitian do not appear in the *Discourses* preserved by the pupil Arrian, but the essential flavor of the reign was distilled by Epictetus into its quintessence: now punishment, now temptation to secure not only external but also internal, slavelike obedience to an autocrat:

> Look you, no one is afraid of Caesar himself, but he is afraid of death, exile, loss of property, prison, disfranchisement. Nor does anyone love Caesar himself, unless in some way Caesar is a person of great merit; but we love wealth, a tribuneship, a praetorship, a consulship. When we love and hate and fear these things, it needs must be that those who control them are masters over us. . . . That is how at a meeting of the Senate a man does not say what he thinks, while within his breast his judgment shouts loudly.[13]

Epictetus, of all the Roman philosophers of whom we have extant works, first explicitly formulated a philosophy with which the individual might consciously face the tyrant, for the arguments in Seneca and Musonius, though tending in the same direction, were not yet fully directed against tyranny as distinct from the other ills of man. The reassurance of Epictetus was the only possible one for the individual face to face with arbitrary power—the tyrant may kill a man's body, but he cannot touch a man's mind (or soul). Or in Stoic terminology, externals are indifferent. Only one's moral purpose counts, and since it comes from God it must be free.

Although Epictetus deliberately noted an essential antagonism between the individual and the state, the freedom of which he talked was an ethical rather than a political concept. He accepted the Principate without question and, albeit ironically, the peace it had brought; he did not preach the doctrine of retirement—for ordinary men—which Seneca had emphasized; and he explicitly rejected the idea that philosophers

[13] Epictetus, *Discourses* 4.1.60, 139 (this section is entitled "On Freedom").

taught contempt of kings. The ruler of this world may have complete control over one's body, property, reputation, or relatives; but Caesar has no authority over one's judgments, nor can he bestow virtue upon those who appear before him.

Yet the ideal of an ethical or moral life which forbids assent to acts contrary to its standard will be enough to bring its adherents into trouble. Helvidius, or, above all, Socrates (who is mentioned by Epictetus more than twice as frequently as any other person), died as martyrs demonstrating inner independence of the state:

> Do you practise how to die, how to be enchained, how to be racked, how to be exiled. Do all these things with confidence, with trust in Him who has called you to face them and deemed you worthy of this position, in which having once been placed you shall exhibit what can be achieved by a rational governing principle when arrayed against the forces that lie outside the province of the moral purpose.[14]

Like a Christian bishop, Epictetus had to face the possibility of martyrdom for being a true philosopher who engaged in silent criticism of the material world; and like a bishop he did not encourage his pupils to rush out to gain the cross. If martyrdom came to them in their execution of their duties as citizens and administrators, he urged them to endure it steadfastly. If a philosopher were called to be witness to God, i.e., to stand up for the freedom of his moral purpose before the state, then "go you and bear witness for Me; for you are worthy to be produced by Me as a witness." [15]

Philosophic thought could not go further than this in constructing a sure support for the individual subject. So strongly did the prescription for the freedom of man sketched by Epictetus, that "eagle among men," appeal to some native of Asia Minor that he had it carved in brief on a Pisidian rock for all to read. Many philosophers, it should be noted, had never felt compelled to censure directly the Principate or the excesses of its worst occupants, nor could those who did stand in opposition draw upon a well-defined doctrine either of political organization or of the place of man in the world. Even the philosophic theory of imperial inheritance by adoption does not have the weight which some modern scholars assign to it, for the Good Emperors of the second century adopted their successors only in default of male children.

All the philosophic opposition in the first century of which we know has an air of the hopeless, of the incomplete, and so reflects the sterility

---

[14] *Discourses* 2.1.38–39.   [15] *Discourses* 1.29.47.

of political thought in the Empire. Thrasea was a martyr, but not a truly noble one. Epictetus, more than any other Stoic, imparted a religious air to his teaching through his devotion to the Stoic God; but, unlike the Christian martyrs dying at this time with perfect faith in Jesus Christ, no philosophical martyr could be buoyed up by the belief either in an essentially mechanical Providence or in the vague future life assured by that principle. He died simply to show his faith in reason.

VIII

The Acceptance of Absolutism

THE answer of Epictetus was actually not needed in the following decades, nor was there soon to be justification for the inner fears of Tacitus that

the passions and the cupidity of rulers are things to be endured like deficient harvests, excessive rains, and other natural evils. There will be vices as long as man endures; but they are not continuous; they are compensated by intervals of better things.[1]

The state of balance under Trajan endured for reign after reign, and the aristocracy was only too happy to forget the grim past and enjoy the blessings of the new era.

Therewith they accepted absolutism, for the long battle of the first century terminated in an essentially complete victory for the Caesars. The Senate, warned first by the unrest of 68–69 and now thankful for Trajan's preservation of order, resigned its independence. Trajan was as complete a master as Domitian and though outwardly modest continued to permit the taking of oaths by the emperor's *genius* and the offer of libations and incense before his statues. The numismatic program of Trajan, which emphasized the emperor's achievements, had more in common with Domitian's issues than with Nerva's weak, well-meaning appeals. The centralizing tendencies of the Flavian dynasty were even intensified.

Reconciliation of emperor and Senate, in other words, rested upon

[1] *Histories* 4.74 (speech of Petilius Cerialis).

a change simply in the personal characteristics of the ruler. The struggle between Caesar and philosopher came to an end not because the former abdicated any of his powers but because the philosopher could at last identify Trajan with the ideal king. No reins, outside those voluntarily imposed by the ruler's own innate goodness and by a vague idea of natural law, had been or could be imposed on this omnipotent figure, the dynamo of the imperial structure. Even in Latin writers the place of the emperor was ever more clearly deduced from the Hellenistic doctrine of divine appointment rather than from the Roman legal theory of the consent of the governed. The hierarchy of the world led from subjects to emperors, and "o'er these in turn rises the sovereignty of Heaven" with its deities who were subject to the laws of the universe.[2] The poet Statius here is speaking of Domitian, but the picture he draws of the imperial system is the same in root as that of Pliny and Dio Chrysostom under Trajan.

"Liberty" no longer denoted the dominance of the Senate; the last serious use of the term in this sense came in 41. For the mass of men *libertas* now meant personal freedom and economic security. Under this title the senators hoped for general freedom of speech, the right to be consulted, and protection of property and position, particularly in the point that the emperor would not independently convict or execute a senator. Not all thinkers accepted without cavil the imperial argument that prince and liberty were indissolubly connected, but in essence freedom now was held not by right but by sufferance and was of a material rather than a spiritual order save for such men as Epictetus. Marcus Aurelius was no less absolute for having been taught by a friend "the conception of a state with one law for all, based upon individual equality and freedom of speech, and of a sovranty which prizes above all things the liberty of the subject."[3]

A general treatment of the difference between tyranny (*dominatio*) and true kingship (*principatus*) is afforded by the contemporary orations of Dio Chrysostom, *On Kingship*. One or more of these he may actually have delivered before Trajan himself; the others he addressed to the East to convince it of the "happy and god-given polity at present in force."[4] Domitian was damned as the tyrant; Trajan was praised as an ideal ruler, brave, law-abiding, a new Hercules. Drawing from a rich background of Cynic, Stoic, and Pythagorean thought (which de-

---

[2] Statius, *Silvae* 3.3.48–55.   [3] *Meditations* 1.14.
[4] *Oration* 3.50.

serves a new investigation), Dio emphasized the divine grant of royal power by Zeus and conceded omnipotence to the emperor, a being "greater than the law" who was limited only by his good character.[5] Like his fellow provincials from the days of Augustus, like even the Christian apologists, who expressed the same strain of thought, Dio was perfectly willing to accept imperial absolutism if it were just and promoted provincial well-being.

Ore from much the same vein was coined in Roman terms in the famous *Panegyric* which Pliny the Younger chanted before Trajan in 100. In delivering his speech Pliny carried out a senatorial request, and at the end he thanked the Senate for his formal election to the exalted dignity of consul. Throughout he maintained a certain dignity and, as he told a friend in a letter, aimed his speech not only at Trajan but also, in revising it for publication, at future rulers. Pliny's adulation of Trajan, covered under the veil of frankness, is so the more remarkable, for it is in essentials as obsequious as that proffered Domitian by Statius and Martial. The Senate was clearly admitted to be second, even though it should be treated with respect as a voice of aristocratic opinion.

What basic difference is there between the toga-clad Pliny, proudly gesturing before emperor and Senate, and the wily Eprius Marcellus, accusing Thrasea Paetus under Nero? Pliny hailed Trajan not as god or tyrant but as citizen and fellow-senator; but he accepted without cavil the overwhelmingly dominant position of the ruler. Trajan was deputy for Jupiter on earth, "a prince most similar to the gods." When Romans pronounced their vows for the eternity of the state and the safety of the ruler, they did not put matters correctly; for the endurance of the Empire, yet more its peace, its concord, its security—all were safeguarded by the strength of their guardian. When Trajan swore to obey the laws, Pliny continues, he learned for the first time that the prince was not above but beneath the laws. The last, most tragic irony is Pliny's observation on the imperial order to the Senate to be free— "he will know when we use the freedom he gave that we are being obedient to him." [6]

Small wonder that the senators scribbled obscene jests on their meaningless ballots in "lazy but unrestrained impudence" [7] or broke forth in rhythmical, repetitious acclamations of the emperor's virtues! On the open political stage official enthusiasm or apathy were the alternatives.

[5] *Oration* 3.10.   [6] *Panegyric* 67.2.   [7] Pliny, *Letters* 4.25.

Compromise with the Aristocracy

One must, however, refrain from painting the picture only in sharp blacks and whites; for by the reign of Trajan the Roman world had also built up an idea independent of personality, the cosmopolitan state termed "Rome," which was no longer a city-state or a peninsula but the entire Mediterranean world. In the early second century the constituent parts of the Empire had risen to a position of essential equality with Italy. The vehicle of this ideal was in large part the wealthy men of the realm, and the tranquillity of the second century rested on a compromise between these men and the Caesars, wherein the former accepted the direction of the emperors and they in turn paid respectful attention to the opinion of the upper classes:

It is true, indeed [said Pliny in a letter], the direction of the public weal is in the hands of a single person, who, for the general good, takes upon himself solely to ease us of the care and weight of government; but still that bountiful source of power permits, by a very wholesome dispensation, some streams to flow down to us.[8]

The old republican aristocracy had essentially died out in the first century. The upper classes failed to propagate themselves; a few families perished in the wide-scale executions under some rulers; but in the main this luxurious, idle class with wealth but without power drifted into oblivion. In its place rose a new aristocracy; some were recruited from the equestrian order, and even more were from outstanding families pushed up by the widening prosperity and increasing significance of the provinces. Cicero's view that admission to the Senate should depend on merit rather than ancestors had won to an extent that might have shocked Cicero.

Economically the aristocracy remained very powerful. The imperial estates swallowed up the fantastically large holdings of the condemned nobles, but private landlords remained the backbone of the agricultural system; quite probably wealth was more equally and widely distributed among the upper classes after the tyrants had wiped out the great Roman magnates of the first century. Socially the aristocracy expanded its domination of life in the Empire, a control which extended to literature, the arts, and education. From the upper classes the rulers drew their top administrators, and only those orders which satisfied this administrative machine were actually executed on a wide scale;

[8] *Letters* 3.20.

Claudius wrathfully observes that "evil men" had prevented the carrying out of one of his orders regarding the imperial post.

In the Empire there was no mobile, well-formed public opinion in our sense—if, indeed, the concept today is not merely a myth. The great majority of imperial subjects were farmers, who had little opportunity to reflect and almost no legal means of expressing any feelings they might have. News traveled slowly in the ancient world, and the completeness with which a provincial might receive it depended on accidents of geography, the reluctance or willingness of the government to publish full accounts, and a person's social status.

The active elements of the Empire, nevertheless, had their private opinions, and these could be intercommunicated by the wide-scale travel of the period. Dio Chrysostom delivered orations all over the Greek East, preaching at once Hellenism and due obedience to the imperial government. Plutarch describes the meeting of two Greeks at Delphi: one was returning to Tarsus from a visit to the islands beyond Britain; the other, a Spartan, had been on a trip of curiosity to Egypt, the Red Sea, and more distant lands. Socially and intellectually the aristocracy of the Empire was a well-defined group. There can be no doubt that the imperial government had to pay attention to the expression of aristocratic opinions, and that it had often to modify its policy to accommodate deep-seated pressures.

The aristocracy, in sum, was a body which the emperors had to try, in the main, to please. Yet it will not do simply to conclude that the suzerain was merely a spokesman for the upper classes. Politically this group had very quickly yielded its independence and had grouped itself about the ruler, from whom it gained honors, wealth, and—in the case of new men—admission to the charmed circle. Caesar might not be able to bestow virtue, but he was the fount of power, the guardian of imperial prosperity, whose virtues were celebrated in panegyric, inscriptions, and coins without shame or limit. Beside him the figures of the Senate, of the people, even of the gods dropped ever more into the background; the emperor, whether tyrant or benefactor, came forward to monopolize the stage, and his majestic utterances rolled back in echo from its farthest corners. Public opinion was at most times and in most places the opinion of the reigning Caesar writ large.

The Empire now was an absolute state. The fact is a grim one, but its reality is clear—clearer perhaps to Pliny than to some modern scholars. If a final proof is necessary it may be found in the catalogue of means by which the developed absolutism of the Caesars could silence men's tongues and warp men's minds. In root the controls go back to Augustus, but by the reign of Trajan the emperors had available a truly impressive, if frightful, machine wherewith to repress divergence.

Machinery of Imperial Control

The wide extent of imperial control reached even to the field of religion. The cult of the Caesars themselves was widely scorned, yet ever more widely spread. Tiberius and Claudius tried to limit the worship of themselves. Other rulers, like Vespasian, mocked the idea they were divine. The upper classes of Rome scoffed at decking out dead men "with thunderbolts and haloes and constellations" and swearing by ghosts in the temples of the gods,[9] and in imperial literature the ruler was commonly advised that his virtue ought to be his best memorial. Nevertheless, the cult was too necessary to be destroyed. Augustus had snatched it up to bind to him the upper classes of the provinces; thereafter the worship of the rulers was conducted mainly by those classes, especially in the West, as a manifestation of their patriotism. About the cult was grouped in close association a variety of imperial honors—celebration of the ruler's birthday, games, festivals, and banquets—which made the emperor's life and career a basic element in the official calendar. When Gaius openly paraded his divine character, he went only a little way beyond what was already conceded; autocracy and deification walked hand in hand.

The old cult of Rome had been brought under the ruler's control by his automatic selection as *pontifex maximus* and his membership in the great priestly colleges. The quaint acts of a minor college, the Arval Brothers, illustrate the attention of the religious machinery to the safety and health of their lord. The Brothers cursed his enemies, who are usually not named, on their downfall; made vows for the emperor's trips and wars; and in every possible way sought divine favor for his acts. The accusation of Thrasea for his failure to perform his priestly functions shows how bound to the imperial system were participants in the official Roman cult.

At times the emperor even seized upon non-Roman faiths. Claudius officially recognized the worship of Magna Mater, and one of the Roman priestly colleges thenceforth directed it at least throughout Italy. The Egyptian deities Isis and Sarapis, too, came close to official

[9] Lucan, *Civil War* 7.458–459.

acceptance and so to imperial dictation. Insofar as this cult had a center, it remained in Alexandria, but here a Roman official oversaw all local Egyptian religions. Under Hadrian it even appears that one of his friends, living in Italy, was appointed chief priest of the Egyptian cults; the tendency to centralize religious activity at Rome was too strong to be resisted entirely. The emperors could discourage as well as encourage faiths; the theory of the state placed political allegiance first and gave no room for true religious liberty.

Those cults which remained relatively free were accordingly careful to express their loyalty, by sacrifices and by decorating their shrines "for the holy days of the Lord Emperor." [10] The Jews from the days of Augustus to the great revolt of 66 sacrificed *for* the emperor in the Temple, bedecked their meeting places everywhere with shields and other tokens of imperial loyalty, and commemorated the great days of imperial victories or anniversaries. The Christians as well protested their loyalty endlessly and were, when once tolerated, to be largely sheared of their earlier independence.

To the ancient mind there were no sharp barriers between human and divine. Supernatural intervention might be gained and the future might be explored, both for terrestrial ends, by a variety of means; here the emperors went far in checking potential trouble. Augustus and Tiberius made very strong efforts to wipe out private possession of prophecies, which all too often expressed political opinions in a religious guise. The latter attempted to close the sources of prophecy near Rome; a confused report would even suggest that the reading of anti-Roman oracles was punishable by death.

Divination through astrology and manipulation of life by magic were arts in which the Empire believed devoutly, but the emperors essayed to keep their practice under strict rein. Augustus had banned individual consultations or any prophecies concerning death; thereafter Tiberius, Claudius, Vitellius, Vespasian, and perhaps Marcus Aurelius expelled the astrologers when political conditions were upset. Many a noble suffered blackmail or went to his doom on the charge of consulting an astrologer about the end of a ruler or his own prospects for rising to august station; the jurist Paul of the third century says flatly that consultants and astrologers, or other foretellers of the future, who investigate the safety of Caesar or state affairs are to be punished by death.

[10] *Inscriptiones Graecae ad Res Romanas Pertinentes* 1.421 (the Tyrians of Puteoli).

Though the practice of magic was even more frowned upon, its popularity throughout all levels of the Empire was immense.

Over the secular media for the expression of ideas the sway of the Empire was subject to little question. Imperial statues and inscriptions honoring the ruler had been ubiquitous under Augustus; the only change thereafter was an intensification of the turgid adulation as the local aristocracies commemorated their obedience to the master of the world. The Column of Nero at Mainz, though erected privately, may justly be called "an imperial hymn in stone" in reference to its grouping of deities and abstractions to show the ruler's mastery of world destinies.

The face of the emperor was to be seen everywhere (see Pls. III, V, VI b). While Marcus Aurelius was still heir-apparent, Fronto wrote to him:

You know how in all money-changers' bureaus, booths, bookstalls, eaves, porches, windows, anywhere and everywhere there are likenesses of you exposed to view, badly enough painted most of them to be sure, and modelled or carved in a plain, not to say sorry, style of art.[11]

So too the lengthy formula of the names and titles of the ruler appears so often in all types of inscriptions—building dedications, milestones, decrees—that one tends unjustly to ignore it, for the intensive repetition of the majestic imperial titles must have had a considerable effect on the minds of the subjects of the Caesars.

Buildings and statues were erected under official supervision; their destruction might stem from popular frenzy but was usually motivated by imperial displeasure. When Hadrian was felt to be hostile to the sophist Favorinus, statues of the latter were destroyed as far afield as Corinth and Athens. Men officially condemned were thus wiped out of public memory as far as the loosely co-ordinated structure of imperial life permitted (see Pl. IV). The revulsion felt after the fall of Sejanus, the minister of Tiberius, is typical in its manifestations, though exceptional in its intensity. No erasures of his name in inscriptions are known, for the entire inscription bearing his accursed name was destroyed. One of the few examples of erasure of names from coins occurs on those struck by the Spanish town of Bilbilis in his honor; and his consulship of 31 was the only one permanently removed from the im-

[11] *Letters* 1, 207 (Loeb).

perial Fasti. The author Valerius Maximus gloated over his fall without mentioning his name, and an Umbrian inscription of 32 referred to the event simply as the removal of "the most baleful enemy of the Roman people." In this same inscription, incidentally, erasure followed this suppression, for the name of one of the consuls of 32 was removed when he revolted against Claudius.[12]

Underlying the phrases of provincial and urban decrees, the sculptural decoration of buildings, and the cast or dress of statues was the shifting imperial policy, laid down in the rulers' edicts and speeches and trumpeted forth to the world by a variety of means. Their acts were undoubtedly the most important, and the emperors took their tasks very seriously; but leaders can never be sure that they read the mind of their subjects rightly—to compensate for errors they make the age-old attempt to adjust their subjects' minds by words as well.

Most direct were the echoing speeches and edicts in which the governors held up for admiration "the majesty of our God, the emperor," as one Egyptian governor put it in publishing an edict of Claudius (which incidentally refused divine honors). In other cases edicts and similar propaganda may have been circulated directly from Rome. Under Domitian a thousand copies of a memoir which the noted informer Regulus wrote on his dead son were sent out, to be read on public order by the most eloquent decurion in each city to the people; though we never hear again in imperial literature of such a step, it may have been patterned on the process of publishing imperial edicts.

Nowhere, however, can modern students better observe the program with which each reign placated its subjects than in the coinage, for the emperors exploited the propaganda qualities of this medium in steadily more supple form. We do not know precisely how the aims of an emperor were transmuted into coin types, but whatever the method the influence of the ruler on the entire coinage was paramount; the imperial mints set a pattern from which local moneyers took now this, now that, element as being of most interest or appeal to their own area. By the second century the coins paid very little attention to the difference between classes or even between Italy and the provinces. To all they presented a general line of imperial propaganda, revolving about the victorious defense against foreign foes of a heartland of prosperity, wherein justice and peace were the gifts of the ruler.

Absolutism was ever more clearly stressed; by the time of Trajan the

[12] *Corpus Inscriptionum Latinarum* XI 4170.

state and the emperors were one. In this magic world the imperial virtues which secured its blessings paraded by in endless sterility, shifting in stately alternation to suit the ruler's will; all the world turned to the emperor and rendered him thanks for every bounty. Here misfortunes found no place. The Roman world of the coins was one of incessant victory and prosperity, and under a weak Caesar like Nerva the Concord of the Armies was most heavily stressed. Beyond doubt the message of the coins was really directed at, and subtly reflects, currents of thought in the Empire; but to gain the true value of this reflection one must always turn to non-numismatic sources, where opposition or commentary on the imperial ideas might at times speak more clearly.

This independent voice is not often to be heard. In the reign of Trajan writers were generally free from curbs, but the bony claws of past specters clutched and slowed men's pens. Many an author had suffered from failing to follow the imperial line; who could foretell what the future might bring? When thought is not truly free, it is always better not to write anything which might be provocative in the least degree— the true tragedy of absolutism is the self-censorship men impose on themselves.

In ancient civilization the means of oral expression were perhaps even more important than written ones. Public vocal criticism of imperial policies or persons did not occur, unless the critic were promoting a revolution or were willing to invite the thunderbolt. The stage, while remaining popular, was carefully regulated. Its audiences were generally watched by imperial troops in Rome, and its actors were handicapped by the continuation of the old republican stigma on their profession; magistrates and imperial officials could deal with them at their discretion. All over the Empire the public gathering of men was largely concerned with official protestations of loyalty to the current ruler, these protestations often having a religious tone; when the Senate met, its members liturgically acclaimed the ruler's wishes. Imperial control of the judicial system increased inexorably. Formal grouping of the well-to-do in clubs was carefully restricted, and private associations were watched. Only the poor were given blanket license, probably under Claudius, to form funerary *collegia;* Trajan even took alarm at the idea of recruiting a gild of firemen in unruly Nicomedia—let each individual houseowner have his own fire-fighting equipment!

As an open means of attesting their loyalty the armies and at times the populace of the Empire in whole or in part were bound to each successive ruler by vows for his safety; the armies at least renewed these vows at the beginning of each year. There survives, among other examples, the oath sworn by the Paphlagonians in 3 B.C., which pledges the individual to be loyal to Augustus and his descendants "in word and deed and mind," to inform on anyone saying or thinking anything contrary to the oath, and to oppose these enemies by land or sea. Tertullian summed up the spirit of the Empire here revealed by asserting that "against those guilty of treason, against public enemies, every man is a soldier." [13]

Another oral proof of loyalty consisted in delivering and in attending speeches of praise for the ruler. Day by day, year after year, the orators of the Empire sent up their chant unto Heaven in gratitude for the virtues of their perfect ruler. So common was the subject that rhetoricians laid down general rules for the treatment and sequence of topics in the praise of Caesars. The cool analysis of imperial panegyric by the third-century Menander and his blunt catalogue of the tricks of the orator's trade sufficiently damn the praises of specific Roman rulers which have survived—"all the lying titles that we have used so long to our masters," said Lucan scornfully.[14] As Menander pithily put it, the auditors must acquiesce without quibble in whatever is said of their lord. He warned also that the encomium of the emperor was not to suggest that the present good qualities of the ruler could be increased, or that any part of his rule was debatable; a fourth-century panegyrist blurted out that "it is not proper for anyone to judge princes." [15]

Modern scholars have often been unduly moved by the confusion and unrest of our world when they wax eloquent on the ideals presented by ancient panegyrics. Their surveys of the Empire have likewise taken too seriously the tremendous mass of flattering inscriptions and statues which the provincials set up to just—and unjust—rulers alike. Jesus spoke ironically, but truly, when He said of the Greeks, "They that exercise authority upon them are called Benefactors." [16]

Only in private dared a man criticize. Here speech was probably as free as under modern dictatorships—but one could never be sure. Even among his friends a member of the upper classes always found it wise

---

[13] *Inscriptiones Graecae ad Res Romanas Pertinentes* 3.137; Tertullian, *Apology* 2.8.

[14] Lucan, *Civil War* 5.385–386.   [15] *Latin Panegyrics* 10.5 (Nazarius).

[16] Luke 22:25.

not to be too violent, for the imperial system of repression was by the reign of Trajan beautifully developed.

The discovery of discontent was the work of the regular machinery of government, of informers, and of the secret police. An emperor opposed to the Senate had only to make clear his attitude, and the senators slaughtered each other in mutual accusations to protect themselves and to secure preferment. Tacitus never ceases to assail the delators and *agents provocateurs* who laid traps for the unwary; under Nero the great nobles quivered in the glare of unceasing scrutiny by their fellows and by their slaves. Good rulers might limit the functions of delators and their informants, could threaten them with punishment in cases of falsehood, and even exiled more notorious sycophants, but no emperor ever abolished this system of amateur prosecution. Few imperial officials dared to silence a man who claimed, however falsely, that he had news of imperial danger.

It is only under the "good"—or efficient—emperors that one can clearly detect a special secret police in operation. Earlier secret police may merely have been detached from the praetorian guard, and soldiers could always be used for the purpose; but by some point in the first century a body of *frumentarii* was being detailed from the legions to serve as couriers and spies in the provinces and also at Rome. Its camp, the *castra peregrina,* had existed close to the praetorian camp from the time of Nero at the latest. Upright rulers and autocrats alike are reported to have been quite interested in the activities of their more important subjects, as gleaned by the *frumentarii* through the opening of letters, spying, and so on.

The activities of the secret police are not often cited by historians of either the first or the second centuries, nor are its methods fully revealed; but this silence proves little beyond the authors' caution—to what extent would novelists or historians living in the police states of today discuss their surveillants? The law is clear: the prefect of Rome is directed "to have detachments of soldiers placed so as to keep the people quiet and to bring to him news of what is going on." [17] That soldiers wore civilian clothes while on duty as spies is attested both by Tacitus and by a papyrus duty roster from an Alexandrian legion; Epictetus, always bold, warns against casual conversation with "civilian" strangers in Rome in a passage which has already been quoted. Going out at night at least in some places and at some times required a special permit.

[17] Ulpian in *Digest* 1.12.1.12.

Although this police was presumably not so efficient as the various gestapos of our modern, advanced civilization, the seizure of Flaccus, governor of Egypt, in his own province would do credit to any secret service. The emperor Gaius dispatched a certain centurion Bassus with his century on a fast ship to Alexandria, which it reached before dusk. The centurion had his ship lie off the port until nightfall, then landed, and tried in vain to get in touch with the commander of the local legion. Finding that the commander and the governor were both dining at a certain house, Bassus moved there swiftly, threw a guard about the exits, and after sending in a soldier dressed in civilian clothes to survey the ground carried out the arrest with complete sureness. The skill with which this operation was carried out in a strange city, after a long sea voyage, speaks eloquently for the ability of the emperor's agents.

Movement in the Empire was not as free as its tales of travel would suggest. Each man, as was noted earlier, had a place where he permanently belonged, his *idia* or *origo*. After Claudius senators could go only to Gaul and Sicily without explicit permission. Departure from Egypt by sea was strictly limited, and an Egyptian law code states firmly that even Roman citizens could be prosecuted for evasion of the rule. So too flight across the frontiers of the Empire was subject to punishment. If a person did quit his *idia*, he could be expelled from his "temporary" home by police action, or he could be required to return to his true domicile for purposes of census or for other reasons. Such a census led to the birth of Christ at Bethlehem, and the papyri have preserved several ukases for Egyptian "farmers" to leave the city of Alexandria. Men who attempted to flee or to hide had apparently little chance of escaping the imperial dragnet. The runaway slave Androcles was caught; during the rule of Tiberius the noble Rubrius Fabatus, who tried to flee from Rome to the Parthians, got no farther than the Straits of Messina before a centurion caught him and dragged the refugee back.

Once the contumelious or dangerous had been seized, they had to be legally convicted. The weapon of widest application was that of *laesa maiestas*. To give only one type of example of its use, the pages of imperial historians are full of instances where charges of insult to a ruler's image were utilized for a man's destruction. If one may credit ancient stories, to carry a coin or ring with the effigy of Tiberius—or later of Caracalla—into a latrine or brothel could mean death. Did careful men pay off their girls in *quadrantes* or pennies (which did not usually bear the ruler's head)? Seneca tells a story of an ex-praetor who took a chamberpot into his hands while wearing a ring with the head of Tiberius; only a quick-witted slave's speed in taking the ring from his master's finger prevented an informer from calling witness to the fact. Under Domitian a woman was reportedly executed for undressing before his statue.

Such farcical accusations were often mere pretexts when a ruler wished to get rid of a dangerous subject. Delators, too, may have used these additional charges to blacken the character of the accused. Jurists specifically warned against the abuse of the charge of *laesa maiestas,* and the better rulers supported the lawyers on the point. Titus went so far as to proclaim, "It is impossible for me to be insulted or abused in any way," and the expression of Tiberius on the violation of oaths sworn in the name of the deified Augustus was famous—"Let the gods take care of their injuries." [18] With this mighty weapon, however, the tyrants of the first century broke the outward display of any opposition. The benevolent rulers who followed laid it away, but the fair-seeming appearance of this era must not blind one to the fact that men were exiled under Trajan and executed under Hadrian for political offenses.

In the Republic trials for *laesa maiestas* had been conducted by a special *quaestio,* but this court fell into disuse under Augustus; later trials took place before the Senate or the ruler. In almost all cases there seems to have been at least the semblance of a judicial procedure, though its extent varied greatly, for the historians sometimes note their surprise when no record of a trial was released. Under those rulers who were more careful of legal forms or of the Senate's dignity the Senate tried cases of treason insofar as they affected senators. Tiberius, and probably Augustus also, gave the Senate some independence of judgment, but in a senatorial trial under Nero or Domitian the Senate was perforce an accomplice of Caesar in sending a man to his predestined doom.

At some points, and generally for nonsenators from all over the Empire, the emperors themselves or their praetorian prefects tried cases of *laesa maiestas;* before the ruler no rules of justice need apply. Intelligent men could naturally often detect absurdities in the imperial records of treason trials:

It is generally believed, at any rate, that many men are unjustly put to death . . . some without a trial and others by a prearranged conviction in court; for the people will not admit that the testimony given or the statements made

[18] Dio Cassius 66.19.1; Tacitus, *Annals* 1.73.5.

under torture or any evidence of that nature is true or suffices for the condemnation of the victims.[19]

Between the Neronian trials in the Pisonian conspiracy and the Roehm trials under Hitler or the Russian purge of 1937–1938 there is little difference in principle.

Augustus had forged not only the weapon to secure conviction but also the punishments which followed. If a culprit were co-operative enough to commit suicide before sentence, he might hope that the ruler would graciously grant his estate to his heirs, for down to Hadrian's reign only serious cases were then pushed to a conclusion so as to justify the trial in the eyes of the public. Those who stubbornly insisted on awaiting sentence might expect death or exile, the latter in either a more severe (deportation) or less severe (relegation) form. On some of the islands exiles seem to have lived reasonably pleasant lives, often with their wives and such friends as wished to accompany them. Two islets, Gyara (or Gyaros) and Seriphos, were so small and so limited in natural resources that exile to them was almost a living death; in the days of Domitian Gyara had the ring which Siberia or Buchenwald carries today.

The supervision of the natives and the imperial grasp of the sea made escape difficult. Where too should a man go? To seek a refuge anywhere in the Empire was hopeless; to leave the Empire involved a long journey, the outwitting of the frontier guard, and severance from "civilization"—and in any event most of the Roman neighbors were obligated by treaty to return refugees. Under many a ruler the world was indeed "a safe and dreary prison" (in Gibbon's phrase), whether men moved in state in Rome or mourned on a rocky island. The accession of a new suzerain often brought the release of those condemned under the previous *princeps*, but the islands of the Mediterranean were never entirely free of exiles from the days of Augustus to the fourth century.

The jurists indicate that only members of the upper classes, the later *honestiores*, were deported or relegated. Individuals of the lower classes might be condemned to furnish a public show in the games, or they too might be exiled; but their exile was in a much more drastic form.

The imperial mines, which were numerous, were always crying out for new hands to replace those who died in the unbearable labor, and the courts—under later rulers if not certainly under Augustus—furnished a part of what was needed. The fearful sentence *ad metallum* put men in

[19] Dio Cassius 55.19.2 (Livia).

chains and gave them no hope of release outside of death; those condemned *ad opus metalli* were not chained and might or might not be assigned a specific length of punishment. Both groups were under military direction and guard. Local gangs carried out all types of state work, even cleaning the public baths. Such punishment might be inflicted for the usual crimes, but those who disagreed with the social order (as Christians) might also be so sentenced. Unfortunately we have no information on which to base a guess as to the numbers of men which the Empire sent to its labor camps.

Absolutism of the Empire

The foregoing survey of the political development of the Empire from Augustus to Trajan has necessarily been long, for its flavor of absolutism has all too often been minimized. The man whom one should invite to pass a judgment on its system of control and repression is Fouché, Beria, or Himmler, or better yet Goebbels; and such an agent of modern despotism might pronounce the absolutism of the Empire to be of the right sort, even if incomplete.

The imperial system was much simpler than our contemporary autocratic structures, but the difference is in large part a reflection of the greater simplicity of the ancient world. Means of expression were scant and not closely integrated. The social structure had only a few important elements. The aims of the ruler who directed the machine were likewise simple and arose primarily from political affairs. To speak of a machine of repression is justifiable chiefly in the necessity of underlining the continuity of precedents and principles.

If the preceding pages have at times drawn or implied a comparison between the Roman Empire and the notorious police states of the present day, I do not thereby intend to argue that the Empire can be simply described as a terroristic institution. The imperial system was not one of unrestrained violence under any ruler of the first two centuries, even though certain classes may have been treated very roughly under a few of the emperors; that terror was yet to come. The Empire rested on the general support of its subjects, vocal and officially enthusiastic in the case of the upper classes, mute and enduring in the case of the lower classes. But is not this situation true in the last analysis of dictatorships at all times?

At its inception the Empire was a world recently racked by disorder and war, which had been only outwardly pacified by Augustus, in which numerous elements still asserted their jarring independence of each other and of the *princeps* himself. By the end of the first century the unified Empire of Trajan had emerged, that bountiful source of power to whom men turned for ultimate decision and, more and more, for initiative. Ever more uniform in civilization, thanks to the penetration of Mediterranean ways beyond the inland sea, ever more tightly reined under an imperial bureaucracy, this structure had grown accustomed to its unity. Frictions still endured, but the centripetal forces far outbalanced the centrifugal.

In part the individual bowed before the Father who could assure prosperity. For some at least the emperor gave a sense of order in the chaotic world; Trajan, like rulers before and after, was compared to Hercules, carrying out mighty labors for the benefit of man. But in part also the unification of the Empire rested on the loss of political freedom by the cities and by the aristocracy.

The voice of the Empire now spoke loudly and in uniform tone through many means. Some men felt bound to differ with it, but whether they were Jews, Christians, aristocrats, or local patriots such as Hellenists and Alexandrians, they all suffered in one way or another for their independent expression of opinion. Most men quietly took the material rewards of stability—prosperity, peace, and security. Was this a world in which thought could flourish?

Part Three

THE INTELLECTUAL
DECLINE OF THE
EARLY EMPIRE

The Intellectual Decline
of the Early Empire

IN THE last century of the Republic men had manifested terrific energies which tended to tear asunder the Mediterranean world; at the very same time they had taken great strides toward a synthesis of Greco-Roman civilization. With scarcely a falter the new fusion surmounted the civil wars which ended the Republic and brought the Principate, and then rose into the Augustan Age (from 40 to 8 B.C.). In the first half of the reign of Augustus Rome poured out its genius more abundantly than at any other epoch; the era is one of the intellectual explosions which stud the development of civilization.

By the later years of Augustus' life Virgil and Horace were dead; they had no successors of equal stature. The history of subsequent intellectual activity is essentially one of the consolidation of the old, of the expansion and unification—but not intensification—of Mediterranean civilization. In the bustle of outward activity lies hidden a decline which becomes obvious in the golden age of the second century; as one looks back from this point, the reign of Augustus assumes a new shape. He stopped the destructive whirlwind of the Republic; but in establishing a veiled autocracy did he necessarily deal a heavy blow to the unfolding of the new synthesis?

At first glance the answer to the problem may seem obvious. The cities lost their political autonomy; all elements abdicated political liberty for the sake of stability—ergo, the Empire became politically an autocracy, and inevitably declined in intellectual activity. The coupling has much to justify it, yet as put it is far too simple. Although the Empire inherited a tradition of state interference in the intellectual, social, and religious spheres, this tradition became weaker rather than stronger in the Empire. When the Caesars broke down one independent political grouping after another, they destroyed the individual's civic powers, but they also released him as a human being from old bonds.

The Early Empire is a period of inexorable decline of classical civilization; to prove this fact is not difficult. Out of the very decay, however, a new system of thought was beginning to arise. Such thinkers of the Empire as Virgil and Seneca not only express the old but also hint at the new; these men are harbingers of a revolutionary shift in the main values of Western civilization.

IX

Letters in the Augustan Age

THE Augustan Age was a Roman age. In the civil wars between Octavian and Antony the poet Horace had not been alone in fearing a
victory of the East, and the natural consequence of Octavian's victory
had been a revival of Roman patriotism. Both the poems of Virgil and
the Altar of Augustan Peace, which form the highest expression of that
patriotism, reflect men's love of Roman antiquities and their search for
the meaning of Rome to the world.

The emphasis on things Roman did not necessarily entail a depreciation of things Greek. The two forces were complementary rather than
conflicting elements in the Augustan pattern, and they were unified in
a way not always comprehended by the modern spectator. Greeks and
Romans had begun truly to accept each other in the age of Cicero; as
Republic passed into Empire, that mutual acceptance continued to
exist. The ruler himself, while basing his rule on Roman and Italian
tradition, paid deep respect to Greek civilization. Symbolic of his protection of the Greco-Roman fusion was his worship of Apollo, who to
some of his subjects was the best incarnation of the radiant Greek spirit
and to others was a native Italian earth spirit.

Men of the Augustan Age had serious thoughts to convey, thoughts
concerned with the values of a civilization restored to peace and order.
In great and small things alike—the lofty aqueduct of the Pont du Gard
and small bits of sculpture, the majestic fabric of Virgil's *Aeneid* and the
lyric odes of Horace—there is that common underlying spirit which we

may detect in eras of true mental exaltation. For its expression neither the emotional unrest nor the pedantic sterility of the Hellenistic Age could furnish the pattern. The Augustan Age accordingly turned away from the Hellenistic Age in every field to the achievements of classic Greece, not to imitate blindly but to gain inspiration in forms. The aim was not a wild, frenzied exploration of new concepts, but the reduction to cool order and perfect form of what had already been accomplished.

No one, to be sure, could eradicate the heavy influence of the Hellenistic Age on Roman arts and letters, and even the most serious work of the Augustan period betrays that influence repeatedly. Nor was the effort of the era to look back past the Hellenistic to the classic entirely desirable, for the resulting emphasis on an intellectual and nonemotional spirit tended to delay the natural course of Roman development. The literary advice of Horace for simplicity of approach and sincerity cannot serve as a measuring stick for the stylistic development of later Latin. When architects imposed balance and proportion on their buildings, they sidetracked the inventive genius of Roman architecture, which recovered its road only later in the first century after the Neronian fire of Rome. In sculpture the sharp, clear work of the dying Republic yielded to the needs of imperial idealization, which is marked in the portraits of Augustus and his associates (see Frontispiece, Pls. I *a*, II *a*, III); and in painting the so-called "third style," which took the wall as a flat surface and preferred restful, classically limited expression, seems a step backward from the illusionism popular in the Late Republic and early decades of Augustus. Culturally as well as politically the Augustan Age was an effort to halt revolution.

The main figure of this era one naturally takes to be Augustus himself; in few eras do the currents of thought seem as closely connected with the policy of the leader. Beneath a veil of outward tolerance Augustus clearly wished the poets and sculptors to handle certain themes, and the arts and letters did deal quite largely with the desired subjects:

one and all they glorify Actium as a victory of Roman culture, of the Roman spirit; one and all they extol plain living and patriotic thinking, the Trojan origins of Rome and the Julian *gens,* Apollo and Mars, the gods of the new order.[1]

Augustus clearly had definite opinions also with respect to matters of style, and could back up his opinions with a native talent of high

[1] A. D. Nock, *Cambridge Ancient History* 10, 476.

order. Alone of all the Roman emperors he was cited by later authors as an authority for literary usage; though he subordinated his literary talent to his political career, the vigor and clarity of the *Res Gestae* demonstrate his command of the pen. His critical acumen in rhetoric was genuinely appreciated by his contemporary Seneca the Elder. Even in the arts, where Augustus eschewed the role of esthete or dilettante, the pattern of his building and portraiture strongly suggests that he had positive views.

The emperor's personal and financial encouragement of the arts and letters extended beyond the accepted fields, where success might be relatively certain, into unfruitful attempts to promote a truly Roman comedy and to revive the old Roman tragedy of the second century B.C. His motives, here as elsewhere, may have been ulterior; but they were backed by real depth of literary appreciation. The first *princeps* established a friendly relation between the Empire and its cultural leaders which was never, save in the field of philosophy, seriously threatened until the third century.

Insofar as the program of Augustus dictated the subject matter of his age, and to the extent that he himself helped to set the return to the classic, he may be accused of opposing the progress of the Roman arts. Yet the fact that the spirit of the ruler often coincided with the spirit of the thinkers does not really justify the common inference that the Augustan Age was a projection of the character of Augustus. The intricacy of the relationships between the program of the emperor and the desires of his subjects has already been suggested in general terms; more specific illustrations can be gained from the writers of the age, first from Virgil and Horace, secondarily from Livy and Propertius. Here can one best assess the true influence of Augustus on intellectual activity and the mingling of old and new ideas in the Augustan Age.

Virgil

Virgil (70–19 B.C.) was born in northern Italy, close to watergirt Mantua. He received a good education at near-by centers and then at Rome, but might have remained all his life a gentleman farmer who dabbled in poetry had not the unrest after Caesar's murder struck him a rude economic blow. In the wide-scale confiscation of land to settle the veterans of Philippi Virgil lost his farm. Other men, thus expropriated, had joined a rebellion against Octavian; Virgil merely wrote the sad First and Ninth Bucolics. The poet of Mantua was more fortunate than the hapless, dispossessed Meliboeus, whom he described in his First Bucolic, for his early verse had caught the attention of several Roman nobles, first Asinius Pollio, and then particularly Maecenas, the great minister of internal affairs for Octavian. Yet the pattern of his previous existence had been forever broken.

From 39 B.C. Virgil lived in Rome or near Naples in the circle of the elegant Maecenas, where he received financial support and artistic encouragement. The days and years seem thenceforth to have rolled by without any great outward mark, for Virgil never married or held state office; his superb quality of delicately reflecting his age required his quiet dedication to his poetry. After the *Bucolics* he wrote four books of *Georgics* and an epic, the *Aeneid*. The latter was left unpolished when he died while returning from an Aegean trip, but his request that it be burned was vetoed by Augustus.

Virgil was a gentle soul with sensitive spirit, the intuitive poet who felt and reflected in his verse more than he consciously knew. Outwardly simple and undistinguished, such a man leads us into the heart of an age if we can but hear him. Although his whispers and hints are not always capable of analysis in cold prose, Virgil reveals underlying forces of the Augustan Age which Augustus could not have suspected, along with others which the ruler could sense and appreciate deeply. Of all the men who wrote in this period Virgil celebrated most clearly and sincerely the manifold aspects of the Augustan program.

Antiquity assigned to Virgil a group of miscellaneous poems entitled the Virgilian Appendix, which presumably represented his earliest poetic efforts. Modern scholars have at times tried to justify this ascription, but not one of the works can be proved to be Virgilian on either poetic or psychological grounds. To argue back from the known Virgil to the hypothetical Virgil of these poems is a most dangerous process which has brought no universally accepted conclusions. The earliest sure view of his mind is to be found in the ten *Bucolics*.

These artificial praises of the pastoral life, which Virgil began to write in the sad days after the murder of Caesar (c. 42–c. 39 B.C.), are skillful imitations of Alexandrian originals, yet not all is copy. The poet's native, lush plains with slowly winding rivers often formed the background, and the political scene was purely Roman. Taken as a group, the *Bucolics* reveal a mind of mixed hope and sadness, where lament for the unrest and the harsh military domination of life after the death of Caesar was mingled with an innate optimism that peace might yet return. The messianic portrayal in the Fourth Bucolic of the happy world to come contrasts strongly, and perhaps intentionally, with the contemporary product of the gloomy Horace, who was at this very time urging true Romans to flee their doomed land for the Isles of the Blest.

Nevertheless Virgil seems to have come but slowly to appreciate the significance of Octavian. His *Bucolics* were patronized initially by Asinius Pollio, whose poetry Virgil praised in the Third Bucolic and whose consulship of 40 B.C. he celebrated in the Fourth. This famous vision of a golden age is linked with the birth of an unknown, perhaps imaginary babe, who "shall rule the world that his fathers' virtues have set at peace." The vagueness of the poet, when coupled with his feeling that a new set of wars must precede the rule of the child, does not suggest that Virgil thus far had visualized Octavian as the savior of Rome. Modern scholars who have tried to prove that the baby was connected with Octavian's house have in my judgment simply predated Virgil's adhesion to the young Caesar.

Like Italy as a whole, Virgil may have begun to move toward Octavian in spirit in 40–39 B.C. By 39 he had become a close friend of Maecenas, who was attempting to win and influence poets, but it was not until Virgil wrote his First Bucolic, chronologically perhaps the next to the last of the entire set, that he revealed his identification of peace with Octavian.

The two characters of the poem, Meliboeus and Tityrus, seem almost to typify the opposed aspects of Republic and Empire. Meliboeus appears first. He has lost his farm to a landless soldier and now is driving his she-goats down the hopeless road, whither he knows not—"lo, to what wretched pass has civil discord brought us!" For a moment he halts beside the languid figure of Tityrus, who is smugly piping of his Amaryllis under a covert of spreading beech. Tityrus has saved his lands, for he had appealed to Octavian. Virgil deftly alludes to Octavian's emphasis on the restoration of peaceful agriculture and in the mouth of Tityrus hails the prince as a very god—"a god brought us this peace; for a god ever will he be to me." [2]

So Tityrus is happy, sacrificing before his god, the emperor, as the Empire was to sacrifice in gratitude for material gain; the linking of peace and the Empire, here quietly hinted, was later to be explicitly stressed by Tacitus. Poor Meliboeus, however, has not enjoyed the master's clemency. Where, he gloomily wonders, are his kind to go, to

[2] Translation by J. W. Mackail.

thirsty Africa, to Scythia, or to remote Britain? No more songs will he sing; and Tityrus can offer only an evening meal and a night's stay to his sad friend, a symbol of the dying Republic. "Already afar the farm roofs smoke, and the shadows fall larger from the high hills."

By the early 30's Virgil was eulogizing Octavian as the giver of peace who restored agricultural life and bestowed something which Virgil called *libertas*. He did not thereafter waver in his allegiance. During the war of propaganda between Antony and Octavian the literary friends of the former seem to have viewed Virgil's mellifluous pen with alarm and attacked him on various esthetic grounds. Virgil is not known to have replied to these attacks, nor was a specific reply necessary. The next poem he wrote, the four books of the *Georgics* (c. 37–27 B.C.), proclaimed clearly enough his faith in Octavian and his reasons for that faith.

The theme of this poem was the practice and glories of Italian agriculture. While later ages have at times tried to use it as a guide to farming, Virgil's work seems aimed primarily to encourage wealthy aristocrats to purchase estates and to consider their lands as more than a source of income. The topic, we know, was suggested to Virgil by his patron Maecenas as one in keeping with the official effort to renew the old basis of Roman economic and spiritual life (see Pl. II).

Although Virgil complained in his *Georgics* that Maecenas' requests "are no light commands," the subject was not one incompatible with his own interests. Three of the *Bucolics* had ended with a recall of the shepherds to their agricultural duty, and in these poems Virgil had broken away from his Theocritean models mainly in his praises of nature. To the modern world, city-bred or accustomed to mechanized farming, the *Georgics* may often seem to drag in their technical detail despite their marvelously turned hexameters and glowing digressions, but even now they convey something of the unremitting toil of peasant farming and the rich pageant of the Italian agricultural world. Again and again Virgil's love of his native land, torn by strife after the ill-fated death of Caesar, shines forth, as in the bitter end of the First Georgic:

For Right and Wrong are confused here, there's so much war in the world,
Evil has so many faces, the plough so little
Honour, the labourers are taken, the fields untended,
And the curving sickle is beaten into the sword that yields not . . .
The wicked War-god runs amok through all the world.

The man who ended this strife is acclaimed with equal sincerity from the opening to the closing lines of the *Georgics*. This poem had no place for Pollio and the other friends of the *Bucolics;* the days of Virgil's doubt were past. The poet was firmly caught up in the Augustan spirit, for better or for worse—and worship at Augustus' shrine was no easy matter. Ancient tradition tells us that Virgil had devoted the last half of the Fourth Georgic originally to a friend, C. Cornelius Gallus; but as we now have the poem this space contains a somewhat frigid fable of Orpheus and Eurydice. The reason? Gallus, first governor of Egypt, took too haughty a position vis-à-vis Augustus, was accused and convicted, and committed suicide in 26 B.C.; his name was erased alike from Egyptian steles and the verse of Virgil.

Upon completing the *Georgics* in 27 B.C. Virgil read the entire poem to Augustus, who was resting at a little Campanian town. Both Augustus and Maecenas must have shown open pleasure in this polished celebration of the ancient virtues of Italian agriculture, in which were so deftly woven the rejoicings of Italy over the peace brought by its savior. Neither, however, was willing to discharge Virgil from further work; what was really wanted was an epic celebration of Augustus.

Varius had composed a panegyric of Augustus and Agrippa, but it died so quick a death that we have only a few fulsome lines which Horace quoted. Horace himself bluntly refused Maecenas' behest to write such an epic; Virgil, on the other hand, had half promised in the *Georgics* to take up the wars of Octavian. He had also, it is true, made remarks about singing of the stars; but this type of subject was obviously useless as far as Augustus was concerned. Though Maecenas was the person who approached Horace—and also Propertius—with regard to an epic, it seems quite clear that Augustus himself urged Virgil to turn to his new work, the later *Aeneid*.

As the news that Virgil was writing an epic spread through Rome, it provoked wide interest. A reference by Propertius in 25 B.C. to the work, "a something greater than the *Iliad*," [3] shows that Virgil swiftly gave up any idea of making Augustus' own wars his central theme. The poet disliked the civil wars; then too, Augustus was by now becoming the prince of peace.

Virgil turned back instead to the legendary character Aeneas. A Trojan hero marked in Homer for his piety, Aeneas was fabled in later Greek

[3] Propertius 2.34.61–66 (Phillimore).

myth to have voyaged after the fall of Troy to north Greece, then to Sicily, and finally to Latium, where he became an ancestor of the Romans. This extension of the legend, which was concocted mainly to give the Romans some tie with the Aegean world, was an inconsistent, uninspired tale when Virgil seized upon it as the kernel for his poem.

At the outset of his work Virgil stated his purpose: he proposed to tell of the tribulations and wanderings of the man who was directed by the gods to pave the way for Rome. Aeneas carried with him the images of his family gods, the Penates, who were to become the inner gods of Rome and the guardians of its rise. The first six books of the work describe his travels; the second six, his wars in Latium against the native Latins, abetted by the Etruscans, in order to found his city of Alba Longa, whence Rome eventually was settled. The earlier books, which contain the famous account of Aeneas' dallying with Dido at Carthage and his visit to the underworld at Cumae, are by far the more famous; but the last half has an even greater significance in the poet's scheme, which culminates in the promise of Jupiter to fuse Trojan and Latin into one great race.

The *Aeneid* is far more than the story of Aeneas, for through this device Virgil was able to state his lofty views of the development of the Roman Republic. In great passages of prophecy Jupiter, then Anchises (father of Aeneas), and others stepped forward to sketch boldly the purpose of Rome and the majesty of its power. The height toward which all Roman history ascended inevitably was the poet's own age, the age of Augustus. Thus the *Aeneid* was a blend of the mythical and the historical, of the past and of the immediate present; all Roman development was seen as a unified block of time which had come to a decisive turning point in the person of Augustus. The *Aeneid* reflects the Augustan Age, not the Republic.

Only if one is to assess the *Aeneid* in purely esthetic terms may one ignore the influence of Augustus on Virgil and his epic. The poem is indeed a mighty vision of Roman destiny, a true reflection of Virgil's own thought, but both in general pattern and in specific details much of the treatment was molded specifically to please Augustus. Some of these touches are apparent in the twists of the plot; others are suggested by the ancient commentators. Though much must slip by us undetected even so, the *Aeneid* admirably illustrates the effect of Augustus on the thought of his age.

The divine paraphernalia of the epic, for instance, clearly betray this influence. As Warde Fowler has pointed out, the necessities of Virgil's plot required him to set up a superhuman opposition to Aeneas, in the form of Juno, and to counterbalance her malevolence with divine aid. Jupiter and the Fates must logically favor the spiritual founder of Rome, but Aeneas needed more personal and dramatic protection.

In the first instance Venus, the ancestress of the Julian house, could be employed, and the poet undoubtedly heightened her role because of this family relationship. Nevertheless Venus had been in the story of Aeneas long before Virgil took it up, and in the *Aeneid* she is merely a personal guardian of its hero. What apparently was new in Virgil's interpretation was his great emphasis on Apollo, who drove the sometimes reluctant Aeneas toward his appointed destination. In magnifying the place of Apollo Virgil was in part reflecting the general interest of the day in the deity of healing and classic balance, but by direct reference to the new Palatine temple, the forthcoming Secular festival, and other touches, he underlined the close connection of Augustus with Apollo and with the god's prophet, the Cumaean Sibyl.

The Ninth Book has a significant interlude when Ascanius, angered by the boasting of an enemy, first kills a man. Apollo appears forthwith to commend the young hero, son of Aeneas, and to prophesy that under his descendants all wars will end in peace; then he descends to earth in human guise and urges Ascanius out of the battle. Nowhere else does the great god Apollo take a direct part in the action, nor do the deities of Virgil generally follow the Homeric pattern in this respect; the interruption of the story and the miscasting of the god were both required to magnify the divine protection of the Julian house, for Ascanius (or Iulus) was the legendary ancestor of that family. In the original story the youth could scarcely have been of any significance, and at times, as in Livy, Ascanius was another son of Aeneas, born after his arrival in Italy. Almost always in Virgil's verse the poor lad seems a puppet, required to show Aeneas' parenthood and even more to serve as a necessary root of the family tree which flowered in Augustus.

Although the indirect influence of Augustus on the *Aeneid* can be seen in other instances than the emphasis on Apollo or Ascanius, there is no need to hunt out such references at length or to engage in the fallacious effort to prove that Aeneas himself is Augustus. The emperor appears in his own person often enough to remind the reader that he is the end-product of the mighty forces beginning with Aeneas. At several points in the *Aeneid* there are brief sketches of Roman history, all of which culminate in Augustus, the peacegiver. Thus in the underworld Anchises shows to Aeneas the future race of Rome, whose stately array reminds one of the great parade of heroes in the contemporary Forum of Augustus. Romulus is immediately followed by Caesar and all Iulus' posterity:

> One promise you have heard
> Over and over: here is its fulfillment,
> The son of a god, Augustus Caesar, founder
> Of a new age of gold, in lands where Saturn
> Ruled long ago; he will extend his empire
> Beyond the Indies, beyond the normal measure
> Of years and constellations, where high Atlas
> Turns on his shoulders the star-studded world.[4]

The most extensive reference to Augustus comes in the description of Aeneas' shield, the work of Vulcan. Unlike the Homeric shield of Achilles, whereon the armsmaker to the gods had worked a panorama of life, Vulcan must produce for his Roman hero a buckler decorated with historical events. Aeneas' shield depicts the story of Italy and the triumphs of the Romans, or more correctly the occasions when Rome was saved from the threat of extinction. The very center is given over to the battle of Actium, and Virgil here canonized the Augustan interpretation of the civil war for later poets. On the one side are the barbarian hosts of Antony and the "shameful Egyptian woman"; on the other stands the true leader of Italy, supported by the Senate and the people, by those very gods of household and Roman state that Aeneas had brought. With the sistrum of the Oriental Isis, Cleopatra calls on her fleet:

> Monstrous gods,
> Of every form and fashion, one, Anubis,
> Shaped like a dog, wield their outrageous weapons
> In wrath at Venus, Neptune, and Minerva.[5]

Then Apollo bends his mighty bow, and the fearful enemies fly in utter rout back to the mourning Nile.

So the god and Augustus have saved Rome, which may now renew itself in a golden age, for Vulcan has yet space to display Octavian's triumph amid popular rejoicing, his vowed offering of three hundred stately shrines to the gods of Rome, and a long file of captives from all quarters of the earth as far as the Asiatic river Araxes, chafing beneath

[4] *Aeneid* 6.791–797.   [5] *Aeneid* 8.698–700.

his bridge. Augustus never reached this stream, much less built a bridge; but Virgil remembered that Alexander had done so, only to have his bridge swept away. As is frequently the case elsewhere in the poetic celebration of the Augustan wars, what appears to be historical fact is only outrageous compliment.

Even more significant than such open praise of Augustus is the reflection of the Augustan political system in the *Aeneid*. The word *libertas* appears infrequently, and the political milieu of the Trojan camp is not that of the Republic. None of the Trojans fail to obey their leader, even at the price of death; for Aeneas, the organizer, the builder or pioneer, bears in himself full responsibility for the fates of Rome. Introducing the Trojans as a group may have been necessary to Virgil's purpose, but in viewing the future of their settlement Virgil often seems to view the family of Aeneas as the stock from which all later Romans descended; so might Augustus, as leader of that family, almost literally claim his later title of *pater patriae*. The masses are disdained, the Senate on the other hand is magnified throughout the epic as an accompaniment of due order. While the *Aeneid* was necessarily a story of leaders, Virgil went far beyond what might have been required in emphasizing the few at the expense of the many—and then the one at the expense of the few!

The emphasis of the *Aeneid* was on peace, not on freedom. Though Virgil had to talk of war, he came hesitatingly to it in the last six books which recount Aeneas' battle against the Latins and Etruscans; the war was an essential job to be done so that Rome might rise. The wars of Augustus likewise had to take place, but only because they brought eventual peace (see Pl. III). Here one reaches the point where the *Aeneid* mirrors some of the most sincere aspects of the Augustan program.

The patriotic love of Italy, apparent in Virgil's other poems, now deepened in both the religious and the historical sense. Unlike earlier —and later—writers Virgil thought of Rome and Italy as quite distinct, yet inextricably joined. The separation of the two was required to some degree by the nature of his plot, which demanded the war between Italians and Trojans, but the earlier historical and legal distinctions between Roman citizen and Italian ally also played their part.

Italy, however, was no longer to be considered as inferior to Rome. In describing the Gathering of the Clans to oppose the Trojans Virgil skillfully put the opponents of Aeneas in a good light; and at the end of the epic Jupiter and Juno made a momentous bargain that the name of Troy should perish and that of Latium remain:

> Let Roman stock, strong in Italian valor,
> Prevail.[6]

A generation earlier the Social War (90–88 B.C.) had resulted in the grant of Roman citizenship to all Italy south of the Po; Octavian had consciously appealed to all Italy in his war against Antony. Ere long men were to pass from considering Italy and Rome as equal to viewing them as one.

The Augustan Age was far from imagining the end of the process, when *Roma* was to mean the entire Mediterranean world. Augustus himself favored the union of Rome and Italy so that this solid core might dominate the rest of the world; in the *Aeneid* the Italo-Roman combination is a unique product of divine forces. Not even all the inhabitants of the peninsula might be accounted a part of this group, for Virgil shared the old Roman suspicion and antipathy to the effete Etruscans; and there is no thought that any people outside Italy might be included in the ranks of the masters. It was, after all, Virgil who coined the well-known phrase "I fear the Greeks, even when bringing presents." [7]

An opposition between Greek and Roman (or Trojan) appears at various points in the poem. In many respects the distinction was a thin, unsubstantial one, a formal inheritance from the arrogance of earlier generations; Trojans and Greeks, indeed, are described as rising from the same stock in the later books of the *Aeneid*. Virgil himself was deeply indebted to Homer's epics, both in details of poetic style and in the general division of his material. The translation of the *Aeneid* into Greek, a rare honor for a Latin work, shows that it could appeal to the Hellenic part of the Empire.

Nevertheless the mission of Aeneas was fraught with cosmic significance far beyond that of Agamemnon or Odysseus, nor will it do to compare the *Iliad* and the *Aeneid* on any but the most restricted points. The *Aeneid* was a Roman poem written for a definite purpose, and Virgil packed into it a wealth of learning about Roman religious and social customs; his hero is the complicated Aeneas, not a half-barbarous Achilles capable of paroxysms of undisciplined anger. Aeneas is brave, divinely handsome, merciful, and sentimental; he is also a cautious

[6] *Aeneid* 12.827.   [7] *Aeneid* 2.49.

builder and lawgiver, the father of his people, and above all pious to gods and parents. As a hero he may not appeal to the modern mind: "pious Aeneas" is merely a vehicle of divine will, and one who needs considerable stiffening to keep to the mark. But to a Roman this characteristic merely showed his divine guidance, and in the *Aeneid* he was ever more clearly driven by the divine mission of paving the way for Rome.

Virgil's sincere belief in the divine support of Rome is the very base of the *Aeneid,* for the essential charge of Aeneas is to bring the gods who will make Rome great. Who these gods were he did not conceive very clearly, and the theological substratum of the divine force could not be sharply stated; like the ancients generally, Virgil could not determine the exact relationship between the gods and Fate. The latter, nonetheless, was assuredly a moral force requiring the creation of Rome, and whether the protecting gods were the ancestral Penates of Aeneas or deities like Apollo and Minerva they united in a common purpose.

Toward the old religious rites many men were skeptical or indifferent in the Augustan Age. The poet Virgil described them lovingly and accepted wholeheartedly the Augustan claim that at Actium Roman gods triumphed over the Oriental deities of Egypt. Only beneath the surface can one sense that the old polytheism was losing its sharpness and that people were posing questions which it could not answer. Though the gods are ethical and punish evildoers in a separate corner of the underworld, Anchises must warn his son Aeneas not to ask what doom awaits injustice in the pagan Hell. A clearer answer to the problems of individual justice had to wait upon the rise of Christianity; Virgil was more interested in the certainty of the justice of the Roman state.

The *Aeneid* is infused with Virgil's sense of Roman destiny, which made that state the inevitable master of the Mediterranean—not for plunder or rapine, but for peace, order, and the growth of equality among the races. Anchises prophesies to his son that the Greeks may excel in sculpture, oratory, or science:

> Remember, Roman,
> To rule the people under law, to establish
> The way of peace, to battle down the haughty,
> To spare the meek.[8]

[8] *Aeneid* 6.847–853.

The idea was far from new, but as Virgil majestically expressed it, it was to echo far down the corridors of the Empire into the great throne rooms of a Christian Roman Empire in a New Rome (see Pls. III, XII). The divine protection of the Romans was canonically stated in the lines of Jupiter in the First Book:

> To these I set no bounds in space or time;
> They shall rule forever. Even bitter Juno
> Whose fear now harries earth and sea and heaven
> Will change to better counsels, and will cherish
> The race that wears the toga, Roman masters
> Of all the world.[9]

Like Livy, Virgil looked to the past of Rome with swelling pride; unlike the historian, Virgil also turned and looked forward into the future with equal certainty of Rome's mighty purpose and essential justice; he had already answered the stinging question of Augustine four centuries later, "Justice being taken away, then, what are kingdoms but great robberies?" [10]

As one reads the great prophecy of Jupiter on the purpose of Rome, which culminates in the bringing of peace by Augustus, or as one views with Aeneas the parade of Roman heroes in the underworld, it is easy to see why Augustus was deeply interested in the progress of the epic. Even while absent in Spain to direct the Cantabrian war of 25 B.C. the ruler kept his eye on Horace and Virgil, and sent frequent requests to Virgil that finished parts, or even rough drafts, of the *Aeneid* be forwarded to him. These requests Virgil refused, and in one preserved letter he went so far as to say he must have been out of his mind when he started so great a work; but on later occasions the poet did read more or less completed sections to Augustus and his companions. One of these literary seances was devoted to the Sixth Book, a glowing mass of allegory and history revolving about Aeneas' visit to the underworld; we are told that Octavia fainted on hearing the passage which alluded to the death of her son Marcellus.

Virgil died before the *Aeneid* was completed, and in the irrational pessimism of his last days begged his friends to burn the work. Gauguin and Byron made the same request more successfully, but Augustus stepped in and ordered Tucca and Varius to publish this epic celebration of his age. So the poem was launched on its great career. Super-

[9] *Aeneid* 1.278–282.   [10] *City of God* 4.4 (Dods).

ficially at least Ovid was correct when he told Augustus that it was "your *Aeneid.*"

The extent to which this phrase is really true is a critical problem. Would Virgil have written his poems, and have written them as he did, had there been no Augustus? Certainly the *Bucolics* would have appeared, for these short works came from a period when Virgil was largely independent of the ruler, was even at times opposed in spirit to the youthful Octavian. The *Georgics* and the *Aeneid* are another matter. It is commonly argued, and I think correctly, that Virgil yearned for peace and was deeply impressed by the restoration of order. The peace of Augustus and his effort to rejuvenate the old Roman ways, especially in religion, struck chords in Virgil which led to his greatest productions. The deep sincerity of Virgil's love for his native Italy, his sense of the religious protection of Rome, his belief in Rome's purpose— none of these could have been assumed like a mask, even though they coincided with Augustus' own ideas.

The Augustan Age was inspiring. It was also corrupting, and the extent to which its greatest poet bent consciously or unconsciously before the imperious ruler was an ominous presage for the freedom of thought in the future. One need not accept the ancient generalization, too often repeated by modern scholars, that Virgil was merely an instrument of the politician. Augustus himself was too intelligent a man to insist on exclusive attention to himself or to his ideas; far more commonly he attempted to interfuse his own person and policies with the great traditions of Roman history and thought. As a pure panegyric of Augustus, direct or indirect, the *Aeneid* could have had little more staying power than the ill-fated poem of Varius. Nor is the open praise of the ruler of great significance, for eulogy, sincere or not, has often been inserted in literary works of all ages without corrupting the general flow of thought. More indicative is the undeniable fact that Virgil warped the plot of the *Aeneid* with Augustus in mind. Examples have already been given; one further, flagrant instance is the adulation of the mere youth Marcellus, the nephew of the ruler, in a passage which mentions the venerable Cato and Fabius Maximus only briefly.

The most significant point is the Augustan pressure on the entire pattern of Virgil's poetry. While the *Georgics* were a response to a request by Maecenas, Virgil might have written such a celebration of the Italian land of his own volition; but in the *Aeneid,* I feel, the poet may have deviated considerably from the path he would have liked to follow. The ancient biography of the poet, it is true, states that he had early thought of writing on Roman antiquities, then shifted to the *Bucolics* "in displeasure with his material"; but there are hints in his own work that he might, by himself, have gone on from the *Georgics* to a great portrayal of the nature of the world. Had he been entirely free, he might have worked out an alternative explanation to that of Lucretius' *On the Nature of Things,* in which Providence could perhaps have played a more significant part. Ancient tradition suggests that even after completing the *Aeneid* he planned to come back to philosophy.

The poet, however, was not to have the long life he had hoped for in the Fourth Bucolic; the suspicion is perhaps not too fanciful that the *Aeneid* was in a way the cause of his death. The trip to the Aegean from which he never returned may have been designed not so much to get local color for his poem—for very little of its action takes place in that area—as to escape for a while from his subject. Not only was the *Aeneid* unfinished on his death, it might never have been completed; and his last wish to burn the poem may reflect more than the gloom of approaching death.

Nevertheless the *Aeneid* has much of Virgil's heart and mind in it; and Virgil sensed deeply the nature of his age. If one goes on through the ivory gates into the secret world of the poet, one must leave Augustus far behind. The emperor saved the *Aeneid* not for its general view of man but for the halo of long-destined purpose which it cast about himself and his efforts at rejuvenation of the Roman world.

In the Second Georgic Virgil proposed to sing Ascraean songs through Roman cities. The comparison which he invites between his work and that of the archaic poet Hesiod is an illuminating one. The briefness and intensity of the Greek are a mark of his early, simple age, while the polish and thoroughness of the Roman seven centuries later reflect the complexity to which civilization had developed. Between the two lies also the meditation of the Hellenistic Age on nature and man's emotions. Hesiod's gaze was unblinkingly fastened on man, but beyond the human for Virgil lay nature, not yet independent in the sense of a modern Romantic poet, but still a force apart from man; it was Virgil, not Hesiod—or Horace—that "fain would see fields that owe no debt to the mattock nor to any mortal care." [11] Again, the main drive of Hesiod's thought—I refer only to his *Works and Days*—was the

[11] *Georgics* 2.438–439 (Mackail).

relation of man with men and the ensuing problems of justice; Virgil was concerned with the working out of Fate's decrees in human history. To the Roman poet of the Augustan Age there was much besides man in the universe.

Lucretius too had felt, even more intensely, the fierce independence of nature, but he had eliminated the Providence which Virgil restored. To the naturalistic, almost impersonal view of nature in Lucretius the *Georgics* oppose the pantheism of a God "from Whom flocks, herds, men, every wild creature in its kind/ Derive at birth the slight, precarious breath of life." [12] In the *Aeneid* individuals may suffer, and Virgil may grieve, but he must press on to express his essential faith in the Roman future, which is based upon the divine plan. The *Aeneid* has an essential optimism which the gloomy Lucretius could never attain, and the relative popularity of the two poets suggests clearly which view of man the Roman world preferred. The Augustan restoration of temples and cults was perhaps a shallow affair, but all the history of thought in the Empire will be read amiss if one fails to recognize that Virgil penetrated deeply into a religious urge of his age.

At this time the poet could go no further than the solemn assertion that the rise of Rome was an act of Providence and that all the world could lean upon its product, the Augustan Empire, for security. The later Christians were yet right in feeling that Virgil was a forerunner of Christianity, and not only because they took his prophecy of the Fourth Bucolic, built about a babe, as referring to Christ.

The inherent optimism of the *Aeneid* must not be construed as meaning that Virgil interpreted life in the simple terms of happiness. More than any other of his poems this epic is infused with his deep pity and brooding upon the world. His compassion for Dido, which almost carried him outside the due bounds of his plot, led to the creation of one of the most striking, deeply felt female characters in ancient literature. Although the Latin Turnus, representing brute war and tribal disunion, had to lose to Aeneas in the end, he was humanely fashioned. Even the piety of Aeneas, frigid though it often was toward the gods, has a new, deeper significance in its relation to man; humanity and pity are characteristics of this hero far more than of Achilles. The popularity of Virgil in his and subsequent ages was the result not of his celebration of Augustus but of his expression of human longings. Mackail does not exaggerate in saying:

[12] *Georgics* 4.223–224 (Lewis).

In no other poetry are the chords of human sympathy more delicately touched, its tones more subtly interfused. In none is there so deep a sense of the beauty and sorrow of life, of keen remembrance and shadowy hope, and, enfolding all, of infinite pity.[13]

That Augustus could penetrate this secret world one may doubt, nor would the cool politician have had any reason to feel deep interest in Virgil's general view of man. The surface of the poet's thought he could, and did, affect in an effort to gain support for those policies by which he thought to shore up the endangered foundations of ancient civilization. That it was far more important to the survival of that civilization to control the hidden ideas implicit in Virgil's work Augustus could never have conceived.

Horace

The other great poet of the Augustan Age, Horace (65–8 B.C.) was the son of a freedman. Raised in the small, South Italian town of Venusia, where he quaked before the bully sons of proud veterans, he was educated at Rome and Athens through the efforts of his remarkably self-sacrificing and upright father. Horace often resembles Virgil in his more Italian than Roman attitude, and reflects his background in his emphasis upon morals; yet, whereas Virgil's intuition might be deep but his mind outwardly simple, Horace had a complicated character. Horace's verse reflects superbly the jarring external aspects of the Augustan Age.

A blackness of outlook bedeviled Horace throughout his life from the beginning of the *Satires* to the last book of the *Odes*. At times he could exorcise the "black cares" of life by song; his only true optimism lay in his proud exaltation of the poet, whose verse might rear "a fame outlasting brass." At other points Horace preached a hedonistic doctrine and drowned his fears in wine; again he tried to withdraw from life and stop thinking. No dodge succeeded; the end was clear. Rich or poor you die, so kiss a maid while you may and enjoy life as best you can, as simply as may be.

Where then could this gloomy soul find an anchor in his upset world? His contemporaries busied themselves in the quest for office or for wealth, but he rejected both scornfully; more clearly than any other Augustan poet Horace voiced a desire for social stability. This personally unambitious freedman's son echoed the aristocratic anger at the breaking down of the old distinctions. The inner worth of a man was inde-

[13] J. W. Mackail, *The Aeneid* (Oxford, 1930), lxix.

pendent of his position—Horace himself lived to speak and jest with the lords of the Roman world—but political office should be reserved for men sprung from noble families. Insofar as the Augustan Age turned from politics to the amassing of money to be spent on gluttony and ostentation, it pleased its critic no more; his attack on materialism struck notes almost absent from Virgil. The Greeks love glory, charged Horace, while we Romans learn to count money; how then can we make poems?

Less crass supports for the making of poems might perhaps be sought, but Horace was too much a creature of the intellect to enter Virgil's magic world where Providence gave serene certainty. Initially Horace was an Epicurean, taught to believe that "the gods live a carefree life regardless of mankind, and that if Nature produces a miracle, petulant gods do not send it down from the high dome of heaven." [14] Later he publicly proclaimed his conversion and his acceptance of the gods who protected Rome.

Modern critics have hotly debated this conversion and now tend to grant it far-too-unqualified credence. The ills of Rome were indeed to his mind a divine vengeance for its sins, and the rise of Augustus was a divine miracle. Patriotically he endorsed the Augustan restoration of temples and old faiths. Toward the rustic gods in field and home he displayed a sympathetic attitude, inherited from his boyhood in a small Italian town and revealed in his delightful encouragement to a rustic maid to sacrifice to her Lares and Penates. All this may establish that Horace was not an atheist in the modern (or ancient) sense, but in the end Horace stood closer to the rationalist Cicero than to the truly religious Virgil.

Both Livy and Virgil drew encouragement from another source of strength, the tradition of the Early Republic. Horace felt the greatness of Rome and looked back occasionally to the simplicity of the old heroes, but the shock of the civil wars, which dyed all plains and coasts with Italian blood, made him fear even more deeply than did Livy for the future of the state. So impressed had he been in his youth that he had joined the army of Brutus as a tribune. Sprung from a town which apparently supported neither Caesar nor the young Octavian, he may have favored the constitutional arguments of the tyrannicides; but even more he must have felt it a Roman's duty to restore order to the tottering state. The side to which he had committed himself was defeated at Philippi; the lands of his native Venusia were expropriated for the

[14] *Satires* 1.5.101–103 (Wells).

veterans of the triumvirs; Horace was pardoned but sank to bitter poverty as a treasury clerk in Rome.

These events stamped Horace for life. Immediately he voiced grim pessimism not only for himself but also for the state. In his Seventh Epode he fiercely indicted the bitter fate which pitted Roman against Roman rather than against external foe. Even blacker is the Sixteenth, written soon after Philippi. By her own strength Rome is ruined in civil strife, mourns the poet, and the barbarian conqueror shall ride in her ash-laden streets; let us launch our boats and fly over the ocean to new lands, to the Isles of the Blest, where nature can still give us a golden age. When Virgil was penning the messianic Fourth Bucolic, the poor treasury clerk could see no ray of hope.

Even as friend of Maecenas and Augustus, Horace nursed a latent fear to the end. The "impious wars" had been a vengeance on Rome for its sins which might not yet be fully expiated; though he rejoiced in the defense of the Roman frontiers, he continued to cast worried glances at the fierce Parthians, Dacians, Spaniards, and other foes round about who might yet drag down the state. Not until the last two books of the *Odes* did he manifest any vision of Rome's destiny, and then only in pale reflection of Virgil. Horace dared not look far either into the future or into the past.

In his inner pessimism and in his need for a support Horace must have resembled many men of his age. Some explained life in terms of money, luxury, or the race for position; others more sensitively fastened on Providence and a sense of Roman destiny. A goodly number must have remained in the quandary of Horace, still seeking a firm foundation on which to construct their lives, and the poet probably had many companions when he found—for a time—the end of his search in the Augustan restoration of peace and order.

First came his introduction to Maecenas by Virgil, most probably in the spring of 38 B.C.; then, after nine months, the wealthy patron of the arts accepted Horace as client and friend. Though Horace's personal life was thenceforth on a firm footing, he did not immediately change his political views; even in 35 he listed as old friends various adherents of Antony. By the later 30's, however, Horace had begun to express in odes his hope that the new Caesar would preserve the Roman state; by the time of Actium he was voicing the attack on Cleopatra as no other could level it. In the conversion of Horace from the black pessimist of the days just after Philippi to the celebrant of Actium one can sense how generally

Italy had swung to the support of Octavian in the 30's and how fiercely men may have clung to his program as an anchor for hope. That Horace genuinely supported Octavian seems clear; the ring of sincerity in his early odes is unmistakable when one compares them to the later frigid celebrations of Actium by such men as Propertius.

The most casual reading of the *Odes* of Horace reveals that the poet accepted Augustus for two main reasons: his protection of the "falling empire" against external and internal foes, and his efforts at social reform. The themes reappear frequently, as does Augustus himself. After Actium Horace engaged in as direct adulation of Augustus as any poet of his age and came remarkably close to making him a god on earth. His rounded appreciation of the Augustan achievement is most compactly expressed in the prayer to Augustus to return to Rome:

> To thy country give again, blest leader, the light of thy presence! For when, like spring, thy face has beamed upon the folk, more pleasant runs the day, and brighter shines the sun . . . For when [Caesar] is here, the ox in safety roams the pastures; Ceres and benign Prosperity make rich the crops; safe are the seas o'er which our sailors course; Faith shrinks from blame; polluted by no stain, the home is pure; customs and law have stamped out the taint of sin; mothers win praise because of children like unto their sires; while Vengeance follows close on guilt.
>
> Who would fear the Parthian, who the icy Scythian, who the hordes rough Germany doth breed, while Caesar lives unharmed? Who would mind the war in wild Iberia? On his own hillside each man spends the day, and weds his vines to the unwedded trees; thence gladly repairs to the feast, and at its close invokes thee as a god.[15]

Here Horace assembled the themes with which later poets were to flatter their rulers for generations to come.

The relations of Horace and Augustus are not to be summed up simply. The poet had a genuine respect for the ruler, and in return he felt that Augustus should respect his poetic pen. Proud of his profession, Horace was not backward in urging that Augustus foster the poets who preserved the reputation of the ruler, formed the youth, and sang due praise to heaven; when a learned lawyer warned Horace that he might be accused of slander in his *Satires,* the poet boldly claimed that Caesar would protect him.

Beyond this confidence in Augustus' report, however, there was always a stiffness between the two, the responsibility for which clearly

15 *Odes* 4.5.5–8, 17–32.

lay with Horace. To Maecenas' requests that he write an epic about the Augustan wars he gave repeated refusals; on feeble grounds he declined the post of private secretary to the *princeps*. Letters addressed to him by Augustus reveal not only the modesty Augustus could assume but also the poet's reluctance to enter a close friendship. "Do you fear," said the master of the world to the freedman's son, "that you will be reproved by posterity for seeming to be an intimate of ours?" [16]

These letters make evident the diffidence which is implicit in Horace's verse. Why then the gulf? The political cleavage is the simplest to see; even to Horace some of the barriers between subject and master were probably apparent. He was the son of an Italian town which had not supported Octavian. He himself had stood by Brutus. His spiritual attachment lay primarily to the noble classes of Rome. The citizen poet might accept phases of the Augustan program insofar as they countered his own deep worry about the future of Rome; he might often slip thankfully into an unpolitical ease of life; but to the extent that he kept in his heart the duties of a citizen he could not blindly move from acceptance of Augustus as a personal savior to an endorsement of the entire Augustan system. Nonetheless, it is also true that neither Horace nor his friends boggled at the fact that Augustus alone bore the burdens of the Roman state.

To the restoration of old cults Horace gave, in my judgment, only lip service. Again, despite his expressed hopes, he does not seem to have felt entirely that the moral reforms of the ruler could actually succeed. The famous Roman Odes (c. 28–26 B.C.), which have often been called a celebration of Augustus, are rather an incomplete reflection by a patriot on the virtues by which Rome had grown great and a warning on the sins to which it and its citizens were liable; scholars have even thought they detected therein criticisms of Augustan policies. Though the last of this group begins by urging the restoration of old cults, it ends:

Our parents' age, worse than our grandsires', has brought forth us less worthy and destined soon to yield an offspring still more wicked.[17]

The grumbling pessimism of Horace was too deep to yield entirely to the vision of a new age Augustus was trying to create; of all the Augustan poets Horace was the least willing to surrender his realistic view of the world to a romantic evocation of either past or future.

These factors played their part in separating the minds of poet and emperor, but another, more basic cause lay deeper in the spirit of Horace, so deep indeed that he may not have been conscious of the manner in which it pushed him away from Augustus. This factor turns up in his later works whenever he assumes the philosopher's garb.

Although a withdrawal from life had always been implicit in Horace's tendency to soft indolence, he devoted himself in his last years ever more to contemplating the purpose of life. In his profession of philosophy, partly Epicurean but now tinged more with Stoicism, he reverted once more to his attacks on wealth, amid which a more somber note began to sound. He rejected his patron's effort to draw him once more in his old poetic vein, and his rejection led him to inquire in one epistle whether it is better to make money by any possible means or to stand "free and erect" before overbearing Fortune. In the end he reiterated the old Stoic doctrine of the wise man with a sardonic twist:

> He's wealthy, he is free,
> Honored, and handsome—king of kings is he;
> And, best of all, he's sound—unless, suppose,
> A nasty rheum has caught him by the nose.[18]

The ideal of *libertas,* not a common one in Horace's earlier verse, appeared repeatedly in the *Epistles.* Generally the word is embedded in Stoic commonplaces. Of the poet's sincerity, however, there can be no doubt, for he himself drew the practical application of these commonplaces to his own life in that insolent yet pathetic epistle to Maecenas in which he refused to return to Rome on the patron's request. Maecenas, he claimed, did not make him rich merely to enforce obedience, but if the poet must give up all to be free he would: "I would not exchange my ease and my freedom for all the wealth of Araby." [19] There lurks in the *Epistles* a feeling that the poet's freedom of thought, the true freedom of man, is seriously endangered by the temptation of gifts of gold.

Horace had begun—unconsciously, I think—to feel that the Empire meant esthetic dictation and to brood upon its results. In his youth the natural resilience of that stage of life had been reinforced by his personal and patriotic relief at the restoration of order; but as his hair grayed and his paunch fattened, the security of his Sabine farm could no longer content him.

From Maecenas, who had tried to direct his pen, Horace turned away in these later years. Augustus he could not escape so easily. The

---

[18] *Epistles* 1.1.106–108 (Murison). [19] *Epistles* 1.7.35–36.

Secular Hymn (17 B.C.) was a command performance, the Fourth Book of the *Odes* (17–13 B.C.) was composed on Augustus' request, and Horace had to write an epistle on literary criticism specifically for Augustus (c. 14 B.C.). In all these later works Horace gave what was desired, even to the point of fulsome adulation; but the formal tone was unmistakable. Horace was no true poet laureate of Augustus.

Against these direct commands of Augustus Horace did not openly rebel. The relation of ruler and poets was nevertheless on his mind; for proof, one needs turn only to the epistle which he addressed to Augustus, for the work is in large part a careful analysis of this very relationship. Horace frankly admitted that poets were in essence bought by Augustus, but he did not consciously object to poets' accepting commissions to sing of royal patrons. Poets must live, and in ancient society they could live only by patronage. So Horace urged Augustus to continue his support, partly on the high grounds that the poet was a seer but more cynically on the claim that Augustus' fame would thus be preserved in enduring verse—Virgil and Varius, for instance, had well merited imperial approval.

In judging the position of Horace one must remember that the poet did not uphold freedom of speech as an absolute virtue. His epistle to Augustus commented on the Fescennine verses of early Rome as being free in nature until they were perverted to cruel license; then a law at last restrained such abuse and men returned to "civil speech and e'en delightful jokes." [20] Here perhaps he might be saying what he knew Augustus wished to hear, but in the *Ars Poetica* Horace bluntly called the freedom of Athenian comedy excessive and violent, "deserving to be checked by law."

The pattern of Horace's relations with Augustus is a most revealing one, even though the evidence may not be pushed too far. Here was a man whom Augustus first won, and then essentially lost; for his return to philosophy in his later days seems to indicate he had not found all that he had desired in the Augustan system. He could not refuse the direct orders of the ruler, but the adulation of his last odes rather made apparent than disguised a certain detachment in his soul.

Only when an act of Augustus appealed to his patriotic spirit did Horace reveal any real emotion. In his patriotism, even more in his disdain for the masses and in his usual emphasis that true worth depends more on birth than on wealth, he reflected the aristocratic ideas of his

[20] *Epistles* 2.1.155 (Murison).

own age perhaps more sincerely than he did the ideas of its ruler. The appeal which Horace has always had in aristocratic societies is not accidental.

Pessimistic in his youth, he was again pessimistic and almost cynical in his old age, for his search for security was essentially in vain. He could sense the serious consequences of the decay of the old group loyalties of family and state, and in proclaiming those consequences he acted as a prophet for the community. Yet he was himself an individual who could not submerge his mind in the pursuit of any ideal. Only in his attack on materialism and in his emphasis on simplicity does Horace link onto the main currents of the next century. The men of this era could produce their own despondency, and they turned to Virgil rather than to Horace for comfort and a humane view of man.

Livy

Virgil penetrated the depths, and Horace reflected the surface, of the Augustan Age. These two men stood closest to Augustus of all the writers of the era, and in their works his program of reconstruction found clearest literary expression. Here too the relations between state and thinker were most direct—and most disturbing. The Augustan Age, however, had in its pattern other threads, not all of which drew so close to the central figure of the ruler.

The greatest prose writer was the historian Livy (59 B.C.–A.D. 17), who fixed the picture of republican Rome for all succeeding generations. Modern scholars have often argued that in his work Livy aimed at a legitimation of the Augustan system; to proponents of this argument Livy was an agent of imperial propaganda in prose as Virgil was in verse. That coincidences do exist between Livy's view of republican history and that of Augustus is undeniable, but these correlations prove very little.

To argue that the history of Livy represented first and foremost Augustan propaganda is essentially to repeat the old attack on Livy's integrity as an historian. His use of earlier authorities was far from the uncritical affair it is sometimes represented to be; and his view of the historian's role was a high one. Not only is there no reason to assume he abdicated his intellectual honesty when he came to the most recent period, but a remark of Tacitus that Augustus called Livy a Pompeian would seem to show most positively that he remained independent of the ruler—and that Augustus openly noted his position.

In his preface Livy ignored the emperor, and thereby departed widely from general practice; even such detached contemporaries as the architect Vitruvius did not fail to invoke imperial blessings on their pens. This preface, moreover, does not seem to reveal a spirit that Augustus would entirely have appreciated. Livy, as he frankly confessed, turned to the past to "avert my gaze from the troubles which our age has been witnessing for so many years." The national character, once so great, had degenerated ever more and had at last tumbled into its present ruin, "when we can bear neither our vices nor our cures"—a statement which would be most puzzling if Livy really endorsed the Augustan plans of reform.

When Livy considered history, he did so as a Roman and not as a blind follower of an Augustan "line." The Elder Seneca, his contemporary, praised Livy as a most impartial judge of character; in Livy's conservative view of the last century of the Republic, in his disapproval of military rule, in his fears for the tottering state, and in his emphasis on the simple virtues which had built up Rome, Livy expressed the judgment of the Augustan Age without thereby being a mere parrot of its ruler.

It would be more just to take Livy as an admirable example of the judicious acceptance of Augustus by thinking men. On the one side Augustus must have appreciated at least the intense patriotism of the historian, who created a panorama of the divinely destined greatness of Rome and emphasized the moral grandeur of the Roman character. The man from Gades who traveled to Rome merely to see Livy and then went back home to Spain was one of many in the Augustan Age who revered the past; Augustus himself did his utmost to bind his own person to this love of old heroes.

Livy, on the other hand, respected the role of Augustus in pacifying the Roman world and felt a certain sympathy with his attempt to restore the ancestral religion of Rome. Livy, unlike Horace, was not averse to moving in court circles, where Augustus welcomed him. The historian encouraged the young Claudius, step-grandson of the ruler, in his historical efforts, though perhaps on the wrong subject, for family pressure stopped the youth from giving a "frank or true" account of the wars of Octavian.[21] If it were really Livy who picked this subject, he seems to have manifested his independence of judgment to a remarkable degree.

[21] Suetonius, *Claudius* 41.1–2.

Propertius

Even further removed from Augustus, both in spirit and in person, was Propertius (c. 50–after 16 B.C.). This Umbrian poet made a name for himself in his early twenties by publishing a volume of elegies, the *Monobiblos*, in honor of his mistress Cynthia. The *Monobiblos* contains no praise whatever of the ruler, though it was presumably composed in the days after Actium. The men and women who bought the book in great numbers had looked upon Octavian's great triumphal procession in 29 B.C.; here they heard of the endless groans of lovers parted, their brief, fiery ecstasies, the incantations of those who can draw down the moon, and all the other themes, always old and always new, which appear in its lines.

Whereas the *Monobiblos* sang almost exclusively of his love, the three succeeding books of Propertius' verse showed a significant change. The course of love ran no smoother than is its wont. Poor Propertius seems to have lost his faithless Cynthia irretrievably by the end of the Third Book, when he rejoiced at finding his wits again and cursed her with the wrinkles of old age. The rejoicing was the appropriate hollow mockery for such an occasion, and Propertius was brought by the whole affair (and perhaps by his passage into middle age) to look with more jaundiced eye upon the state of morals and life in the Rome which lay about him.

Not for him, however, Horatian, philosophic disquisitions on avarice; Propertius attacked the immorality of his day with a vigor which betrayed an all-too-close acquaintance with the subjects of his castigation. Why quiz where one slut got her money? "Too happy Rome in our day, if it is a question of one single girl transgressing good behaviour. . . . You shall sooner be able to dry up the waters of the sea and with earthly hand pluck down the high stars, than avail to make our girls eschew their sins." [22] Against the Propertian backdrop of moral corruption and goldseeking the Augustan efforts at social reform become more explicable, even though Propertius did not endorse them.

Another major reason for a change in Propertius' tone lay in his acceptance of the patronage of Maecenas. The linking together of this poet of love and the minister of Augustus appears extraordinary; yet Maecenas not only took the poet into his friendship after the publication of the

[22] 2.32.43–44, 49–51 (Phillimore).

Monobiblos but also did his utmost to bend the new addition to the support of the Augustan program.

Outwardly Maecenas was successful. Though Propertius never refers to a direct acquaintance with Augustus, he named him frequently in the last three books of elegies, which cover the period to at least 16 B.C. This praise was of a conventional order, halfway between that of the Horatian odes and the heavy-handed adulation by Ovid; but in his very conventionality Propertius may reflect more clearly than any other Augustan author the picture which the Augustan Age drew of its leader—the victor in foreign wars from Parthia to Britain, to whom even India bent; the protector of Rome against rascally Antony and vile Cleopatra; the merciful in victory; the new Romulus descended from Aeneas; the very god in person. Two elegies repeated in developed detail the Virgilian picture of the threat of Cleopatra; at other points, too, Propertius' verse shows how Rome turned to Virgil for illumination on its purpose.

Although skillful of pen and guided by Virgil, Propertius inevitably marred his praise of Augustus and of Rome by jarring notes. Throughout the Second and Third Books Cynthia kept turning up to distract Propertius, but even when she was absent or dead he could not screw his spirit up to the right tone for long. Nor would Propertius write on the aspects of Augustus' prowess which Maecenas suggested. More stubborn even than Horace, the poet affectionately but obstinately rebuffed his patron's persistence in no less than five elegies, which may owe something to Hellenistic models but yet ring true. The modern argument that Propertius really opposed Augustus is made of thin cloth, but certainly of all those who sang for Maecenas and Augustus he had the least sympathy with or understanding of the Augustan program— and was too ingenuous to mask his opinion.

After cheering on the men who were to fight in the East against Parthia, Propertius announced he would stay home and clap his hands on the Sacred Way when the triumphal procession swung by; hard upon an elegy ordering Rome to pray for long life to Augustus, the conqueror of Cleopatra, Propertius did his best to sap the morale of an Augustan warrior by picturing what his wife would think and feel in his absence. His heroines eagerly desired peace, but not that peace envisaged by Augustus which first required wars on the distant frontiers. To the line of Horace, " 'Tis sweet and glorious to die for fatherland," Propertius replied in covert defiance of Augustan social views, "None of my blood will ever be a soldier." Small wonder that in two epistles Horace took sharp issue both with the hedonistic philosophy and with the style of this Roman Callimachus!

His comprehension of the religious and moral reforms of Augustus was as scant as his belief in devotion to the state. He sang of Apollo in proper style, cursed Isis—because she kept him from his mistress' couch on certain nights—and mourned the spider's webs on the temples; but the celebration of religious antiquities in the Fourth Book was no more than dutiful. On the moral reforms of the ruler he could not go even this far. Earlier he had expressed his joy at the repeal of one part of Augustus' social legislation which might have forced him to marry and so to part from his love; Jupiter himself, said the poet, could not part two lovers against their will, or could Caesar's laws. When his interlocutor interjected that "Caesar is mighty," the lover retorted, "Nay, Caesar is mighty in arms; conquest of nations is worth nothing in love," and asserted he would rather lose his head than give up his adored one.[23] The flippancy does not entirely mask his obduracy; and his doubt of the efficacy of official reforms is clear in his question, "What is the good for girls to found temples of Chastity when any bride may be anything you please?"[24]

The view of this poet was a limited one, and his reflection of contemporary Rome, though clear in some aspects which do not appear so well elsewhere, was far from complete. Only once did Propertius reveal any independent sense of the wellsprings of Roman power. His last elegy commemorated with stately dignity the memory of a noble Roman matron, faithful to husband and family blood, remembered in the sons and daughter she left behind. Propertius portrayed her as admonishing her daughter to copy the mother and hold fast by one husband:

And you all must support the breed by your line: I put out from shore in my bark with a cheerful heart to think there are so many of my people to enlarge my destinies.[25]

From the frank delight in sex of the *Monobiblos* to this noble reflection of the enduring strength of the Roman aristocracy was a mighty leap, which Propertius could make only once. Pressure from above may have forced him to produce one more book than otherwise we would have, but it could not drive him, as it had Virgil, on to an epic; nor, on the other hand, was it an outside effort to direct his verse which made him

[23] 2.7.1–10 (Phillimore).   [24] 2.6.25–26 (Phillimore).
[25] 4.11.69–70 (Phillimore).

stop. His great passion ended, this poet of the tender warfare of Venus had nothing more to say and so was silent.

Tibullus and Pollio

Virgil and Horace, Livy and Propertius are the loftiest peaks in an age which saw much writing. Most of the other authors of the era, Latin and Greek, in court circles or outsiders, fell quickly into a convention of eulogizing Augustus. The one Roman who knew Augustus but yet spoke of him in a reasonably neutral tone was the biographer Cornelius Nepos (c. 99–24), who was a hang-over from an older generation. Those who did not care to flatter judged it best not to name the ruler in their works; thus the second Roman elegist, Tibullus (c. 48–19), never mentions Augustus or his lieutenants.

Tibullus, Lygdamus, Sulpicia, and various anonymous authors whose works are preserved in the Tibullan collection and the Virgilian Appendix formed a literary circle grouped about M. Valerius Messalla Corvinus (64 B.C.–A.D. 8). Messalla Corvinus had fought for Brutus and Cassius and then for Antony, but transferred his allegiance to Octavian in the 30's. Nevertheless, he resigned the post of governor of Rome after holding it only six days in 26 B.C., on the grounds that the position was incompatible with the republican constitution. The conjunction of this spectacular event with Tibullus' silence on Augustus has often led modern historians to suspect that the circle was opposed to the *princeps*.

Such an argument pushes silence farther than it can safely be construed. Messalla Corvinus undoubtedly felt that the position of "first citizen" must have its limits, but that was the very attitude Augustus tried to take; and this great noble was quite willing to serve in a variety of other capacities under Augustus—it was he who eventually proposed the title *pater patriae* for Augustus in 2 B.C. Several literary figures who praised Augustus, including not only Valgius Rufus and Ovid in later days but also Horace himself, had connections with Messalla Corvinus.

Again, Tibullus was not completely devoid of appreciation for certain achievements of the Augustan Age. While for the most part he sang only of his patron, of love, and of idyllic country life, he could also comment on the rusting of arms and the joy of peace. In one elegy of his Second Book he summoned Phoebus Apollo as the guardian of Actium and urged him to be gentle with Rome. His servant, the Sibyl, had not deceived Rome in giving the prophecy of its founding to Aeneas; now the wars were ended, and peace could come. If Tibullus had not heard the *Aeneid,* at least in part, he betrays a clear knowledge of some of its main themes.

All that can be argued from the existence of a circle about Messalla Corvinus is the fact that the emperor did not entirely dominate the literary scene in Rome and that some poets, like Tibullus, felt no need to flatter the ruler even while attached to other patrons. In this sense Messalla Corvinus and Tibullus are survivals from the Late Republic, which had had many literary cliques; but the mere fact that they were anachronisms does not necessarily imply that they consciously opposed the towering figure of Augustus.

To detect any literary antagonism to Augustus, even in veiled terms, one must turn to Asinius Pollio (76 B.C.–A.D. 4), though even here the extent of antagonism has often been much exaggerated. Pollio had followed first Caesar and then Antony, down to 39 B.C., when he retired from public life. His retirement perhaps expressed a political judgment, for in the rise of Octavian he apparently saw the end of any hope for *libertas* (in the sense of senatorial domination). He seems, nevertheless, to have trusted Octavian's moderation far enough to feel secure in reverting once more to his literary studies. Pollio was really a scholar, who had been forced out of his study in the civil wars because he desired "peace and liberty." [26]

His history of the civil wars is lost, but enough survives in later writers to show that he adopted a remarkably independent attitude; the war between Octavian and Antony to him was merely a contest to see who would be the master. It is probable, however, that he was careful not to stir up too far the "fires hidden beneath treacherous ashes" by making his charge of slavery as explicit as Dio Cassius was later to put it; [27] Pollio, indeed, seems to have been more interested in the nature of leaders and their interplay in events than in ideas as such. Nor did he venture to bring his story down to the war of Actium. By the date of this event he had definitely broken with Antony, but we have no reason to assume that he accepted Octavian's picture of his defense of Italy against an Oriental menace; in such a situation he may have found silence the best solution.

Pollio was the complete critic. His biting remarks about the literary works of Caesar, Sallust, Cicero, and Livy and his lukewarmness toward

[26] Cicero, *To His Friends* 10.31 (Asinius Pollio, 43).
[27] Horace, *Odes* 2.1.8, on Pollio's history.

the conservative senatorial wing warn us against taking too seriously the stories reported of his defiant independence before Augustus; Pollio would have found flaws in a saint and enjoyed being in opposition to the currents of his day. He affected an archaism ill in keeping with the literary trends of the Augustan Age, and in later years he patronized grammarians and declaimers rather more than poets, even though he was a perceptive critic of poetry. Virgil eventually threw off Pollio's effort to turn him to imitate the Alexandrian poets; Horace, however, remained on good terms with Pollio down into the 20's.

The deft judgment of Augustus neatly manifested itself in his tolerant endurance of the grumbling Pollio, who may have attracted to himself whatever there was of literary opposition in Augustan Rome. The unsavory historian Timagenes, for one, turned to Pollio when he was barred from the ruler's house, even though previously the two had been at odds. Augustus merely quipped that Pollio was keeping a menagerie and neatly sidestepped Pollio's assertion that he would ban Timagenes if Augustus so desired.

Seneca the Younger, who tells us the story in the days of Nero, was obviously impressed by the fact that Rome still lionized Timagenes despite Augustus' disapproval. The really remarkable aspect of the career of Timagenes, however, is not the popularity he may have gained from opposing Augustus but the fact that he was able to voice a very critical view of Roman domination of the world and yet remain a favorite of Rome's upper circles. As Seneca reports in another place:

[Timagenes] used to say that the only reason he was grieved when conflagrations occurred in Rome was his knowledge that better buildings would arise than those which had gone down in the flames.[28]

Augustan Literature

Both Pollio and Timagenes have their importance as a source of Augustan history independent of the major, official tradition. Plutarch and Appian certainly utilized Pollio later; within Augustus' lifetime Pompeius Trogus drew on Timagenes and echoed his hostility to Rome. Yet Augustus could afford to tolerate such manifestations of independence, for they were trifling stuff. The general conclusion to be drawn from a survey of the literature of the Augustan Age—that period down to the death of Horace—remains unaffected: like the architects and sculptors, the writers celebrated both the benign person of Augustus and

[28] Seneca, *Epistles* 91.13.

his program for the restoration of Rome, and in their celebration make clearer to us the meaning of the temples and statues. The literary men were, in the main, willing to portray Augustus in the most glowing terms; of divine character in Horace and Virgil, he was an outright god in Propertius. Almost without exception they had the same view of the history of the Late Republic and of the civil wars as that which Augustus took over from the aristocracy. At least outwardly they accepted his projects of restoration which arose inevitably out of that interpretation of moral and religious decay.

The facts are obvious, and the conclusion seems all too simple: the men of the Augustan Age were merely hireling mouthpieces of imperial propaganda. The charge is common, but those who levy it fail either to comprehend the inner drive of these writers or to understand the relations of the political leader and his *milieu*.

Even though such writers as Horace and Propertius echoed an old claim when they foresaw that they would live forever in their works, they were nonetheless sincere in asserting a high place for the poet as an independent prophet of society and servant of the state, who propitiated the gods for Rome. If the major Latin authors displayed an intense feeling of Roman patriotism, it does not necessarily follow that Augustus taught them to speak thus. Augustus neatly linked his own claims and aims to much that was implicit in the Augustan Age; and at times the poets themselves may have led the way in showing to the ruler the true value of Rome. Poets such as Horace and Propertius and Ovid quoted the *Aeneid;* so too did the rhetoricians of the Augustan Age— and so too did Augustus.

In fine, the quality of sincerity cannot be denied to these men merely because they and Augustus sounded the same notes. The outpouring of genius which we call the Augustan Age was a product of the earlier synthesis of Greco-Roman civilization in the days of Cicero, of the deep relief of men at the salvation of the Roman state and the return of peace, and only in third degree of the financial and personal encouragement of the ruler and his aides. When a humble provincial proclaimed Augustus as savior and worshiped him, when the great poet Virgil sang his thanks to the man who restored peace to Italy, both may have had in their hearts kindred feelings.

And yet there are somber tones to the reign of the first *princeps*. Augustus did consciously exert pressure on the thinkers of his age by methods which have already been partly suggested; to these I shall return shortly. This pressure, again, did warp them. Virgil did not write under Augustus as he might otherwise have written. The pen of Horace faltered as the poet reflected upon the world about him, and finally halted. With that halt the Augustan Age came to an end, and the dull mediocrity of the Empire began. Worse yet, before Augustus died, Ovid's verse had helped to bring him exile, and the prose of other men had been officially burned. The Augustan peace promised fair when it helped to produce the *Aeneid,* but that promise had withered decades before Augustus died; taken as a whole, the reign of Augustus foreshadows the Early Empire.

X

Emperors, Aristocrats, and Thinkers

TO THE thinkers of the Early Empire that structure gave the benefits of peace and prosperity. Men wrote endless verse and prose; emperors and cities built lavishly; sculptors turned out works in great profusion. Some of this product has come down to us and has its modern admirers; but in imperial Latin literature or sculpture after Augustus there is no Virgil, no Altar of Augustan Peace. The simple truth is that classical civilization was treading a dreary path which led to the pompous sterility of the second century.

Against its thinkers the Empire also erected restraints by which their thought was curbed and canalized. These restraints, both social and political in nature, had evil effects, but the potency of such limitations must be assessed judiciously; above all one must not rashly lay the forthcoming sterility exclusively to their account.

Aristocratic and Imperial Controls

The sources of these pressures were essentially twofold—the emperors and the upper classes. In many respects both elements followed the same lines, for the Caesars long sprang from the cultured classes; but if one must have place ahead of the other, the pressure of the upper classes is surely far more significant. The thinker who desires to be understood by his age must always bend his thought to suit the attitudes of the dominant classes of society.

In the Empire class distinctions were sharp, and were based on culture as well as birth and wealth. The local upper classes thus tended in the first two centuries of the Empire to make themselves appear as Greco-Roman as possible in name, in mode of life, in architectural and sculptural styles, and so on. Since these circles bought most of the items made in ancient markets, local cultures tended ever more to sink out of sight below a veneer of dull copying of old Greek and Roman motifs. Though the uneducated in Asia Minor, for instance, still spoke Phrygian, Lycaonian, and other native tongues, the language of inscriptions was almost invariably Greek, rarely Latin; in families holding Roman citizenship even Greek names disappeared temporarily. In Asia Minor as on the Rhine and elsewhere the old cultures were still actually present and can still be detected, especially in art, in the heyday of the Empire. Later they reasserted themselves more strongly and in that assertion heralded the breakup of the Empire. For the nonce, nonetheless, it is still true that the dominant classes generally frowned on local ways.

The extent to which men who adhered to old customs suffered an indirect persecution cannot be estimated. The central government encouraged but did not require Romanization except in the case of the army and the administration. The Empire, like the Republic, tended to protect cultural and religious minorities against overly violent attack by their neighbors, while yet standing squarely behind the effort to turn villages and tribes into cities and to give these municipalities a Greco-Roman dress. Most local cultures, at least in the West, were not vocal enough to furnish conscious opposition; those elements in the East which dreamed of an Oriental deliverer expressed their dreams in surreptitious winks and whispers. Conservative adherents to non-Mediterranean ways, one suspects, found themselves frequently passed over in admission to Roman citizenship or election to local office and suffered other forms of the petty persecution which men visit on their nonconforming fellows. Culturally as well as politically the Empire appeared ever more unified, and local variation decreased as men looked to the cosmopolitan center, Rome, for the latest fashions in thought.

In the arts the upper classes—and the Caesars—influenced both style and substance, for they were the men who gave commissions to artists and architects. The congregation of men in law courts, baths, and palaces required buildings on a grand scale; in its domed structures and vaulted basilicas Rome created new architectural types of significance for the future. So too an imperial style of portraiture quickly arose, which cast both imperial personages and their friends into a common mold everywhere. Though Roman art never created the image of a god, it did throw up the symbol of an earthly savior, the emperor (see Frontispiece), and gave to that ideal "something of the quality of great religious art." [1]

Within the general frame of imperial art the esthetic preferences of each emperor had a considerable influence on the official art of his reign, whether the material was statuary or coins. Nero's coins, thus, rose to a very high artistic level through the combination of Roman vividness with Greek modes of expression; the same quality and, to a considerable extent, the same spirit can be seen in the frescoes of Nero's Golden House, which furnished inspiration to Raphael and other painters of the Renaissance, and in Neronian statuary. Few of the emperors, however, supported the arts for abstract motives, and their stylistic preferences seem rarely to have countered the general trend of their era. The turn to the classical in the Augustan Age was one which Augustus shared, rather than instigated. The imperial system did not draw styles of art into the political sphere as Nazi and Communist ideologies have done in more recent times.

In a broader sense the taste of the Empire ran to the exploitation of lines already established in the Hellenistic world; the archaistic sterility of the second century was the product not of imperial pressure but of aristocratic attitudes. There were, indeed, vigorous debates over esthetic issues. Under Augustus the architect Vitruvius roundly disapproved of the appearance of monsters in paintings and shuddered at the impressionistic style, where thin stalks replaced columns and candelabra supported shrines from which tendrils twisted in all directions; like the old-fashioned critic he was, Vitruvius bluntly stated, "Pictures cannot be approved which do not resemble reality." [2]

This unreality, nevertheless, meets one again and again on the walls of Pompeii, which were decorated under the Julio-Claudian rulers, and early imperial art manifests other aspects which heralded an artistic revolution in the future. The governing elements of the Mediterranean world desired to be conservative, but unwittingly fostered esthetic developments which were irreconcilable with the basic premises of Greco-Roman civilization.

Of music little can be said. There may be revolutions in symphonies,

[1] Eugénie Strong, *Cambridge Ancient History* 10, 562.
[2] Vitruvius, *On Architecture* 7.5.4.

as the saying goes, but we do not have the necessary material to judge the, music written and played either in the Auditorium of Maecenas or in any other concert hall of the Early Empire. In its serious works music undoubtedly had to satisfy the taste of the aristocratic classes, which frowned, as always, on the looser, more seductive ditties that appealed to the common folk. Dio Chrysostom thus urged Trajan to banish

indecent dancing and the lascivious posturing of women in licentious dances as well as the shrill and riotous measures played on the flute, syncopated music full of discordant tunes, and motley combinations of noisy clanging instruments.[3]

Such moralists were willing to sell every intellectual freedom—especially of the lower classes—for the sake of improving their fellows, but the emperors did not venture as a rule to deprive their subjects of the "lascivious melodies of our effeminate stage"[4] or to control the stage save as a source of political disorder.

The one exception, Nero, was a virtuoso on the lyre whose efforts to secure applause were at once amusing and terrifying. One may doubt the stories that a man had to feign death to get out of one of Nero's concerts or that once the door was shut pregnant women had to give birth to their young within the hall; still, absence was dangerous, and the faces of those present were scrutinized by open and secret agents. The later emperor Vespasian could not help falling asleep at one imperial recital; on this count he was rebuked by a freedman, or in another version was banished from the court for a time.

Rhythmical acclamations of famous men had been known since the Republic and had been rendered to the rulers from Caesar's day, but to improve the quality and certainty of this praise Nero formed in 59 an organizing cheering section, the Augustiani, from the younger equestrians and plebeians. Numbering five thousand, dressed in distinctive fashion and carefully subdivided, the group was trained in the Alexandrian mode of rhythmical applause, which must have been its main practical objective; it has also been suggested that Nero thus was attempting to group the young nobles about him in Hellenistic style as a bodyguard and to lead them from military training of the Augustan type to emphasis on music and Greek games.

Throughout the rest of his reign this band of young bullies appeared at his musical recitals. In 66–67 it accompanied him to Greece, where the

---

[3] *Oration* 2.55–56.   [4] Quintilian, *Institutes* 1.10.31.

four great games of ancient dignity were arbitrarily crowded into one year so that the emperor might receive their awards; for this purpose Olympia held a musical competition, contrary to its custom. Here or elsewhere the emperor forced an old master of the lyre to compete against him; not content with the glory of victory, Nero mutilated the statues of his rival.

To ensure an even wider circulation of his songs, some were inscribed on the temple of Jupiter Capitolinus in gold letters, and a collection of the works was published under the title *Domenicum.* The scholiast on Persius asserted that Nero's poems were used in school; the third-century author Philostratus has a tale that in Neronian Rome some unspecified source had hired a man to go about the city singing Nero's songs. "Anyone who neglected to listen to him or refused to pay him for his music, he had the right to arrest for violating Nero's majesty." [5] Though the story is probably fabricated, the atmosphere does not seem entirely fictitious. No other emperor went so far in the arts and in music.

On literature the pressure of the Caesars was more conscious and continuous from the days of Augustus. To some degree the first *princeps* had been interested in matters of style and had brought the subject into the field of politics by criticizing the style of Antony as rhetorical, over-luxurious, and given to the use of old words. When Maecenas instigated Virgil to find a new style in the *Georgics,* not overrich nor overthin but of common words with hidden tones, his advice may have had political as well as literary significance; so too the archaistic affectation of Asinius Pollio may have been a political manifesto.

Augustus, however, was concerned chiefly with substance. Horace clearly had this conception in mind in advising the ruler that poetry was of purely practical value not only to the state but also to the emperor, and Augustus' writings displayed the same practicality. The one tragedy which he composed, the *Ajax,* he never published; his hero, he jested, had fallen on a sponge. What did see the light of day were his early autobiography, a political pamphlet on Cato, a life of his lieutenant Drusus, and the summation of his reign, the *Res Gestae.* When he fostered "the talents of his age," he was essaying to win men's minds and to influence the judgment of posterity, or alternatively to turn men from political activity.

[5] Philostratus, *Life Of Apollonius* 4.39 (Kayser ed., p. 158).

This effort was far from crude, for both Augustus and Maecenas were skillful men. By jest, friendly letter, or gentle hint they conveyed their desires, and if the poet were temporarily unreceptive these patient patrons were willing to wait and try again another time. The *Aeneid,* the Fourth Book of Horace's *Odes* and his *Secular Hymn,* the later elegies of Propertius—all these are to some degree the necessary payment by the client to his patron.

The sordid note of financial support had an undeniable place in the relations of ruler (and upper classes) and author. Many of the Augustan writers—Virgil, Propertius, and Tibullus for instance—had lost their land in the confiscations of 41–40 B.C.; Horace and others had never been well endowed with this world's goods. Both then and later most authors found it necessary to attach themselves to a patron if they were to have an entree into the upper circles of society and were to live well.

The author who could live by his sales was rare, even though publication for the market reached unusual heights in the Empire. Literacy expanded in the cities of the Caesars to a degree which it did not reach again until the eighteenth or nineteenth century, and there seems to have been a great deal of publication of the usual trash for cursory readers. The poet Martial talked much of his publishers and their prices, and groaned at the ever-present friends who requested free copies; he boasted that his works were read in the distant provinces; but he also dryly commented that lawyers, not poets, gained the riches—the latter got only the chink of kisses.

The higher the patron, the greater was the glory of the client—and at least under the first *princeps* the rewards of clientage were considerable. By his largess Maecenas made his name a synonym for literary patronage, and Augustus, unlike some later rulers, drew freely on the riches of the Empire to support the arts. "If you must write," a friend advised Horace, "have the courage to take as your subject the deeds of invincible Caesar. You will get ample pay for your trouble." [6] From Maecenas and Augustus these authors gained also that sympathetic encouragement which is always necessary for men who think, and they enjoyed the certainty of a wide audience at least in their own day. Few writers can have refused such advantages, and many sought them; the minor poetasters hoped, as Horace ironically advised Augustus, "that, as soon as you hear we are composing verses, you will go so far as kindly to send for us, banish our poverty, and compel us to write." [7]

[6] *Satires* 2.1.10–12 (Wells).   [7] *Epistles* 2.1.226–228 (Fairclough).

Subsequent Caesars continued to grant some patronage, though few were as lavish as Augustus or Nero in his earlier years. The born syco-phant Martial, for instance, caressed Titus, Domitian, Nerva, and Trajan in turn, but he gained only a legal privilege here, the grant of a water supply there, or again a little cash and the intangible stamp of official approval. Vespasian had little interest in the arts; even the emperor Claudius, himself a historian, gave little support to the works of others. From his reign comes the bleak advice of the patronage-hunter Cal-purnius Siculus: let the rustic poet break his pipes and peddle milk.

To interpret imperial patronage as all powerful or even to assess the client's product as a mere *quid pro quo* overlooks a great deal. The indi-vidual patron, whether Maecenas or Prince Esterházy, necessarily bends the artist's mind by the very act of giving, but the influence may not consciously go further. In any case the weight of patronage may be far less than the mighty economic pressure exerted by the anonymous public of today. The author who refuses to give that public exactly and always what it wishes soon finds modern publishers obdurate, but Horace or Propertius might refuse Maecenas' requests, at least in part, and yet continue to gain support. One finds extraordinary divergencies in style and thought in the circle about Maecenas, and between its mem-bers and their patron.

To control every utterance of a poet was obviously impossible, nor did it seem necessary. Neither in poetry nor in sculpture did Augustus, for example, insist on sole attention to himself; it was enough if within the general bulk of a work the picture of his person and his program was generally favorable. When a poet spoke occasionally in an unpleasing tone, Augustus at least went no further than trying to secure a later off-set; he thus requested Horace to address to him an epistle on literary criticism like those he sent to the Pisos. Horace and Propertius—and Livy too—show clearly that they were not in sympathy with various aspects of the Augustan system and particularly that they doubted the efficacy of his moral reforms, as did most of the upper classes of Rome. Horace and others seem to have desired more warlike action toward the Parthians and the British than Augustus was willing to undertake, and Augustus had carefully to justify his limited steps in these areas by edict and coins.

If one may give Augustus the intelligence which he usually showed, he surely realized that in the long run neither official patronage nor attention to the deeds of Augustus were sure guarantees of the survival of a literary work: Varius' panegyric of Augustus vanished long ago with many other honeyed chants, but the *Aeneid* still lives. To endure, an author's product had to have that true quality which comes from the author's mind, not from outside pressure; to survive even through the Roman Empire a work had to satisfy the upper classes above all.

This fact is a cardinal point in assessing the influence of the Caesars on letters. The rulers may have encouraged obsequious authors, but they wisely did not try to create an antiaristocratic faction of literary men; the absolutism of the Empire did not extend beyond the political field far into matters of culture. Men of letters were always dependent primarily on the aristocracy, both directly as their patrons and as buyers of books and indirectly as the masters of the schools.

The accusations of repression and loss of liberty which rose in imperial authors were directed primarily at the same quarters as those singled out by Horace—at the nobles who resented personal attacks and at the patrons who hired men of intellect only to prostitute their abilities. In his essay *On Salaried Posts in Great Houses* Lucian, the satirist of the second century, asserted repeatedly that one who sold himself, dazzled by the luxuries of a great Roman mansion, left behind his freedom and soon sank to such ignobilities as lecturing his patroness while she was having her toilet. Literary clients might be treated scurvily by their aristocratic "friends," but to be successful poets such as Horace and Martial had inevitably to hearken to the interests of the wealthy leaders of the Mediterranean world. Though the satirist Juvenal might apparently deviate from the pattern in excoriating the vices of the rich or in moaning the obligations of the client, he too had to seek a patron and rejoiced when Hadrian was friendly; one suspects that it was the smug rich who bought his work.

A scholastic process of literary selection and rejection is apparent on the walls of Pompeii, where schoolboys scratched lines from Virgil and Propertius. A more formal treatment of this selection was indited by the great teacher Quintilian, who devoted some space in his *Institutes* to a discussion of works which should or should not be read in schools. This treatment undoubtedly influenced many a schoolmaster's choice, and the schoolmasters were powerful in shaping the thought of the Roman Empire. The schools, moreover, always depended primarily on the aristocracy. Neither Augustus nor any of his successors in the first two centuries seriously challenged this situation; rather, they supported the structure of education by granting to teachers various exemptions from taxes, quartering of troops, and other duties, and Vespasian went further by setting up chairs for Greek and Latin rhetoricians at Rome, one of which Quintilian was the first to fill.

Very little control accompanied this imperial support; the one certain instance is an edict assigned to Domitian, which warned teachers and physicians not to teach slaves on penalty of losing their exemptions. The schools, after all, were careful to uphold established authority. Even the school of Epictetus inculcated obedience on the political level, and few other philosophers, one may be sure, would have gone even as far as Epictetus did in indicating that this obedience had moral limits. The fictitious cases of the rhetoricians carefully eschewed the political or contemporary scene; we know of only isolated instances in which Gaius and Domitian punished rhetoricians for perhaps overstepping the bounds in their fulminations against tyrants.

Between them aristocratic patrons and schoolmasters determined the survival of literature. Martial frankly admitted that his works would not be chosen by schools, but he consoled himself that the boys would read his filthy epigrams outside of class; to such extracurricular interest various Latin writers owe their preservation.

The whole tendency of the social and educational structure was to encourage writers who disseminated virtues of the aristocratic stamp. The literature of the Empire was consequently cast in a uniform style and ignored or scorned the common people. Variations in emphasis existed, but the degree of such variation was really narrow; outside that limit one may find at Rome itself only such works as the earliest Christian literature. Not only was there little addressed to the lower classes but also apart from scattered works such as the history of Velleius Paterculus the interests of the bureaucracy found little reflection. Originality in thought was not to be expected in such a world, even though the schools of the Empire were to be remarkably successful in forming a mold of civilization from which they stamped out many generations of gentlemen of a common culture.

Literary Flattery

If the authors of the Empire also made their obeisance to the Caesars, that was, from the point of view of the schools and the aristocratic readers, quite secondary though acceptable. From the point of view of the authors flattery of the emperors seemed necessary, and there were few writers from the reign of Augustus onward who did not proffer their adulation. The tendency is evident in Propertius but became overwhelming in the verse of Manilius and Ovid, both of whom eulogized the aging Augustus in extravagant terms.

There is as gross adulation in Horace as in Ovid, but between the two came a distinct change in tone which no one has ever mistaken. While Horace really sensed the values in the Augustan reforms, Ovid rolled out conventional flattery. The later historians of the reign of Augustus seem in the main to have followed the same road; Tacitus commented that "due talents were not lacking to describe the Augustan period until they were discouraged by growing adulation." [8]

The gulf between ruler and subject implicit in this obsequiousness grew steadily wider, for Augustus in his later years no longer made any serious effort to cross it and to gain the friendship of new authors. Possibly he felt he had done enough in securing his perpetuation in the verse of Horace and Virgil; the forced compliance of Propertius and Horace may have been unsatisfactory; or again he may have been too old and tired to make the effort to understand the newer men. Whatever the reason, the last years of Augustus marked the establishment of an attitude of stock adulation of the ruler which persisted in later literature. Never again did a poet take the position of Horace or Virgil, who accepted much of the Augustan program but claimed an independent vein of prophecy; thenceforth the authors of the Empire rarely ventured to demand real partnership in the establishment of ideals. Subjects rather than citizens, they eschewed matters political and filled the gap by praising the virtues of their master.

Whether the ruler desired or disliked the flattery made little difference. Tiberius rejected divine honors and frowned so harshly on senatorial references to himself as Master and the like as to interrupt orations in this tone. No author could expect any reward for fulsome flattery from Tiberius, but the literature of his reign is significantly unctuous. The pressure to elevate the ruler into the divine protector of the Roman Empire clearly came not from above but from below; deep-seated urges drove the subjects to idealize the figure in whom they embodied their hopes for order and security.

So a city in Cyprus dedicated to Tiberius both a temple and sacred image, against his general order, and others had priests for his cult; Cyzicus went so far as to hail him as the "greatest of the gods." [9]

Valerius Maximus, who had no contact with the emperor, and Velleius Paterculus, who had very little, engaged in what appeared to be the most nauseous toadying, but the remarks of neither author can be ascribed to ulterior hopes of patronage. Since the work of Valerius was designed to be a handbook of rhetorical examples for general use, one must conclude that wide elements of the Empire were quite ready to accept a book filled with praise of the ruler. Even the heir-apparent Germanicus, in translating Aratus, proclaimed that while his Greek original began with lauding Zeus he must commence by extolling Tiberius, through whose peaceful government he could write his work. One can imagine the dour face of Tiberius when he read such remarks —but they or their kind were to be addressed to one ruler after another.

Under the Caesars who sought autocracy and deification this flattery may reach a higher pitch; even so it is always difficult to weigh the desires of the ruler against the natural bent of the subjects. At the end of the century Martial and Statius attempted to perfect the sycophantic style which ran back through the Neronian poets to Ovid and even to Horace and Virgil, but it is not without significance that they redoubled their adulation of Domitian after the revolt of Antonius Saturninus in 89. The sober and sensible Quintilian, official tutor of Domitian's grandnephews, had at the beginning of his *Institutes* failed to mention the emperor; about this time he decided to repair his initial omission by inserting in the middle of his work on oratory an eulogy of Domitian. Flattery, in sum, was always raining on the master of the world, but when men felt less secure they attempted to gain security by fawning even more.

Authors who scraped the ground also inevitably gave lip service to the views of their master. Men of the Empire recognized and frequently commented on the fact that each emperor set the standards for his reign, though after his death—as in the case of Nero—those standards might be attacked. Lesser men of the court as well as provincial aristocrats shifted as he shifted—"nearly all of us live according to the standards of one man." [10]

Imperial Limitations of Literature

This conformity did not always pass beyond the superficial, and it is not proper to assume that the emperors and the upper classes were always in accord. Since the rulers moved toward absolutism during the

[10] Pliny, *Panegyric* 45.5.

first century, tension frequently arose between the emperors and segments of their subjects. Some authors redoubled their flattery, and survived; others could not always mask their thoughts, and suffered.

Although Augustus had sought conformity from the writers of the Augustan Age, he had realized that thinkers are delicate instruments and that their adhesion is better secured by blandishment than by the rude shock of sheer compulsion. In his later decades, however, he had gone further. Ovid he had forced into exile, and the books of Cassius Severus and Titus Labienus were burned with his approval. To his successors he left more than a tradition of literary patronage; they inherited also a considerable arsenal of means for applying imperial pressure.

To control books it is possible either to limit their circulation or to prevent their initial publication. Imperial supervision of the libraries of Rome continued. Tiberius gave a prominent place in the public libraries to the busts and writings of certain minor Greek authors; Gaius is reported as having planned to remove the works of Virgil and Livy from all libraries, as well as abolishing Homer's poems. These steps, however, cannot have had great significance, and we do not know of many bans on the possession or circulation of books, once published. In a few cases the burning of books was ordered after the reign of Augustus, but copies always escaped.

Hence [says Tacitus on the burning of the history of Cremutius Cordus] one cannot but smile at the dulness of those who believe that the authority of to-day can extinguish men's memories tomorrow. Nay rather, they who penalise genius do but extend its power: whether they be foreign tyrants, or imitators of foreign tyranny, they do but reap dishonour for themselves, and glory for their victims.[11]

Gaius himself revoked the senatorial bans on the works of Cassius, Labienus, and Cordus, with the unctuous remark "that it was wholly to his interest that everything which happened be handed down to posterity." [12]

There is very little evidence that the Caesars interfered in the copying halls of the publishers. The Empire had no system of censorship before publication, and the works which were condemned were usually banned *in toto*. The authors themselves had the responsibility of sensing the ruler's preferences and rewriting history in accordance therewith. A tendency, for instance, to react against the tremendous praise lavished

[11] *Annals* 4.35.6–7.   [12] Suetonius, *Gaius* 16.1.

on Augustus in his lifetime can already be detected in the Tiberian period, but under Gaius, who boasted descent also from Antony, this reaction received official sanction. The victory of Actium and the defeat of Sextus Pompey were no longer to be celebrated "on the ground that they were disastrous and ruinous to the Roman people"; [13] any reference to Agrippa, the lowborn grandfather of Gaius, immediately called down the despot's anger.

One may suspect that publishers were careful not to handle frankly seditious material, which could be accused of damaging the ruler's majesty, but very rarely did the condemnation of a man for *laesa maiestas* affect his works. Only in the case of anonymous tracts was there a legal provision against the publishers, correctors, and sellers of books; and only in one instance, under Domitian, do we hear of punitive measures against publishers. Otherwise the vast publishing business of the capital, which circulated books far afield to the provinces, seems to have been free of any legal restrictions, including copyright.

Penalties for the expression of improper thought lay primarily against the authors themselves, for the law of *maiestas* and other provisions could be directed at thinkers as well as politicians. The extent to which these means were applied depended on the rulers and their aides, and followed generally the pattern of shift between autocracy and toleration which was described earlier. Tiberius, thus, permitted men to write as they wished, while Gaius was erratically despotic and Claudius relatively indifferent. Nero was intolerant on both political and esthetic grounds; Vespasian again was tolerant and Domitian rigid; then came the relative freedom of Trajan's reign, which ushered in the second century.

Of the twelve rulers from Tiberius to Trajan, the most interesting from the point of view of their pressure on thinkers are Tiberius and Nero. The reputation of the former was thoroughly blackened by the later historian Tacitus, though Suetonius has preserved quite a different picture of his policy:

He was self-contained and patient in the face of abuse and slander, and of lampoons on himself and his family, often asserting that in a free country there should be free speech and free thought. When the Senate on one occasion demanded that cognizance be taken of such offenses and those guilty of them, he said, "We have not enough spare time to warrant involving our-

[13] Suetonius, *Gaius* 23.1.

selves in more affairs; if you open this loophole you will find no time for any other business; it will be an excuse for laying everybody's quarrels before you." [14]

Tacitus, however, brooded much on the moral and mental degradation of the victims of autocracy. When he came to write of the reign of Tiberius, he found, as he thought, adequate evidence to paint a brutal picture of the punishment of men for literary activity. In particular he singled out the most outstanding case of the era, that of A. Cremutius Cordus, and used it as a point of departure for the greatest defense of freedom of pen which we possess from the Empire.

Cremutius Cordus was a senator who had begun to write history under Augustus. Though he had read some of his work before that ruler, Cordus seems to have had a rather reserved attitude toward the Principate. He praised Brutus and called Cassius the last of the Romans (in a speech ascribed to Brutus), attacked the proscriptions, and repeated some stories unfavorable to Augustus. Under Tiberius he opposed the rise of the imperial favorite Sejanus over the heads of the senators and thus brought his undoing; in 25 Sejanus let loose two of his clients to remove this possible obstacle to his further plans. The charge against Cordus was that of *laesa maiestas;* the proof, the tone of his history of the Augustan period and particularly the remarks about Brutus and Cassius.

From the account of the contemporary Seneca the Younger, it appears that Cordus starved himself to death before the trial could get under way. Tacitus, who wrote ninety years after the event, apparently assumed there had been a trial, and made up for the defendant a stirring speech.

The theme is the proposition that acts might be accused, but not words. Cordus questions rhetorically whether he is in arms with Cassius and Brutus on the plains of Philippi—or is he inflaming the people to civil war by his harangues? Far to the contrary his history is recounting the deeds of men dead seventy years, and historians have always been free to write as they would of the dead. To support his praise of Brutus and Cassius, Cordus adduces the freedom with which Livy, Asinius Pollio, and Messalla Corvinus spoke under Augustus; or Cicero, Catullus, and Bibaculus under Caesar—to say nothing of the Greeks, "who tolerated not liberty only, but license." [15] In fine, as words his statements

[14] Suetonius, *Tiberius* 28.   [15] Tacitus, *Annals* 4.35.1.

should not be accused; his words did not offend the ruler's *maiestas;* Caesar and Augustus did not destroy hostile literature; and he was not upsetting the tranquillity of the state.

This speech is a superb illustration of the vehemence with which Tacitus felt it necessary to defend freedom of speech in the Empire— and also of the limitations thereon which he was forced to accept. In point of fact one may question whether its eloquence does not sweep the reader entirely down the wrong path. Tacitus built it entirely on the assumption that to praise Brutus and Cassius could *ipso facto* be considered treasonable. This is a puzzling position, for Augustus had made every effort to avoid crowning the pair with a halo of martyrdom. Historians of his age inclined to judge the tyrannicides charitably, and their praise continued in authors of the Tiberian age; even the proimperial historian Velleius Paterculus, who wrote after the death of Cordus, did not fear to speak well of them.

While Sejanus was undoubtedly ready to twist his opponent's words, it still appears probable—as Columba has argued—that Cordus went too far in his work. One possibility is that in revising his history under Tiberius he openly attacked the Senate and people for their lassitude in enduring Sejanus and immediately turned to laud the republican hero Cassius *as tyrannicide.* In the absence of the original work this explanation cannot be proved; still, the fact that in a later reissue of the history his remarks on Brutus and Cassius were removed suggests that they were really objectionable.

If this suggestion is correct, one can see why a charge of *laesa maiestas* was tenable, and perhaps also why Tiberius supported Sejanus —if indeed the emperor played any part in the trial itself, for on this point we have only casual assertions by the later, hostile historians. Other charges also may have lurked in the background which were never advanced due to the abrupt end of affairs.

The *cause célèbre* of Cordus thus took its rise from the initiative of Sejanus, not that of Tiberius. As an attack on freedom of speech it was inflated by Tacitus for his own ends. Yet, whatever the cast of Cordus' language, the servile Senate did order that his works be burned, in Rome by the aediles and in the other cities by the local magistrates. Another burning of the books had been added to the two Augustan examples of Cassius and Labienus; later in the reign the orations of Scaurus were also to go up in smoke.

In neither case did the emperor Tiberius halt the fires. That failure cast a pall of impenetrable ashes over his very real efforts to maintain freedom of speech; for sober examination of his reign leads one to conclude that literary repression therein was due entirely to the initiative of other elements than the emperor. Nevertheless, men of importance must have cast an anxious glance at their writings and vowed to be circumspect.

It remained for the reign of Nero to show what the ruler himself could do if he wished to chastise the arts. The first years had a fair appearance as the young, openhanded Nero smiled on poets and his ministers Seneca and Burrus guided the state. In so friendly an atmosphere, where anything—or almost anything—could be said, men of letters expanded joyously and scribbled furiously.

Ere long autocracy began to display itself, and the last years of the reign attained a height of despotism which was in some respects not thereafter surpassed. The aristocracy was no longer a partner in the government and from the fate of Thrasea Paetus learned that it could not even be neutral. Men might not attack the ruler or his servants; they might not even engage in philosophic criticism of autocracy or of the ruler's moral qualities. Worse yet, by the middle sixties Nero was an emperor turned artist, and had progressed beyond the support of other artists to the policy that no one should be considered his equal. Particularly in music and poetry he was to be *princeps* not only of men but of the arts; his mastery had to be applauded; and rivalry was dangerous.

The most famous victim of this intolerant spirit was the brilliant nephew of Seneca, the poet Lucan. His major work, the *Civil War* (or *Pharsalia*), outwardly concerned itself with the war of Caesar and Pompey but developed into the most bitter attack on the Principate from the circles of the Roman aristocracy which has survived. Most anguished of all his lines is his cry that at Pharsalus

we were overthrown for all time to come; all future generations doomed to slavery were conquered by those swords. For what fault of their own were the sons or grandsons of the combatants at Pharsalia born to slavery? Did *we* play the coward in battle or screen our throats from the sword? . . . To us, born after that battle, Fortune gave a master; she should have given us also the chance to fight for freedom.[16]

[16] 7.640–646.

Whoever won at Pharsalus ended freedom of speech, and in the resulting tyranny one kept the semblance of freedom only by acquiescing in each behest of the tyrant.

Like his uncle, Lucan considered the Principate inevitable, but unlike Seneca, who accepted it while opposing only unworthy holders of the supreme direction, Lucan rather counseled opposition, however hopeless, and virtually alone of all first-century thinkers was a real republican. That Lucan's opposition was a mere rhetorical exaggeration is to deny all sincerity to the poem; of rhetoric and digression there is indeed a superabundance, but the work seems in basic pattern of thought to be a unified structure. The kernel is the successful effort of Fortune, operating through Caesar, to exterminate Roman virtue and so Rome itself. Lucan was particularly intent on displaying the constant struggle of Stoic virtue, embodied in Cato, against the slings and arrows of outrageous fortune.[17]

Both of the ancient lives of Lucan indicate that the poet read part of his work to the public while he was still a friend of Nero; one life goes so far as to say he had published Books One through Three. Though men could handle the past with relative freedom in the Empire, one may doubt if the later books saw the bookstores before the death of the poet. Like the even-more-direct assault of the *Octavia*, they must have come out after the suicide of Nero.

As it was, the parts which Lucan did publish helped to contribute to his downfall, but more through their popular acclaim than through their tone. Nero, himself a poet, disliked the popularity of his young friend and seems to have forbidden Lucan to engage in poetry or legal pleadings. Too young to be politic, Lucan retorted by such childish acts as reciting a line of Nero's verse at an apposite point in the public latrines—whereupon the other occupants fled in great haste!—and by a direct attack in verse on Nero and his friends. In the end Lucan joined the Pisonian conspiracy of 65. When named as an accomplice and taken prisoner, he swiftly confessed the whole affair, accused his mother as a participant, and secured the right of opening his veins in suicide. With him fell also his father, his uncles Seneca and Gallio, and many other Roman nobles; but it was on the silencing of Lucan that

[17] I am much indebted in my views on Lucan to the unpublished doctoral dissertation of Mary Roberta Irwin, "Republicanism and Freedom of Speech in Rome in the First Century" (Cornell University, 1945), a copy of which was lent to me by Professor Harry Caplan of that university.

later men of letters such as Martial and Statius looked back in detestation of Nero.

Nero's very real interest in the arts had led him down a path which no previous emperor had followed far, that of esthetic dictation. His attempt to coerce cultural judgments brought outward acquiescence, but beyond this lay hatred—not so much for the affront to freedom of speech as for the ignominy of having an emperor so emphasize literary pursuits. Eventually the generals were able to turn their soldiers against the singing emperor, who whimpered in his last moments, "What an artist dies in me." [18]

Influence of Imperial Pressure

The evidence for the pressure of individual emperors upon freedom of thought is considerable and has led many scholars to visualize the intellectual decline of the Early Empire primarily in terms of the direct relations between thinkers and Caesars. Without accepting this overly naïve simplification one may agree that the emperors had a double effect on letters, at least superficially.

On the one hand, they spurred literary production by their patronage, by their institution of festivals as a "stimulus to men's minds," [19] and by other means. On the other, they also curtailed the outward independence of that work. Augustus did not try to reach deep into men's minds, though if he had had prescience he might have made the effort; but by affecting even in minor degree the surface he placed a cold hand upon freedom of thought. By the end of his reign men had suffered for their productions, though purely on chronological grounds one cannot attribute the end of the Augustan Age (c. 8 B.C.) solely to this repression, which came in his last years. Seneca the Elder put matters very well in saying that the punishment of genius began in that very period when genius began to be lacking.

In more autocratic reigns authors were forced to silence or turned to innocuous forms of literature. Pliny the Elder first wrote biography and then a history of the wars in Germany, but in the last years of Nero he composed eight books on *Linguistic Queries* "when the tyranny of the times made it dangerous to engage in studies of a more free and elevated spirit." [20] In bitter epigrams Tacitus summed up the effect of Domitian on thought:

[18] Suetonius, *Nero* 49.1.   [19] Tacitus, *Annals* 14.21.5 (of Nero).
[20] Pliny, *Letters* 3.5.

In those fires doubtless the government imagined that it could silence the voice of Rome and annihilate the freedom of the Senate and the moral consciousness of mankind; it even went on to banish the professors of philosophy and exile all honourable studies, so that nothing decent might be left to vex its eyes. We have indeed set up a record of subservience. Rome of old explored the limits of freedom; we have plumbed the depths of slavery, robbed even of the interchange of ideas by the secret police.[21]

Very frequently, it is true, the judicial charges which were drawn from the literary or rhetorical activities of a thinker were mere pretexts, and often they were far-fetched. When the foolish, pompous Mettius Pompusianus was charged with *laesa maiestas* under Domitian, the grounds included his horoscope, his map of the world, and his excerpting and reading of speeches of kings and other leaders in Livy—as practice, perhaps, for his own imperial efforts, come a lucky day. One may not take too seriously these picturesque charges, with which later historians delighted to whip the autocratic rulers of the century; but in truth it mattered little whether men's words were used against them as pretext or in reality. By the opening of the second century men who thought must certainly have realized the truth of Musonius Rufus' observation:

to many people, nay to most, even though dwelling safely in their native city, fear of what seems to them dire consequences of free speech is present.[22]

Nevertheless none of the first-century emperors had essayed to wrest control of the ancient intellectual system from the aristocracy, and in more cases than one might suspect at first glance the imperial structure itself was a vehicle for that aristocratic dominance. Cassius Severus and Titus Labienus so suffered; under Nero a senator who was convicted of having attacked his peers and the priests in a fictitious will was exiled and his works were burned; Domitian sought out the authors of pamphlets attacking the nobles. The aristocracy as a whole had as little concept of freedom of speech in the first century as it had had under Augustus; not until the days of Tacitus did a representative of the upper classes see, and then incompletely, the need for such an ideal.

Nor, again, had any of these emperors directly attacked the basic characteristics of classical civilization. None of them had even detected, much less opposed, the secret springs of change in the Greco-

---

[21] *Agricola* 2 (Mattingly).
[22] Translation of Cora E. Lutz, *Yale Classical Studies* 10 (1947), 74–75.

Roman world. Civilization in the first century of the Empire was still a turbulent sea in which the waves apparently moved in one direction while hidden currents were setting in a diametrically opposed direction; the fury of the Caesars and the constant, even flow of aristocratic pressure affected only the surface.

Seneca the Younger

No man of the first century better illuminates all these facets of civilization than Seneca the Younger, the greatest pagan intellect of the era. Few philosophers have had such a chance to direct the politics of their day, for Seneca was both an adherent of the Stoa and a member of the highest circles of the imperial aristocracy. Born of Spanish stock, he tended to co-operate with the imperial system, particularly under Nero, for whom he was first tutor and then minister of state with the praetorian prefect Burrus.

After the death of the latter in 62 Seneca realized that his influence with Nero was waning and unwillingly retired in "apprehension and weariness." [23] His last weary years he devoted, as Cicero had done, to pouring out a great mass of works. In 65 Nero seized the occasion of the Pisonian plot, in which Seneca may or may not have had a part, to force him to suicide.

Seneca was more than a senator, a figure of state, an apologist for the Neronian regime, or a millionaire. He was also a philosopher of unquestionable sincerity and ability of mind; a masterful essayist with a rushing, epigrammatic, tricky style and a willingness to expand Latin vocabulary by using common words; a dramatist of repute; an expert in natural science of the period—in short, one of the most rounded figures of the Empire.

In his tragedies Seneca wrote works to be read rather than performed; these vehicles he utilized for an intense psychological portrayal of man, as seen through Stoic eyes. Otherwise it is difficult to employ the tragedies for illumination of his world, for both the plots and many of the more striking observations came straight from Greek models. His *Moral Essays* and his *Moral Epistles* are a different matter, even though not all the *Essays* can be placed within exact chronological limits. Here at times Seneca struck notes of real moral grandeur; at other points he served up the stalest rehash of Stoic doctrine; but always he considered directly the ethical problems of the noble class, to which

[23] Seneca, *Epistles* 56.9.

he primarily addressed himself. Not as lofty a Stoic as his younger contemporary Musonius Rufus, or as influential in molding disciples, Seneca was more in tune with his fellow aristocrats.

He reveals the frightened inner uncertainty of that class which was only in part the result of man's general inherent insecurity. Seneca viewed the Empire as a reign of force, in which his readers often had to bear their tyranny in silence. Like many another imperial subject he saw that the republican *libertas* could no longer exist "where the rewards both of supreme power and of servitude were so great, or that the earlier constitution of the state could be restored after the ancient manners had all been lost." [24] The only alternative was the Principate, which, in my judgment, he accepted as a vital bond for the Empire; but he feared the unchecked liberty which the rulers enjoyed.

For a time Seneca hoped, as tutor of a ruler, to be able to bend his charge toward true virtue. With this aim in view he prepared in 54–55 a powerful essay *On Clemency,* which began with a spectacular portrayal of the absolute power of the ruler:

Have I [muses Nero] of all mortals found favour with Heaven and been chosen to serve on earth as vicar of the gods? I am the arbiter of life and death for the nations; it rests in my power what each man's lot and state shall be; by my lips Fortune proclaims what gift she would bestow on each human being; from my utterance peoples and cities gather reasons for rejoicing; without my favor and grace no part of the wide world can prosper; all those many thousands of swords which my peace restrains will be drawn at my nod; what nations shall be utterly destroyed, which banished, which shall receive the gift of liberty, which have it taken from them, what kings shall become slaves and whose heads shall be crowned with royal honour, what cities shall fall and which shall rise—this it is mine to decree.

With all things thus at my disposal, I have been moved neither by anger nor youthful impulse to unjust punishment, nor by the foolhardiness and obstinacy of men which have often wrung patience from even the serenest souls, nor yet by that vainglory which employs terror for the display of might —a dread but all too common use of great and lordly power. With me the sword is hidden, nay, is sheathed; I am sparing to the utmost of even the meanest blood; no man fails to find favour at my hands though he lack all else but the name of man. . . . Today, if the immortal gods should require a reckoning from me, I am ready to give full tale of the human race.[25]

To mitigate this fearful absolutism and re-enforce the virtue of the vicar of the gods, Seneca adduced various arguments, all designed to

[24] *On Benefits* 2.20.2.   [25] *On Clemency* 1.1.2–4.

encourage the ruler voluntarily to limit his power. The last and most powerful was the only theoretical defense one can offer against misuse of absolutism: the ruler, though all-powerful, holds his power only for the good of the state and is subject in its use to natural law. Even slaves are guarded by the principles of equity and right; so much the more are free men committed to the ruler by the gods not as slaves but as wards. "In dealing with a human being there is an extreme which the right common to all living creatures refuses to allow." [26]

Although Seneca paraded his exhortations in the essay *On Clemency* merely as a mirror of Nero's own self, his real fears are obvious. In actual fact Seneca and Burrus had to concede one piece of deviltry after another to their ward, including the murder of Nero's mother. Easy was the descent, but the philosopher after a time was no longer able to "adapt good morals to the occasion." [27]

When his effort to reform the ruler failed, Seneca had two options. One was to attack the increasing autocracy of Nero's later years; and this, I have already argued, he did in the *Octavia*. The other was to advise his fellows ever more insistently on the way they should live, and whence they might obtain an inner freedom from the ills of the world. To this purpose the weary, fearful man shut himself up and wrote night and day for posterity; the product was the *Epistles to Lucilius*, or *Moral Epistles*.

The burden of his prophecy was the futility of action. The prescription which he offered was essentially that of Epictetus, not quite as sharp in dogmatic clarity but more directly linked to the political problems of existence. The Roman living in Nero's world should be a Stoic wise man, who would live a life of reason in retirement and give as few hostages as possible to Fortune. This he might do by distinguishing carefully between goods of the body, which were unimportant, and goods of the soul; in man's virtue lay his freedom, which was unassailable by torture or death. Seneca talked much of torture in the *Epistles*, and not idly.

In an earlier essay *On Tranquillity of Mind* Seneca had frowned on the idea that the individual must give up his public duties if he were to secure his own true ends in life. One must, rejoined Seneca, do as much as one can as soldier or official or pleader; if that were dangerous,

---

[26] *On Clemency* 1.18.2.

[27] Lactantius, *Divine Institutes* 3.15 (quoting a general observation of Seneca) (Fletcher).

then by silent support; if entrance even in the Forum were dangerous, then by friendship at home. "The service of a good citizen is never useless; by being heard and seen, by his expression, by his gesture, by his silent stubbornness, and by his very walk he helps." [28] Yet even in the *Essays* this was almost an isolated note; for in at least three other places Seneca expressed the equally Stoic idea that one should retire unless required to serve the state.

In the *Epistles* there is no doubt that retirement was vital, first to avoid giving offense to the people, the Senate, or "individuals equipped with power by the people and against the people"; and secondly not to expose oneself unnecessarily to the fears of want, sickness, or "the troubles which result from the violence of the stronger." [29]

A man, however, was to retire gradually lest he call undue attention to his abstention or appear to condemn what he avoided. Seneca did not as a rule approve of the distinctive cloak and long beard which would-be philosophers assumed as outward marks of their inward holiness and which led men to look upon philosophers generally with a certain scorn. To disassociate oneself so from the multitude whom one was trying to improve, argued Seneca, was to frighten them away; but another important reason was the fact that "philosophy when employed with insolence and arrogance has been perilous to many." [30]

Seneca's underlying distinction between body and spirit (*animus*) and his subdivision of the latter into irrational and rational parts went back to Aristotle. The argument of internal independence which he based on these distinctions was likewise old, but in repeating it as incessantly as he did he underlined its application to life. His very lack of originality, which he admitted in one letter to be deliberate, stemmed in part from the fact that, particularly in the earlier *Essays,* he was applying philosophy to the main issues of the day so as to aid a man who would go no further in theoretical research. The study of philosophy was the height of human endeavor to Seneca, but he, like Demetrius the Cynic, would have a man possess a few cardinal points by which to live rather than much but barren learning. His line of thought in the *Epistles* remained typical of philosophical thinking in the Empire: it was conventional, eclectic, and flat; yet it continued to exhibit Roman practicality, and the end product was a great step forward in ancient self-scrutiny.

The difference between the philosophical positions of Seneca and

[28] *On Tranquillity* 4.6.   [29] *Epistles* 14.7, 14.3.   [30] *Epistles* 103.5.

Cicero brilliantly displays the pressure of the Empire on men's minds. Cicero, though in the main an Academic skeptic, was much more optimistic than the Stoic Seneca could be. One feels that by the time of Seneca the social structure had deteriorated and afforded less security; Seneca, too, wavered between making man the chief creation of the universe or depicting him as an utterly contemptible thing. Seneca was more personal, less interested in—or hopeful about—political problems. Despite his fears of the political system under which he lived, he wrote no *Republic* or *Laws* to sketch an ideal state, and while he kept the Roman Stoic idea of civic duties, his whole tone was against participation in politics. The outlook was not positive, but negative; through a self-contained life, indeed, a philosopher might not be able to escape the troubles of this world, but his chances were better. If fear of sickness or the pressure of the political system affected one, there was always the opportunity of suicide, which Seneca praised and in the end adopted himself.

This introspective emphasis on the individual is a highly significant mark of the intellectual temper of the Empire. In numerous other respects as well, Seneca reveals more clearly than any other man of his century the hidden drift of civilization, for he had real powers of intuition and coupled with them an ability to view the life about him frankly.

The freedom of his criticism is outstanding in imperial writing. Seneca himself noted in a biting passage of the late essay *On Benefits* the cringing obsequiousness of the public which drove rulers to misjudge their capabilities and so destroy themselves, and he urged that one could repay the favors of masters by telling them the truth instead of cant. Here he seems to express his own policy in advising Nero, for amid that "well-bred urbanity" which Tacitus singles out among his characteristics he could yet be fairly open in trying to direct Nero on the lines of virtue. In his essay *On Clemency* he certainly was far franker than were the imperial tutors Fronto and Ausonius of later centuries, and in his last words to the emperor he justly asserted that "he was not a man addicted to flattery: and that no one knew better than Nero himself, who had more often found him too free than too servile in his utterances." [31] Unlike his contemporaries he was remarkably open in judging the acts of past emperors and in exposing their omnipotence for good or for bad.

[31] Tacitus, *Annals* 13.2.2, 15.61.3.

Nor was it alone in the political field that Seneca so frankly criticized his own age. He is often accused of hypocrisy in that he was fabulously wealthy and yet preached against the evils of wealth; but Seneca, if any man, could appreciate the dangers and trouble of money, which he tried in vain to resign to his master. His philosophic disdain for this world's goods, "the diploma of slavery," did not extend as far as that of Musonius' advocacy of downright poverty, for so much his wealthy readers could not be expected to stomach; but Seneca delivered strong attacks on the zeal of men in the Empire for wealth. The attempt to set up earthly goods as the aim of life, so marked in Neronian Rome, he assailed with equal contempt: "Pleasure is the good of cattle." [32] Not only wealth but the pursuit of culture was, in Seneca's eyes, a false diversion which led men away from their true objective, living well. In his accusation of the delusions of this life he struck a note common to many thinkers in all ages, but the appearance of the attack—and its width—has a deep significance here as prelude to later thought in the Empire.

An outstanding aspect of Seneca's views is his compassion and humanitarianism, and here he beat his own path. Seneca was bitingly opposed to the games in which even in the intermission "men were strangled lest people be bored." [33] In his essay *On Anger* he painted a horrendous picture of the cruelty and faithlessness of man to man in his world, and elsewhere went so far as to say that "the first thing which philosophy undertakes to give is fellow-feeling with all men; in other words, sympathy (*humanitatem*) and sociability (*congregationem*)." [34]

Seneca, however, could not go as far as his contemporary Musonius, who argued that daughters and sons should receive the same education and that a single standard of virtue should apply. Nor do we find in Seneca the conclusion of Musonius that the home was the rampart of society, and that the first step in the home was marriage, to be followed by many children and perfect companionship. This warmth of social feeling, akin to that of the Christians, is entirely alien to Seneca's rather coldly intellectual nature.

With slaves, nevertheless, Seneca could be deeply sympathetic—more so in fact than any other pagan of the first century, unless one includes the Jew Nicolaus of Damascus, who educated his slaves as his friends. Seneca was as devout as any Christian in believing that each man had a spark of the divine within him:

[32] *Epistles* 92.6.   [33] *Epistles* 7.5.   [34] *Epistles* 5.4.

God is near you, he is with you, he is within you. This is what I mean, Lucilius: a holy spirit indwells within us, one who marks our good and bad deeds, and is our guardian. . . . No man can be good without the help of God.[35]

From this to the intensely religious spirit of Epictetus is only a short step, but like many other aristocrats of the Empire Seneca's religious feelings arose more from philosophy than from the official Roman cult. In a lost work *Against Superstition,* which Christian fathers approvingly quoted, Seneca evidently assailed the gods and their rites more freely than Varro had done a century before and ridiculed the worshipers of images as being boys with dolls.

As Christians of later ages read Seneca, they were struck by the extent to which he apparently echoed Christian ideas on the relations of man to man and of man to God. The apologist Minucius Felix deftly interwove Seneca's phrases with those of St. Paul; others assumed that he had known Paul and had imbibed his ideas from the contemporary missionary of the Church. By 400 a fictitious collection of letters between the two had even been composed and was widely circulated. Actually Seneca's humanitarianism and cosmopolitanism emerged from the deeper currents of the Empire, and if Christianity had the same ideas the parallelism was merely a reflection of the widespread nature of those ideas.

Christianity, in truth, could offer much more, for though Seneca looked to the future the past still limited his vision. Thus Seneca's humanitarianism was largely theoretical. On the one hand men were all members of one great state, the state of Nature under God. They must support each other like the stones of an arch, or as he said in a noble passage, "You must live for your neighbor, if you would live for yourself." [36] Since we are all wicked and all must meet the same end, the man who is wise will cherish his fellow human beings with indulgence.

The individualism of the Roman aristocracy, on the other hand, so seriously affected Seneca that he did not consistently display a true feeling of brotherly love. In the long work *On Benefits* the analysis was the usual pagan one of social duties and good turns on a rather cold plane of utility, whereas the Christian supports the needy and unserviceable of society in brotherly love and in hope of reward only from God. Seneca argued that if a man were *dignus* the philosopher

[35] *Epistles* 41.1–2.   [36] *Epistles* 48.2.

would share his peril; if the threatened man were *indignus,* he would
go so far as to raise an outcry to save him from robbers!

In his *Epistles* Seneca dedicated himself to working for later generations. His exhortations to retirement, nonetheless, conveyed the idea
that in these parlous times each man could do little publicly for others
but must save himself; the Christian virtue of brotherly love, though
suggested in spots, was much overladen by the concentration on the
individual who lives within himself. Seneca shared the Stoic doctrine
on the "apathy" of the wise man to evils befalling his friends and
family, a doctrine which was criticized as heartless by pagans and
Christians alike.

In his broader view of the nature of man and the world Seneca
displays the same curious mixture of old and new. He had an almost
Christian attitude of resignation before the will of God, for the Stoics
too believed that the universe was an orderly pattern under God's pur-
poseful control. Fortune, though outwardly chaotic, was only His way
of testing us. Life in accordance with reason, which brought virtue,
was nothing else than understanding and accepting that divine pattern
of the world which was partially sketched in Seneca's *Natural Questions.*

The product of resignation, however, is almost incredibly different
to the Christian and to the Stoic, for Seneca could not couple his endurance with the joy of the Christian in the sureness of rewards. He
displayed, instead, the underlying pessimism characteristic of pagan
philosophers. The golden age lay in the past, and man had fallen from
it through the introduction of wealth and luxury; the useful things of
the world had been corrupted by man's depravity. The idea that a
divine will has predestined all could comfort the Christians, but to this
weary man on the old, old treadmill of classical civilization the chaotic
malevolence of Fortune remained a potent, practical force.

On the lower level this pessimism was rooted in Seneca's advancing
age and in his sadness over contemporary politics, for a senator could
not, like the Christian, disengage himself from political activity. On a
higher plane it arose from basic flaws of pagan thought, to wit, the
view that personality is static, the belief in the necessity for the individual to save himself by his own efforts, and the inability to visualize
life after death.

Seneca now and then pictured man as enduring patiently his life on
this earth, a sort of inn, in the knowledge that a better abode waited

beyond the grave, when the soul had shed its body. In one work, the *Consolation to Marcia,* he depicted a mortal ridding himself of the body and speeding away to join the souls of the Stoic blessed in the stars. Here his style was almost ecstatic, and he revealed for a moment the yearning of men for "salvation," for a future happiness, which recurred more forcefully in Epictetus. Yet this Stoic heaven was a vague place, and in arguing against the fear of death and the pagan stories of the underworld Seneca suggested, like Pliny the Elder, that death might be the end of all. This dilemma the pagans could not resolve: "The fear of going to the underworld is equalled by the fear of going nowhere." [37]

Having stripped from his Roman audience their usual aim of life, i.e., to get wealth, Seneca could offer no real reward for the cheerless joy of fighting against evil. His ethical preaching he had to ground generally on the need for a man to live by reason, which was given to him by God as the mark of man. He sounded like a Christian in asserting, "Let man be pleased with whatever has pleased God," but the immediate sequel is totally unchristian in its emphasis on the necessity for man to save himself:

Let him marvel at himself and his own resources for this very reason, that he cannot be overcome, that he has the very powers of evil subject to his control, and that he brings into subjection chance and pain and wrong by means of that strongest of powers—reason. Love reason! [38]

Although Seneca sneered at the sophistic arguments of the Greeks, he resorted frequently to Stoic paradox, and the method of inquiry and proof in his *Natural Questions* was the rational rather than the empirical. Seneca was also bred in the rationalistic school of Greco-Roman civilization, which tried to cut away the emotions and to rely only on the mind, and his philosophy could not allow the emotional appeal of Christianity. The pleasures of the wise man he sketched as "calm, moderate, almost listless and subdued, and scarcely noticeable inasmuch as they come unsummoned." [39]

How different are the jubilations of Paul or Clement! The one needs only to understand the world and to live resignedly within it; the other feels that Heaven is always being built, and by our efforts. The assertion, "We are all bad," appears incessantly in Seneca, but he can offer no guarantee of salvation; the static mournfulness of pagan civilization

[37] *Epistles* 82.16.   [38] *Epistles* 74.20.
[39] *On the Happy Life* 12.2.

was summed up in the cry, "There is, believe me, great happiness in the very necessity of dying." [40]

Even a brief summary of Seneca's views suggests a number of important conclusions about his intellectual position and, by extension, about the character of first-century civilization. In the first place, Seneca drew heavily from the Greeks for his basic ideas. His criticism is merely one of details; of truly original philosophical twists there is almost nothing.

Yet, perhaps more in his attitude than in his words, this man sensed new ideas on the place and nature of man and was moving from philosophic meditation to religious contemplation—but he was unable to express these new ideas clearly within the old intellectual framework which he inherited. That basis of thought in turn depended on a political and social scheme of life which was disappearing in this very century as the independent aristocracy vanished, and the city-states were subordinated to a centrally organized empire. The dejected retirement which Seneca urged is at once a mark and a further cause of the destruction of the old ways. Repeatedly Seneca reflects the essential weariness and gloom of this civilization.

Secondly, the work of Seneca is a monument to the freedom of thought in certain areas in first-century Rome. Seneca could attack the officially accepted religion as stupid and unfounded and could at least at times lay open a vision of future happiness. He could direct a withering blow at the popular games for their inhumanity. He scorned the prevalent emphasis on wealth. In the bitterness of old age he looked back over his life and pronounced its devotion to public affairs erroneous—to save himself man must retire. The emperors who were dead he damned, all save one; the emperor who was living he first advised, then criticized with remarkable boldness, even if one accepts no more than the essay On Benefits as his work. Though Seneca's originality was limited, his work is a proof that the lack of political freedom did not yet—at least—connote the destruction of all ability of men to think.

Thirdly, the grounds on which Seneca met opposition from his contemporaries and finally was condemned by Nero were essentially superficial. The attacks from his senatorial peers, which linger on in Tacitus and Dio Cassius, revolved primarily about his imperial preferment and the inconsistency of his philosophy with his life, particularly as

[40] To Polybius 9.9.

regarded his acquisition of a vast estate. When Nero finally ordered his tutor to commit suicide, it was primarily to assert his own independence and to remove a frank critic. Although Quintilian and Aulus Gellius engaged in more general criticism of Seneca's work after his death, they attacked mainly his style and his hostile literary judgment on writers from Ennius to Virgil. The fact that he embodied in his works ideas which were in the end destructive of the ancient view of man brought neither his downfall nor serious reproach.

And lastly, it is significant that Seneca did die as a victim to Nero's anger. In talking of philosophical martyrdom Epictetus later urged that new martyrs be added to the old examples.[41] Epictetus himself named only Helvidius Priscus of his own age, but beside and perhaps ahead of this fanatic one might justly place the figures of Thrasea Paetus and of Seneca, both of whom believed that the human mind could not yield entirely to outside compulsion.

The Empire as a whole—army, provinces, and Senate alike—turned ever more to the emperors for final decision and for initiative, but in estimating the power of imperial absolutism one must not forget the tired old aristocrat who wrote in his study, "Let us thank God that no man can be kept in life" [42]—or again the Christian preachers expounding the meaning and limits of the text, "Deliver unto Caesar the things that are Caesar's."

[41] *Discourses* 1.29.57.   [42] *Epistles* 12.10.

XI

The Sterility of the Second Century

THE second century of the Roman Empire was outwardly a happy, serene age. Nero and Domitian were dead. The tribulations of Cremutius Cordus, of Thrasea Paetus, of Seneca lay far in the past. Now came the famous Good Emperors, a series of conscientious rulers from Trajan to Marcus Aurelius (98–180) such as few states have had the fortune to enjoy.

The absolute position of the emperor, which had been defined in the struggles of the first century, was accepted under Trajan. One of his successors, Marcus Aurelius, could calmly admit to himself the virtues of the first-century rebels Thrasea and Helvidius, and of the earlier tyrannicides Cato and Brutus, and could view his own reign as one "based on individual equality and freedom of speech . . . cherishing above all things the liberty of the subject." [1] Apart from minor troubles under Hadrian the Senate and *princeps* were in essential accord. All the world looked to its master as protector; about that ruler had grown up a court and court procedure, adapted largely from Hellenistic and Eastern practices and developed mainly through the pressure of the subjects to elevate their savior and benefactor.

The tensions of the Empire, which had underlain the feeling of insecurity of many first-century rulers, had diminished in other ways as decade after decade of firm provincial government and military maintenance of order did their work. In this prosperity local differences sank

[1] *Meditations* 1.14.

into the background of country life. Men of the cities dropped their native names and took on Roman-sounding appellations as they rose in imperial society; in Gallic and Syrian cities alike they moved and died against a background of Greco-Roman civilization. The gods were not everywhere the same, nor did the statues and buildings exhibit exactly the same flavor; but to our eyes the differences, though important, are less essential than are the similarities. Down to the reign of Antoninus Pius (138–161) the background was ever more uniform; then local attitudes began to reassert themselves. The civilization of the Mediterranean was on the verge of a great swell of change.

Sunlight and Shadows in the Second Century

In the reign of this monarch a young, enthusiastic orator of Smyrna, Aelius Aristides, traveled to Rome. There he delivered, in or about 144, a great eulogy of the Empire. This speech is rhetorical, at times frigid; its author was neither critical nor original; but the very banality of its commonplace phrases aids in fashioning a superb picture of the prosaic second-century Empire as seen by the self-satisfied upper classes of the provinces.

First appeared the city itself, notable in the quality of its citizens, in its size, and in its magnificence, the focal point to which flowed all the riches and luxuries of the great realm centering about the Mediterranean. Outside the Empire was nothing but what the Romans considered useless; within it was the "inhabited land" (*oikoumene*), an egotistical term often used by imperial authors. The boundary between civilization and barbarism was defined for Aristides by the Roman *limes,* that definite frontier marked by a wall or patrolled road which was solidified by Hadrian all about the Empire, and this *limes* was defended by the superbly organized Roman army. Unlike Horace, our orator of the second century had no fears of the outside barbarians.

Within this charmed precinct lived the happy subjects of the emperor. The ruler was an autocrat whom all obeyed instantly and silently without thought of objection; when his name was mentioned, all rose, bowed, and prayed—to the gods on his behalf, to him on their personal behalf. A contemporary inscription from Ephesus puts much the same platitude in asserting that Antoninus Pius had "restored to health the whole race of mankind." [2]

Since Aristides was not a senator like Pliny, his speech rarely referred

[2] *Orientis Graecae Inscriptiones Selectae* 493 (trans. by Wilhelm Weber, *Cambridge Ancient History* 11 [Cambridge, 1936], 332).

to the Senate, but both Roman and Greek agreed in emphasizing the virtue of the imperial system and the freedom which resulted therefrom. Unlike the Persian realm of old or the Athenian Empire, the Caesars ruled over free men—free in the sense of such private rights as sanctity of marriage, protection of life, security in the fruits of their labor, and certainty of justice. Law and order were maintained by all parts of the bureaucracy; if any echelon failed, appeal to the emperor was always open. "Is not a political regime of this sort," asked Aristides triumphantly, "above any democracy?" [3]

To each area and to each class the emperors gave their proper due. The upper classes received the Roman citizenship they coveted and were permitted to take part in the government. The rest of the world was granted social and economic justice, particularly against local oppression.

The conclusions which the orator drew from this distribution of privileges are engaging. He saw correctly that in the expansion of Roman citizenship the term *Roma* too had expanded to include not merely a city or the peninsula of Italy but the entire Empire; moreover, he ventured to assert, "A common democracy of the earth has been set up under one man, the best, as ruler and orderer, and all come together as in a common market place, each to receive what is worthy of him." [4] We may shudder at the destruction of political values implicit in this argument, and even in the Empire some men knew their system might better be called "equitable servility." [5] Nevertheless the view of Aristides was one which reappeared in later thinkers; and the humanitarian attitude of the second-century rulers which underlay it was a significant force in the felicity of the times. By and large Aristides was correct when he asserted that

the political system at present has at once the approval and defends the interests of the poor as of the rich, and it seems now that no other regime were possible—a harmonic politico-social organization has been formed which coordinates all. By your work that has become reality which once might appear an unrealizable Utopia—in your government are mingled firmness, magnanimity, and human clemency, and discipline without the necessity of coercion. [6]

It is small wonder if the inhabitants of this charmed circle, to which the golden age had returned, prayed for the eternity of the Empire. The concept of *aeternitas* bulked ever larger in the thought of the

[3] *On Rome* 38.   [4] *On Rome* 60.   [5] *On the Sublime* 44.3.
[6] *On Rome* 66.

second century. Its complement, the fear that Rome might eventually fall, even the Christians grimly coupled with a nightmare of universal war and the ruin of civilization.

By the time of Marcus Aurelius clouds were beginning to draw across the sky. If the subjects of the Empire had momentary alarms, they were perhaps reassured by the imperial coinage, which emphasized the victories of the imperial armies and the protection of the imperial peace. Order was safeguarded, but only because the emperor spent a great part of his reign on the northern frontier, hurling back a variety of barbarians who penetrated at one point as far as Aquileia in north-eastern Italy and at another ravaged the Balkans; his coemperor Lucius Verus was called to the East by a long-protracted, difficult Parthian war. Still, Marcus Aurelius had restored the frontiers by the time of his death and was even thinking of annexing a part of modern Hungary across the Danube. Only to us do these attacks appear the forerunners of the ever-increasing pressure from the North and East which broke the imperial dikes in the following century.

Modern scholars can likewise detect shadows in the glowing picture of the economic prosperity of the Roman world with which Aristides concluded his oration. The Empire reached an extraordinary height of economic well-being in the reigns of the Good Emperors, and the evidence for a wide interchange of goods is extensive. Roman rule, how-ever, was no longer expanding; Hadrian had even given up some of Trajan's ephemeral Eastern conquests. Down to this point the ever-widening circle of the Empire had been a potent spur to commerce and industry, and the wars which accompanied that growth had pro-duced a vital supply of manpower in the form of slaves.

Others changes were equally ominous. Specialized, slave-style farm-ing tended to yield in many areas to less efficient operations by well-nigh hereditary renters (*coloni*); in other districts independent farmers gave way to great landowners. There were no significant improve-ments in industrial techniques or in the use of credit in commerce. Though we have no comprehensive statistics, modern students seem agreed that both industrial production and the level of commerce tended to rise until the second century, then reached a plateau, and began slowly to slip, more particularly in Italy and the West than in the East. Local manufactures, which were fostered by the great costs of transportation and the easy transmission of the simple methods of production, copied established wares in ever-grosser forms and with little originality; economically as well as culturally the Latin West and the Greek East were drawing apart by the end of the century.

Since the army was under ever-heavier pressure on the frontiers and the bureaucracy continued to swell, the financial demands of the state did not fall off in compensating fashion. Trajan had had to step in to correct financial troubles of various cities; Hadrian had found the Empire unable to bear the burdens of Trajan's wars. In meeting the barbarian threats Marcus Aurelius could not choose between war and peace, but the expenses of his wars had forced him to depreciate the currency; in one period of financial stringency he had even gone so far as to sell off a great amount of palace possessions.

Increasing the burden of taxation met stubborn popular resistance, and so the government was slowly driven to extraordinary exactions of food, animals, and other supplies from the population of areas traversed by the armies. State compulsion on the urban rich to take up public office and burdens (*liturgies*) begins to be obvious as early as the reigns of Trajan and Hadrian; another threat to urban economy, though far less clearly seen, was the increasingly centralized exploitation of the ever-enlarging area of state lands. In the end the lower classes bore the brunt of the pressure and slowly began to vent their desperation in complaint, in revolt, and in the rejection of aristocratic political and cultural standards.

Socially also there were signs of approaching trouble. Inscriptions seem to suggest that the size of families decreased not merely in aristocratic circles but also among the people. When a great plague swept the Empire in the reign of Marcus Aurelius, contemporary observers felt that the losses in population were not replaced. In deserted areas along the northern frontier the emperors settled captive barbarians, and to fill their armies turned—as yet in small numbers—to recruits from beyond the frontiers, though to explain this phenomenon one must also remember the increasing pacifism of the docile, materially minded subjects of the Empire. By and large, the curve of imperial population was apparently following the general curve of economic activity and was turning downward by the reign of Marcus Aurelius.

Intellectual Activity

Only casually, almost unconsciously, did men of the second century refer to these difficulties; if they had heard the modern voices crying Doom, they would have listened in incredulous amazement. In one field alone were the subjects of the Good Emperors worried by an evident decline—after a century and a half of imperial peace the mind of the Empire had sunk into an appalling sterility.

The sterility which they saw was one only in terms of classical culture, the dominant system of thought thus far in the Empire. Movements in art and in thought were already in the second century heralding the rise of a new system of thought, but these harbingers of the future were not entirely visible. The decline in intellectual activity, it may also be noted, did not at first express itself either in an abandonment of classical culture by society or in an absolute decline in production.

By the second century classical civilization had become an almost measurable quantity which could be communicated by the conventional system of rhetorical education, not perhaps painlessly but assuredly with some guarantee of success. Throughout the vast reaches of the Empire it was so conveyed to the sons of Roman aristocrats, Gallic nobles, or Syrian magnates and formed a great bond of unity among the middle and upper classes; as men of low birth rose, they put on the necessary veneer. Acquisition of this cosmopolitan culture admitted a man like Lucian, who began as sculptor's apprentice, to the governing classes of the Empire, and its possession was considered a necessary mark of the gentleman. "Culture" was coming to enjoy the position of a conscious concept which was to be even more marked in the immediately following centuries.

Both public and private aid to education was considerably expanded, and Quintilian at least could feel that every man's child deserved equal attention from the educator. The spread of the Greek and Latin languages in East and West, the wide circulation of literary works and the foundation of libraries, the truly remarkable extent of literacy in the cities of the Empire—all these are marks of the attention which men paid to their intellectual heritage. The thinkers may not have thought as well, but more persons made the pretense of thinking—and their reflections were transmitted more widely and more speedily than ever before in human history.

The wealth of the Empire supported an extremely active artistic and literary life; measured externally, the second century pullulates with a hurly-burly of intellectual activity. To put the "intellectuals" in their proper light one must remember the savage remark of Juvenal that poets would do well to rent a bakery to support themselves, or the caustic observation of Martial that a favorite racehorse was as well known in Rome as he was; even so, the arts and letters appeared to thrive. The abundance of artistic work is staggering. Over three hundred statues have been unearthed in Hadrian's villa at Tivoli; monuments to emperors and private citizens abounded; the cities of the Empire put on a new marble dress of baths, amphitheaters, forums, and other majestic buildings (see Pls. V–VII).

Men of letters continued to be busy well past the end of the century. Some of the popular writers neatly epitomized long works of the past; others drew up lists and brief biographies of notable figures in history; yet others wrote or orated at great length. The works of the physician Galen fill twenty quarto volumes; Dio Chrysostom, Plutarch, and others wrote at almost equally great length. In all these cases, to be sure, the bulk was attained by piling up numerous fairly short essays and orations. The great storehouse of ancient learning—and a mighty one it was— lay open to systematizers or ragbag anthologists like Aulus Gellius, who jotted down twenty books of notes from his wide reading. To such men we may be thankful for preserving earlier knowledge which otherwise would be lost.

Just as the lack of originality did not necessarily bring a reduction in production, so too it did not immediately entail a decay in technical skill—perhaps even the reverse was true, inasmuch as authors did not have to hammer out their own ideas. If a poet like Statius was overpedantic and rhetorical, as well as sentimental and mystical in a fuzzy fashion, he could improvise technically proficient verse rapidly and handled the Latin language skillfully. Greek letters, which had long been in a slump, revived notably as the East gained new economic and political importance in the second century; emperors like Hadrian the Greekling and Marcus Aurelius even favored Greek over Latin.

Much of this work exemplifies a "desire for knowledge" (*curiositas*). The emperor Hadrian sought to explore all fields of learning and the arts and to be adept therein; the hero of Apuleius' *Golden Ass* was propelled primarily by his passionate curiosity in the specialized field of magic. To an appallingly great extent this drive led merely to the collection of bits of knowledge for their own sake, to the random assembly of notes based not on observation but on reading—a spawning of books from books which the modern world knows too well. As Henri Marrou has recently suggested, one may view the erudition of the second century in a more favorable light by interpreting it as an effort to cling to the real and concrete rather than lose oneself in the cloudlands of theory which lay close at hand over every field of knowledge; yet the emphasis on the bizarre led men to accept the marvelous easily. Some scholars did now and then break out of their study to see nature or to travel about the known world, but their number was few.

More common was the complete abandonment to fantasy, for the romantic novel of antiquity began its phenomenal rise about the end of the first century and reached its apogee by the early third century. The most famous product of this type is the romantic, picaresque novel just noted, the *Golden Ass* of Apuleius. Others dealt with Alexander or other great figures of the past, but most typical were the romances in which a couple fell in love, were separated or pursued, and finally were reunited. Into such plots were mixed magic, sudden death, witches, and other extraordinary ingredients, all cast against the fascinating background of Egypt, Babylonia, or other exotic lands.

The popularity of the novels has been argued to be a mark of decay of thought, befitting an urban, shallow-rooted population, where education was widespread but superficial, where the requirements of formal style were no longer endurable, where the individual took his own pleasures by himself; and it is true that formal tragedies and comedies, long the marks of a common urban culture, were no longer composed or performed after the first century. Yet in these romances there is also a note of the future in the emphasis on redemption and conversion through love, the stress on Oriental cults, and the general air of the transcendental.

The trades of the philosopher and rhetorician were also outwardly active. Philosophers were to be found everywhere, tramping the roads, preaching their sermons full of rough jokes and low badinage and passing the hat in busy ports or at the great games, mixing gravity with affability in their endeavors to uplift the aristocrats—though Lucian scornfully put their place in noble households below that of athletes and jesters—even occupying the throne, as Marcus Aurelius. Four official chairs of philosophy, one each for the Stoic, Epicurean, Academic, and Peripatetic schools, were established at Athens under this emperor; but to be a philosopher required no degree or official permit. Anyone could read the works of Plato or the Stoics for himself, form a new but eclectic system, and then adopt the fraternity's guise of beard, cloak, and sober mien.

Throughout the Early Empire rhetoricians and philosophers continued their old battle for pre-eminence, partly to gain the practical rewards of patronage and students, partly to assert their theoretical superiority. Although rhetoric could never quite dethrone philosophy, the two subjects often merged in practice, and in general popularity rhetoricians were easily foremost.

Their art had its practical uses in the courts and councils and offered greater opportunities for the display of ability. Ancient civilization was a vocal one, and occasions for speaking increased, rather than diminished, as the prosperity of the Empire mounted. The rounded phrases of Greek and Latin eloquence rolled through the law courts and declamation halls of imperial cities as majestically as ever. Now Pliny chanted the praise of his emperor, now Dio Chrysostom rebuked and uplifted men of the Hellenic tradition; and everywhere grown men took the imaginary themes of the rhetorical schools and twisted them about in great or little displays.

In the Aegean a variety of rhetoricians called sophists flourished throughout the century and eventually became the subject of an extant work by Philostratus, the *Lives of the Sophists*. No single type of intellectual activity better illustrates the temper of the age.

The sophistic movement of the Empire, according to Philostratus, began with a certain Nicetes of Smyrna, who flourished under Vespasian. The innovation consisted essentially in dropping the old Greek idea that oratory was directly concerned with the life of the state, for this was an anachronism in the days when the boot of Rome was poised above the cities. Sophists converted their speeches into displays of rhythm and style, which borrowed heavily from tragedy and attempted in general to be Attic in outward appearance. Rising from the schools, the new oratory caught popular attention particularly among the rich and well-born of the Asiatic cities, who craved a genteel means of occupying their time as well as a mode of competing with each other. Throughout the second century men of consular families, patrons of their cities, perfected themselves in sophistic oratory and gave public exhibitions of their ability which remind one of the competitions of late medieval troubadours.

A fine instance of the fervor aroused by sophistry was the visit of Alexander of Cilician Seleucia to Athens. On the news of his arrival the Athenians eagerly gathered in the theater of Agrippa and settled down to hear the visitor, who began appropriately with a panegyric of Athens. Then the audience gave him a theme: "The speaker endeavors to recall the Scythians to their earlier nomadic life, since they are losing their health by dwelling in cities." [7] Pausing a moment, Alexander sprang from his seat with a look of gladness, and began his discourse—only to interrupt and recommence when that nabob, friend of emperors, and virtual despot of Athens, Herodes Atticus, arrived in aristocratic tardiness.

Later Herodes himself spoke in rivalry and, as befitted a lover of the past who used old letter forms on his inscriptions and rejected new words, addressed himself to a theme derived from the Athenian invasion of Sicily five centuries before. The fulsome compliments of his rival he repaid by bestowing on Alexander ten shorthand writers, twenty talents of gold, and other presents. At Rome, we are told, the Senate adjourned when the sophist Adrian spoke at the Athenaeum, a hall built by Hadrian to foster such displays of Greek learning; and Pliny the Younger rhapsodized over the performance of an earlier member of the sophistic fraternity who could argue on either side of a question at will.

Successful sophists were honored by their cities, by wealthy auditors, and especially by the emperors. Trajan gave one orator the right to travel free by land and sea; Hadrian went even further in presenting Dionysius of Miletus with equestrian status, a governorship, and the privilege of free meals at the Museum in Alexandria. Marcus Aurelius and subsequent emperors chose sophists for their secretaries of correspondence (*ab epistulis*)—with the result that imperial letters thereby sometimes became obscure and rhetorical—and two imperial chairs of rhetoric were established by Marcus, at Athens and at Rome. Adrian, who held the chair at Athens for a time, went down to his lectures in a carriage with silver-mounted bridles, and would return home escorted by those "loving Hellenic culture"; this paragon of professors, who was later elected to the Roman chair and then was made on his deathbed *ab epistulis* for Commodus, gave games, parties, and hunts to display his magnificence. Even teachers in private schools could build handsome estates and were much sought by the cities of the Aegean coast, for they enticed students from all over the East.

Marks of Intellectual Decline

The ferment of intellectual and artistic life in the second century was a notable one in terms of quantity. The revival of Greek letters in the era, which produced Plutarch, Lucian, and others, is perhaps a mark of the extent to which the peace of the Empire could fructify letters—

[7] Philostratus, *Lives* 572.

and of the limits of the fructification. We may not sneer at such an epoch, yet, to put the matter briefly, classical culture was rapidly declining in the second century. The first marks of this decline are archaism, erudition, repetitiousness, affected style, emphasis on collecting the wisdom of the past, and romanticism. All of these center about men's inability to engage in original, fresh thinking within classical frames and, in our eyes, are made more dangerous by the serious lack of interconnections between cultured and uncultured classes. Later, but still in the century, more positive indications attest an unconscious turn by some men from classical culture as a whole.

In literature there is no pagan writer of consequence during the two decades of Marcus Aurelius' reign apart from the *rara avis* Lucian, and perhaps also Apuleius. Such a situation was not novel. Since the outburst of literary activity under Trajan and in the earlier years under Hadrian, writers of note had been few; and men of the period felt that even the first century of the Empire had been poverty-stricken in comparison with the great days of the past. To find originality in the frigid, sterile intellectualism in the *Attic Nights* of Gellius or the mellifluous orations of Dio Chrysostom is difficult; even Plutarch, who has shaped the modern view of ancient heroes more than any other classical source, was essentially a sober, judicious collector of earlier knowledge which he embalmed in his flowery style, and some of his *Moral Essays* were confessedly compendia of the opinions of authority.

The emperor Hadrian preferred to Homer the almost unknown Antimachus of Colophon (c. 400 B.C.); other men of the second century quoted Ennius and Cato about as often as Virgil and Cicero, and passed over more modern writers. Though these thinkers criticized the old structure, often on grounds which they themselves did not fully sense, they could offer nothing to replace that which they attacked; their arid scholarship and emphasis on form can at best be described as an unconscious summation of the past in preparation for a new age of thought.

Neither philosophy, nor rhetoric, nor science was in better shape. The eclectic philosophical systems of the second century, while insisting that materialism was not enough and that man had a genuine significance, could not furnish a real substitute for materialism or expound satisfactory answers to the problems of the subjects of the Caesars. Since philosophic thought is a touchstone by which one may assess with rough justice the intellectual level of an age, it is significant that at this time

philosophy reached its lowest point in the ancient world. Its practition-
ers juggled the old ideas in eclectic combinations or haggled over
verbiage in learned conclave. Many of these men were serious and
tried desperately to enlighten those who still turned to them for advice,
but in this cure of souls they could only repeat in new words the
intellectual cargo of the past.

In the religious tone of Epictetus, in Plutarch's mystical belief in
demons, in the individualistic drive of Seneca and Epictetus, and even
in the desire of men for an "authority," one may sense powerful new
ideas striving to break forth, but they were not to emerge into the open
day in this period. Neoplatonism, which came closest to providing a
new answer, did not arise until the third century; Stoicism was becoming
the thin structure which we find in the *Meditations* of Marcus Aurelius;
Epicurean materialism was no longer the stuff to offer many men a
"quiet citadel." The physician Galen tells us that he progressed through
the philosophical schools, seeking for some rule of truth of unquestionable authority, but failed in his search. As a result, he asserts, he might
have fallen into Pyrrhonian skepticism—Sextus Empiricus' exposition
of this was very popular in the period—had he not been able to cling
fast to mathematics!

No one in this period exhibited the relentless drive, the delight in
rational achievement, or the sureness in the value of preaching which
Lucretius had displayed in the last days of the Republic. The Stoic self-
scrutiny which led one to true morality was much practiced but did not
lead to the proper end. Men from the Latin West seem to have been
more impatient than ever before of the closely reasoned, logical subtleties of the Greeks; even Marcus Aurelius, the philosopher king, openly
thanked his tutor Rusticus for steering him away from sophistry and
speculative treatises, and he expressly scorned syllogisms and the
physical theories of philosophy. The methods of classical thought were
no longer entirely satisfactory, but what was to take their place or reinvigorate their earlier power?

Not only the principles but also the defendants of philosophy were
subject to attack. While the lines of criticism were not new, the accusations of earlier ages were now redoubled. Authors of the period ridiculed
unmercifully the philosophic fakirs, who concealed avarice and corruption beneath their academic garb. Lucian went further in sensing the
hopelessness of the intellectual tradition of the philosophers of his day.
While respecting their aims and unconsciously yearning for solid ideals

of his own, he satirized the impostors of the day, attacked the logical hairsplitting as relentlessly as any Latin, and jeered at the revered Socrates. His dialogue *Hermotimus* is a superb statement of the skeptical attack on the idea that philosophies can lead men to their goal of a happy, serene life. The poor butt of the argument, who had spent twenty years in study and was promised another twenty before he reached the goal, is finally made to agree with the devastating criticism and decides to lead an everyday life guided by common sense like the multitude of the Empire. On purely intellectual grounds Lucian demolished the philosophies of his day as effectively as did the Christians on other bases of argument.

In some respects the rhetoricians fitted men for the practical life of the Empire better than did the philosophers. Certainly the Empire brought no decline in educators' attention to the subject, and rhetoric continued to enamor men down past the days of Augustine, who was himself trained as a rhetorician. With the study of rhetoric itself one can scarcely quarrel; the danger lay in the overly great concentration upon the subject by itself and the backward gaze of its teachers—though these men were in truth merely reflecting the attitude of the classes they served. In the schools of rhetoric, we may feel, men gained closed minds, steeped in the learning of the past, which refused to face the changes of the day. These were the decades of little creatures, timid in mind, good in details but weak in over-all perception, mouthing "commonplaces" rather than thinking.

Insofar as the echoes of imperial oratory have come down to us, they are sorry stuff. Sophistry was one of the last flowers of the Hellenic spirit and kept alive the Greek pride in the intellectual, artistic approach to life, but the unreality of the subjects treated by the sophists has already been suggested; of the themes given in the account of Philostratus not one refers to any event after the death of Demosthenes (322 B.C.). Latin rhetoric was in no better shape on the adult plane. Quintilian adopted an air of optimism and enthusiasm, and his *Oratorical Institutes* breathe a judicious, sober common sense which makes the work one of the freshest and most progressive of all Latin literature in the Empire. Still, he emphasized his subject at the expense of all other learning, and even he could not avoid displaying the unreality of declamatory practice, the overattention to the niceties of style and the search for old words, for paraphrases, for obscure allusions. Men regard it, he groaned, as a sign of genius if they cannot be understood. In these interrelated charges of unreality of subject and emphasis on style rather than substance, Quintilian unconsciously gives the impression that oratory was expected only to delight the auditors, and that even where lawsuits presented a real challenge the insidious poison of fantasy and essential indifference to truth was entering.

In view of the importance of rhetoric in the educational curriculum it is not surprising that we have several analyses of the reasons for the decline of oratory in its higher, public aspects. Generally men agreed in putting the blame on points of style, such as the overemphasis on declamations, and on the luxury of the era. Wealth leads to indolence and luxury, asserted the anonymous author of the essay *On the Sublime*, and so step by step men slide into bribery, legacy-hunting, and the laying of traps for others. Sometimes the critics went further and suggested an interrelation between the imperial structure of government and the deterioration of oratory; to this idea I shall revert shortly.

In the field of science the Roman Empire inherited the vast mass of knowledge and fanciful theory created by the classic Greek and Hellenistic eras. This material it passed on to later times in voluminous compendia such as the *Natural Questions* of Seneca, the *Natural History* of Pliny the Elder, the botanical studies of Dioscorides, and the geographical and astronomical surveys of Ptolemy. The scientific treatises of the Empire, in full or in epitome, were to be the last composed in ancient times and accordingly dominated medieval learning for over a millennium.

Neither the peace of the Empire nor its unification of the Mediterranean world led to wide-scale scientific advance; there is a lack of true criticism, of willingness to disagree with tradition, of breadth of view. In the second book of his *Natural History* Pliny commented in surprise on the fact that more than twenty Greek authors had published works on meteorology in an earlier period when the world was disunited and pirates disturbed the transmission of information. Yet now, he continued, when peace was so secure and letters and arts flourished under the encouragement of the emperor, nothing at all had been added by new investigation; not even the discoveries of old were handed on. In earlier days the rewards of discovery were not greater:

Age has overtaken the characters of mankind, not their revenues, and now that every sea has been opened up and every coast offers a hospitable landing, an immense multitude goes on voyages—but their object is profit not knowledge; and in their blind engrossment with avarice they do not reflect that knowledge is a more reliable means even of making profit.[8]

Pliny (and along with him Petronius, who explained the decline of the arts in similar vein) is harsh; his moral tone is querulous; but his criticism is not unjustified. Although Roman merchants, or at least Roman goods, penetrated to Scandinavia, to the Sahara, to China, Roman scholars gained far less knowledge of the world beyond the frontiers than one might expect; Ptolemy did little but consolidate contemporary knowledge of the Empire itself. The Romans remade the face of their earth more than any earlier people, by creating artificial harbors, by cutting tunnels and building roads, by constructing canals; they made extraordinary practical advances in architecture; yet here again theory failed to progress, and even labor-saving devices were not encouraged. In part the classical system of rhetorical and ethical education was responsible for the lack of scholarly investigation of the world. Ordinary education had never given much attention to scientific subjects, but in the Empire the scope of the school tended, if anything, to narrow; knowledge of the world was mainly expounded to illuminate passages in Virgil and other authors. The generally educated man probably paid as much attention to numerology and astrology as to mathematics and astronomy.

More serious, however, were several basic flaws in the classical approach to nature. Though one need not accept the modern Marxist argument that the decline of ancient civilization was due to the repressive influence of slavery on technological advance, there certainly was a great gulf between the scholar, a gentleman, and the active man, a slave or a person of the middle class. The chief tool of the former was by this time the citation of authority, backed primarily by the logical power of the human mind but also in such cases as Galen and Ptolemy by a very limited amount of observation. As Marrou has pointed out, one must not calculate the number of modern hypotheses held by any ancient man and so estimate the degree of his scientific spirit, for when placed in their philosophical or literary context these theories lose much of their significance in modern eyes. If Cicero knew that Hicetas thought the earth revolved, it was merely a piece of information of the same order as the name which Achilles carried in the court of Lycomedes, a nugget of pure erudition which led to no greater knowledge of the forces of nature.

[8] *Natural History*, 2.117–118.

Natural phenomena, moreover, were still essentially manifestations of the divine, almost a projection of the human being, i.e., they might be used to point moral lessons for humanity. All creations had a teleological purpose, and physical theory was secondary to the superstructure that one might erect upon it. Even the atomism of Epicureanism was essentially a base for ethical and theological argument.

The dominant impression to be gained from the architecture and sculpture of the second century is much the same as that which one must draw from the literary and intellectual trends. The famous revival of Hadrianic art, which has its modern admirers, is really one of the most saddening artistic aspects of the century. Its resuscitation of Greek models was artificial, apart from the creation of the idealized, deified type of Antinous (see Pl. VI *a*); its perfection of technique and style cannot mask its absence of content. Everywhere one finds the same fauns and sleeping hermaphrodites and all the other types which fill the museums of the modern world in their ineffable dullness. Earlier local styles of architecture gave way increasingly to a uniform imperial architecture, grandiose in size, lavish with marble, but academic in spirit. Pottery, jewelry, bronze work, and other household items, which turn up in great numbers in excavations from the second century, are solid but inert replicas of earlier, more inventive eras. The very quantity of the material is significant as showing the wide expansion of Mediterranean civilization, which afforded a base for later development, but in themselves artistic products of the era are rarely exciting.

Amid this general banality, to be sure, the art and architecture of the second century hint more temptingly than any other media at the new stirrings of thought which led to the future; intuitive perception revealed much to the artist which a more plodding intellectual approach hid from the thinker. We might without grave exaggeration begin the phase of late Roman art with the reign of Marcus Aurelius, especially with the remarkable reliefs of his Column.

Marcus Aurelius

Men's bodies were in general better nurtured by the Empire than by any previous structure of government in the ancient world. Their minds were better educated than ever before, and the intellectual and artistic output of the second century was probably as great, quantitatively, as that of any other ancient century. By this very epoch, however, men were becoming intellectually discontented, and in their weariness were unable to lift the Greco-Roman synthesis to new levels in literature, philosophy, rhetoric, science, or the arts. Some men were by now turning away toward fresher views of life; among the upper classes and the emperors the old classical pattern was still dominant at least outwardly, though its roots among the people were quietly rotting.

In his sculptured representations and in his own writings Marcus Aurelius beautifully illustrates at once the sway and the essential failure of the classical structure. One of the best portraits of this ruler is the famous bronze equestrian statue which commands the serene Piazza del Campidoglio in Rome (see Pl. V). Bareheaded, bearded, Marcus Aurelius looks downward and to his left in a weary, kindly fashion; the sculptor has made of him not an individual of flesh and blood but a symbol—and what the symbol means is not very clear.

To the right of the statue is the Palazzo dei Conservatori, along the stairs of which are imbedded three reliefs taken from an arch of Marcus Aurelius' day, companion pieces to eight others now on the Arch of Constantine. In one relief the emperor is again on horseback, stretching out his hand in pardon to two suppliant barbarians, while his generals and soldiers look on (see Pl. VI *b*). In a second the emperor is entering Rome in triumph, drawn in a four-horse chariot while a flying Victory crowns his head; in the third the ruler is sacrificing before the Capitoline Temple (on this very spot) in gratitude for his victory. Still bearded, compassionate, the emperor stands out sharply from the other figures in higher relief and accentuated position.

Again the reliefs leave the spectator puzzled. The story in each slab is clear, and technically both statue and reliefs are competent in the classical sense, though a purist would note that the composition of the reliefs is becoming flatter; the individual figures, too, are tending to fall apart in isolation and to turn more toward the spectator. Nonetheless the symbolic acts are chilly, hard, without an inner meaning or sense of movement.

Marcus Aurelius wrote to himself twelve books of *Meditations,* which have survived as an example of the self-scrutiny practiced by men of the Empire for the first time in history. The product of a weary man after his day's labors (in camp for the most part) were done, its pages are a series of repetitious, abrupt aphorisms. The general tone is not one of imperturbable optimism, as many scholars would have one believe; the ruler is writing not so much to keep himself from vanity or from abuse of power as to remind himself of his duty. As one penetrates through his own self-revelation behind the mask of the statues, one finds in Marcus Aurelius a man who, while kindly and seeking the good, was insecure as to his purpose in life, even afraid. He was tired and, though desperately sincere, able to think only in the stale mumblings of Stoic thought; there is perhaps no single original thought in the entire work, nor are there any extensive contemporary references: the *Meditations* are curiously timeless and disassociated from the events of the ruler's life.

From this work it is a long distance in time and spirit back to the only other extensive product of an imperial pen which has survived from the Early Empire, the *Res Gestae* of Augustus. The ruler who begins the Empire and the successor who essentially brings to a close its halcyon period are singularly different. The one wrote a stale, choppy rehash of old thoughts by which his weary soul, isolated as an individual, consoled itself; the other addressed an imperial, impersonal document to the world and in it displayed his pride in his achievements and the security in his purpose.

As great a contrast permeates the sculptured representations of the two. Augustus, in the Prima Porta statue, stretches out his hand in command and lifts his head proudly (see Frontispiece); on the reliefs of the Altar of Augustan Peace he is lightly distinguished from his companions while taking part in a solemn religious event which is charged with significance even to the casual glance of a bystander. Alike in statue and on relief, on the other hand, Marcus Aurelius masks his wistful face in a beard and is portrayed in hieratic stiffness. On the Conservatori reliefs he looms forth baldly and claims the spectator's undivided attention; static rite has replaced the action of faith.

The change is obvious, and in it is manifested more than the decline of classical civilization. To explain the origins of that change requires a sympathetic penetration, beneath the outward decline, into the depths of imperial thought.

Part Four

STERILITY
AND   FERTILITY

Sterility and Fertility

IN THE fifth book of *The Brothers Karamazov* Dostoievsky imagines a fleeting return of Christ to life in the public square of sixteenth-century Seville. When He gently performs miracles, He is arrested, and the Grand Inquisitor interviews Him by night before condemning Him to death. In the diatribe which ensues Dostoievsky expresses superbly the spirit of the material world, so nearly master of man—weak, ever sinful, and ignoble—and yet so irritatingly balked by the irrational spirit which lurks within humanity.

More particularly the aged fanatic upbraids his Prisoner for refusing those temptations of the Devil in the wilderness (bread, performance of miracle, and universal rule) by which man might easily be led in the way of subjection. At one point he bursts out in anger:

Thou didst reject the one infallible banner which was offered Thee to make all men bow down to Thee alone—the banner of earthly bread; and Thou hast rejected it for the sake of freedom and the bread of Heaven. Behold what Thou didst further. And all again in the name of freedom! I tell Thee that man is tormented by no greater anxiety than to find some one quickly to whom he can hand over that gift of freedom with which the ill-fated creature is born. But only one who can appease their conscience can take over their freedom. In bread there was offered Thee an invincible banner; give bread, and man will worship Thee, for nothing is more certain than bread. But if some one else gain possession of his conscience—oh! then he will cast away Thy bread and follow after him who has ensnared his conscience. In that Thou wast right. For the secret of man's being is not only to live but to have something to live for. Without a stable conception of the object of life, man would not consent to go on living, and would rather destroy himself than remain on earth, though he had bread in abundance.

No, he continues, instead of taking men's freedom from them Christ made it greater than ever. Christianity furnishes, not a simple, easy basis for life, but the enigmatic gift of freedom of conscience and will, than which nothing is more seductive, nothing the cause of greater suffering. The Church itself has contracted an alliance with the Devil and has attempted by miracle, mystery, and authority to make its flock mere sheep, who lay their freedom at its feet in return for material food; but this is not the way of his Prisoner:

Hadst Thou accepted that last counsel of the mighty spirit, Thou wouldst have accomplished all that man seeks on earth—that is, some one to worship, some one to keep his conscience, and some means of uniting all in one unanimous and harmonious ant-heap, for the craving for universal unity is the third and last anguish of men. . . . Hadst Thou taken the world and Caesar's purple, Thou wouldst have founded the universal state and have given universal peace. For who can rule men if not he who holds their conscience and their bread in his hands.

The three temptations of the Devil embodied for Dostoievsky "all the unsolved historical contradictions of human nature." In his biting, somber novel he allegorized the eternal clash between the material and the spiritual drives of man, a significant example of which is to be found in the history of the Roman Empire.

To their subjects the Caesars gave bread, someone to worship, and a sense of unity. Men, in turn, sacrificed their political freedom of thought to their earthly savior. So far there can be no question; but it is also true that those who enjoyed the golden age of the second century were no longer able to think seriously in the classical pattern. Is one to conclude that the Empire had grasped men's consciences and so had paved the way for the decline of classical civilization? Dostoievsky's novel may warn us not to accept this proposal too easily.

The historian of the Empire, like Dostoievsky, may justly feel that men are not easily satisfied by bread; beneath the surface the subjects of the Caesars were fashioning a new system of thought, wholly untouched by state pressure. Hints of this development have already been noticed; in the third century the tremendous shift in man's views of the world and of himself became obvious even to contemporaries. Sterility and fertility are closely interconnected in the later centuries of the Empire, for both arose out of the same pattern of causes.

XII

The Causes of Sterility

INTELLECTUALLY the second century was a plateau of outward activity and hidden decline, when viewed in classical terms. This decay has long exercised men's minds, though not perhaps to the degree that the social, economic, and political dissolution of the Empire has attracted speculative inquiry. If one may rightly assume that the intellectual decline was prior in time and also led logically to these other signs of the decline and fall of the Empire, the common distribution of interest is not just. Anyone who proceeds on this assumption, however, must very carefully consider the forces at work in classical civilization.

Modern scholars frequently avoid the problem of true explanation by labeling the Romans as men incapable of true culture. When the Romans destroyed the promising bloom of Hellenistic thought, they were incapable of providing a substitute; the true bearers of ancient civilization, the Greeks, could not hope to push ahead under barbarian masters. To this really extraordinary view, which often attributes a magic genius to Greek blood, I shall return later; and other similar mystical ratiocinations may be disregarded for the moment. The most tangible and seriously argued interpretations of the intellectual decline have revolved about two poles: the character of the imperial political structure or changes within the major classes of the Empire. Both solutions are superficially appealing. They have certain merits if they are not pushed too far, for to the root of the matter neither can penetrate.

Effects of the Imperial System

The evidence of the pressure by individual emperors and by the imperial system itself on freedom of thought has already been noted. By the reign of Trajan the conflict between freedom and absolutism on the political level had been settled by the victory of the latter. The Roman Republic had interrupted the pattern of monarchy established in the Hellenistic world, but that interruption had not endured. Once more one man ruled, and his power had now been erected on a wider and more solid footing.

Both this victory and the battles which had led to it did in truth have a serious effect on *political* thinking in the Empire. Many men had suffered, and under tyrannical, suspicious rulers a subject could never tell what degree of independence in utterance or act might bring swift punishment:

At all times under the sway of dictatorship, conformity means security and safety, non-conformity a thousand fateful possibilities of insecurity, of a shadowed future or of complete annihilation.[1]

The pages of Tacitus, lit by wars and lurid persecutions, show how devastating an effect intermittent repression had had on the more sensitive minds among the aristocracy, for if his work had utility, it was to teach men how to live under autocracy and maintain their internal dignity. He burst out once, that his theme

is narrow and inglorious . . . to record a succession of cruel edicts, of prosecutions heaped on prosecutions; to tell of friends betrayed, of innocent men brought to ruin, of trials all ending in one way, with a uniformity as monotonous as it is revolting.[2]

Tacitus, to be sure, could not really decide as well as Seneca or Epictetus what principles would safeguard both honor and life under an autocrat; while he accepted the Empire as necessary, he could neither endure its practice nor suggest a remedy for the decay of the people, the Senate, and the rulers. His indecision appears best in the words he attributes to Galba (addressing Piso): "You will have to rule over men who are neither fit for entire liberty, nor yet can tolerate entire servitude." [3]

Nor did he fathom any underlying purpose for the world. The vision

---

[1] E. K. Bramstedt, *Dictatorship and Political Police: The Technique of Control by Fear* (London, 1945), 229.

[2] *Annals* 4.32.3, 4.33.3.　　　　　[3] *Histories* 1.16.

of Rome's destiny which had fired Virgil and Livy is almost utterly missing in the works of Tacitus. In his own day the Roman ideal was broadening out to embrace the Empire, and a love of one's fellows was beginning to appear; but this man born out of time could draw no inspiration from either. Tacitus represents the bankruptcy of the old political ideals perhaps more completely than any other literary figure of the Early Empire.

Other illustrations of the intellectual hypnosis of the imperial system are not far to seek. The new age which Augustus had celebrated in his Secular festival was not the renewal of youth for which he had hoped, but rather the beginning of political senescence. His restoration of order necessarily entailed a limit on senatorial initiative; above all he brought a calculating, cold spirit to the system of government. The unexpected, the gay abandon, the zest of life went rapidly under a ruler whose motto was "make haste slowly." Mockingly but justly Tacitus compared the decorum of his funeral, which was carefully guarded by soldiers lest any irregularity occur, with the wild funeral pyre of Caesar in the Forum.

While the people and the provincials united in hailing Augustus as a savior and looked to him for all earthly benefits, the aristocrats deserted politics to an ever-greater degree; they amassed riches and lavished them on a hedonistic life. Tradition long drove the aristocrats to seek the honorific magistracies, however devoid of content these became, but from true political life they withdrew in a manner which alarmed even the emperors, who tried repeatedly—and in vain—to reinvigorate the Senate.

The extent to which men generally abstained from political thought is displayed in the curiously unhistorical or even antihistorical frame of mind of authors. Ancient thought often used history merely as a quarry for examples, but insofar as rhetoricians and philosophers of the Empire cited from history they drew almost exclusively from the days of the Greeks and the Roman Republic. Now and then Plutarch and Gellius set down the names of Tiberius or Nero—chiefly to date an event—but very rarely in contrast with the names of men dead when Augustus came to power. In reading imperial literature one feels that time stood still when once the Empire was established, and that the events of the first century had been dismissed from men's minds. The age was a conservative one, and its scholars were in part overcome by the weight of ancient knowledge; the jurist Cassius, for one, had no doubt "that all matters had been better and more wisely ordered in days of old, and that any changes would be changes for the worse." [4] Still, in failing to refer to incidents of imperial history, men may also have felt it wiser not to enter a potentially dangerous ground.

Another mark of the decay of political thought is the decline of rhetoric. Ancient explanations of this decline sometimes are cast in political terms, though usually with great care. Seneca the Elder commented that public rewards for the profession of rhetoric had disappeared when the Empire took over the bestowal of offices. The speakers in a carefully argued *Dialogue concerning the Orators* (assuredly the early work of Tacitus) accepted without cavil the peace and ease of the imperial government; but they all, save one, drew the inevitable conclusion that great oratory could not flourish in such an epoch. Lucian was more succinct in calling rhetoric a harlot which had lost its independence; an anonymous essay *On the Sublime,* perhaps of the first century, was bolder in quoting a philosopher:

In these days we seem to be schooled from childhood in an equitable servility, swaddled, I might say, from the tender infancy of our minds in servile ways and practices. We never drink from the fairest and most fertile source of literature, which is freedom, and therefore we come to show a genius for nothing but flattery.[5]

This "hackneyed" view the anonymous author rejects—would he have dared do otherwise?

In his *Dialogue* Tacitus was more polite, but scarcely less frank. One speaker asserted that by the middle of the reign of Augustus,

in consequence of the long period of peace, and the unbroken spell of inactivity on the part of the commons and of peaceableness on the part of the Senate, by reason also of the working of the great imperial system, a hush had fallen upon eloquence, as indeed it had upon the world at large.

Or again:

What is the use of long arguments in the Senate, when good citizens agree so quickly? What is the use of one harangue after another on public platforms, when it is not the ignorant multitude that decides a political issue, but a monarch who is the incarnation of wisdom?

In sum, men had fallen away more from the old-fashioned outspokenness (*libertas*) than from eloquence; as William Pitt once translated a pregnant phrase of the *Dialogue:*

4 Tacitus, *Annals* 14.43.1.   5 *On the Sublime* 44.3.

It is with eloquence as with a flame. It requires fuel to feed it, motion to excite it, and it brightens as it burns.[6]

In writing his historical works Tacitus was impelled in large part by a sense of opposition, and he ventured to speak his mind about the past in an era of relative freedom. Thereafter the fires of hate were utterly damped in the dullness of a secure life; the placid second century had no outstanding historians. Insofar as a subject mentioned or addressed the reigning emperor, he displayed reverence of a most abject nature —"subdued by unending slavery," as Ambrose later put it.[7] When the imperial tutor Fronto wrote a history of the Parthian war of Lucius Verus, he made his pupil a greater general than Trajan; we even have a letter from Verus in which the emperor quite clearly suggests the tone he wished to have followed.

In such a structure, where the rulers by their controls on thought and the subjects by their desire to set up symbols collaborated to replace thought by vapid rhetoric, true freedom of thought in the political sphere, and particularly in history, seems almost impossible. If this conclusion were correct, it would lead to even more sweeping—and dangerous—corollaries on the general decline of thought, for mankind cannot permanently sunder its political and nonpolitical thinking. Not all men, however, had given up their consciences for bread. One example will suffice—that of the Syrian satirist of Fronto's own day, Lucian of Samosata.

Lucian was a man of fertile imagination but not of great originality, for he, like his fellows, quarried in the classic past. His great gift was a love of truth and an ability to penetrate shams. And so he warred relentlessly in his cool, clear style against the mystic quackery of Alexander of Abonoteichos, one of the greatest religious charlatans of all time, against the romantic perversion of the truth in travelers' tales, against the endless study of the philosophers which brought them no closer to enjoying the world in which they lived. In the work entitled *Nigrinus* he bluntly attacked Rome as producing flattery and servitude of mind; but even more in the delightful essay *The Way to Write History* he reveals abundantly that at least one man of the second century understood scholarly objectivity.

In general outline the argument of the essay is directed first to show the faults of contemporary history, as marked in the various Greek

[6] *Dialogue* 38.7, 41.7, 36.1.
[7] *Exameron* 5.15(52) (*Corpus Scriptorum Ecclesiasticorum Latinorum* 32.1, 179).

accounts of the Parthian war; then the author expounds the qualities of the true historian. In the first part Lucian castigated the undisguised, clumsy flattery by men in search of patrons, which blurred the distinction between panegyric and history. His victims, we learn, engaged in the baldest of imitation of Thucydides and other classic models, while corrupting their style by inserting Latin terms for weapons and military engines; they portrayed the emperor as Achilles and dilated upon his shield; rhetoric marred all, and trifles such as the wanderings of a Moorish trooper were exaggerated for romantic interest at the expense of the important events.

To Lucian the prime quality of the true historian is this: "First and foremost, let him be a man of independent spirit, with nothing to fear or hope from anybody; else he will be a corrupt judge open to undue influence" (trans. Fowler). In oblique reference to the imperial pressure on thought Lucian argues that the historian is not to falter in fear that Alexander will be irked by a true account of his murder of Clitus, nor is Thucydides to be silent in describing the follies of the popular leader Cleon. "The historian's one task is to tell the thing as it happened." On the other hand Lucian discourages his student from carrying private prejudices into a historical account, and in one brief warning on overextensive praise or censure he gives advice which many later historians could profitably have heeded: "Historical characters are not prisoners on trial."

The historian will collect his facts carefully, order them in logical fashion so as to bring order out of chaos, and recount his story in a lucid, poetic, yet restrained style. Above all the historian must write with an eye to eternity and ask from it his reward. "And that reward? That it be said of you, 'This was a man indeed, free and free-spoken; flattery and servility were not in him; he was truth all through.'" To emphasize his final point Lucian tells the story of Sostratus of Cnidus, who built the great lighthouse at Alexandria and carved thereon his name. Over the inscription he put plaster and inscribed on this the king's name— when finally the plaster fell off, the true builder was revealed. "So too should the historian write, consorting with Truth and not with flattery, looking to the future hope, not to the gratification of the flattered."

Further than this essay by Lucian there is no need to go. As he hints, the emperors stood at the gates through which men passed into the realm of wealth, official position, and contemporary esteem. A great part of the cultured elements of mankind, weak as always, found it both safer and more profitable to ape the attitudes of the ruler of the moment, and in seeking their "bread" they were not always conscious of their servility. In another essay Lucian tried carefully to rebut the charge that by entering state service he was giving up his boasted freedom of thought, and he himself actually composed a panegyric of the mistress of Lucius Verus!

To an extraordinary degree men were bent by imperial pressures and, we must always add, by their own desire to throw up a lofty, perfect symbol of the man-become-God, and so they engaged in panegyric. Those like Tacitus, who refused to laud, were unconsciously warped by the imperial system to the point where they could not reconcile the truth and their prejudices. The hot vigor with which Lucian hammers at his central idea that history is truth is a bitter indictment of the historiography of his epoch—but his essay also attests that even in the intellectually poverty-stricken second century a reverence for the truth still survived.

After all, the belief that the state can by force or skill gain complete mastery over the mind and the emotions of mankind is false. The pessimistic calculation of the limitations of the human being which underlies the modern experiments in this direction, the autocratic certainty that man's nature can be measured and so controlled—these are hobgoblins firmly to be rejected.

That conditions such as the state control of thought described by George Orwell in his horrible fantasy 1984 may exist for a time cannot be denied, but that such conditions could long endure is impossible. The mind of man, though dominated by his basic emotional and physical necessities, has never permanently been suppressed either by these internal factors or by outside pressures exploiting his lusts and fears; in the myth of the Grand Inquisitor Dostoievsky saw far deeper into the complex, contradictory drives of man, who will reject bread for conscience at the most unexpected points. Man is neither entirely rational nor merely an animal—therein lies his enduring strength.

From this point of view it is incidental that the imperial system did not actually attempt to dictate all aspects of thought, for the system would have failed had it tried to do so. Even as far as imperial control went, it raised in opposition the assertion of the inner freedom of man by the philosophers Seneca and Epictetus. In very fact, however, the state interfered less openly and less arbitrarily in the second than in the first century. We cannot entirely discount the assertion of Tacitus that the reign of Trajan was a happy one where man was free to think what he wished and to say what he thought, or again the brief celebration by Plutarch of the Roman peace, where there was neither war nor civil strife, where agriculture and trade were secure, where "we may speak or act, be silent or at leisure, as we choose." [8]

Only within the political sphere, and there incompletely, did the Caesars seriously limit freedom of thought. It must always be remembered that the arts and letters generally depended far more directly on the upper classes of the Empire than on the emperors. The attitude of a wearer of the purple in Rome cannot be used to explain the pervasive quality of sterility—in classical terms—in provincial architecture and art; nor does an effort to couple the presence or absence of writers with the character of a ruling emperor carry any real conviction. When one man in Rome acted or spoke in a certain fashion, those of his subjects who wished to ape—or feared not to do so—might act like automata, but not all were thus impelled.

In the Empire, indeed, a new system of thought was secretly arising. This important development is an invincible rebuttal to any argument that state control was the direct, sufficient cause of the sterility of the second century, and that imperial pressure on thinkers had destroyed the capacity of thought of the subjects of the Empire. The essential problem is the fact that within the classical system of thought men had nothing to say.

Effects of the Class Structure

A more direct explanation of the intellectual decline which has gained many adherents in recent decades revolves about the class structure of the Empire. Essentially this solution postulates a decline of the upper classes and a rise of the masses and of "mass thinking." Superficially this is a winning type of interpretation, but it takes us in the end no farther than the explanation in terms of political autocracy.

There can be no doubt that civilization in the Roman Empire was expressed primarily in upper-class terms by members or clients of those classes. If one views the Empire purely as a period of decay, it is tempting to picture the process as one where the cultured classes were supplanted by other, less intellectual elements, which brought with them their primitive notions. The Orient, the barbarians, the military, the

[8] *Moralia* 469E.

masses—any or all of these can neatly be cast as villains. Seeck described the ensuing tragedy as "die Ausrottung der Besten"—the extermination of the best—which he laid at the door of the more tyrannical emperors; Rostovtzeff speaks in a less personal tone of the dying out of the old upper classes and the rise of men and ideas from the masses.

In terms of the actual historical development of the Empire this theory has little support. During the period men did move upward from one class to another with greater ease than had ever before been possible, even though class distinctions were steadily sharpened. While men could gain money with comparative ease through commerce, industry, and other occupations, this process continued; a fine example of a parvenu, the rich freedman Trimalchio, is sketched in the *Satyricon* of Petronius. Such men rose, and the more elevated classes tended to die out through execution, loss of property, or natural failure to reproduce themselves.

By itself, however, this movement would scarcely have had any serious effect on the intellectual activity of the Empire. In Western provinces like Gaul or Britain, where whole districts had thus to rise or where families came up quickly and then disappeared, cultural originality could not be expected. In the older areas like Asia Minor, on the other hand, the framework of civilization was more deeply set, and parvenus were absorbed with remarkable speed. Trimalchio had his Greek and Latin libraries; if he had had sons and grandsons, these offspring would have been molded by the system of imperial education into persons indistinguishable from scions of older families.

While it is true that the imperial aristocracy of the second century differed in family background from that of the first, and also was less "Roman" in many ways, its basic attitudes toward culture do not appear to have been radically different from those of the Roman and provincial aristocracy of earlier decades; and such changes as can be detected are to be found just as much in Virgil and Seneca as in Dio Chrysostom and Plutarch. In any case, not only did older families tend to hang on longer than some scholars realize, but also the imperial escalator tended to slow down and even to halt in the second century, the very period in which intellectual decay becomes noticeable.

Rostovtzeff broadens out the explanation in terms of classes by noting that more men of the Empire than ever before sought the fruits of civilization, and at the end of his famous *Social and Economic History of the Roman Empire* queries, "Is not every civilization bound to decay as soon as it begins to penetrate the masses?" To answer this pessimistic question, one might perhaps do no more than put a counterquery: Is not every civilization already decaying when it begins to penetrate the masses?

Such an answer, however, accepts certain basically false assumptions in the initial query. Actually, the man of culture in the Empire became ever more separated from the masses; this very separation was probably more devastating than the expansion of the cultured circles. Moreover, when we face basic movements of human history, their analysis in terms of classes carries us but little farther than that in terms of Great Men. Are men of the lower classes necessarily lacking in intellect, especially those men who do rise? We are all descended from the lower classes, but we create ever afresh for ourselves a myth that birth and intelligence go together—and just as constantly the myth is disproved, now by Socrates in Periclean Athens, now by Shakespeare in Elizabethan England. If the Christian achievement in the Roman Empire is to be taken as primarily a product of the lower classes of the cities—and this is certainly as valid as its ascription to the upper classes—who can feel that these elements were intellectually incompetent?

Nor is it just to argue that civilization is the product of the upper classes. The more learned, more wealthy circles mainly express and give form to civilization at all times, but this fact does not necessarily imply that they "make" the civilization in question, however arrogantly they may feel that they do so. The rise of the new order of thought in the Empire, for instance, can be shown to be a matter essentially independent of classes—or of geographical areas.

The upper classes are never as significant as they assert themselves to be. One may grant that they have considerable importance as a vehicle for the thoughts of their age, and the historians are forced to concentrate on these elements inasmuch as they alone speak clearly to the modern world. The problem still remains that in the second century of the Empire the upper classes were no longer capable of intellectual advance within the framework of classical civilization.

As men rose to this circle, they found sterility; as influences went out from it to the lower middle and lower classes of the cities, they were likewise found to be sterile. To this fact may be ascribed the emergence anew of local tongues, cults, and customs in the late second century. The failure of the cities to continue their Romanization (or Hellenization) is not due to the upward movement of the lower classes: it reflects the failure of the urban classes themselves to be satisfied by their inherited culture.

Rise of Individualism

A complete explanation of a major historical phenomenon is never afforded by the statement of any one single factor as its sole and sufficient cause. One may, however, justly feel that the source of an explanation must be sought in a certain sphere: assuredly if human history arises out of the actions of human individuals, the historian must seek its basic motive forces within the psychological changes of the human. In this very place there is one great key which unlocks for us the understanding of the basic pattern—though not of all the ramifications—of the progress of ancient civilization.

The Empire represented a final, catastrophic completion to the individualizing movement of the ancient world. Man lost his political significance as an active member of a political group; the political and social units which had enfolded and supported the individual, from which the thinker had gained his vital strength, were broken down. Humanity, thus liberated and made individual to an extent never known before—or again until the present century—was even less able to bear its position than can modern man; and the initial sign of that incapacity was the collapse of the classical intellectual system.

This collapse first affected the upper classes, which led the way in individualization, and then passed into the rest of the population. From this root, far more than any other factor, came the political, economic, and social decline of the Empire; by the late second century the emperors were finding the more advanced urban classes inadequate to support the Empire and were turning to the peasants, who themselves felt ever less satisfied by the stale answers of classical civilization. The way had been paved for the twin nemesis of the third century, internal dissension and external invasion; and thence arose the final collapse.

The whole of ancient intellectual development in this view is one great swing, the causes of which lie within the human being himself. For the Empire proper the value of this explanation lies in the basic simplicity with which it can embrace both the sterility of the second century and the intellectual rebirth which was to follow. To analyze the tension between individual and group in general philosophical terms is beyond my province, for the virtue of history lies primarily in its attention to the concrete fact of past development; nor is it possible to consider in detail the rise of individualism as a historical reality down to the Empire. In treating only the broadest outline, the existence of crosscurrents will perhaps be unjustly neglected, but the main course of ancient civilization may appear the more clearly.[9]

The opening phases of this great swing were noted above in the first chapter. After the display of magnificent individualism by the leaders of the Mycenean world, reflected for all later time in the epics of Homer, the Greek world had settled back into a life of tradition and of group ties. But these ties began to break as the Greek world started to expand physically and intellectually (about the eighth century B.C.).

Although old groups yielded their dominance over their members very slowly—first politically as the clans lost their power and then in other fields—the urge of man to assert himself practically against his group ties proceeded inexorably. Along the coast of Asia Minor, where Greek culture first flowered and Greeks first began to sense the wider world, the power of the human mind found ever-greater scope for its individual display. In this earliest breakdown of group life, significantly enough, thinking men began to explore the idea of afterlife; here too there occurs a pessimism of the human cast adrift in an uncertain world.

At about this same time Hebrew thinking was turning to more individual terms, but the main line of Greek philosophical inquiry failed to take up the practical development of contemporary society and to carry it to a firm establishment of the human as an unique object, of importance to himself and to the world generally. The old patterns of thought could not be thus abruptly broken. The earliest Greek philosophers considered nature first, and moved from nature to an explanation of man as being of the same substance. From early days, too, the Greeks conceived all existence in general terms as a fixed quantity. The individual was merely a "type" of an ideal; time as such had no real significance in the sense of development or differentiation. Heraclitus might assert that in forming his philosophy he "searched himself," but he came in the end to a pantheistic view of life in which all was changing and the individual had no real basis.

Although Greek culture emphasized the human far more than Oriental civilization; its theory could not advance to the Christian stress

[9] At various points in the following pages I am greatly indebted to the interesting, if bold, survey by Georg Misch, *A History of Autobiography in Antiquity* (Cambridge, Mass., 1951).

on the individual. As Aristotle put it, poetry deals with the universal and history with the particular; therefore, "poetry is a thing more philosophical and of greater import than history." [10] The idealist theory of Plato, which canonized the tendency of classical civilization, was not seriously breached until the rise of Christianity.

Nevertheless man was slowly coming to examine himself as an individual and made great strides toward virtual emancipation from the old bonds in the Hellenistic Age. In this era the Greeks poured out over the eastern and then the western Mediterranean. Whether at home or abroad they concentrated largely on economic matters and lost the greater part of their political capacities, first to the Hellenistic monarchs, then to the ruthless march of the Roman Republic. For long, many clung to the old gods and to the little cities, but as the Hellenistic world collapsed they found themselves ever more adrift in an incalculable universe. The Jews, who were faced by the same problems in large part, threw up appeals to God in the Psalms. Some Greeks turned to Oriental cults which could give them personal assurances, but more adopted the new philosophies of personal conduct, the Stoic, Epicurean, and others. In general, all these means of comfort emphasized the inner independence of man as the base upon which he must build his view of the world.

The idea of *autarky* under natural law was not new. The accompanying subjective emphasis on self-criticism and self-education toward perfection had appeared at least a century earlier. Where the Hellenistic philosophers broke new ground was in their disregard of the state and the family; they concentrated upon the human as a cosmopolitan member of the brotherhood of man and correspondingly as an individual who was subject only to the laws of nature.

The personal values of mankind, it must be noted, were an internal matter to these philosophers. Man might have internal freedom of thought, but he did not need to express that thought externally; each individual was concerned essentially for himself and not for his fellows. Stoics might at times find that their "conscience" or sense of duty drove them to voice moral opposition, and their doctrine urged them to perform their duties to the state; but the only school which consistently felt a necessity to speak out was the Cynic, whose members barked like dogs at powerful and poor alike under the shield of complete contempt for wealth and comfort. Here Greek individualism reached its highest

[10] *Poetics* 9.1451b.

point, one with which Christian thinkers were later to find themselves in agreement in many respects. Cynicism has been well described as a levelling attack upon the city-state and all its typical social institutions. It looks not so much to the setting up of a new social principle as to the destruction of all civic ties and the abolition of all social restrictions. It aims at a return to nature in a sense which makes nature the negation of civilization. The Cynic philosopher, dirty, witty, contemptuous, shameless, a master of billingsgate, is the earliest example of the philosophical proletarian.[11]

Other Hellenistic philosophies constructed a more widely suitable pattern of internal independence, but their autarky could be neither complete nor entirely helpful. The basic reason for this limitation is the fact that the schools continued the idealizing tendency of earlier Greek thought. Accordingly these philosophies could give man neither an ethical nor a theological basis for belief in the significance of the individual; only in the first century B.C. did the shadowy figure Posidonius begin to point the way toward a less rational, more religious interpretation of the world and of humanity.

The Roman Republic interrupted the process of liberation of the individual. One of the most distinctive marks of early Rome was its long-enduring, close-knit system of social and political groups ascending from the family, under the father's control, to the state linked by its piety to the gods on high. As in earlier Greek society men were so attached to these groups and so governed by group tradition and customs that the citizen had very little scope for assertion of his personality; freedom of thought and action alike was severely limited.

The Republic, to be sure, was not of quite the same character as preclassical and classical Greece. The aristocrats, in particular, had vied in establishing the pre-eminence of their families—so a Scipio proclaimed in his epitaph that his public honors had ennobled his house and that his ancestors might accordingly feel proud of their offspring, and Appius Claudius the Censor (c. 300 B.C.), in erecting a temple, placed therein the portraits of his ancestors. Funerals of notables included the praise both of the dead man and of his ancestors, who were represented by persons wearing appropriate masks.

Thus far the aristocrat felt himself to be a representative of his family and ancestors rather than an individual in his own right, but this unity

[11] G. H. Sabine and S. B. Smith, *Cicero's Commonwealth* (Columbus, 1929), 18.

of living and dead led also to the pride of the living and their assertion of freedom of action to attain glory, the highest mark of which was the celebration of a triumph. When one of the great men of the great families died, his heirs emblazoned not only his name but also his deeds upon the tomb. By the second century the aristocracy had begun to snap the ties which restricted its individuality, and in the next century, which brought the end of the Republic, men vied ruthlessly for their own pre-eminence.

By the age of Cicero Rome had gone far in catching up with the general trend of the ancient world toward a greater factual liberty of the individual and even had taken steps toward a philosophical appreciation of the dependence of the human being upon himself. While the emergence of biography and somewhat realistic portraiture can be traced back into the Hellenistic Age, first-century Rome fostered both in unwonted zeal; and the great men of the post-Gracchan period poured out a spate of autobiographical writings. Cicero, who was one of this group, went on to justify in more general terms the variety of human character; in his treatise *On Duties* he rejected the Platonic mold in part by asserting that "each must cling to what is his own" and not imitate the nature of others.[12] The one literary form to which Rome may lay credit, the satire, is a mode of detecting human reality and diversity. True lyric, again, has been called a product of the Hellenistic world, but it found its perfect representative in the fiery young Catullus, pouring out his own soul in true love.

In the Republic the Romans still moved forward hesitatingly on the common path. Even though they had progressed rapidly, and in part on their own terms, toward an individualization of humanity (see Pl. I *a*), the old corporate feelings did not entirely disappear even on the upper levels. Cicero, for example, felt a clash between the tendencies of Hellenistic philosophy and Roman tradition, and tried to unite a concern for the unity of the state with the due welfare of the human; the judicious though unconscious balance and tenacity of the Romans enabled them to conquer their empire and again, unconsciously, to create a frame of life in which the individual became ever more liberated.

Only with the institution of the Empire did the drive of ancient civilization attain its culmination—or its abyss. In the first century after

[12] *On Duties* 1.31.110–14 (whether borrowed from Panaetius or not, this view fits the Roman experience).

Christ the senatorial aristocracy tore itself to pieces in its rivalries and was replaced by a new, imperial aristocracy. The emperors did not consciously try to destroy the class system of their world—its distinctions were, if anything, sharpened as the Empire wore on—but they did attempt to break down the independence of the upper classes, to destroy independent means of expression for groups of their subjects, and to reduce these subjects to the status of individuals standing alone before the state. Groups conscious of their unity might be dangerous; atoms, whatever their ideas, could either be ignored or more easily suppressed.

By the reign of Trajan the emperors had achieved their ends. Roman society now was one in which the individual operated for himself, scrambling for crumbs from the tables of the rich patrons, who in turn danced attendance on the ruler to get their provinces and consulships or retired in individual isolation. The emperor's court, with its "friends" of first and second degree in his council, was a shifting hierarchy where men, not groups, had their influence through personal ties to the master; beside adulation and flattery stood inevitably "that deadly poisoner of a true heart, self-interest." [13] The individualism of these nobles is apparent in the philosophical teachings of Seneca and still more of Epictetus, both of whom tried to establish a basis for the liberty and dignity of the human outside the political field.

In the provinces the urban form of organization was widely expanded in the Empire. Outwardly this development suggests the rise of a firmer political structure; but in fact the true spirit of the ancient city waned as the upper classes gained complete dominance over the local governments, and the lower classes and peasants felt themselves to be exploited by an institution in which they had no part. Here again, by the time of Trajan, the huge concentration of power in imperial hands was sucking out of the cities their local autonomy. Increasingly men felt their destinies determined from above, and local groups lost their significance.

Even within the families the same process of atomization may be detected as the world grew more civilized. Within Roman law, the sway of which widely increased, the emperors came to direct and also to limit the powers of the family head, especially from the time of Hadrian. Sons and wives alike became steadily more independent agents, and Musonius Rufus even asserted that both sexes must be governed by the same standards of morals. Slaves remained chattels in the eyes of the law, but Hadrian deprived owners of their power

[13] Tacitus, *Histories* 1.15.

to execute slaves; and the increasing humanitarianism of the Empire brought other mitigations of their position. Plutarch bitterly condemned Cato the Elder for working slaves until they were useless and old, and then selling them off, "thinking there ought to be no further commerce between man and man than whilst there arises some profit by it." [14] The human body, indeed, became ever more significant in men's minds in the Empire, a reflection of internal character according to the theories of the physiognomists, a precious object which must be protected in life and properly buried in death.

The liberation of the individual from old ties and supports is a towering phenomenon of imperial social history which has never been fully analyzed in all of its manifold illustrations; the fact itself is most certain even though the wide range of supporting evidence cannot here be adduced. This liberation is not to be taken as a complete negation of society. The aristocracy had a vigorous, even hectic life at the baths, dinners, and soirees, and family groupings continued to have hidden political influence. The masses everywhere came together in associations for religious and funerary purposes on a remarkably wide scale, for such groupings of the poor were given blanket legal authorization by a senatorial decree of the first century after Christ. Nor, to take the most important political instance of group organization, could the emperors afford to destroy the *esprit de corps* of their armies even though they earnestly tried to link themselves to that spirit.

Nevertheless, apart from the army—and Christian congregations— the groupings of men in the imperial age, as for instance "the Epicurean band full of joy," strike one as a weak expression of social urges.[15] As Hegel put it, the Empire was a duality—"on the one side, Fate and the abstract universality of sovereignty; on the other, the *individual* abstraction." [16] That the conflict of the two could lead to the essential misery of the human, Hegel also pointed out; individualism and the decay of public life were correlated.

It is notable that the Empire almost universally accepted man's right to kill himself in "boredom with life" when he found the world no longer palatable, for the attitude of an age toward suicide is often a touchstone by which its individualism may be measured. The treatment of suicide as a right first became evident when old group attitudes broke

[14] *Cato the Elder* 5 (Clough).
[15] *Corpus Inscriptionum Latinarum* X 2971.
[16] G. W. F. Hegel, *Philosophy of History* (New York, 1944), 317.

down in the Greek world from the fifth century onward. In Stoic theory suicide was even at times a duty—like the death of Cato—to display or preserve one's freedom. In the Empire Pliny the Elder termed suicide "the supreme boon god has bestowed on man among all the penalties of life," [17] and it was often preceded by public debate as to one's justification. Only as a new concept of the individual's place in the world emerged did pagan (and Christian) thought begin to deny men this means of exit.

Imperial Substitutes for Earlier Ties

It is true that the Empire offered its subjects certain substitutes for the support and control which men of earlier ages had derived from political groupings, from close social and religious ties, and from the traditions and customs of the group. These substitutes were essentially three: the ideal of an eternal world-state in which all men were members and from which they could receive social and economic justice; material well-being for the individual's body; and the improvement of the individual's mind.

The creation of the first of these, the ideal of the world-state under a benign ruler, has already been inspected, and its inadequacy can easily be demonstrated. The joint concepts of the divinely appointed ruler guarding his flock and of a unified world destined to confer its blessings of peace, prosperity, and justice to all in perpetuity are a sweeping, magnificent vision, perhaps even a noble one (see Pls. II–III). Certainly this cosmopolitan state was a culminating point of ancient thought, from which further progress in a direct line would have been difficult; and the ideal of Rome has in numerous aspects greatly influenced the thinking of all later ages.

Many a eulogy of this ideal, however, fails to consider the price that had to be paid for its institution in the Empire, insofar as it was actually realized—the loss of political liberty, of local autonomy, of all the groups and institutions which had previously supported mankind. Cosmopolitanism and its individual parallel, individualism, rose hand in hand to frightening heights. Man now had justice and security, but could he rely upon this lofty, distant ideal for strength and support?

The second substitute for the old groupings of life, material prosperity, had been emphasized since the days of Augustus. Tacitus linked "peace and the prince"; Dio Chrysostom more bluntly spoke of "peace

[17] *Natural History* 2.27.

and servitude," the one of which all men wanted while the other was no longer a sign of baseness.[18] This famous "Roman peace" was construed by contemporaries quite largely in terms of security of property, of marriage, and of children. These things are always the most important objects in normal life, but despite—or perhaps because of—the overvaulting ideal of the world-state the dominant impression one gains from a survey of life in the Empire is that of rampant materialism, of concentration on the petty ends of human life. The inscriptions blatantly emphasized the wealth and generosity of the upper classes; social position within the imperial hierarchy depended to a tremendous extent upon one's financial position; and the literary descriptions of life prove the concentration of imperial man on its practical, material aspects. The fortunate man gained security, but he forgot liberty.

To interpret the spirit of the Empire solely as one emphasizing the goods of this world would be an undue simplification; the historian must always be cautious in lending his ears to the ever-present castigations of society by the censorious. It is true, nonetheless, that the world-state of the Roman Empire was founded on a material prosperity, the blessings of which bulked large in the praises of its subjects. Insofar as this underpinning placed temporal things above the human being and his ideals, it is scarcely to be lauded, nor could it serve as an enduring foundation for life. Long afterward Gregory the Great looked back and observed of the Empire:

There was long life and health, material prosperity, growth of population, and the tranquillity of daily peace, yet while the world was still flourishing in itself, in their hearts it had already withered.[19]

Most men were content with the role of placid sheep under the care of the good shepherd. Those few who were not could turn to the inherited resources of the Greco-Roman intellectual synthesis and from this source might strive to gain some purpose for their existence and a direction to their efforts. Culture, in sum, might replace politics.

Learning did spread widely in the Empire. That this extension of Greco-Roman civilization was praiseworthy in itself, was a potent force for medieval culture, and provided a powerful means for unifying the Empire I should be the last to deny, but that it justifies the Empire, as modern scholars (following in the footsteps of Virgil) often argue, is

---

[18] Dio Chrysostom, *Oration* 31.125.

[19] *Homilies* 28 (Migne, *Patrologia Latina* 76, col. 1212); quoted by Christopher Dawson, "The Dying World," *A Monument to St. Augustine* (New York, 1930), 25.

a conclusion which is open to criticism on many grounds. Even more important, this intellectual heritage had serious weaknesses as a crutch for the dissatisfied individual. Its idealist tinge provided no sound justification for his individuality. At best it could satisfy only his mind, for the Stoic creed, and the other schools in lesser degree, attempted to excise the emotions from the governance of human action. Man stood alone, separated from nature and from his body; if he felt dissatisfied, the cure lay in ever-greater concentration on the mind alone.

A further, even more critical weakness of Greco-Roman civilization was its limitation to life in this world. Mankind had long had naïve ideas of the survival of some part of the human after death, and these ideas had occasionally bubbled up into more conscious arguments by the Orphics and others. As classic Greece passed into the Hellenistic Age, and this in turn yielded to the Empire, man hearkened ever more to the promises of the Dionysiac mysteries or of the Neopythagoreans, who preached that the soul might be purified by prayer and discipline—i.e., by purely human means, not by faith or rite—and so be separated from the body.

The current was a natural one, given the increased dissatisfaction of restless men, but the thinkers of the age frowned on detailed portrayals of this afterlife and especially on ideas of the resurrection of the body. While even the Epicureans conceded a soul to man, neither they nor the Stoics could accept the idea of personal immortality in any real sense of the term. If a man were dissatisfied with his life in the present world, it was considered comfort for him to meditate on the fact that when he died, all was over, Pliny the Elder assaulted the idea of immortality as fiercely as had Lucretius a century before:

Plague take it, what is this mad idea that life is renewed by death? What repose are the generations ever to have if the soul retains permanent sensation in the upper world and the ghost in the lower? Assuredly this sweet but credulous fancy ruins nature's chief blessing, death, and doubles the sorrow of one about to die by the thought of sorrow to come hereafter also; for if to live is sweet, who can find it sweet to have done living? But how much easier and safer for each to trust in himself! [20]

Collapse of Classical Civilization

The ideal of the world-state, the physical rewards it offered, and the extension of Greco-Roman civilization based on its prosperity were

[20] *Natural History* 7.190.

inadequate for the great bulk of mankind. The complacency of modern egalitarian liberalism can perhaps yield no more to modern man; if that be so, there is a frightful lesson in the experience of the Roman Empire. The goals which that state offered to its subjects were inadequate, and in that fact lay the turning point of ancient civilization.

The process of development had freed the individual ever more from the ties and customs of the groups in which he had been encompassed; in the Empire the human stood forth, independent and isolated, dependent upon his own powers for the construction of a pattern of life. Men found their individual powers inadequate to their terrific tasks. Most men could not comprehend the sweep of the philosophic systems, designed for the upper classes, and could gain only temporary assuagement from the diatribes of wandering Cynics; in the world of culture generally they had little place and little interest. Deprived of voice in local and imperial affairs, they could not feel themselves to be vital parts of the great imperial ideals. The blessings of imperial prosperity did not benefit all men equally. Even those who were materially successful were not thereby necessarily relieved from a gnawing, unconscious uncertainty as to the place of man in the world; the hidden canker may have been suppressed by the pleasures of life, but it could not be eliminated.

Hence came that sense of gloom which overhung the Empire; and hence arose the intellectual sterility of the second century. It is not accidental that the collapse of classical civilization becomes apparent in the very century which marked the height of material prosperity for the Empire.

This collapse is obvious on all levels of society. The intellectual sterility of the second century has already been described; abundant pagan evidence indicates that contemporaries could recognize it. Another testimonial, often investigated, is the great popularity of magic, astrology, the cult of Fortune, and some forms of mysticism. None of these were invented by the Empire itself; rather, all appear to be debased inheritances from earlier cultural levels, taken up by a despairing, advanced civilization from late Hellenistic times onward. Magicians and astrologers operated on the highest level of society; capricious Fortune was shudderingly worshiped by men fearful of their individual freedom, in hopeless uncertainty as to the processes of the world. "We are," said Pliny the Elder, "so much at the mercy of chance that Chance herself, by whom God is proved uncertain, takes the place of God." [21]

The intellectual tradition of the ancient world fought hard against these encroachments of nonintellectual attitudes, but the stand of rationalism was a desperate, futile battle.

As the old order collapsed, the field was left open for nonclassical ideas. The rise of a new system of thought becomes apparent in the third century, although one can already see here and there in the second century that rational meditation was proving inadequate and that men were pushing on into metaphysical contemplation in which they exposed their weaknesses, expressed their development, and even announced their conversion to some new way of life under transcendental influence. Accompanying this rise was a vast surge of older ideas. Enthusiastic modern portrayals of the Romanization of the Empire sometimes fail to admit the rural survival of native ways and tongues beneath the urban veneer of Greco-Roman civilization. To a considerable extent natives had taken up Latin and Greek ways, but the fact that not all did so becomes more evident to our eyes as the second century waned. The Rhenish provinces had enthusiastically aped Roman art forms; now the native patterns reappeared on the Rhine as well as in the Balkans. Native deities turn up in inscriptions on a wider scale. In Asia Minor tombstones at times bear native names; in Syria the vernacular Syriac rises into a written tongue, and the Syrian Christian Tatian expresses a hatred of Greek culture. Though the common stamp of classical civilization was not usually challenged so fully, local variations were subtly asserting themselves.

To sum up, the second century was an epoch of decay and sterility from the point of view of ancient civilization. To a minor degree political causes may be adduced for this decay. Men did learn to talk discreetly of the present ruler, though they might be boldly witty about those dead, and they tended to eschew matters political. To an even-more-minor degree the decline in ancient civilization was the product of changes in the composition of classes in the Empire. The major factor was the isolation of the individual and his inability to support his isolated position.

That position was a product of the general tendency of ancient civilization and more specifically of the creation of the world-state under its absolute ruler. Since neither this ideal nor the more practical rewards of the Empire could lastingly satisfy the individuals contained therein, classical civilization inevitably declined, and from this decline

21 *Natural History* 2.22.

principally sprang the ensuing social and economic deterioration of the Empire, which in its turn worked grievously anew on intellectual activity.

The appalling weakness of second-century civilization shows clearly in the last emperor who truly dwelt within its halls. A weary, fearful man, crying desperately for certainty, Marcus Aurelius recognized that his must be the cheery face, independent of help from without and independent of such ease as others could give. Upon the bull depended his herd. Yet the burden of individualism was too much for the over-worked, despondent man who wrote, "Everything above and below is ever the same, and the result of the same things. How long then?" [22] and felt that even his own intimates wished him gone from his imperial post.

If thought were useless, if reflection were as empty of content as it was in the pages of the *Meditations,* if the actions of life were of no avail even for the emperor, what must have been the position of his subjects? Man's individualism had reached the depths, not the heights; from the pessimism of the second century was to rise a juster assessment of the nature of man and a deeper recognition of his dependence upon his fellows.

[22] *Meditations* 6.46.

XIII

Toward a New Order

IF ONE stands by the deathbed of the philosopher-ruler Marcus Aurelius and looks forward over the ensuing century and a half of turmoil to the death of Constantine in 337, a phenomenal change can be detected in the Roman world. The disguised absolutism of Augustus became the open autocracy of Diocletian. Economic production declined, and the state proclaimed an ever-more-rigorous control, at least in the theory of the imperial edicts. The social system ossified as the distinctions between classes were simplified and hardened.

Very soon after the death of Marcus Aurelius his son Commodus (see Pl. IX *a*) turned to capricious autocracy, which endured twelve years. Then came his assassination and a series of bloody civil wars (193–197), which ended in the victory of the Balkan legions under Septimius Severus. The civil wars and the reign of Severus opened a century of violent upheaval, during which the fabric of the Empire and of ancient civilization appeared doomed to extinction.

From the murder of Commodus down to the final victory of Constantine (324) some thirty-six men occupied the imperial throne, and a host of claimants must also be reckoned. To 235 members of the Severan house held power, save for one interloper; under them the Empire was still able to beat off the barbarian attacks on the northern frontiers and the threats from the East. From 235 to 284 the emperors changed rapidly, and the Empire fell to pieces to the extent that independent states emerged in Gaul and the East during the reign of Gallienus (260–268). This capable but ill-starred ruler and his immediate successors, especially Aurelian (270–275), then put the Roman world back together. Finally, the reorganization of the Empire by Diocletian and Constantine (284–337) succeeded in restoring an appearance of stability and preserved its unity for another century.

The third century is one of political, social, and economic unrest and misery which may be justly termed decay from the point of view of the earlier structure of the Empire. The intellectual collapse of the second century bore its fruit inevitably, though slowly, in the collapse of the Augustan Principate. Among the outward marks of its decay are the rise of the army and a parallel depreciation of the aristocracy, the increase of violence and terrorism in the conduct both of political affairs and of life generally, a greater emphasis upon the agricultural elements as against the cities. While the bureaucracy was centralized under the praetorian prefect and Rome and Italy were leveled to a provincial status, the major blocks of the Empire increasingly drew apart; in their cleavage was foreshadowed the medieval and modern significance of the Mediterranean Sea as a dividing rather than a unifying factor.

Economic production continued to decline in an era when life was insecure, communications poor, and the currency inflated; there can be no doubt that the population of the Empire shrank in the century, perhaps by even one-third. The needs of the state, however, steadily increased. Its altruistic, paternalistic interference in social and economic life in the second century now passed into dictatorial exactions as the leaders thrown up by the army necessarily, ruthlessly seized an ever-greater proportion of the production of the Empire.

Persistence of the Classical Structure

The era is a gloomy one, but its course attests the tenacity of the inherited framework of life; in the end the Empire came back together under Diocletian and Constantine. The rulers made vital changes almost unknowingly, under the sheer pressure of ineluctable need, while doing their utmost to preserve the old ways. The classical structure of ideas remained outwardly dominant through most of the century, for behind it lay the power of tradition and a well-ensconced system of education. Though the structure of ancient civilization was deteriorating, we must sit by its deathbed for another two centuries.

If the basic ideas of the old synthesis were failing, the decline was due far more to inherent decay and to the chaos of the era than to imperial opposition. The emperors of the third century accepted the value placed on classical culture by its own exponents—even though they were not always on good political terms with the aristocracy. Septimius Severus thus encouraged proper literary and artistic activities, and not without some success; his wife Julia Domna had a famous salon of her own, where doctors, philosophers, and rhetoricians abounded. Although later emperors gained their real strength from other sources than the civilized layers of the empire, only Caracalla and Elagabalus obviously moved outside the Greco-Roman synthesis, the former toward the soldiers and the German barbarians, the other toward his ancestral Syrian sun-god and customs. Neither was successful in carrying the Empire with him.

Throughout the third century schools were still state supported and existed even in villages; historians, poets, and others continued to receive imperial posts and largesses; pagan rhetoricians delivered panegyrics before the rulers which stressed not only their divinity but also their devotion to the good of their subjects and their high level of culture. Possession or absence of this culture, indeed, became a powerful basis for judging the quality of rulers, administrators, and other notable men. Historians coupled "birth" and "education" as related marks of virtue; against Caesars whom they disliked they were wont to hurl charges of hostility to civilization.

Culture thus was elevated into a positive criterion almost independent of the state. This process was a defensive reaction by aristocratic adherents of the antique, facing as they were the rise of barbarism and smarting under their own loss of political position, but one must not underestimate its effects either on imperial policy or on the Christian attitude toward pagan letters in the third and fourth centuries. Long ago, when Rome was conquering Greece, it had been valorous but uncivilized; now its military power was failing, but it boasted ever more of its culture.

In truth a sensible ruler had quite good practical reasons for cherishing that which he could not fully understand. The unity of the Empire rested in the last analysis not only upon its maintenance of social and economic justice but also upon its common culture, manifested outwardly in the extension of Roman citizenship and expressed in succinct form in the ideal of Rome. A sophist might still compare the Roman Empire to the sun, and Eternal Rome became a motive ever more stressed on the coinage both of emperors and of pretenders in the prov-

inces. The restoration of unity by the predecessors of Diocletian depended largely on the desire of Roman subjects to remain under Roman
rule; when in the early fifth century men in the West accepted Germanic invaders at least with resignation the end of the Empire in that
area was near. The ideals of Mediterranean civilization and of the
world-state as a political expression of that civilization continued to
exercise a strong power over men down into the fourth century.

The sway of these ideals became steadily more external; to scholars
imbued with classical standards of judgment the developments of the
third century must be viewed as serious marks of decay. Pagan literature, already sterile in the second century, withered away. Scholarship
and learned commentary on the works of the past decreased tremendously in quantity during the third century and declined in quality;
even the collection of bits of learning in anthologies disappeared after
the works of Athenaeus and the Christian Julius Africanus early in the
century. Pagan art forsook the old emphasis on harmony and beauty;
as the efforts to maintain classical form halted, so too did the copying
of classical statues. A cultural split between East and West became
obvious. Although Greek had gained a definite, almost exclusive as-
cendancy as the language of culture, Latin aristocratic education devoted ever less attention to the inculcation of Greek. Men were inclined
to give up letters and arts, so hopelessly sterile in their classic forms,
and this tendency was relentlessly encouraged by the political and economic decline.

New View of Man

This same period, however, Christian historians from the days of
Eusebius have viewed as one of great advance. Modern students have
sensed in the changes of the third century a mighty step toward modern
thought, for new ideas now emerged into the open. Some men greeted
them with puzzlement, others occasionally opposed them, but ever-
widening circles unconsciously accepted them: eventually they became
the basic postulates of civilization.

To define succinctly—and so with dangerous precision—the character
of these new ideas, man during the third and fourth centuries came
to visualize himself as an individual entity. He was sharply distinguished
from all other humans and was also clearly set off from the physical
world about him. Nonetheless, he had vital links to two outside forces,
the divine power above, and his fellow humans; for he now advanced

to the capability of intimate union with his brothers. So he might work for common aims in a group without sacrificing his individuality, and while separated from the physical world he was certain that it too was divinely governed.

In achieving this view men had finally arrived at a destination toward which ancient civilization had long been working. In the earliest days of Greek thought man and the world had been united, as had man to man; then the thinker in his pride separated himself from the world and burst one by one the ties which had held him within the city-state. As the new view emerged, it overcame the ruthless individualism of the second century after Christ, which had been restrained only by the purely mechanical bonds of family and state. When the new view triumphed, men felt themselves once more secure in the world, even while their political and economic framework was falling to pieces; from God and from the new groups enfolding them, individuals—while still individuals—could gain the support they needed. On a visible plane these groups were the agricultural community and the Christian church, but the true bonds of life were psychologically imbedded within the minds of men. Therewith the basis for medieval and modern civilization had been laid.

This shift was not entirely visible in all its implications during the centuries when the Empire was dying. Many aspects of classical civilization still survived. Some of them were even incompatible with the new ideas; in this sense the period after 300 may rightly be called Late Classical. Since modern observers know the end objective of the shift, they must necessarily describe the new view as "transcendental," and to explain the character of the Late Empire they must use other modern terms which in their modern connotations do injustice to the unique quality of that era. Neither in art nor in thought was it simply "medieval."

It is also true that the medieval period, taken as a whole, was one where the brute necessities of keeping alive prevented much play of individuality or much exploration of the world. The purely physical requirements of increased production, reviving commerce, and establishment of internal order did not exist in sufficient measure until after 1000. The essential individuality of man was an underlying factor which bided its time; the progress of modern civilization has been a release of the human very much akin to that of his ancient liberation, but starting from a higher view of the relations of man to his fellow men and to nature. One may, if one wishes, still make much of the Renaissance liberation of mankind, but historians have come to realize that the Renaissance of the fourteenth and fifteenth centuries had its roots far back in prior development. If human history is, as I take it, the expression of the capabilities of the human being, then the most vital forces of that history must be looked for in the psychological development of humanity, one of the greatest phases of which took place in the third and fourth centuries after Christ.

The magnitude of this change has inevitably drawn the attention of modern historians from many points of view. The classic concept of "decay" has unfortunately dominated most discussions of the third century, but some men have seen more clearly the new forces involved. In considering the unfolding of the new view of the world and of man, one must tread a path which at least a few have trodden before, and one must stick to its main course; limits of space and proportion prevent a deep exploration of many half-hidden manifestations of the new view. The limits are regrettable, for here especially subtlety of interpretation yields the greatest results. Even a brief summation, however, may have its value; for the intellectual shift of the third century has not often been described as an entity and placed in its proper light as a mark of human advance.

New View in the Arts

The most obvious illustration of the shift is the triumph of Christianity, but this is too majestic and blinding a phenomenon with which to begin. It is better to commence more humbly with the tangible subjects of architecture and sculpture and then turn to the philosophic and religious changes of the third century. To set the stage for this analysis I may first adduce two concrete illustrations of the new architecture and sculpture of the fourth century.

A well-known walk in Rome is that along the Sacred Way from the round temple of Vesta at the end of the Roman Forum, up to the Arch of Titus, and down again to the majestic bulk of the Colosseum. High to the left as one strolls up this path is the Basilica of Constantine, begun by Maxentius and dedicated shortly after 312. This mammoth structure consists of a nave of three square bays, a structure adapted from the central hall of a Roman bath. Each bay is crossvaulted with buttresses, and opens out into side bays in an aisle on either side, which are likewise vaulted on a lower level. On the vaults and arches gilding was lavishly employed, and the lower walls were originally covered by marble linings.

The relative immensity of the basilica is impressive, now as it was in the fourth century. There is also a less conscious emotional impact when one moves slowly but freely about the great interior of the basilica, senses its complex yet unified structure, and gazes upward at its soaring brickfaced vaults against the sky. The impact is quite different from that of the columns and horizontal architraves of the Forum temples. As a recent critic has put it, the observer is "relaxed and strangely subdued by a feeling of his own small insignificance and a sense of beneficent calm descends upon his spirit, a feeling distilled from the greater unity into which he has entered and of which he now becomes more thoroughly a part." [1] The spectator, if sensitive of spirit, may feel that the builder of this basilica and an architect of Augustus must have had very different views of space and structure, of man's relation to the world; and if he stands a moment in contemplation, he may sense that the new view embodied in the basilica is somehow akin to that which modern Western architects have consciously expressed from the days of the Gothic cathedrals.

Horace often traveled the Sacred Way; if he had suddenly seen this basilica in a vision, he would probably not have liked it. When pressed for the reason of this dislike, he might have commented on the riotous color of pavement, walls, and vaults, which far surpassed that customary in the Augustan Age. He might have objected to the lighting by the huge arched windows of the clearstory, which produced effects of light and shade unknown to his own era. If extraordinarily perspicacious, a contemporary of Augustus might have expressed his distaste for the complexity of the structure, in which carefully graduated units were combined; the lack of that firm connection with the ground which classic building ensured in its platform and horizontal lines; or the failure of the whole work sharply to delimit space as did a temple. In the basilica all shifts in rich and varied aspect as one walks from nave to aisle and back again.

Beyond the basilica and the Arch of Titus stands another work, hard by the Colosseum, which shows more distinctly a new view of man and the world. This is the Arch of Constantine, erected in 313–315 to celebrate Constantine's defeat of his rival Maxentius just outside Rome

[1] Emerson H. Swift, *Roman Sources of Christian Art* (New York, 1951), 198.

(see Pl. VIII *b*). As one stands by the Colosseum looking at the three archways of the arch, its projecting columns, and its relief-covered walls, one may sense again that its builders, though essaying to be classical, had a different sense of space than did those who erected the simple, harmonious Arch of Titus two and one-half centuries earlier; but more obvious differences, both political and esthetic, come quickly to the eye.

Although the inscription emblazoned over the central archway incorporates the elements to be found in the inscription of the Arch of Titus—the dedicant Senate and Roman people, and the emperor—Constantine has precedence, and the other element is reduced to the abbreviation SPQR. Such a reversal is inconsistent with the spirit of the Augustan Principate; that Principate was gone, and Constantine was an openly accepted autocrat. The inscription also gives as the cause for the erection of the arch the fact that Constantine had delivered Rome from a tyrant (Maxentius) "at the impulse of the divine spirit." This emphasis on religious motivation of human acts would have surprised a man of the Early Empire, and he would have been puzzled by the ambiguous generality with which the divine power was described. Even if one takes the phrase as referring no more than to the cult of Sol Invictus, tokens of which can be detected in the reliefs, the expression is remarkable; but if Constantine were thus covertly referring, as I believe, to the God of the Christians who had helped him to victory, the inscription is a truly extraordinary testimonial to the change in spirit from the second century, when Christianity was a despised, illicit sect.

The clash of esthetic style in the reliefs of the arch is another impressive mark of the alteration in men's intellectual views. In the haste of erecting the arch its builders sought out suitable earlier panels and incorporated them in their general scheme at appropriate points. The medallions above the side archways are Hadrianic; the reliefs on either side of the main archway and at the ends of the attic are Trajanic; the captive Dacians crowning the columns are likewise Trajanic; and the scenes on either side of the inscriptions were taken from an arch of Marcus Aurelius, other pieces of which, now in the Conservatori Museum, I have already noted. In these works the classical conventions of proportion and harmony are still strong, though our taste may call the product frigid; the emperor's figure stands out, but all the participants in the scenes have a lifelike, if idealized, cast.

Other reliefs were carved at the time of the erection of the arch. Over the left archway on the north front, for instance, Constantine is depicted addressing his troops; over the right archway he manifests his *liberalitas* by distributing a donative to the Senate and citizens of Rome (see Pl. XII *a*). In these reliefs the human figures are squat and poorly proportioned, and their garments are roughly indicated by deep grooves. Unity of composition is achieved not by subtle balance but by an emphasis on the seated, towering figure of the emperor (in the donative scene) to whom all others turn with uplifted head and arm. These sharply defined, undercut symbols no longer merge skillfully one into another, as on the second-century reliefs, but, though thronged, stand apart individually; yet from a distance one finds these low reliefs of Constantinian workshops less sharply defined than the Hadrianic medallions immediately above them.

Most modern spectators tend to ignore the later work or at most find in it "a gravestone of the arts of Greece and Rome," a mark of that barbaric decay with which many historians of art still condemn fourth-century sculpture. Others have seen more correctly that here, as in the basilica, a new view of the world is embodied. The present problem is to clarify the bearing of that new view and to determine how it came to dominate architecture and sculpture in the third century.

To solve this problem is not altogether easy. The pattern of third-century artistic development will always be especially difficult to understand, for this upset period has left us very few architectural and sculptural remains. Worse still, the history of Roman art is yet to be written. In the last half century signposts have been erected with greater rapidity to show the way, but some scholars still refuse even to accept the existence of Roman—or perhaps more properly, Mediterranean—art as a thing apart from Greek art.

While in architecture the contribution of Rome is more generally accepted, there are those who would consider Roman sculpture as merely a continuation of Greek principles and forms. Others, though admitting the importance of the Greek outward impress, look more to the spirit and try to discern in Roman sculpture and painting the introduction of new, Roman ideas such as realism, depth, illusionism, and the like. Even this line of argument appears to an outsider to have been conceived in far too narrow terms and to smack of modern nationalistic views of "race"; if once one admits the existence of that Greco-Roman synthesis which had emerged by the time of Augustus, or of a truly Mediterranean civilization, it is possible to rise above the futile efforts to trace esthetic developments to innate principles of the Roman race, of the Greek race, of the *Volkstum* of this or that area or layer of Mediterranean population.

The sculptors of the Altar of Augustan Peace and many other monuments of the Late Republic and the Empire may have been almost exclusively Greek, Syrian, and so on in name and Greek in speech. The men who commissioned the works were undoubtedly Latin in tongue and origin. Both elements may have felt the same impulses and, though of differing social quality, may have shared the same changing views of the nature of man. Do American artists of foreign origin express only European ideas?

Often the new tendencies of imperial sculpture and at times even the developments in architecture appear before us first in nonofficial art emanating from Italy or the provinces, but the new modes all soon turn up in products of the capital itself. Rome was, as the center of imperial social life and government, the most important artistic center of the Early Empire—more than Roman roads had their focus in Rome. Since the term "Mediterranean art" may be misleading, I shall call the architecture and sculpture of the main imperial tradition "Roman" art, especially since Greek areas tended to follow classical traditions and so to flatten out the new waves which swept more freely in the Roman milieu. However scornfully connoisseurs of things Greek may condemn this art, it must be recognized that the esthetic idiom of the Empire had within it a spirit that appealed mightily to the Middle Ages and to the Renaissance.

The use of art to illustrate history always remains a dangerous practice for the layman. Not only may he misread the signs, but also the consideration of esthetic matters is all too often a subjective one, where the observer may construe, in arbitrary fashion, his documents to prove anything he wishes; so he glides into a mystic interpretation which obfuscates that which he essays to illuminate. Yet in these esthetic developments one may perhaps sense the pattern of the future earlier than anywhere else, for artists unconsciously often express future trends before any other element of society.

Changes in Architecture

In the field of architecture it is an obvious truth that the way in which men fashion their buildings reflects their view of the world in which these buildings rise, and also mirrors their concept of the relations of man to that world. In moving from the Greek temple through such structures of the Early Empire as the Pantheon, and on down to the Christian basilicas of the Late Empire, one can see even at a superficial glance that the architectural principles of the ancient world underwent a great shift.

To speak in the most general terms, this shift was toward an acceptance and expression of space and an attempt to release buildings optically from their ties with the ground upon which they rested. Though late Roman architects could not quite shake off classical concepts, they paved the way for the complex medieval view of space as an infinite, immaterial fluid into which man's structures could merge in separation from the physical world and within which man could feel himself at once insignificant and unified with the infinite. As we shall see later, these two aspects of man are not incompatible. The Christian might proclaim himself to be a miserable sinner, a small part of the world of God, just as a man in the great Basilica of Constantine might appear to be a mote. Still, the Christian also knew that he was a thing apart from the material world and that he was firmly attached to God.

When a modern man looks at a Greek temple, he must inevitably think first of a box, for the vertical lines of the columns and the horizontal lines of the base below and the architrave above the columns form a sharply limiting outline for the structure. The Greek architect, in other words, took a part of chaotic space and gave it a definite form (see Pl. VII a).

Space itself could not be truly suppressed, but as far as possible it was confined within two rather than three dimensions. The temple architect was not interested in the interior; as many critics have pointed out, he was far more concerned with limiting space by his walls and columns and tried to suppress any idea that his interior room had any connection with the infinite air. The cella, where the cult statue of the deity stood, was dimly lit, for windows might give a feeling of such a connection; the façade received a plastic treatment in the form of frieze and metopes which emphasized its existence. One will not push matters too far in asserting that the temple was viewed as a physical, material, individual entity radiating the spirit of the god within. It is noteworthy also that while the architect thus tried to reduce the chaos of the world to clearly defined order, he did not try to separate the temple from the ground. Greek temples were set on a stepped platform as if they were statues to be touched and felt.

The temple was an old form, and modern critics may go too far in positing its ideals as those of all architecture throughout the long history of Greek civilization. Hellenistic art shows that its creators—perhaps even the men of the fourth century—were becoming more interested in tridimensional space, but a clear indication in architecture that men's views were changing is given first in Roman buildings of the Late Republic and Early Empire. Roman architects still concentrated their efforts on the façade, the exterior limitation of space; but behind the façade, and not always directly connected with it, the interior area now began to play a consciously conceived part. The Romans took over the vault and employed it far more freely than the Greeks had ever done; they also invented the dome; but even within the Greek frame of horizontal and vertical lines they emphasized the third dimension.

In private homes the Romans shifted after 100 B.C. to the famous second style of painting, where the walls were covered with panoramic or stagelike landscapes within architectural frames (see Pl. I b). Men of Cicero's age somehow felt that internal space existed, must be expressed, and must be connected with an ideal world as represented in the landscapes of the walls. Though the third style, which perhaps arose in the last years of Augustus, reverted to treating the wall as a purely flat surface, artists by the time of Nero were dissolving wall surfaces in fantastic landscapes and painted architecture. Windows, which became a necessity in the apartment blocks of Rome and Ostia and then were incorporated in public buildings, also brought the feeling that internal and external space were connected.

The same forces were at work in the basilica, an Italian invention as far as is now known. In essence this building was a large square or rectangular structure, usually roofed over and designed for the transaction of public business ranging from lawsuits to business operations and even to the sale of goods. Here, obviously, internal space was an object of architectural planning, though it cannot be said that the architects of the vast, vaulted basilicas and baths of the Early Empire clearly felt the internal space as a positive object which must direct the whole pattern of the building. Eventually the basilica—in its simpler, unvaulted form —served as the point of departure for the Christian Church and so for the cathedral, but one must be wary of applying medieval concepts of space to the forms of Roman times.

Augustan architecture tended to emphasize faultless proportion and sureness of taste in its effort to recapture a mood of peace and order; the work of the Augustan Age thus stands in a lull between the creative developments of the Republic and the structures of the first century after Christ. In all the arts the serene poise of the Augustan era was sacrificed in the eager experiments of the Neronian period, which were tinged with that emotional realism marking the tragedies of Seneca. Nero's gigantic Golden House, which used crossvaulting, and his ambitious replanning of Rome after the Fire seem to break the earlier barriers. The interest his architects showed in the manipulation of space passed on to those of the great palace of Domitian and to the ingenious experimenters of Hadrian's villa at Tivoli; it is also evident in the temple to Venus and Rome, which combined vaulting with a columned exterior, and in the Pantheon, originally constructed by Agrippa but rebuilt in the reign of Hadrian (see Pl. VII *b*).

This domed, round building is famous, for it is the first extant ancient structure to show a clear architectural vision of an organic internal space. Externally the Pantheon has little pretensions. There is a columned porch; behind this the cylinder bulk of the main mass supports a low dome as sharply set off from the circumambient atmosphere as was the box of a Greek temple. When one crosses the porch, however, and enters the interior, one senses immediately a tremendous change from the cella of a Greek temple. The rounded walls and the vast vault overhead contain a part of space which has been molded and shaped into a harmonious, restful unity. On the ground level the circle of the wall is broken by regularly spaced niches, which give an effect of minor alteration of shadow and light, an emotional or "coloristic" effect in modern esthetic terminology. These niches also serve as a subtle means of emphasizing the central space, and one may perhaps see in them a means of detaching that space from the ground plane. This separation, however, is purely an internal matter, for the cylinder exterior of the Pantheon does not betray the existence of the niches; the internal space, moreover, is still cut away from the world outside. Even the great circular window at the height of the dome, though admitting a stream of light, serves more as a boundary or chandelier than as a conscious connection with the air above.

Throughout the third century the amount and, in some respects, the quality of building necessarily declined, but architects decisively broke with the usual dull level of the marble structures of the second century.

The so-called temple of Minerva Medica in Rome, a landmark in this advance, has recently been dated in the early decades of the fourth century (see Pl. VIII *a*). Here internal space is not only a conscious substance but is also clearly reflected in the exterior, for the niches surrounding the central, ribbed dome project externally from the central wall. The distinction between façade and interior has withered away; the façade is losing its importance and is deprived of the plastic treatment a Greek would have felt necessary. The arched windows, set in a drum above the niches, directly connect the internal space with the air and admit light in a coloristic manner; through the unbroken swelling of niches the central mass tends to separate itself from the ground far more than does the Pantheon.

No longer does the Greek concept dominate, that a building is an essentially static unit in which the movement of columns and architrave is mutually compensatory, in which all action is confined within the frame of the structure. In the complex frame of Minerva Medica the swelling and receding niches and the lofty central dome with its piers and buttresses give an impression of movement which is almost, but not quite, bursting the boundaries of the physical ground plan.

Here one has arrived essentially at the late Roman architectural concept of space. The size of these imperial structures and the companion development of arch and vault are further marks of a break by Roman architects with Greek concepts. The tremendous structures of imperial Rome cannot be ascribed entirely to the megalomania of the emperors and the wealth of the Empire, nor does the use of domes reflect merely superstitions about the mystic significance of that form. In the great audience hall of Domitian's palace the barrel vault, spanning over 100 feet almost 150 feet above the ground, stood far higher than that of Ctesiphon. Its architect Rabirius perhaps designed it to display the grandeur of his Master and God, and Domitian may have approved its erection as an imitation of the dome of Heaven; but beneath any conscious intentions of emperor and architect lay an unconscious approval of an expression of the new view of the world. The demand for space which dwarfed the individual and yet immersed and identified him with itself had deep roots, which have been suggested above in the consideration of the Basilica of Constantine.

In technical details, in opulence of decoration, and in general plan the step from Minerva Medica to Saint Sophia in Constantinople is a direct one. To drive farther was difficult, and in the West architecture seems for a long moment to have halted. There is even an apparent retrogression in the Christian barnlike basilicas with wooden roofs and simple exteriors which began to rise in numbers; for these structures tend to be an agglomeration of parts which do not form a true unity and in which conscious ideas of space seem to disappear. The same tendency is manifest in sculpture, where the background and tridimensional space virtually disappear; when men had succeeded in freeing their creations from a connection with the ground, they were not immediately able to form them in a new unity with the infinite.

The essential step, however, had really been taken. Medieval art derives its "character in the last analysis from the factor of infinitude which came with Christianity into the ancient world, and opened spiritual vistas through the crumbling walls of Greek materialism." [2] When the European world began to quiet down after the barbarian conquests, a new vigor, fertilized by the Late Classical experiments, led to the dynamic movement we call Romanesque, where the arched naves and aisles of the cathedrals drive forward irresistibly toward the altar. Here the whole internal structure has a clear unity within itself and yet is bounded by the space about. The soaring vaults and towers of the Gothic cathedrals were to be an even-more-successful manifestation of the transcendental unity of man with God.

Changes in Sculpture

Imperial architecture moved from two dimensions to three or, we might dare to say, from the rational to the transcendental. Since this development in architectural forms is not always easily sensed by the layman, it is fortunate that the same pattern can be detected in the restricted compass of sculpture, which places more direct emphasis upon the human than upon his world.

Greek sculptors concentrated upon the human being as a physical, material object, viewed as he actually appeared to the eyes and representing more or less completely an ideal perfection. In the classical Greek period (roughly 480–323) the human was almost never conceived as an individual different from all other humans; even the vaunted realism of the Hellenistic sculptors, though going much further at times, had usually quite definite limits.

Greek statues, again, stood apart from the space about them and formed a unity within themselves in which the parts were harmoniously

[2] C. R. Morey, *Medieval Art*, 17.

welded together. In viewing a relief one rarely turns one's attention away from the panel; by the skillful turning inward of the figures at the edges and by the internal balance the sculptors shut off the outside world. Nor do these reliefs have depth in any true sense; classic Greek reliefs very rarely contain an indication of any background.

Roman sculpture, as recent scholars have begun to argue, emerged in the lifetime of Cicero together with landscape painting and Roman architecture (see Pl. I *a*). In the Empire the development of sculpture was not along a straight line, for the potent influence of the classical tradition rose repeatedly to camouflage for a time the general direction of the movement. From the time of Marcus Aurelius the current began to run ever more forcefully and unalterably away from the classic. "New and peculiar elements, unknown to Flavian or Trajanic art, are apparent," says G. Rodenwaldt about the Column of Marcus Aurelius, erected to commemorate his northern wars but not completed until well after his death; and the judicious critic goes on to give these elements more precisely:

In place of broad presentation there is a concentration of action, Roman pride of conquest, helpless barbarian submission, the solemn representation of the Emperor himself are strongly stressed, and a transcendental element comes into the scene depicting the Miracle. The Italic centralizing method of composing single scenes and the un-classical repetition of identical figures, like those of marching legionaries, are employed to intensify effect. Lines and alternations of light and shadow heighten the expressive character of the whole work.[3]

The style foreshadowed here is that of late Roman art; its earmarks are frontality, colorism, immobility, symbolism, and an accompanying dissolution both of general composition and of the general form. These marks appear both in imperial works and also, perhaps even more distinctly, in the previously subsidiary, almost hidden provincial styles which began to reassert themselves from the end of the second century as the cosmopolitan culture of the Empire slackened its hold. To gain a true picture of developments one must look not only at the great imperial monuments but also at the private sarcophagi and tombstones now buried away in basements and garrets of museums all over the erstwhile Roman world.

Frontality, that is to say, the tendency of major figures in reliefs to turn straight to the front in static pose and to draw toward themselves

[3] *Cambridge Ancient History* 11, 796.

the gaze of other figures in the composition, has far too generally been called an Oriental innovation in Roman art. Oriental relief before the Christian era actually made very little use of direct frontality, for heads were usually shown in profile; in the first century after Christ frontal figures appear in a painting at Dura on the Euphrates and thereafter turn up in Palmyrene sculpture. This Eastern trend may have had its influence at points within the Empire, but unmistakable, outwardly quaint examples of this same tendency can be found at just as early a date in popular art in Italy and elsewhere. In both areas one may often sense that the sculptor was essaying to convey a feeling of reverence toward the central figure.

As the emperor rose to a position of accepted absolutism, the use of frontality received a powerful impetus in imperial art at Rome and in the provinces, for the place of the ruler in reliefs grew ever more prominent and demanded reverence from the spectator. A comparison of parallel scenes on the Columns of Trajan and Marcus Aurelius where the emperor is addressing his troops attests a considerable advance: Trajan stands to one side or is partially masked by his soldiers; Marcus Aurelius is frontally elevated above his men, who stand in part before him with their backs turned to the spectator. The observer thus is led toward identifying himself with the men as a part of the crowd attending on the ruler and is impelled to feel that he is taking part in the excited, at times supernatural, activity which distinguishes these reliefs from the calmer presentation of Trajan's deeds. On the Arch of Septimius Severus occurs a similar scene, and here, unlike the Column of Marcus Aurelius, the minor figures are a flat, undifferentiated mass before their lord. On a contemporary arch at Lepcis frontality is even more baldly dominant.

Men of the third century completely accepted frontality. On medallions of Severus Alexander a four-horse chariot is represented frontally, even though the sculptor had to spread out his horses, two on each side, in an awkward fashion. The famous Philosopher Sarcophagus of Gallienic date (in the Lateran) is dominated by a serious, monumental philosopher seated on a chair in the center of the scene (see Pl. XI *b*). To face him squarely to the front, the sculptor had to shorten the philosopher's thighs virtually to the point of their disappearance. Such a violation of reality was impossible when sculptors had a strong sense of plastic reality, but by the third century the psychological necessity of expressing reverence had broken this sense. This relief is, as Rodenwaldt observes, a mark of an epochal change in European relief-sculpture; his suggestion that this may have been the sarcophagus of the great transcendentalizing philosopher Plotinus is fanciful but fitting.

An analysis of third-century sarcophagus reliefs, to which one must turn in the lack of monumental state reliefs, also illustrates the rise of colorism, or of the play of light and shadow in which the background often disappears. This emotional effect, which has already been noted in architecture, was secured by various devices in sculpture, chief among which was the drill. The use of the drill for undercutting or outlining figures by a groove may be traced back to the Column of Marcus Aurelius and on into the first century—but not to the contemporary Orient, which made little use of colorism. In imperial reliefs drapery tends to become a matter of deep grooves and flat highlights; for a time faces are polished while the hair and beard are deeply drilled or otherwise colored, an effect which becomes obvious in the busts of Hadrian and lasts into the third century (see Pls. VI *a*, IX).

In keeping with the emphasis on colorism the figures on reliefs increasingly distinguish themselves from each other, as on the Philosopher Sarcophagus; later they are isolated in niches. In other works the humans press closely upon one another, as on the famous Ludovisi battle sarcophagus (c. 235), yet even here the individual figures are sharply undercut and so stand distinct (see Pl. XI *a*). The vigor of the scenes first increased as classical poise gave way. One finds an untamed restlessness and even an impressionistic treatment, in which men's hair flares up like flames in the wind, but soon this vehement activity tends to sink as the figures become more and more immobile. Eventually figures are outwardly stiff and wooden, and the use of the drill declines; the background essentially disappears, and the individuals are isolated, not so much in space as outside it. Unity of composition depends mainly upon the coloristic play of light and dark surfaces and upon the content which the observer's mind attributes to the scene.

The humans, in short, have become symbols, spiritually connected with each other and charged with moral significance. Beside them stand personifications of moral virtues of a type not prominent in earlier centuries, figures of Salvation and the like. Artistic thought so betrays a symbolic, transcendental, yet simple, attitude which is bent ever more on an analytical, subjective study of man's position and deeds. On the Ludovisi sarcophagus, for instance, the restless action throws individual figures into a strained agitation, but the general who presumably was interred within the sarcophagus is depicted frontally, calmly demanding our respect for his triumph.

If figures are to become symbols, there is less need to observe the realities of life in their proportions. The warriors on the Ludovisi sarcophagus vary considerably in size, even in the foreground, depending on their importance. On most work the ordinary mass of humans shrinks in scale and flattens out in relief, just as the men themselves appeared dwarfed in the great spaces of the buildings of the period; in sculpture, on the other hand, there is also a tendency from the time of Trajan to exaggerate the size of the ruler and from that of Commodus to create colossal statues of the Caesars, superhuman in size as in significance. Concern for proportion even in the parts of the body wanes; individual figures as well as the whole composition lose their unity as the third century moves on. Much of the head becomes dull and flat while expression is confined to a few of the features. The result is such work as the Arch of Constantine, where the stubby figures of men with their oversize heads are simply puppets (see Pl. XII a).

Yet the realism of earlier centuries did not entirely die away. In shaping the colossal heads of the emperors of the fourth century—and in private busts as well—the sculptors formed schematized, simplified presentations of ideas, but they were still looking at specific human individuals (see Pl. X). On a visit to Rome the emperor Constantius moved calmly and imperturbably through the streets, looking straight ahead without rubbing his face or nose; but, as Ammianus Marcellinus neatly comments, the emperor was really not a bloodless symbol, for he ducked his head on going through the lofty gates.

Throughout the third century there were little flurries of opposition to the direction in which sculpture was moving. The drift of imperial taste toward a new style which was directly connected with the new view of man was a slow, unconscious process which often reversed itself temporarily as individual artists—and writers too, I may add—harked back to classic models, or as a whole generation, like that of Gallienus, turned back briefly. One cannot even describe the development of late Roman art simply in terms of an advance, retreat, and then new advance, for the crosscurrents break up any such pattern which one may try to establish; men in Constantine's era were able to put their own work side by side with reliefs of the second century. The old classical tradition, nonetheless, had been broken in its essential points by this date; and though its influence still shows itself in some fourth-century busts, the sculpture of the future was to be largely in the vein of that on the Arch of Constantine.

To assess fourth-century sculpture objectively, one must wipe out of one's mind classical standards of judgment and must disregard the old critical attacks on the work of the Late Empire as barbaric and decadent. Viewed after this preliminary purgation, the solemn, static reliefs, the colossal heads of the rulers, and the other surviving pieces convey an impression of tremendous vitality. This work has a new feeling of the significance of life which cannot be matched in intensity at any previous point short of the classic Greek period.

Artistic output declined greatly in quantity, in keeping with the impoverishment of the ancient world. There was also, in my judgment, a downright decline in technical skill which can be seen in the lesser arts too. The emphasis alike on internal content and on the immateriality of the divine tended to destroy men's interest in creating or erecting statues; free-standing figures decrease significantly in Christian (and also pagan) art of the fourth century and almost disappear in the fifth. Still, the powerful force which shines quietly through the colossal head of Constantine in the courtyard of the Conservatori Museum is something new in human experience (see Pl. X *a*).

The nature of that force is not difficult to detect. In their sculpture men of the third and fourth centuries were expressing their turn away from the physical, rational, material to an inward emotional meditation which led to a communion with a superhuman force. So the human form became symbolic; the physical had in itself no value and yielded to a pattern. The eyes of the philosopher on the Philosopher Sarcophagus appear to stare into remote space, or rather into an imaginary world, an impression which was secured by marking the pupils with deep outlines and a shallow, beanlike indentation. This accentuation of the iris and pupils in the wide-open eyes emerged on sculpture and mummy portraits of the early second century and reached an advanced stage in a famous head of Commodus in the Terme Museum (see Pl. IX *a*); thereafter it was customary, and it lends to the heads an impression of inner spirit communing with an outside, invisible world.

Heads of figures tended to tilt upward in the late second century and still more in the third century, as if seeking communion with Heaven. Action eventually halted; men's mouths closed, instead of opening in breathless emotion. Their feeling of reverence expressed itself outwardly in the simple gestures of an uplifted hand or a turned head. Physical activity meant less and less, inner, incorporeal activity ever more. L'Orange thus comments on a head from Ephesus:

All physical movement has ceased in the deep stillness. . . . Beneath the deep shadows of the brows and eyelids, the eyes shine upon us with phosphorescent light—reminiscent of the descriptions of the gaze of inspired men. Here, more than ever, the expressional features have been abstracted from the physical context of the head, as though liberated from the body, from the corporeal man himself.[4]

In fine, the development of imperial sculpture is an expression of the triumph of a new view whereby man was moving toward the nonmaterial world of the Redeemer. To avoid the use of the term "transcendental" is impossible.

Sculptors could not yet entirely overcome the conventions which they inherited from classical civilization; in fourth-century work the physical approach wars with the spiritual introspection. As a result, scenes tend to lack physical unity; but in many products of the era one can sense the unity of the individual figures, themselves sharply distinguished, in a spiritual reverence toward a central object, emperor or God (see Pl. XII). Plotinus, it may be noted, considered that the beauty of man lay not in due proportion but in his illumination and uplift. Literary descriptions both of emperors and of saints often emphasized the godlike serenity of their faces as reflecting the radiance of the soul in visual form; sculptors achieved the same results in their timeless masks. In both appears "the sphinx-like calm of a never-ending vision." [5]

Sources of the New View

The development of imperial sculpture and architecture, even when considered in a general, unspecialized manner, throws a powerful light on the major intellectual shift of the Empire. Not only does the esthetic pattern illuminate the actual shift; it also suggests vital conclusions about the underlying forces behind the change in men's views. There can be no doubt, for one thing, that the roots of artistic technical devices and modes of composition—frontality, colorism, and all the rest—are apparent in the second century; they can even be traced back into the beginnings of the Empire. Clearly the turn to the transcendental, which

[4] H. P. L'Orange, *Apotheosis in Ancient Portraiture* (Oslo, 1947), 106–108.
[5] L'Orange, *Apotheosis,* 111.

underlies these devices, was not simply a product of the economic and political chaos of the third century. The new ideas had begun to flower long before; the unrest of the era following the Severi merely promoted the speed with which the turn becomes apparent.

The esthetic development of the Empire, again, cannot be ascribed either to the rise of the lower classes or to Oriental influence. As regards the former, we cannot distinguish to any major extent a style of art favored by the rulers and the aristocracy from that fostered by the lower classes. The statues and coins of the emperors, the great reliefs, the architectural monuments erected on imperial commission embodied new ideas essentially to the same extent as did those of private individuals; at the most, the imperial monuments, being larger and more public, were more polished and refined, and their outward gloss may at times conceal the presence of the new ideas.

That men of the lower classes who rose in imperial society dragged up with them certain deep-hidden concepts may be possible, though one can as easily ascribe the emergence of these views to the breakdown of classical standards. What is significant—and what still remains to be explained in this view—is the sure fact that the upper classes were unconsciously willing to accept the esthetic and other manifestations of these ideas from the very beginning of the Empire.

The frequent ascription of late Roman art mainly to Oriental influence is just as nonsensical. During the third century the art of Mesopotamia and Persia, as preserved at Dura and in Sasanid work, was likewise moving to frontality and spirituality, and one area may at times have influenced another in minor points; Rodenwaldt, however, has sensitively pointed out that the similar transcendental end was achieved in quite different fashions. Instead of the passive, absolute symmetry and repetition of identical features of the East, the Philosopher Sarcophagus and other frontal work of the West still turn the central figure slightly in one point or another and replace symmetry, as on the Arch of Constantine, by a balance of dynamic forces in which the individual figures vary. In drawing its stiff, bulging figures with almond-shaped eyes the truly Oriental art of the Eastern Roman provinces and of Persia pursued another path than the coloristic flat relief characteristic of Roman art.

At the most one might affirm that the Roman Empire received a slight assistance from the Orient in clothing its own political and intellectual developments, for the factors here under consideration were driving all the known world of ancient times in the same direction at the same period. The Sasanid state, which replaced the Parthian, was far more centralized in its government and its hierarchical society, just as the third-century Roman Empire was more centralized than the Augustan system. Sasanid Persia, too, was shifting from the earlier Parthian religious toleration and erected a state cult of Zoroastrianism in the very years when the Empire was experimenting with the cult of Sol Invictus. The Roman Aurelian, no less than the Sasanid Shapur, was on his way toward becoming "partner of the stars, brother of the sun and moon"; [6] and toleration slowly yielded to persecution in both areas.

To assert that Christianity was an Oriental cult is to make a statement which is not altogether justified. It must be remembered that Oriental cults as a whole did not succeed in conquering the minds of Mediterranean inhabitants. Christianity, again, showed remarkable indifference to borrowing from the worship of Mithra or Isis while opening itself easily in its dogma to Greek philosophy and in its organization to Roman political influence. But even if one grants the dubious and calls the new creed Oriental, the victory of Christianity must be ascribed on historical grounds to the fact that it rose at the very time when the Empire was ready to receive such a faith. Christian art as such was merely a continuation of the styles already rising, whether in Rome or in the Orient; for there was no *one* Christian art—the Christian faith did not bring with it an inevitable art form.

In sum, the intellectual revolution of the Empire was not the product of barbarian workers or of uncivilized concepts introduced from the north, or of the rise of the lower classes in the Empire, or of Oriental influence. These explanations seem to rise out of the naïve feeling that classical rationalism was good, and medieval transcendentalism bad; therefore the vandalic Germans, the riffraff of the Empire, or the Orient—the sink of all iniquity—must be held responsible for the introduction of "nonrational" ideas into Western civilization. Neither chronology nor logic can support this frame of thought.

There is no need to explain away the shift of Mediterranean civilization as something innately bad. Rather than leading Western civilization down a side track, the men of the third and fourth centuries were preparing the way for the development of the modern world and were working on foundations laid by the Early Empire. The movement, moreover, of the Roman Empire toward a new view of the individual

[6] W. Ensslin, *Cambridge Ancient History* 12 (Cambridge, 1939), 357.

and of the world was a product of its own conditions, which affected all classes.

Literature and Philosophy

The conclusion that imperial development was unified and was essentially independent of alien, distorting influences is a vital but inescapable result when one analyzes the artistic pattern of the Empire. The same processes were at work in literature and philosophy and also in religion. Almost every product of an imperial pen is in some degree an illustration of the decay of classical civilization and of the pressure of the state upon the thinker, and as such the major writers and philosophers have already been considered. The very same products, however, also contain manifestations of the emergence of the individual as an entity in himself, the turn of these individuals to a superior power, and the equally important realization that man is bound to man in a common humanity.

In the field of literature one example will suffice to show that these ideas go back at least to the Augustan Age. In his majestic epic, the *Aeneid*, Virgil sang of the mythical origins of Rome but viewed all the earlier history of Rome as a divinely inspired progress toward the security of the Augustan Age. After the unrest and black concern of his earlier years Virgil had found his savior in the form of Augustus. Now he voiced a serene optimism in the future of Rome: the world has purpose under the guidance of the gods. Besides divine providence, there are men and things in the universe, and it seemed not unreasonable in my earlier discussion to argue that to Virgil the physical world is set apart from man to a greater extent than it is in the work of Hesiod. Virgil also had a deep sense of the tears in life and a sympathy with the human lot; the lines of his epic breathe a greater sense of humanity and pity than one can find in his contemporary, Horace. Alike in his optimism and his gentleness Virgil clearly struck chords in the minds of his fellows and of later generations which his gloomy friend could not reach. Augustus had paid little attention to these deeper notes, but men of the Empire quoted Virgil for other reasons than for his celebration of the Augustan system.

Both in his turn to supernatural power, which was embodied only in part in the emperor, and in his sympathy with mankind, Virgil had predecessors in the Republic, but his intuition plumbed depths they never reached. Thereafter pagan Rome produced no more poets of the depth and sincerity of Virgil; the search of the individual for ties outside himself spilled over in three major channels: philosophy, especially of the Stoic and Neoplatonic varieties; religion, both the Greco-Roman and ecstatic cults; and the idealization of the emperor.

When the effective sway of the Greek city-state had declined, the philosophers of the Hellenistic Age had evolved divers answers to the desperate needs of mankind. These answers all stressed the individuality of the human being, who must by self-scrutiny raise himself to the ideal; he must, in other words, live by his mind and accept death as the essential end of his personality. In the second century after Christ the sessions of these philosophers revolved wearily in old, old terms about the problems of duty and the like; the systems had become hopelessly eclectic; and all seemed dismally sterile.

New ideas, however, were rising beneath the surface, and men were turning to more basic issues. Before dismissing classical civilization as dead, one must always take account of the remarkable accomplishment of those imperial thinkers who linked philosophy and religion and so gave a new direction to philosophy for centuries to come. Ancient thought had still the potentiality of one more adjustment to the urges of mankind, though in the end that adjustment proved not quite supple enough to be all-conquering.

Preliminary steps toward the last answer of philosophy were taken by the Stoics and Neopythagoreans. In Stoic thought the Empire witnessed an increased emphasis on humanitarian and religious ideas. Amid the blackest pessimism over man's fate under autocracy Seneca yet expressed a real humanitarianism and an almost Christian resignation before the will of God. Epictetus went on to a well-nigh mystical celebration of the divine wisdom and of divine governance of human affairs. Self-scrutiny began to pass beyond rational meditation into a search for transcendental control and enlightenment. Sextus Empiricus still preached the skepticism of Pyrrho to a wide audience, Lucian still scoffed, but repeatedly in other thinkers of the second century one may note in a narrowing concentration on ethical problems a turn toward the religious, an effort to *believe*, an emphasis upon authority.

Of all the second-century thinkers the humane and practical Plutarch perhaps shows most clearly the main course of thought. On the one side he assailed the black aspect of Stoic thought, the harsh and callous doctrine of *apatheia*, and argued that the ties of men to their fellow men and to their families, which resulted in emotions distressing to the perfect Stoic, should not be ruthlessly excised; in a dialogue *On Love* he sounds almost a modern note in his just appreciation of the physical and spiritual unity of marriage. His reproof of the heartlessness of Cato to slaves, which has already been quoted, may be placed beside Dio Chrysostom's attack on prostitution. Both his *Lives* and those of his *Moral Essays* which really deal with moral questions betray, amid their quotation of early opinion, a remarkably strong emphasis on the need of morality for the individual and society.

On the other side Plutarch, like Apuleius and others, took up from Plato's pupil Xenocrates and the Pythagoreans an old doctrine of "demons" or divine beings which were visualized as intermediaries between perfect divinity and imperfect man, in need of supernatural care or revelation. This doctrine he evolved in ways which pointed directly to the Neoplatonist doctrine of the following centuries. Plutarch had a truly pious cast of mind even though he strongly assailed "superstition," i.e., an emotional belief in the supernatural outside the paths of Greco-Roman religion, for this led to a fear "which utterly humbles and crushes a man." [7]

Other men tapped more directly the placid yet sincere Pythagorean combination of moral and religious doctrine. In the Empire the most famous example was Apollonius of Tyana, but many thinkers assisted in an interesting fusion of philosophic and religious doctrines which took up both magic and ethics into a single package, according well with the increasingly moral tone of the late second and third century. The pagan emphasis on morality, one may note in passing, often smacks of Christianity while rising entirely independently thereof.

Men of the third century found in Plato the chief root for their merger of religious and philosophic views, which reached its pagan consummation in the teachings of the third-century master, Plotinus. This fascinating, yet somehow frightening man was a pupil of an Alexandrian philosopher, Ammonius Saccas, who had been a Christian but had turned back to philosophy. It is not without significance that the greatest Christian scholar of the third century, Origen, had earlier been a pupil of the same teacher and drew most directly from Plato in his mighty efforts toward the *rapprochement* of Christian doctrine and pagan philosophy.

The great work of Plotinus, the *Enneads*, rests directly upon the

[7] *Moralia* 165B.

writings of the master, i.e., Plato, who had pictured the toilsome upward progress of the human mind by stages to the concept of the perfect idea of the Good—and had found that only through transcendental revelation could man attain that vision. Yet in many respects there is a tremendous gulf between Plato and Plotinus. The one tried primarily to fit his fellows for life in the ideal city-state; the other was a master of contemplation who sought to lead his contemporaries into retirement so that they might gain individual communion with the divine force. The same gulf becomes visible in the contrast between a bust of Plato and a portrait of a Neoplatonic philosopher, for the face of the latter is a mask displaying by upturned eyes the search of the soul for a vision.

In essence Plotinus utilized the rational method of inquiry into the nature of the world to establish the existence of a universal power, pure intelligence yet transcendentally divine, which could be apprehended in its lower stages by reason but in its full manifestation only by a mysterious, rapturous contemplation by the elect who could soar so high. From this divine force emanated a number of subsidiary beings, demons and the like, which intermediated between its purity and imperfect man; but in contrast to the teachings of the mystery religions, the gnostics (in part), and Christianity, Plotinus asserted that the human soul could by itself, without divine aid, rise to see that purity and gain an ecstatic union with the One.

Although so intimately addressed to the individual, Neoplatonism tended in the main to sweep away the individualism of earlier philosophy and of imperial life, for the self merged into the One, or highest divine force. Plotinus himself did not believe in individual survival after death. The last ancient philosophical explanation of the world afforded a release for the human from his fear of Fate or Chance and his sense of atomization, but only at the danger of wiping out his individuality; that this threat was partly seen is suggested by several essays in the *Enneads* wherein Plotinus came close to formulating a metaphysical explanation of human individuality. In the end he failed to establish this vital point clearly, and a true comprehension of transcendental unity and human diversity was to come only after the Christian debate on the Trinity.

A full outline of the growth and ideas of Neoplatonism would require far more space than can be given to it, nor is Plotinus the only Neoplatonist. Its popularity in the Latin West was great throughout the fourth century; Plotinus himself had the favor not only of senators but even of the emperor Gallienus. From the Christian point of view the significance of this stream of thought looms up at first glance. As Augustine notes repeatedly, the pagan philosophers came close again and again to Christian doctrine; by the fourth century Christianity itself was a fusion of religion and philosophy, though in somewhat different proportions. The Neoplatonists exercised a powerful influence on Christian thought by criticism of its doctrines and by their independent constructions, and we cannot take their teachings as entirely opposed to Christianity. Though Augustine spent much ingenuity in combating the philosophers—far more than in opposing the absurdities of pagan cult—it was through the entrycourt of Neoplatonism that he himself came to visualize a nonmaterial explanation of the divine soul and so to approach the Church.

Christian scholars felt a great danger in this last effort of classical thought to erect its own positive explanation of man's place in the world, but in the end the philosophers were always led away into blind alleys by their inheritance of negative rationalism and materialism. The pride of the human mind still had to give way to Christian humility. Nor could the pagans exorcise the crushing weight of mythology. Plotinus had uttered the puzzling statement that the pagan gods should come to him and, like his disciple Porphyry, rejected sacrifice. Later adherents of the sect refused to accept this dangerous excision of tradition and were as credulous fanatics as any Christian monk. The fourth-century popularizer of Neoplatonism, Iamblichus, fitted almost all previous religious and philosophical systems into its doctrine of subsidiary divine and semidivine creations.

From the thinker Augustine to the conjuror Maximus any type of man could find a temporary or permanent home within Neoplatonism. Yet this abode was not designed for the ordinary man, whom Plotinus' chief disciple Porphyry warned away; and with this dogmatic product classical philosophy had reached the end of its creative potentialities.

Doors of Religion

The aims of philosophy and of religion had become much the same by the time of Plotinus, though the methods might vary. Some of the most interesting men of the third century sought inner certainty through the old paths of philosophy, but most tried to gain their individual salvation by passing through the doors of religion. The roads, once one passed the gates, were many, and their course has often been charted by modern scholars.

The starting points were mostly old, for the framework—if not the spirit—of Greco-Roman paganism continued to endure. Some of its gods were officially accepted and supported by the state. During the third century certain Caesars were even to emphasize the practical duty of a citizen to worship these deities, and the religious calendars of the time show that the Empire scrupulously maintained the cult of its great gods down to the economic chaos of the late third century. Apart from Jupiter and his confraternity, but within the same frame of paganism, were other deities of more ecstatic appeal. The processions of Cybele or Magna Mater, whom Claudius endorsed as a goddess of state, were famous; the mysteries of Dionysus exercised a pervasive influence which extended even as far as the decoration of Christian sarcophagi. These gods were Hellenized; others, like Adonis of Syria, Mithra of the Iranian world, and Isis and Sarapis from Egypt, retained an alien air and were not officially supported. These latter cults gained adherents at times among the Roman aristocracy and emperors, but they never won the majority of the people or even a deep hold widely in the West.

Throughout the second and third century thinkers essayed to pour a new spirit into this old framework. The feeling that godhead was essentially one and indivisible was an old one in classical thought, but in the unified Empire, under its one master, men ever spoke too of God in a more singular, abstract sense. The multiplicity of gods was not directly assailed, but a syncretistic effort was apparent, in which the followers of each deity attempted to gain the mastery for their god by equating other divinities with it.

The most successful essay revolved about the sun-god and stemmed largely from Syrian sources; its aim was to erect at least a monophysite faith on the concept of the sun-god, who was the generative principle and master of human destinies and who supported and justified imperial rule. In the novel *Aethiopica* by the Syrian Heliodorus, in the reported order of Gallienus for the erection of a colossal statue of himself as the Sun, in the inscriptions and coins of many third-century rulers, and in a host of other evidence the worship of the sun is obvious. A specific example of the resulting syncretism is given in an inscription from the Mithraeum in the Baths of Caracalla, dedicated to Zeus, Helios,

Sarapis, and Mithra, all associated and confounded in one supreme god, "the invincible master of the world." [8]

Finally the worship of the sun debouched on the highest level under the emperor Aurelian, who erected a temple to Sol Invictus as embodying Apollo, Sarapis, Mithra, and other deities, with the great pagan gods as assistants. The state established a new priesthood and cult, which celebrated the Sun's birthday on December 25; mints struck coins with the legend "Sol master of the Roman Empire"; and Aurelian considered himself the vicar of this power. With this last truly pagan religious effort the Empire had thrown up almost as exclusive a force as Christianity, and at his death Aurelian was moving toward persecution of the Christians. Constantine was later to find it easy to step from worshiping the Sun to revering Christ.

In all this activity the little gods continued to live close to men's hearts, but the great deities receded farther and farther from the call of a desperate man. Although some thinkers, such as Plutarch and Porphyry, felt they were stripping away dross from true belief when they ascribed pagan mythology to the faulty views of the poets and dramatists or when they reduced the lecherous, deceitful deities of these stories to the status of lower divinities or "demons," they were actually helping to kill the spirit of Greco-Roman cults no less than Lucian, who mocked the paraphernalia of paganism. Such a critic as Porphyry was wildly superstitious in many respects, but he was unable to accept the emotional drive of the new creeds. As men grew sicker, they pushed their rationalism ever further.

All sorts of strange constructions were invented by the gnostics to link the purity of divinity and the baseness of man. To many others communication with the divine force became less a matter of formal sacrifice and more a mystical union in the form of dreams, visions, and miracles. Socrates had had visions, and Plato had had a mystical experience of the highest Good; but these transcendental communings shine palely beside the developed imagery of the famous dream of Apuleius in the *Golden Ass* or the repeated revelations recorded in the next century in the Hermetic corpus and elsewhere.

This drive of mankind toward a view of God as unique, as an ethical guide to mankind expressing himself through visions, in short, as a transcendental force on which man might rely, was quite independent

[8] *L'Année épigraphique* 1913.188.

of Christianity. As expressed in the brittle framework of paganism, however, the effort had serious defects. It loosed some men from the grim powers of Fate, primarily in terms of the ills of this life, but only rarely did the loosing rise into a promise of personal immortality of the soul. None of the pagan faiths could become a completely rounded religion, with a central organization and an independent moral and political standing. One and all, they accepted subjection to the state gods and to the imperial cult; the latter of these became ever more developed and transcendentalized in the third century.

Christianity

Although philosophers and rulers alike were unconsciously moving in a direction which led them far from the old ideas of the city-state and of classical culture, they were unable to advance rapidly or to shake off the limitations of the past. Philosophy could not escape its rational, materialist outlook; religion had still the dross of paganism; the Caesars, while shifting toward an effort to maintain morality and to uphold social obligations, were beset by the problems of the political, economic, and social decline of the third century. The most perfect exposition of the new view of the world and of man was to be found not in the teachings of the philosophers, not in the practice of the emperors, not in the esthetic development of architecture and sculpture, but in Christianity.

By taking up this tremendous force last, one can appreciate more fully that Christianity was a perfectly logical outgrowth of imperial development. Since the days of Augustus the men of the Roman Empire, of whatever creed or philosophy—or of none—had been making their way toward the same goal as that of Christianity. The concept of the individual as a distinct entity, the idea that the physical world and man were things apart though under identical governance, the belief that man had a soul and could through it claim access to a divine power —all these had been evolved by Mediterranean civilization independently of Christianity. That evolution had been expressed in the buildings, in the reliefs and statues and paintings, and assuredly also in the music which men of the Empire produced; it had manifested itself in their writings and in their thoughts. Historically speaking, the triumph of Christianity was but the culmination of the entire trend of the Roman Empire; even ancient Christians could feel that the emergence of the Empire and of Christian truth at the same time was not accidental.

Understanding the pattern of development of imperial culture does not detract from the unique character of the Christian faith. While many scholars have explored the deep differences between Christianity and classical civilization, others have drawn our attention to the absorption of classical culture by the Church. Either view is one-sided and is likely to disguise how uniquely, yet how fully the new faith provided the perfect embodiment of the search of imperial man for a justification of his individuality together with a firm establishment of communal life and sense of divine guidance.

The individualism of imperial man was satisfied by the new faith in at least three ways: the proffer of an individual as the center of the cult, the establishment of a theological basis for individuality, and the assertion of the essential equality of all men. Although the early Church paid little attention to the human figure of its founder, Christianity was historically rooted in an individual who lived, died, and rose again within historical times. Christianity, again, refused to offer to the men who lived in the Empire a far-off emperor, who was supported by the upper classes of the Empire and who bestowed purely physical rewards which might be all too obviously ashes. Its hero was One who was Himself sprung from the masses, whose promise of salvation through His own sacrifice was of eternal value.

To this divine mediator came the despondent individuals of the Empire one by one, for conversion to Christianity was an individual matter in which the person so saved had often to break his ties with the groups about him; thence arose a great series of apologies, in which Justin and others explained their radical change of mind and tendered the liberating doctrine to the pagan world. Each of these men could be confident that he had an individual soul, which could be saved by this break with the world and which would survive in its uniqueness after his death. The Christian was a miserable sinner, but he was also an object of individual value in the sight of God.

In the essential equality of all men before their Maker the Christian faith expressed in simple yet sublime terms a powerful tendency of the Empire to treat all subjects as individuals worthy of imperial protection. Far more than the emperors, the Church broke in essential theory with the aristocratic domination of all ancient society. Although the bishops steadily became more distinct from the laity, and men of wealth came into the Church from very early days, Christians could always look back to the humble men of Galilee who had formed Christ's first disciples; they could call all Christians, whether slave or rich, man or woman, their brethren; and they could dream of a heaven where rank depended on virtue rather than on earthly position. Herein lay one great stumbling block to the conversion of the intellectually arrogant layer of the Empire, for even the Neoplatonists felt that only the few could aspire to the highest immortality; against this human arrogance Augustine reverts again and again to the essential requirement of humility in the Christian faith.

Christians also lived together in groups, partly because the pressure of outside society drove them in upon themselves, but partly because they had their duties to their fellows. Christ had commanded His followers to love God and to love their neighbor as themselves. Toward the unjust and the heretic Christians could display an appalling hatred, but throughout succeeding centuries the Christian communities under their bishops exhibited within themselves a standard of mutual love and support which appealed strongly to the dissatisfied atoms adrift in the mist of imperial society. The heretics whom Ignatius denounced "have no care for love, none for the widow, none for the orphan, none for the distressed . . . none for the hungry or thirsty." [9]

Accordingly Christianity, unlike any other cult of the Empire, furnished man and society with a real motive and basis for morality, which did not rest simply on the rational instincts of mankind. Placing the soul first, Christian leaders could yet grant more leeway to the passions and emotions of the body than could a Stoic, and they could criticize Stoic *apatheia* more sharply even than did pagans like Plutarch. Jesus, says Augustine, had emotions. Lactantius puts the Christian view beautifully in calling mad those who deprive "man, a mild and sociable animal of his name; who, having uprooted the affections, in which humanity altogether consists, wish to bring him to an immovable insensibility of mind." [10]

From this new view of the human ensued the Christian condemnation of gladiatorial games, of exposure of newborn infants, of licentiousness under religious guise, of suicide, and of other evils which pagan philosophers could dimly sense as wrong but, apart from the Cynics, could not firmly attack. Thence too came that sympathy with others which passed beyond pagan compassion into Christian charity and social responsibility, virtues which the pagan emperor Julian felt to be worthy of imitation by pagans.

[9] *To the Smyrneans* 6.2.   [10] *Divine Institutes* 6.17 (Fletcher).

In another, complementary aspect Christian metaphysics continued an attack on pagan thought already delivered by numerous pagan thinkers, and brought to the battle a new thrill of certainty. Christians, that is, rejected the grim fatalism of Tyche or the stars, for Christ's sacrifice had liberated the individual from this awful impasse of ancient thought. Each man might save or damn himself; at the same time he also must assist in saving his fellows. In a word, the Christian as an individual inherited and incorporated all the advances of the ancient world in this respect, and yet as a member of a definite group had the certainty of support and ties with his fellow humans.

The Christian had also his ties with God the Father—an aspect of God which comes into prominence in the teaching of Jesus in contrast to the earlier Jewish view of Him as judge. The Christian deity was an ethical force which rewarded virtue and punished sin both in this world and hereafter; for the deliverance even of the sinner He had opened out a way through the voluntary sacrifice of His own Son, a human being. Whereas other cults expected the individual first to purify himself, Christianity embraced a man, whether ignorant or learned, whether good or bad, and offered him salvation on the conditions of repentance, faith, and the execution of certain rites.

For proof of this assurance of salvation, the Christian could turn to a divinely inspired work in the form of the books of the New Testament, which in turn rested on the prophecy of the Old. The unquestionable authority of the Bible had been clearly accepted as a principle by the end of the second century. In the last analysis a Christian thinker had to believe in assumptions unprovable by the pure exercise of reason; but once having believed he could build his thought upon solid foundations.

The tremendous vigor of Paul's mind cannot be denied even by those who detest his influence on Christian doctrine. Of the origins of the leaders of the Church in the next few generations after Paul we know little, but we cannot deny to Clement, Ignatius, and Polycarp independence and sureness of mind, clarity of pen, and force of character. Though Christianity was only one manifestation of the rise of the new order of thought, it was to end by being the dominant form, the vehicle by which that new order was passed on to the modern world; and if one wishes to derive the Christians from the lower strata of society, that level must be admitted to have had great intellectual potentialities when fired by a new idea.

XIV

The Empire and Christianity

WHEN men of the third century looked at the world, they had their choice of a new pair of spectacles or the old set of classical manufacture. Some preferred the old, some the new; most switched back and forth from one to the other in a bizarre fashion. In their selection men acted unconsciously, for not until the end of the century did the more penetrating thinkers begin even dimly to see the true outlines of the new view of life.

Neither society nor the emperors were quick to realize the drift of their world. The new structure of thought rose independently of the imperial autocracy, and in this fact is a majestic proof that political systems cannot entirely harness the thinking of their subjects. More can be said: the emperors, like other men, tended to promote the speed of the current, and themselves embodied many of its tendencies. At times the social system did scent dangers in the infiltration of new ideas and reacted blindly against them, as a human organism counters a virus. The reaction was never sufficiently broad or enduring—and in its more violent aspects it was limited by the very emphasis of the imperial system on peace and order.

The Empire, to be sure, had joined with the aristocracy in supporting classical civilization. Both elements essayed to keep the lower classes in subjection and to muzzle the uncouth or the barbarian. The weakness of the defense, however, lay in the insidious penetration of the new ideas into the minds of men of all classes. Augustus surely did not comprehend the ramifications of Virgil's thought; and, though Seneca fell, Nero had not condemned him for his humanitarian sympathies. The philosophic martyrs during the last half of the first century generally suffered not because they possessed radical notions but because they were conservative. They refused, that is, to accept the autocracy of the imperial position, which was in itself a mark of the turn of mankind to a savior outside its own circle.

The emperors, one and all, offered themselves to the Empire as an embodiment of that savior, even though some might refuse actual worship. Most of them expressed actively in their policy that sympathy with humanity which Virgil had voiced. They supported the poor and protected the underprivileged elements of society; under the Good Emperors and the Severi the humanitarian tone of imperial legislative and administrative activity was conscious and extensive. Whereas emperors of the first two centuries had become largely resigned or indifferent to the moral shortcomings of their period, the Caesars of the third and fourth centuries took an ever-more-positive attitude in essaying to promote morality; the human was rising in imperial legislation to be an individual of ethical significance, even though the rulers might try to dictate his political and economic status.

Down to the third century the old pagan cults were the only ones officially recognized in the army or supported in public life, but besides them deities like Isis or Mithra were openly worshiped. The emperors often led the way in revering such gods, and eventually promoted the search for a deity under whom all others could be subsumed. In art, in architecture, and in literature the works commissioned by the emperors breathed the spirit of their times. The only emperor who may possibly have tried to withstand the new esthetic tastes was Gallienus, but the Gallienic Renaissance was not only a superficial affair but also, as far as it went, a phenomenon to be found outside the districts which he ruled. When the same emperor thought of endowing Plotinus with a city in Campania, we are scarcely justified in construing the plan as an effort to combat Christianity with Neoplatonism; and in any event the philosophy of Plotinus was itself shot through with the new order of thought.

At only one point did the Empire directly place itself in opposition to the intellectual revolution. This point is the rise of Christianity, for the new view of the world, of man, and of God was most fully embodied in Christian thought. To speak of the area in question as a "point" is to minimize it greatly: the conflict between Church and state was protracted over two and one-half centuries. The persecutions illuminate many aspects of the imperial structure of government, not least of which are the actual machinery of repression and the reluctance of the central government to give a free hand to the cities. In the present connection the prime necessity is to determine the extent to which intellectual grounds underlay the persecutions, either at the outset or later. Did the Empire oppose Christianity on ideological grounds?

Treatment of the Jews

To solve this complex problem one must look beyond Christianity itself. The experiences of the Jews are particularly illuminating, and beyond these one must consider the general relations of state and religion in Roman thought.

At the end of the Republic various cities in the Aegean were exerting strong local pressure against the Jews. For protection the Jews appealed to Rome, first in the days of Caesar and then once more in 14 B.C., when Agrippa, the chief agent of Augustus, was in the East. King Herod of Judea came up to Asia Minor to meet his old friend; with him traveled his adviser and orator, Nicolaus of Damascus, who delivered before Agrippa a great oration in favor of Jewish liberties.

The speech, as reported in Josephus, stressed the Roman principle of freedom of worship. Nicolaus argued that the Jewish rites were already protected by Roman decrees, were not inhuman in any respect, and needed only the same protection as was given to other cults. The local Greek steps against the collection of funds for the Temple, against Sabbath observance, and so on (he asserted) were merely indirect attacks on the Jewish religion itself and were, he also argued, a manifestation of hostility to that Roman benevolence and good government which he praised in glowing terms.

This plea is perhaps the greatest defense of freedom of religion in ancient literature; against it and against so well-supported a pleader the Greeks could make no defense. In the end Agrippa confirmed once more the privileges of the Jews and promised them anything else they desired —if it did not injure Roman rule.

The whole affair, which nicely illustrates the practical Roman policy, is the compound of a number of complicated elements: Jewish hopes, Roman religious theory and political practice, and local anti-Semitism. The local pressure against the Jews, sometimes hidden, here open, is perhaps the easiest to explain. In the first degree it was a manifestation of the renascent Hellenism of the politically weak Greek cities in the last century before Christ. Anti-Semitism, then as always, rested on one main factor: the Jews, scattered widely abroad in other lands as farmers and city-dwellers, refused to give up their own way of life and to accept completely that of the community in which they lived; in reaction, the community tended to try to enforce its standards on this alien element, which often in the East grouped itself into a tightly knit unit.

The religious and ethical practices of Judaism differed far more sharply from the dominant cultural pattern of the ancient Mediterranean world than they do from Western civilization today. Whereas the Christian God is much akin to Jehovah and the Old Testament is accepted by both Christianity and Judaism, the Jewish deity had little in common with the anthropomorphic, numerous gods of the pagan world who had almost no influence on the ethical views of their worshipers. Further, Judaism was an exclusive faith which could not easily be held along with Greek cults. To be a citizen of any Greek city, one had to partake in the state cults of the city, and all pagan social life was closely intertwined with the worship of the gods. At the games, at the public festivals, at the banquets—where the meat had first been sacrificed to the gods—even at the law courts, which met on the Sabbath, no Jew could feel entirely comfortable. The practice of circumcision, the dietary requirements of the Mosaic law, the Jewish view of the sacredness of the family—all made their adherents stand apart from the general pattern of Greco-Roman life as no other element of the ancient world did.

"Religion governs all our actions and occupations and speech," asserted Josephus,[1] and though the Jews abroad frequently adapted themselves to local customs to an extraordinary degree, those who kept their faith always remained marked off. In more or less direct fashion Jews had always to deny the charge of the pagan world: "It behoves you, if ye would live with us, also to revere our gods."[2] The intensity of the resulting pressure varied from mild social ostracism to vehement literary attacks and even to physical assault.

Matters were made worse by the positive tone of Judaism. Down to the end of the second century after Christ the Jews made some effort to expand their faith among Gentiles. In Palestine itself the Jews had a political center which had been free from the middle of the second

[1] *Against Apion* 2.171.   [2] Josephus, *Antiquities* 4.137.

century B.C. to Pompey's conquest and had thereafter been recognized as a political entity, whether ruled by client kings, split up, or governed by procurators. Here Judaism tended to press for real political independence to secure its religious way of life; in Palestine the Zealots seem to have caused much of the recurring troubles and to have exploited to the hilt any provocation by the Greeks. Abroad the Jews seem to have pressed hard for citizenship in the Greek cities, even though they could not take up all the burdens of that citizenship, and in retaliation for opposition were not backward in polemic, apologia, and even revolt.

The Romans themselves despised the Jewish cult and disliked its universal claim, yet generally they protected the Jews much as Agrippa had done in 14 B.C. To explain this position one cannot make an arbitrary use of the principle of religious toleration which Nicolaus postulated, for Roman thought failed to recognize that citizens—or subjects —had any inherent right to religious liberty.

In particular, the Romans might protect unpleasing local customs abroad while resenting their introduction into Rome itself. In the Republic, as I noted in the first chapter, Roman citizens were expected to worship in public only gods approved by the Roman state. Citizens had little practical opportunity to demonstrate this loyalty, for the magistrates conducted the public ceremonies; Cicero and Varro could be skeptical of the inner meaning of the cults while still going through outward forms. Yet, in the last analysis, I am sure, citizens could be required on the orders of a magistrate to manifest their worship of the gods of the state, who safeguarded the sway of Rome and the lives of its citizens, and to abstain from foreign temptations to "levity" and "superstition."

During the Empire foreign cults were able in practice to spread their beliefs among Roman citizens, but the Roman spirit still showed itself occasionally. Augustus banned the cult of Isis and Sarapis from the city proper; under Tiberius the Senate repeated the ban and extended it to Judaism. Some four thousand Jewish and Isiac freedmen were shipped off as soldiers to Sardinia. Josephus tries to lay the blame for this wholesale expulsion on a fraud perpetrated on a Roman noble by two Jews, Philo accuses Sejanus, Dio Cassius asserts that the Jews were converting Romans. The latter account best explains the sweeping nature of the punishment—as an old Roman Tiberius was not inclined to permit such conversion, which was always legally barred. Under

Claudius the Jews became riotous, and their associations were banned, for Claudius found them too numerous to be expelled easily.

Thereafter the practical significance of the Roman opposition to foreign cults in Rome itself waned considerably, and the cosmopolitan capital became equally cosmopolitan religiously. The emperors, nonetheless, never abrogated the idea that Roman citizens should worship Roman gods; in the days of Trajan Rome was still proclaimed a "state dedicated to religion and always meriting the favor of the gods by its piety." [3] Marcus Aurelius ordered the exile of men leading others to superstitious fear of a deity; not long thereafter state intolerance of non-Roman cults was to re-emerge on a practical level and seriously to embarrass the Christians.

To its subjects Rome applied in general the same rules as to itself, that the citizens of a state should worship its local gods, that it was as impious for these citizens to desert their gods as it was for Romans to neglect theirs; and so the Romans tended to protect local religious activities which they found at the time of their conquest. In Egypt, thus, the Romans made the killing of a sacred animal a capital offense. To this extent one may accept Claudius' description of Augustus "as willing that all subjects could continue in the observance of their own customs, and not be forced to transgress the ancient rules of their own native religion." [4]

Deep beneath the surface, however, the Romans disliked manifestations of a religious spirit which radically differed from their own. The subjects were quite generally allowed to worship as they desired, but the Roman state occasionally banned religious activities which ran counter to the practices of Greco-Roman religious thought or the conduct of which led to unrest among the masses. When Augustus conquered Egypt, he felt that his hold over the sullen populace was insecure; among other steps he confiscated the land of the Egyptian temples and placed the priests on the state payroll to ensure their subservience. A Roman official at Alexandria became the head of the Egyptian state cult; under Trajan the coinage of this city, which depicts a great variety of local Egyptian gods in an Alexandrian, official interpretation, suggests the reworking of local cult which could take place.

An even-more-outstanding example of imperial interference is the

---

[3] Pliny, *Panegyric* 74.5.
[4] Josephus, *Antiquities* 19.283 (paraphrased in Philo, *Legation* 153).

Roman attitude toward the decaying Druid worship of Gaul. Augustus barred citizens from partaking in this religion of "dread inhumanity" which burned men alive, and the more extreme, backward rites were generally forbidden. Tiberius went farther, and under Claudius the survivals of the cult, already much weakened by the cultural advance of Gaul, were stamped out.

The ancient evidence shows that the ban rose only partly, if at all, from the motive often asserted by modern scholars—a possible political role of the Druids in opposing Roman rule. At least as powerful was the Roman dislike of human sacrifice, which was practiced elsewhere, especially in the slaughter of young children. Pliny the Elder, in discussing human sacrifice, argued that the Romans should be thanked for their abolition of such horrible rites; the Senate had barred human sacrifice in 97 B.C.; and Hadrian placed a general imperial ban on the custom. Circumcision was likewise a religious rite which the Romans found distasteful; priests in Egypt who had to be circumcised were forced to petition the government individually for permission, and the Jews were commonly permitted only to circumcise born Jews.

The story of the Jews in the Empire is a sad one, but it may at least be said that the emperors, while barring the main drive of Judaism, might have treated it much worse. They could not accept its claim to universal domination, and they would not permit even political independence in Palestine; by various edicts they attempted to confine Judaism within the bounds of the Jews. The Jews had to acknowledge that the state was primary by accepting the imperial cult, but the emperors generally exempted Jews from those aspects of imperial worship which conflicted with the Mosaic ban on graven images. Although the state, again, did not give the Jewish communities as wide jurisdiction as is sometimes stated, it usually tried to accommodate the requirements of secular life to the peculiar dictates of the Law. Augustus thus permitted Roman Jews to claim their grain on the following day if the regular distribution fell on a Sabbath, and specifically safeguarded the dangerous right of the Jews to collect and transmit Temple funds to Jerusalem.

Of all the Roman Caesars down to Hadrian, only two deliberately thought of attacking the Jews outside Rome, if we may omit Philo's suggestion that Sejanus planned a mass persecution in the name of the emperor Tiberius. One of these was Gaius, who essayed to set up his statue in the Temple at Jerusalem and looked harshly upon Jewish complaints of ill-treatment at Alexandria. The other was Domitian, who appears in his later, more autocratic years to have contemplated a general repression. Both rulers were autocrats who had an exalted view of the divine, imperial position; and their dislike of Judaism was motivated more by the scruples of Jews in this respect than by the general moral and religious nature of the religion.

Some Jews, like the historian Josephus, were willing to put the state above their religion; rabbinical literature sometimes even praised the ideals of the Empire. Others were unwilling to make this simple but devastating sacrifice. Revolts broke out twice in Palestine and at other times in other parts of the East; more generally the malcontents surreptitiously set afloat prophecies based on the old messianic idea, the dream of the four kingdoms in Daniel (which Josephus treated very gingerly), and so on. Some attacks on the ideal of the Empire as an institution beneficent in practice and divinely ordained made their way into the Talmud and other purely Jewish works; some were couched in outwardly classical forms, such as Sibylline oracles, and have come down to us in the Greco-Roman stream. Although the riddling obscurity of oracles and Talmud cannot always be penetrated, the indictments of the avarice and social corruption of Rome are at times of a bitter intensity.

From the practical point of view the Jews were saved by their numbers. It was dangerous to permit local persecution to drive them often beyond discontent to rebellion; in any case, the state frowned on the display of independent violence by the subject communities. Neither the destruction of the Temple in 70 nor the ban on Jewish settlement in Jerusalem under Hadrian brought an end to the general privileges of the Jews throughout the Empire; bloodshed and outward legal discrimination were forbidden even at the cost of interfering with the powers of the local units of government.

Thus the emperor Claudius tried to hold the scales evenly in his settlement of the great riots at Alexandria, where the Greeks had vented their hatred on the Romans by assailing the Jews as Roman pets and the Jews had in turn sprung to arms after the death of their oppressor Gaius. In an extant letter the new emperor refused to decide which side had caused the commotion or, rather, the war, but he warned that if this trouble did not cease he would be "compelled to show what a benevolent prince can be when turned to just indignation." [5] Like many another ruler Claudius found it impossible to allocate the responsibility for anti-Semitic outbursts or to remove the causes; all that could be done was to clamp down the threat of force on its open manifestation and to tread an uneasy path of compromise between privilege for and limitations on Judaism.

The hidden forms of social and economic persecution the emperors could not touch; but in most areas Jews were able to live, to rear children, and to die in their faith without serious danger. Against Alexandria, where local conditions long kept the Jews on tenterhooks, may be placed the Phrygian town of Acmoneia, where a Jewess served as eponymous magistrate; in their turn some Jews were fanatical, but others even took up the trade of actor or gladiator. Whenever local repression did become too violent, the imperial government cast its cloak of protection about the Jews. Here, as in the case of Christianity, the imperial government was unwittingly safeguarding the "wave of the future" and enforcing toleration for creeds which were themselves intolerant.

Pagan society, then, reacted against Judaism largely because it was alien; the conflict, in root, was ideological. As regards the Empire, however, Judaism ran into trouble outwardly on the political plane, for the emperors asserted that the state must be dominant. No serious efforts were made to root out any parts of Jewish religious doctrine which applied to the Jews themselves, though this doctrine was legally banned at least for Roman citizens who were not born Jews.

Ban on Christianity

Pagan society likewise soon became suspicious of the Christians. The aristocratic Tacitus scented in the new creed a dire superstition unfitting for Romans, and in frothing against it he was typical of the bulk of pagan thinkers, insofar as they had occasion to mention the Christians.

In the first two centuries of the Christian era Christianity and classical civilization realized that a difference lay between them, and both outwardly had little to do with each other. At times it would appear that conversion to Christianity meant a complete separation from the temporal world, a passing over to a "third race," as the Christians called

[5] *London Papyrus* 1912, ll. 81–82 (H. I. Bell, *Jews and Christians in Egypt* [London, 1924], 28).

themselves; yet in the physical sense this separation cannot have been complete. Despite their clannish attitude the Christians lived in this world among their neighbors, they shared the same form of education and had their intellectual ties with classical civilization, they earned their daily bread in pagan society.

In particular, they either converted or exceedingly irritated their fellows by their uncompromising attacks on the customs of pagan life. Although Christian preaching was not necessarily carried out in the market places, Christians were not to be deterred from expressing their beliefs "by the noise of human indignation." Christians in this period may not have made good neighbors in practice nor always good wives. When Plutarch advised bride and groom, he was probably thinking of pagan Greek cults in urging a wife to "know only the gods that her husband believes in, and to shut the front door tight upon all queer rituals and outlandish superstitions." [6] His remarks, however, would apply well to the Christian wife described by Justin, who was always trying to reform her dissipated husband by picturing the hellfire in wait for sinners. When the emperor Julian tried to restore paganism in the fourth century, he discovered the obnoxious power of Christian women, who cried all night over their backsliding husbands.

Christians, again, were atheists in the sense that they denied the gods of their pagan neighbors and refused to consider the heavenly bodies divine; they failed to carry out many of their urban duties; they even at times seemed to disagree with the pagan views on marriage. Between Christian premises and classical civilization, moreover, lay a gulf. The depths of this gulf were not yet fully seen, but it yawned widely enough at the surface to bring down on the Christians a pagan dislike in which such men as Bishop Ignatius gloried: "Christianity is not the work of persuasiveness, but of greatness, when it is hated by the world." [7]

Even in the lifetime of Christ the vigor of His attack on contemporary ethics and social customs, which resulted in the dramatic expulsion of the moneychangers from the Temple, inevitably led to serious unrest in Jerusalem and to the Crucifixion. Within a generation came the great fire of Rome in 64, whereupon the emperor Nero singled out the Christians as scapegoats; it is clear that he would not have taken this action had not the Christians already been disliked or capable of being disliked. He might have seized the Jews, but they were protected by his

[6] *Moralia* 140D.   [7] Ignatius, *To the Romans* 3.3.

wife Poppaea and in any case were so numerous that persecution might be dangerous. The Christians, on the other hand, were probably not very clearly known, though growing fairly rapidly in numbers, yet they were already distinguishable from the Jews and were "detested for their abominations." [8] In the trials they could be charged with "hatred of the human race," an absurdly sweeping term which sums up well the attitude of pagan society toward the Christians.

Modern scholars have at times been puzzled by the fact that the successors of Nero did not reverse the policy which he laid down—that being a Christian was a crime in itself. Confession of the "name" was enough for condemnation, and there was no need to prove that the culprit had also committed a generally recognized delict. In truth, the remarkable step would have been an act of toleration for the Christians; imperial persecution was the course which one should rightly expect. Once the Empire had sensed something quite dangerous in Christianity, the religious policy of the state permitted it to move quite arbitrarily against citizen and noncitizen alike; to Pliny the Younger the Christians deserved punishment simply for their pertinacity and inflexible refusal to obey his orders to recant.

How the official ban was promulgated we do not know; nor do our surviving records indicate directly the reasons which moved the Caesars. One, I believe, was the feeling that the tenets of Christianity were opposed to those of imperial society and that the spread of these tenets might cause unrest among the lower classes. The union of Christians into exclusive groups with their own judges and customs appeared to imperial eyes far too much like the *hetairiae* or drinking societies which plagued the larger cities.

To this extent the persecution of the Christians, like the troubles of the Jews, was basically due to ideological differences, but the surface manifestations of those differences were political. The Church kept its groups firmly tied together in an Empire-wide web and insisted upon a complete moral dominance over its members. The outward mark of the latter was the refusal of the Christians—attested repeatedly in the *acta* of the martyrs—to obey the orders of imperial officials on certain matters, such as the worship of the emperors and the pagan gods of state. This refusal showed that the Christians put their religion above obedience to the world-state; when the jurist Ulpian came to analyze

[8] Tacitus, *Annals* 15.44.

their position, he located their punishment under the provisions of *laesa maiestas*.

Partially to offset this basic clash the writers of the Church emphasized their obedience to the state in all other particulars. Paul had set the tone, far more than Christ, in his celebrated passage in Romans on the theme "the powers that be are ordained of God." Though Christians might not pray *to* the ruler, Clement of Rome prayed to God, who had given sovereignty to the Caesars, that Christians might be obedient to "our rulers and governors upon the earth" and that these rulers might have "health, peace, concord, firmness that they may administer the government which Thou hast given them without offense." [9] Thus also Bishop Polycarp of Smyrna offered to defend his faith before the proconsul of Asia, for Christians had been taught to render honor "if it hurt us not, to princes and authorities appointed by God." [10]

Despite the violently anti-Roman tone of Revelation and some of the Christian Sibylline oracles, the Church as a whole damped down the revolutionary seed implicit in the idea of the Second Coming; and it would not curse its oppressors or the upper classes who held the bulk of its members in economic subjection. Christian doctrine, in sum, offers a fine illustration of the degree to which the subjects of the Empire had accepted absolutism. Yet the Christians served a jealous God Who permitted worship to no other but Himself. The emperors saw no reason to accept the compromise which such Christian leaders as Polycarp dared to offer them, or to accord the Christians the privileges of the Jews, who were ancient in their peculiarities and were also numerous.

The reasons for imperial disapproval of Christianity were of a weak, almost theoretical nature so long as the emperors felt reasonably secure in their position. During the first two centuries after the coming of Christ the Empire made no serious effort to stamp out the cult; in a famous letter to Pliny, then governor of Bithynia, Trajan really discouraged the use of imperial machinery to support local persecutions. From the days of the Passion on it is obvious that the agents of the emperors, when they met Christians, desired chiefly to preserve peace and order in their districts. Pontius Pilate yielded up Christ to quiet local agitation, and in various other instances the proconsuls or other officials sanctioned the torture and death of Christians to appease the mob.

Even in such investigations we cannot be sure that execution always

[9] *I Clement* 60–61. [10] *Martyrdom* 10.2.

followed automatically for confessing Christians, for the correspondence of Pliny and the brief remarks of Tacitus suggest that the aristocracy as a whole shared the imperial attitude of disliking yet tolerating the benighted Christians. In Africa, thus, one proconsul avoided the last resort by asking Christians only to take an oath for the safety of the ruler, a request which they could obey.

Frequently the attempt of local society to oppress thought which challenged its accepted standards must have met a check at the hands of the emperors and their deputies. When the silversmiths of Ephesus roused the city mob against Paul, the town secretary warned them bluntly that "we are in danger to be called into question for this day's uproar," and the agitation stopped abruptly. A sarcastic edict by Hadrian to a governor of Asia, usually accepted as genuine, ordered that Christians be punished only after a due trial in open court; execution merely on popular clamor was discouraged, and accusations for the sake of blackmail were to be penalized.

As the Christian Lactantius looked back from the days of the great persecution under Galerius, he was not entirely unjustified in praising the Good Emperors of the second century, under whom the Church began the necessary consolidation of its doctrine and organization after the hectic excitement of the days of the Apostles. That this expansion, which offered a universal god to a universal realm, was promoted by the peace and roads of the Empire has often been noted. Equally significant was the imperial tendency to discourage local opposition of a violent nature; the weakening fiber of classical civilization could not support an inquisition.

In the second century Christians might even venture to emerge into the daylight and engage in fairly open apologetic for their faith and appeal against the judgment and canards of pagan society. The earliest apology is that of Quadratus, addressed to Hadrian; then come the *Apology* of Justin and other works, in all of which appears the self-consciousness of the Christian Church as an independent, yet usually compatible force with the Empire.

Persecutions of the Christians

The hopes of the apologists met a bitter disappointment in the third century. Truly imperial persecution on a large scale now appeared for the first time, and local repression was no longer firmly checked by the imperial machinery, which was itself deteriorating. The Christians often suffered as scapegoats; as Tertullian observes, whenever a plague or famine struck, the cry arose, "The Christians to the lion!" [11]

Christian-hunting was, to be sure, only one aspect of the greater violence arising out of the economic and political decay of the era. Riots and civil wars broke out repeatedly in Antioch, Alexandria, and Rome. Brigandage and rural revolts against oppression occurred all over the Empire and foreshadowed the more serious troubles of the fourth century. In a desperate effort to keep order the cities and the army spread over the countryside a net of police, which was turned on occasion against the Christians. The misery of the masses was alleviated neither by riots nor by Christian pogroms, and in the end the unrest of the century drew more adherents to the Church than it took away.

More significant is the intensification of imperial hostility to the Church. Down to the last great persecution under Diocletian the motives of this opposition continued to be primarily political: in brief, the inability of the Christians to worship either the emperors or the gods of the state. Along with these factors the increasing organization and self-assurance of the third-century Church played a part in arousing imperial ire; its growing wealth, in promoting imperial covetousness.

In the peaceful decades of the second century the state could almost ignore the Christian reluctance to worship a material redeemer in the form of Caesar. As the imperial position worsened in fact and was exalted in theory, the rulers began to cast more worried glances at this nonconforming element whose firm, virtually intolerant position could now be detected in the apologies addressed to the pagan world; for these works attacked pagan virtues fully as much as they defended Christian virtues. Efforts at compromise on imperial worship as a sign of patriotism were occasionally made both by Christian moderates and by provincial governors, but Christian extremists were unwilling to accept these offers. Even a judicious thinker like Origen, in his great rebuttal to the pagan Celsus, clearly put his church first and judged outward loyalty to the state by Christian ethical requirements—a Christian might pray for the ruler only if he were good. In any case, so long as the ruler was a pagan, distinction between sacrifice and reverence was difficult to establish; not until the reign of Constantine could a true compromise be worked out on this one point.

Christians were also unable to sacrifice to the gods of the Roman state, a duty which was still technically incumbent upon citizens. This

[11] *Apology* 40.2.

difficulty seems to have played a large role in the third century, when the Roman emperors, especially those of Balkan stock, were trying to keep the Empire together by emphasizing the ideal of Rome. In his famous grant of Roman citizenship to the city-dwellers of the Empire, Caracalla, "the most pious of all mankind" in his own words,[12] asserted, if we may believe a fragmentary papyrus, that his motive was to increase the number of worshipers of the state cult and so to demonstrate his piety. Whether or not P. Giessen 40 is an actual record of the grant of citizenship, it corroborates other evidence for the idea that the gods of Rome were officially encouraged and were to be worshiped by Roman citizens.

Coupled with the increasing weight of these factors was the growing autocracy and violence of political life in the third-century Empire, which led the emperors to look with disfavor upon any open opposition to their wishes. The rivalry of would-be emperors, for instance, resulted in an erasure of names from inscriptions and in a pitiless treatment of the defeated side which cannot often be paralleled in the first two centuries of the Empire. Caracalla, who quarreled with his brother Geta, ended by murdering Geta in their mother's lap and destroyed his partisans wholesale; thereafter the damnation of Geta's memory brought the erasure of his name all over the Empire in inscriptions, and some cities in Asia even hammered out Geta's name and bust on their coins.

In view of the increased violence of the third century and the autocratic ruthlessness of the rulers in exacting compliance and money, one must marvel not that the Christians were persecuted but that they were attacked so rarely. The major persecutions of the third century were few and brief, and the available evidence indicates that the actual punishment of Christians was an almost haphazard affair, in which the state seized upon examples from the leaders, the wealthy, and the more forward members of the Church. When such a notable "confessor" as Bishop Cyprian of Carthage was in prison or on his way to death, he could be comforted and attended by other Christians without serious danger to the latter; many who were arrested were quietly released after the furore had died down. The proclamation of a persecution by imperial edict did not necessarily mean that all imperial officials immediately sprang to implement the policy of their master. Nor did all rulers sense in Christianity a clear and present menace which could draw their attention away from all their manifold problems in other

[12] Dio Cassius 77.16.1.

fields; not until the reign of Diocletian was the opposition of the state based on a perceived clash of old and new views of the world.

Since the motives for the persecution were political, it must also be remembered that the overwhelming bulk of Christian congregations continued to cling to the Empire as a political institution almost as fervently as any pagan could have done—and not only because they expected Antichrist to come upon the fall of the Empire. The fiery Christian of Africa, Tertullian, gave in his *Apology* a notable statement, couched in truly Roman legal views, of Christian loyalty to the Empire in temporal matters; in this work as well as his address *To Scapula* Tertullian argued for religious liberty within the state: "It is assuredly no part of religion to compel religion—to which free will and not force should lead us." [13]

Later Tertullian turned toward an attitude of opposition to the state, to marriage, to pagan culture, to the orthodox hierarchy of the Church; but others were not shaken in the obedience to Caesar which their leaders had inculcated since the days of Jesus. Throughout the century Christians continued to address the emperor and his subordinates in hopes of assistance against local opposition or in prayer for the recision of imperial bans.

The immediate groundwork for the persecutions of the mid-third century was laid by the house of the Severan emperors, who emphasized their autocratic, semidivine position. A new attention to the religious duties of citizens is also to be found in contemporary law. The jurist Paulus reiterated the earlier rule that those who introduced new kinds of worship contrary to reason—i.e., to Greco-Roman notions—"and thus disturbing men's minds," were to be exiled or executed.[14] Even worse, Septimius Severus reissued in 201–202 a ban on Jewish proselyting and on the conversion of citizens to Christianity. The rescript, which virtually swept away the earlier factual toleration, led to a spate of "splendid martyrdoms of the champions of piety," for which our evidence is fullest on Carthage and Alexandria.[15] Yet neither this brief flurry, nor Caracalla's announced intention of gaining worshipers for the pagan gods, nor the Oriental fantasies of the emperor Elagabalus immediately produced a full-scale explosion; the later emperors of the

[13] *To Scapula* 2 (Thelwall).

[14] *Sentences* 5.21.2 (*Fontes iuris romani anteiustiniani* 2 [2d ed.; Florence, 1940], 406–407).

[15] Eusebius, *Ecclesiastical History* 6.1.1.

Severan dynasty were religiously eclectic and tended to be friendly to at least some Christian divines, such as Origen and Julius Africanus.

By the middle of the century the internal and external difficulties of the Empire rose appallingly. The emperor Decius (249–251) courageously opposed the Gothic invaders in the Balkans, but he felt that arms alone could not withstand the winds of dissolution. In desperation he turned to the gods of the state, and essayed to unify his world in devotion to those ancestral protectors. At the end of 249 or in the first months of 250 Decius issued an edict which apparently ordered all citizens to appear before a local commission and make public profession of worship of the gods of the state, this profession consisting of the offer of incense and sacrifice. Since the edict itself has not survived, we cannot be certain whether all sacrificants received a certificate of compliance (*libellus*) or whether only those who were delayed beyond the stated time were so certified upon completing their sacrifice. Thus far the sands of Egypt have produced over forty *libelli*, dated between June 12 and July 15, 250, but the edict may have been enforced tardily in this province.

The great profession of public loyalty was probably designed in the first place to awaken the gods of Rome to their duty to protect the state and ruler and to manifest the unity of the Empire. Decius thus took a significant step beyond the effort of Caracalla to secure more worshipers for the gods. By such a profession men were not debarred from worshiping other gods as well; one *libellus* was issued to a priestess of an Egyptian deity.

True Christians, however, could not thus "worship devils" and were forced publicly to deny the gods of the state, an act of recalcitrance which may have been foreseen in the original order. The Jews likewise must have been unable to sacrifice but do not seem to have been persecuted as a result, for by this time the pagans tended to support the Jews against the Christians. One contemporary account of a Christian martyr, the *Acta* of Saint Pionius, suggests that the Jews were legally exempted from the original requirement by Decius, just as Diocletian later excepted them from a similar order.

The Christians, on the other hand, were already outside the pale and, according to Origen, were hated at the time as bringing wars, famine, and pestilence. So they paid for their refusal to sacrifice by the most violent attack they had ever suffered; Decius first hurled the bolt of empire-wide persecution at the Church. The bishop of Rome was executed in January, and his position had to be put into commission for a term; Origen, who had recently finished his tract *Against Celsus,* a firm defense of Christianity, was tortured; Cyprian of Carthage and Dionysius of Alexandria fled to rural hiding places from which they could keep their churches alive. For the first time the state attacked the laity as well as the clergy; and both groups of the Church often purchased their lives by bribing commissioners to issue *libelli,* or they even engaged in open sacrifice. In Alexandria men who had withstood a local outbreak the year before bent reluctantly but submissively before the edict of the august emperor and by sacrifice kept their public positions or privileged rank.

In Africa the persecution waned by the beginning of 251, and Cyprian could return to Carthage for Easter; persecution had come to a virtual halt everywhere by the middle of the year. There was no official termination; the first flush of official and popular hostility to Christian dissent had ebbed, and the emperor was now busy with the Goths, before whom he was to fall. His efforts had made manifest the unpatriotic refusal of the Christians to join with the rest of the Empire in sacrifice. Sporadic persecutions continued, and the next decade saw two more direct imperial attacks.

The persecution of Gallus (251–253), which was minor, was quickly ended by his death; the second attack was that of Valerian (253–260). This assault was far more serious, for to prejudice now was added both the general failure of Valerian's administration—which may have tried to turn popular discontent against the Christians—and his serious financial needs. The Church itself had become steadily wealthier during the century, and its adherents included, not for the first time but in greater degree than in earlier centuries, men and women of wealth as well as the poor; Dionysius may be justified in indicating that Macrianus, minister of imperial finances, played a great part in instigating the persecution of Valerian. The old attempt to make citizens worship the gods and emperors also appears in several accounts of individual interrogatories.

The first edict of Valerian, in August 257, struck only at the Church proper, by ordering its clergy to sacrifice on pain of exile and by banning Christian assembly or entrance to their cemeteries. The second, of 258, went on to order the confiscation of the property of upper-class adherents of Christianity. These persons were also to be punished by degradation from rank and by exile, forced labor, or even death, while the clergy was to be executed outright. No effort was made to gain the ordinary laity; deprived of its leaders and forbidden assembly, it was expected to scatter. The financial spur led to a rigorous application of these edicts, and the faithful had the glorious opportunity of confessing for Christ in all quarters of the Empire until 260, when Valerian was taken prisoner by the Sasanid ruler of Persia. His son, Gallienus, halted the attack, ordered the restoration of churches and cemeteries, and even addressed a rescript to the bishops which was virtually a *de facto* acceptance of the existence of the Christian hierarchy.

For the next four decades the Church enjoyed an uneasy peace, which appeared on the verge of rupture under Aurelian. His death postponed the last trial of Christianity until the closing years of the reign of Diocletian. By this time both the Church and its pagan opposition had changed considerably in relative strength and also in intellectual position.

The early third century had been one of great bloom for the Church. The troubled decades after 250, while halting many pagan religious activities, seem to have brought converts to Christianity in even greater numbers. The considerable expansion of Church property was usually winked at by the civil authorities; and the organization of the hierarchy became ever tighter, at least on a provincial level, through the preeminence of certain bishoprics and the assembly of bishops in councils.

Intellectually the Christian leaders drew closer to the pagan world during this century, which marked the open turn of classical civilization itself toward a new view of the world and of man; as the philosophers grew more religious, the preachers became more philosophical. Tertullian would seem to deny the uses of reason or pagan culture in general and put the famous question, "What have philosopher and Christian in common,—the disciple of Greece and the disciple of heaven?" Yet he must permit Christians to attend pagan schools and could not deny "the necessity of literary erudition"; [16] and Christian scholars ever more willingly incorporated pagan learning into their system of thought. The deep roots of the Church saved it from an overintellectualization and decay in the process, though men at times wandered off into unorthodox, overly classical alleys.

Already marked in the second century, the accommodation of Chris-

[16] *Apology* 46.18; *On Idolatry* 10 (Thelwall).

tian and classical thought has often been traced through Clement, Origen, Africanus, Hippolytus, and others. The high point of Christian liberality is perhaps the assertion of one of Origen's pupils that in his school

No subject was forbidden to us, nothing hidden or inaccessible. We were allowed to become acquainted with every doctrine, barbarian or Greek, with things spiritual and secular, divine and human, traversing with all confidence and investigating the whole circuit of knowledge, and satisfying ourselves with the full enjoyment of all pleasures of the soul.[17]

Christian and pagan thinkers thus were actually drawing closer to each other, but neither realized, as a rule, the common ground of thought. Instead, the intellectual leaders of the pagan world turned more openly against Christianity in the third century and fiercely assailed the nonclassical aspects of its creed. The first great polemic against Christianity as a body of doctrine was launched by the philosopher Celsus under Marcus Aurelius, at a time when the expansion of Christianity began to be noticed generally and to alarm pagans. His work on *The True Word* we know largely through its quotation by Origen's dignified defense of Christianity, *Against Celsus;* in the main it appears to have been a vehement attack on the follies of the new faith as measured by ancient philosophical doctrine, especially that of Plato.

Celsus stressed the illogicality of a god's descent to mortal pains and death and the immutability of the laws of nature. He bluntly denied the Christian emphasis on man as the ultimate end of the workings of the universe; and as an ancient rationalist he deplored the Christian reliance on faith, which Origen in turn skillfully defended. Worried also by the contemporary problems of the state, Celsus appealed to the Christians to recant and perform their duties in society so that all Roman subjects might unite under the emperor to repel external foes.

The lofty discourse of the greatest thinker of the third century, Plotinus, passed over Christianity, but his pupil Porphyry wrote a long, slashing attack *Against the Christians,* in which he spoke well of Christ Himself but assailed His followers, above all the incoherent, coarse Paul. Porphyry, who was well acquainted with the sacred books of the

[17] Gregory Thaumaturgus, *Panegyric on Origen* (Migne, *Patrologia Graeca* 10, col. 1096A–B); trans. by M. L. W. Laistner, *Christianity and Pagan Culture* (Ithaca, 1951), 61.

Christians, devoted much sarcastic attention to criticizing their inconsistencies and the nonrational character of Christian doctrine; he also addressed himself to the eucharist (which he termed cannibalistic), baptism, resurrection, and other facets of Church ritual. The skill and vigor of his attack are attested not only by the numerous Christian replies thereafter, but also by later bans on his work by Christian emperors.

Where Porphyry led, a number of others followed, and pagan opposition soon sank from the philosophic plane to that of mob fanaticism. By 300 a considerable body of directly anti-Christian material was in circulation, ranging from the analytical treatises of philosophers to oracles and scurrilous innuendo; in rebuttal the Christians had invented so-called Sibylline oracles and other material which circulated in similar fashion.

These defenders of the old order were in fact far removed from the classic spirit. Men in the more philosophical wing of this group, such as Porphyry, gave up a great deal of pagan mythology and cult in attempting to form a supreme divinity who could match the attractiveness of the Christian God; others insisted on keeping every last scrap of ancient cult, but they had really turned from the outside world to internal, mystical contemplation of the divine. The intellectual currents of the fourth century, either in art or in religion, cannot be plumbed unless one recognizes that it was an age of faith, among pagans as well as among Christians.

In this climate of opinion men had to believe in some god or gods, both their own and those of their opponents, for even the Christians conceded that the pagan "demons" actually existed. The question lay on the issue as to which divinity the state would recognize. The issue seems prejudged as we look back, but the overwhelming pagan majority of A.D. 300, in control both of the state and of culture, might hope otherwise.

The emperor Diocletian (284–305) was an autocrat who consciously exercised his despotic powers in ruling the Empire, as, for instance, in the most thoroughgoing—but unsuccessful—effort known in the Empire to limit prices. The first general prohibition of astrology came in his reign. The alchemists of Egypt were banned and their writings burned. Diocletan had fulminated against the Manicheans (a Persian sect indebted to Christianity but believing in the coexistence of good and evil) in an edict probably to be dated to 297 and rising out of his efforts to repress a serious rebellion in Egypt. This edict asserted his "great desire to punish the obstinacy of wicked mind among most evil men" and underlined the foreign origin, incitement to unrest, and new-ness of Manichean superstition, "For it is the greatest of crimes to re-tract those customs ordained and defined by the ancients." [18] The leaders of a sect so infecting the tranquil Roman world were to be executed, their books to be burned, noble adherents to be condemned to the mines and their property confiscated.

Diocletian assuredly liked Christians as little as had any of his pred-ecessors. At some point prior to their persecution he had barred them from his palace service and then from the army on the complaint of the haruspices that the presence of Christians vitiated their attempts to determine the will of the gods. Nonetheless I must agree with a number of recent scholars that his persecution was not as inevitable as it is sometimes put. Though Diocletian was devoted to the old gods, there is little evidence that he truly tried to impress the same unity on reli-gious matters which he employed in the political field, and even in the latter he had treated political foes with a clemency rare in this violent epoch. In banning both the Manicheans and the alchemists, Diocletian may have been motivated by the troubles in Egypt and by his antag-onism to Persia, for Manicheism was of Persian origin, even though its founder Mani had been executed by a Persian king. In sum, Diocletian was an autocrat, he disliked Christianity, but to find the causes of his persecution one must look to outside pressures—principally to his vio-lent, ambitious lieutenant Galerius, and secondarily to the court council, fired by the spirit of men like Porphyry.

The Diocletianic persecution was a battle of faith against faith far more than any earlier attack. In the opening blow, on February 23, 303, the Christian basilica at Nicomedia was invaded and burned, and the Holy Scriptures found within it were deliberately given to flames. The first edict of the persecution banned assembly of Christians, ordered the destruction of churches, and also required the surrender and public burning of the Scriptures and liturgical works. Punishment to the person of Christians at first was limited to legal and judicial restric-tions, but it rapidly sank to death and forced labor for those Christians who refused to sacrifice to the gods.

[18] *Comparison of the Laws of Moses and the Romans* 15.3 (*Fontes iuris romani anteiustiniani* 2, 580).

Although Diocletian had had some scruples about kindling this holocaust, Galerius had none and continued the assault intermittently down to 311. On April 30 of that year, broken by his sense of failure and by an excruciating disease, Galerius issued a spectacular edict of toleration, an anguished plea which casts his motives in bold relief:

Among other steps which we are always taking for the profit and advantage of the State we had formerly sought to set all things right according to the ancient laws and public order of the Romans and further to provide that the Christians too who had abandoned the way of life of their own fathers should return to sound reason. For the said Christians had somehow become possessed by such obstinacy and folly that, instead of following those institutions of the ancients which perchance their own ancestors had first established, they were at their own will and pleasure making laws for themselves and acting upon them and were assembling in different places people of different nationalities.

After we had decreed that they should return to the institutions of the ancients, many were subjected to danger, many too were completely overthrown; and when very many persisted in their determination and we saw that they neither gave worship and due reverence to the gods nor practised the worship of the god of the Christians, considering our most gentle clemency and our immemorial custom by which we are wont to grant indulgence to all men, we have thought it right in their case too to extend the speediest indulgence to the effect that they may once more be free to live as Christians and may re-form their churches always provided that they do nothing contrary to order. Further by another letter we shall inform provincial governors what conditions the Christians must observe.

Wherefore in accordance with this our indulgence they will be bound to entreat their god for our well-being and for that of the State and for their own so that on every side the State may be preserved unharmed and that they themselves may live in their homes in security.[19]

Galerius clearly moved more in the realm of belief than of reason. All men must worship some god, and in the existence of the Christian God he clearly believed. For the first time since Nero's attack a Roman emperor had publicly, though reluctantly and with dangerous limitations, stated the right of obstinate Christians to worship that deity. The hopes of Galerius for Christian intercession were in vain, for five days later he was dead.

[19] Lactantius, *On the Death of the Persecutors* 34; Eusebius, *Ecclesiastical History* 8.17; trans. by Norman H. Baynes, *Cambridge Ancient History* 12, 672.

Victory of Christianity

Although a few flurries of persecution were yet to come, the main wave had broken itself. Surveying the whole course of imperial opposition, one may assert that the persecution of the Church was always due in the last analysis to its embodiment of a view of life strange to the prevailing classical pattern, for the Empire was dedicated to the political defense of this pattern. Yet only slowly did the rulers come to appreciate that difference in some measure on an intellectual as well as on a political level. In the last attack the destruction of Christian literature was stressed, and the ruler of the East after Galerius, Maximinus Daia, attempted to spread the apocryphal *Acta of Pilate,* which were officially used in the schools of his provinces. The pagan rulers turned, however, to their ideological attacks far too late.

Under Constantine, who rose to full mastery of the West in 312 and of the whole Empire in 324, the state surrendered its efforts to suppress the new view. During his earlier years Constantine had been an adherent first of Hercules, then of Sol Invictus; but he was tolerant of Christians as his father Constantius Chlorus had been. Before the battle of the Milvian Bridge against Maxentius in 312 Constantine had a famous dream in which, says Lactantius, the worried general was bidden to mark a Christian emblem on the shields of his soldiers. His victory in the battle sealed his conversion, though the ruler continued outwardly to respect the pagan beliefs still held by a majority in the Empire.

Only a truly internal experience could have impelled Constantine to take up a faith which was very much in the minority in the West, but his step was one from which there was no turning back. In the long run it was one of tremendous significance in the history both of the Empire and of the Church; immediately it resulted in a policy of universal toleration, which was announced in the so-called Edict of Milan. So mild a view consorted ill with a believing age or with the basic unity of church and state which had been implicit in ancient political structures; inevitably paganism was to decline in the future and to become illegal.

Only in its Christian manifestation had the emperors opposed the emergence of a new order. That the Caesars could have succeeded in destroying Christianity was impossible, but even had they won this limited battle they would have lost the major war which they never tried to wage. The pagan world itself was irresistibly thrusting its way to a nonclassical view of the relations of man to his fellows, to the surrounding world, and to the divine force above; against this general drive, as manifested in art, religion, and philosophy, the emperors did not even struggle.

In one respect, then, whether Christianity endured or fell in the persecutions mattered little. In many others it was of tremendous significance that Christianity, rather than Neoplatonism, was the vehicle by which the new concepts were transmitted to later ages.

Neither the Christian Church nor Christian dogma, to be sure, were the same in 324 as they had been in the days when the disciples of Jesus walked the earth. Imperial political persecution had had little effect on the Church, but the almost unconscious opposition of society had bent the Christians tremendously. This or that deviation of Christian creed and organization in compromise with the pagan milieu may be regretted as one surveys the lasting effects of those compromises; on the whole, however, it was fortunate that the new cult made so successful an adaptation to its world. The Church, after all, passed on to modern times some of the most important advances of classical civilization.

The Christians had never been truly isolated from the secular world, but by the fourth century the outward appearance of isolation had waned. On the one side the Christians had adapted their way of life and moderated their disciplinary rules to fit the fallibility of mankind; on the other the pagan world had moved to a new plane of morality. During the Diocletianic persecution Christians in extraordinarily large numbers were willing to surrender their Scriptures—or heretical books or works of medicine instead—or even to engage in pagan sacrifice. The pagan populace, on the other hand, as a rule no longer led their masters in demanding persecution but tended to sympathize with the victims in many districts, though not in all; this sympathy was possibly a reaction against the arbitrary exercise of imperial power which had so burdened them in other respects. Governors themselves were quite frequently reluctant to carry out the more savage imperial orders.

Even politically the Christians had adapted themselves to a remarkable degree to the needs of the Empire and had patterned their structure on that of the imperial autocracy. In the fourth century bishops took an ever-greater part in the governance of the Empire, while creating a series of ranks within their order akin to those of the Diocletianic bureaucracy. The essentially unaristocratic tone of Christian thinking was muffled in practice. From its earliest days Christianity had refused to preach social revolution and the liberation of slaves; by the fourth century the upper classes of the Empire stood predominant in the great hierarchy of bishops, priests, and other clergy which led the laity and managed an ever-greater amount of Church property. The secular tone of the Church in the era was marked by the luxurious life of the bishops and by occasional armed wars over election to the desirable episcopal offices; one of these outbreaks scattered bodies in the church of Santa Maria Maggiore in Rome. As a host of new converts flooded into the Church, its moral level sank to the point where the truly religious turned away to seek the individual salvation offered by the monastic way.

The doctrine of the Christian Church was far from perfected as yet; to paraphrase C. N. Cochrane, Christianity had won as a way of life but still had philosophical deficiencies. In the turmoil of the third century, nevertheless, great strides had been made in the evolution of this doctrine, in which the Church made large drafts on pagan thinking. Not until the Protestant Reformation did segments of Christianity throw off, and then incompletely, the effect of pagan thought and of imperial organization upon the Church. Some steps in this accommodation of Christian ideas to pagan forms have been noted; the same process can also be studied in detail in the painting and sculpture, which are cast in pagan symbols and style.

The Christian adjustment to the world was extensive, but there were very important limits to its concessions. Despite the compromises, the purer stream of Christian development never forsook the compassionate view of humanity expressed by Christ, and the leaders of the Church stubbornly fought off those infusions of the dying concepts of classical civilization which would fatally have weakened Christian tenets.

The most insidious and dangerous attacks on the new structure of thought were delivered not in the realm of local prejudice or imperial persecution but on the battleground of ideas. The vehicle of the attacks was the throwing up of heresies within the Church itself—those heresies, I mean, which attempted to preserve the rational, corporeal presuppositions of classical thought. Christian divines endured the persecutions by the state with patience and humility, for they could sense that the blood of the martyrs was the seed of the Church and that political pressure could not disrupt their communities or destroy their beliefs. Their reaction toward "the federation of godless error" created by heretics was far different. Here they detected—and rightly—threats to the preservation of a truly Christian view and the seed of rancor and of fatal disruption.

From the gnostic constructions of the third century, which resembled Neoplatonism, to the arguments of Arius in the fourth, the leaders of heresy tried to draw Christianity toward a philosophic view by creating a chain of divine emanations from the Perfect One to the human soul imprisoned within the body, and by eliminating the historic individuality of Christ as merely an emanation of God subject to later replacement by another emanation. If these thinkers had had their way, Christianity would have become a mystic, transcendental matter reserved largely for the educated classes. Had they won, the Church would have discarded the broad sense of human equality before God, the grounding of belief squarely on faith and the authority of the Bible rather than on reason, and the humanitarian love of man for his fellow man; and in doing so it would have perished.

In attacking the idea that a perfect God could speak directly to imperfect humans, particularly to the humble fishermen of Galilee, and that He might embody Himself in a man who could endure the punishment of slaves on the cross, the gnostics displayed an intellectual arrogance which was one of the worst parts of the classical inheritance. Lactantius puts this stumbling block well in talking of the men of his day:

They say, in short, that it was unworthy of God to be willing to become man, and to burthen himself with the infirmity of flesh. . . . The majesty of heaven could not be reduced to such weakness as to become an object of contempt and derision, a reproach and mockery to men.[20]

The efforts to transplant the root ideas of the old harvest in the new garden failed, and in that failure is clearly manifest the essential death of the ancient structure of thought. A more fruitful but less extensive harvest of ancient ideas was to be made by the Christian leaders themselves, especially in the fourth century.

[20] *Divine Institutes* 4.22, 4.30 (Fletcher).

XV

The Potentialities of the New Order:

Augustine

THE fourth century looms Januslike at the threshold of the Middle Ages. For a time the reforms of Diocletian and Constantine and a momentary decline in the barbarian pressure gave a breathing spell to the Empire, in which there was a striking amount of intellectual activity. Scholars today call the period the Late Empire and its culture Late Classical or Late Roman, but no formula can entirely sum up the puzzling, unhappy mixture of old and new, of gentle and violent in this epoch. Contemporary materials illuminate its developments remarkably well, though most historians unjustly ignore it; in this era one can see, for a brief moment, the potentialities of the new order of thought.

Men's ideas were still clothed in classical forms, and the frame of life remained essentially ancient; the ghost of classical culture appeared still to rule life through its mastery of education and its hold upon the aristocracy. In this period, too, vital steps were taken in the transmission of classical knowledge to the Carolingian Renaissance and thence to the later Middle Ages by the copying into parchment codexes, the emendation, and the illustration of classical authors. Both pagans and Christians were active in this work. The devout Theodosius, in ordering the end of pagan sacrifice, specifically kept open the temples and preserved their statues as works of art, an attitude toward "our country's fairest ornaments" which was enthusiastically seconded by the deeply pious Christian poet, Prudentius.[1] Modern museums are indebted to the discouragement of iconoclasm by the fourth-century Church, as are our libraries and minds to its distinction between pagan practice and pagan letters. Had the radical wing of the Church gained control, it would have added premeditated destruction to the ravages of economic decay and popular disinterest. What then would we have left today of classical literature and art?

In considering the transmission of classical letters and arts one must speak in a minor, somber key. Classical rhetoric was declining. Although the state attempted to shore up education by subventions and by announcements that "culture" was indispensable for promotion in the civil service, fewer and fewer men went through the regime of classical instruction. The adherents of the old order were fighting a desperate but hopeless rearguard action in maintaining paganism, in asserting the glory of Rome against the attraction of the new Christian capital of Constantinople, in repeating the commonplaces of classical letters.

The spirit of life was basically new. The only serious effort to combat its victory was the persecution of Christianity, and this was drawing to a close. Once the third century had been traversed, the Roman Empire could not have turned back to the Augustan synthesis even if it had desired to do so. Neither Augustus nor Marcus Aurelius could have understood the extent of piety, mysticism, and intolerance in their fourth-century imitator, the emperor Julian. The ivory diptyches of the Nicomachi and Symmachi toward the end of the century are deliberately classical in form, but Alois Riegl is right in asserting that no student could mistake the time of their creation; this is revealed in underlying, unconscious reflections of fourth-century style.

Pagan Manifestations of the New Order

Pagans as well as Christians felt in some degree the invigorating blasts of the new wind. The shift toward individualism, humanitarianism, and transcendentalism had been a general movement within the Empire; one must not fall into the common error of setting off pagan thought too sharply from that of the Christians. The fourth century accordingly saw more pagan thinkers than had the third, not only because economic conditions were now temporarily stabilized but also because life had a new intellectual vigor. Most of these poets and orators were overpoweringly

[1] *Against Symmachus* 1.502–505.

affected by ancient forms, and so walked in the ruts of tradition and conformity; but at least a few pagans tapped the new stream more directly.

In the fields of architecture and sculpture secular and Christian thought coursed in virtually the same channel. The Christians devised a new form of structure, the basilican church, but the view of space inherent in the basilica was essentially the same as that of secular buildings. Although the Christians began to form their own iconography, the mixture of classic form and transcendental spirit is apparent both in the figures of the Christian epic on sarcophagi and in the colossal bust of Constantine at Rome or the stern head, probably of Marcian, from Barletta (see Pl. X *b*). When one views the full-length statue of Saturninus in Rome or the highly transcendentalized head from Ephesus (now in Vienna), one needs not ask whether these men were Christians; pagans and Christians alike drew from the same spring.

In literature the difference in subject matter between Christian and pagan writers tends to hide the common source for their reinvigoration. After the long drought of the third and early fourth centuries really competent Latin verse reappeared in the pagans Claudian, Ausonius, and Rutilius Namatianus—and also in the contemporary Christians Paulinus, Ambrose, and Prudentius. The latter, who is justly considered the greatest Latin poet since the Augustan Age, must be a puzzle to those who see only decay in the fourth century.

Equally surprising from the purely classical point of view must be the emergence of a major pagan historian, Ammianus Marcellinus. In this man one can see most clearly the working of the new yeast within pagan circles. Sprung from the middle class of Syrian Antioch, Ammianus Marcellinus wrote his history of the Empire at Rome in the last decades of the century. The surviving books, on the period 353–378, show him to be worthy of being ranked for honesty and balanced judgment beside Livy and ahead of Tacitus. Both Tacitus and Ammianus Marcellinus had good reason to feel hopeless, the one at seeing the victory of absolutism over the Senate, the other at witnessing the barbarian incursions of the fourth century, the ruthless violation of justice in the *maiestas* trials, and the internal decay. Not even the accession of Trajan could restore the confidence of Tacitus; the outward brilliance of his style does not mask his inner despondency and lack of a firmly held basis for judgment and interpretation of the historical pattern of the Early Empire. Ammianus, on the other hand, had also to chronicle gloomy events, but his spirit rose above the gloom with an inner certainty of faith.

The fourth-century historian could see a purpose in the Empire which justified and explained its existence. Ammianus had a firm belief in the divine protection of Rome. Fortune might vacillate and bring affliction, but in the end the Empire would rise again. The concept of the eternity of Rome, which had gained ever-wider expression in the third century, had helped materially in bringing the restoration of the Empire under Aurelian, and still lurked in men's minds; at the end of the fourth century the pagan poets Rutilius and Claudian were to express the concept in the most glowing terms it ever received. Ammianus also shared the fourth-century respect for culture, and tended to judge men according to their education. The urban prefect Orfitus, for instance, is termed arrogant, wise, skilled in the law, "but less educated in the splendor of the liberal arts than befitted a noble." The praetorian prefect Modestus was bluntly accused of "a countrified intelligence, unpolished by any readings of antiquity"; and so Ammianus proceeded, awarding praise or censure to the learning of his characters.[2]

These attitudes are ancient, but in the case of the barbarian Nevitta, chosen as consul by Julian, another basis for judgment entered. Nevitta did not have high birth, experience or renown; rather he was "unpolished and rude and—what is less to be borne—cruel in his high power."[3] Ammianus had a distinct sense of justice and ethics, based partly on class attitudes but also on general standards. The historian was not a Christian, though he could praise the purity and moderation of some provincial bishops as opposed to the luxury and ambition of the great urban bishops; yet the standards of Ammianus were not far removed from those of Christianity. He opposed the castration of eunuchs, the love of cruelty of a ruler in the games, the murder even of unjust men, and the violence of contemporary punishments. At times he countenanced sharp practice against the barbarians, but elsewhere he censured the murder of barbarian leaders at a Roman banquet, and he spoke very harshly about the poor treatment of the Gothic supplicants which led, indeed, to the disastrous battle of Adrianople. In one remarkable sentence which Tacitus could scarcely have written Ammianus asserted that if a ruler is "to pass judgment affecting the life and breath of a human being, *who forms a part of the world and completes the number of living things,* he ought to hesitate long."[4]

[2] 14.6.1, 30.4.2 (Glover).   [3] 21.10.8 (Glover).
[4] 29.2.18 (Rolfe, as henceforth; my italics).

To penetrate beneath these beliefs in Rome, in culture, and in the ethical conduct of life to determine Ammianus' view of the divine forces in the world is difficult, for Ammianus was capable of pagan inconsistency. He believed in the wheel of Fortune and yet felt that men had guardian spirits, a concept on which he referred explicitly to the doctrine of Plotinus. Since Ammianus was a historian and not a theologian, the critic may excuse his failure to outline his conception of the world; the important points are that he did have a faith and that his history in consequence rests upon a firm standard of judgment. The great intellectual change of the third century lies manifest in the contrast between the hopeless hesitation of Tacitus and the certainty of Ammianus.

The atrociously crabbed prose style affected by Ammianus has tended to hide his essential honesty and his effort to search out the truth. Whether portraying his villain Constantius or his hero Julian, he noticed both virtues and faults; his brief sketches of other figures are extraordinarily incisive. That they are at times partial is true, the innuendo and rumor to which Tacitus gave vent are found here too, but besides the prejudice are also sobriety, essential fairness, and withal frankness in criticism of society and of individuals. Though Ammianus supported the senatorial aristocracy in the main, its most severe criticism comes from his pen.

This combination of virtues is the more remarkable when one places it against the growing intolerance of the later fourth century. Ammianus himself observes that, had he written under Valentinian, he could not have published an impartial account of political events; but, "Since I have a free opportunity of saying what I think," he bluntly censured that emperor's elevation of the military element.[5] Originally he halted at the year 363 "to avoid the dangers which are often connected with the truth,"[6] but after 393, in the reign of the strongly Christian emperor Theodosius, he wrote six more books. Here he had to pick his way very carefully, yet even in the field of religion one may detect the essential honesty of the man beneath the surface. His concluding sentences on Valentinian's character thus seem to be an indirect rebuke to Theodosius' repression of paganism:

Finally, his reign was distinguished by toleration, in that he remained neutral in religious differences neither troubling anyone on that ground nor ordering him to reverence this or that. He did not bend the necks of his sub-

[5] 27.9.4.   [6] 26.1.1.

jects to his own belief by threatening edicts, but left such matters undisturbed as he found them.[7]

Pagan thinkers as a whole could rarely shake off the dross of the past. One must not expect to find many pagan works of the fourth century which can show an advance over the sterility of earlier centuries. Here and there they do appear, and pre-eminent among them is the history of Ammianus Marcellinus. No less than the sculpture and architecture of the era it reveals the capacity of men to think in new lines outside the fold of Christianity; once again men had a support for intellectual activity.

Christian Manifestations of the New Order

For a fuller revelation of the intellectual advance which was now possible one must turn from the pagans to the Christians. In its Christian statement the new view of life was one which could incite even men of moderate capacity like Lactantius and Eusebius and lead them to intellectual achievements of an order not seen for many generations. The sublime heights to which it could elevate the mind attracted the most able thinkers of the fourth century, who were accordingly lost to paganism.

To toil gradually upward through the foothills of the earlier fourth-century Christian figures is too arduous and lengthy a labor here to be undertaken, nor is it possible briefly to discuss the development of the abstruse debate over the nature of the Trinity and the underlying Incarnation. This argument, however, was a landmark in the progress of thought, and its conclusion at least can be summed up with fair certainty.

Men of a less believing age may regret that their forefathers spent so much time on an abstract, perhaps artificial creation, that blood was spilled and men's lives were ruined on this theoretical point. In the argument no resource of mud-slinging or appeal to passion was spared; each side vindictively and unscrupulously essayed to turn now the mob, now the state against its opponents. Still, so vigorous a debate had not been seen for seven centuries, since the days of Plato and Isocrates. Arius, Athanasius, and their followers were exercising their minds on matters which seemed vital and which were in truth of the greatest significance to the structure of Christian dogma of later centuries—and of Western thought generally. In the fourth century men overcame that weakness

[7] 30.9.5

of Christian thinking which was still apparent in the third century and which was even visible in Lactantius at the beginning of the fourth; thus they paved the way for the mighty structure of Augustine.

The new view of man and the world here broke decisively with classical concepts and gained the upper hand in Christian theology. Arianism was the last serious attempt of classical idealism and rationality to implant its ideas within the Church; with the victory of Athanasius an interpretation of Christ, the god became man and redeeming man by His death, won in spite of its apparent irrationality.

The definition of the Trinity which was embodied in the Nicene Creed, as finally adopted at the Council of Chalcedon in 451, is a mystery, inexplicable in terms of classical logic or the classical view of nature. The divine essence is to be found by man, not by a search of nature as classical thought had argued, but by a direct perception through the spirit. The Church thus grounded its essential beliefs upon faith—how reluctantly, the struggle of the fourth century shows—but the direction of the solution is all-significant.

Having believed, the good Christian was led by his faith to a view of man as an individual, though dependent upon a transcendental divinity; to an understanding of the world and man as being on the same plane under the law of God and yet distinguished from each other; to a denial that the world and the flesh were inherently imperfect. The orthodox view paid little attention to Christ as a human, but it never forgot that He *had* lived. The factual insistence of the Nicene Creed upon His life and death is in sharp contrast to the theoretical existence of the "demons" of Plutarch or Plotinus.

Work of Augustine

Most of the participants in the Arian controversy came from the Eastern provinces of the Empire, for the Greek-speaking thinkers continued to display the intellectual pre-eminence they had enjoyed since the second century after Christ. Urban life was more deeply entrenched in this area; the inherited resources of civilization were greater; and to some extent the tendency of Hellenic modes of education to encourage subtlety of thought and grace of expression had persisted. The West also played some part in the controversy, at least in its more practical aspects, and threw up toward the end of the century a group of Latin Christian thinkers which can justly be compared to Athanasius, Basil the Great, or Gregory of Nazianzus in intellectual capacity and in literary ability.

In little more than a decade the West gave birth to Jerome, Ambrose, Prudentius, and Augustine. Of these great figures the youngest and greatest, Augustine of Tagaste (in Africa), is a superb example of the new individuality and of the intellectual achievement of which the new structure of thought was capable.

Augustine was born in 354 to an urban family of moderate estate. Educated first at home, then at Carthage, and finally at Rome, he was firmly grounded in the classical learning of the century, which revolved primarily about the reading of a few authors and rhetorical exercises; later he was to groan at this erudite bookishness, "multiplying toil and grief upon the sons of Adam." [8]

Augustine himself took up the profession of rhetorician in the old capital. When the chair of rhetoric at Milan fell vacant, the prefect of Rome, the pagan author Symmachus, examined the young man's qualifications and endorsed him for the post, in which he delivered at least one panegyric before the ruler. He also came under the influence of the bishop of the city, Ambrose, and was converted to Christianity in 386. Thereupon he gave up his professorship, with its considerable chances of worldly success, and his intentions of marriage.

The *Confessions* of Augustine throw a clear light upon his life to this point. They reveal him as a man who liked other men and gained their affection, as a keen and wide observer of nature and life, as an individual human who could write simply, even naïvely. Such a relentless revelation of personality no classical author had ever thought of exposing—Augustine is often called "the first modern man." [9] In this sense his work may justly be termed the first autobiography, despite the earlier essays at the exploration of the self in the fourth century and before.

In the internal struggle of this human being, searching with his powerful intelligence for the meaning of life, is beautifully symbolized the search of all the Roman Empire, for the stages through which Augustine passed were essentially those of the Empire. For practical purposes Augustine accepted rhetoric and never lost his ability in this field; he also studied the pagan classics which had been standard fare for the past three centuries and, as he confesses, wept over the death of Dido.

[8] *Confessions* 1.9 (14) (Pusey).

[9] As by William James (C. N. Cochrane, *Christianity and Classical Culture* [rev. ed.; New York, 1944], 387). For secondary guidance to the manifold aspects of Augustine's thought I have drawn heavily upon Cochrane and the works of H. I. Marrou.

The sympathy of Virgil, however, was not enough to stay his passionate drive, born of heart and mind, to get an all-satisfying answer. At the age of nineteen he made the acquaintance of Cicero, in the essay *Hortensius*—an invitation to philosophy.

Later Augustine wrote that this event awakened him to the study of wisdom, but in the first flush of teaching his study proceeded slowly. First it led him to Manicheism, which afforded a clear interpretation of good and evil; from this he moved to skepticism and then to Neoplatonism, the last and greatest answer to the problems of the world which ancient philosophy erected. Here he gained a relief from Manichean—and, one may add, all ancient—materialism which had made him think in corporeal terms, for the Neoplatonic doctrine of God showed him another, incorporeal concept of reality. Even Neoplatonism was too cold a faith and its god too remote for this man of the fourth century, and at last he discovered his safe harbor, with Ambrose as pilot, in Christianity, his mother's faith.

At the age of thirty-two Augustine had found his answer to the problems which had long harassed him; forty-four years of life remained. His ceaseless intellectual energy drove him on to explore the depths of his soul and of Christian doctrine, first in a retreat from the world at Cassiciacum, then in Africa, where he shortly became bishop of Hippo. There he remained until his death in 430. The results of his exploration he communicated to his fellows in tracts, sermons, and letters, which poured from his pen in profusion. Addressed both to the scholars and students and to the faithful flock whose practical needs served always as a check upon the bookish tendencies of his earlier education, the pages of Augustine formed a mighty foundation for Christian thinking, both Catholic and Protestant, for all the future.

The most famous single work in this corpus is the *City of God,* in twenty-two books, composed between 413 and 426. This treatise arose out of Augustine's efforts to rebut the pagan charge that the abandonment of the pagan gods had produced the Gothic sack of Rome in 410, but his meditation led him inexorably into a majestic treatment of the intervention of God in human history and a contrast of the earthly plane or "city" with that of the eternal. His course of thought prompted Augustine to point out the defects of earthly society, especially in pagan times and particularly on the intellectual level.

On the basis of his presuppositions this attack is superbly executed, and his estimate of the relative place of reason and faith essentially concurred with that of other Christian fathers. His stand has not always pleased modern rationalists, who have frequently blasted the "evil effects" of Augustinianism—or even of Christianity—on thought, and who, in their faith in the powers of the human mind, have denied the necessity of faith. The charge that Christian doctrine was a destructive solvent to ancient thought or is theoretically incompatible with any system of thought is a serious one; fortunately it is not difficult to show that the indictment is misconceived, at least as far as Augustine and his confreres are concerned.

In the *City of God,* as elsewhere, Augustine easily swept away the crudities and abominations of pagan cult, but he had a more formidable task in dealing with the errors of the philosophers. The root of their defects he located in the fall of Adam, i.e., in man's putting himself first and seeking in his pride to exalt himself as an end. The doctrine of original sin, which was a mighty force in subsequent Christian thinking, was here cast partly in the intellectual, Faustian terms of undue zeal for mere knowledge, partly in the moral terms of desire for domination and carnal lusts; but either aspect manifested a subordination of the spiritual to the material "desire for this world."

God accordingly abandoned man to himself, "not to live in the absolute independence he affected, but instead of the liberty he desired, to live dissatisfied with himself in a hard and miserable bondage to him to whom by sinning he had yielded himself." [10] To Augustine this master of earthly man was the devil; for our purposes, and in less theological terms, the Fall of Man might be construed as a parable of the historical drive of ancient civilization toward individualism, whereby man gained his own liberty at the price of dissatisfaction and subservience to an earthly autocrat. "By craving to be more, man becomes less." [11]

The intellectual result of the undue exaltation of the individual apart from society and God, Augustine pointed out, was the pride of the pagan philosophers, who could not stoop to be called Christians and so bear a name which common folk also bore. The true Christian must subordinate himself to God and thereby place faith before reason. At the outset of his treatise *On the Trinity* Augustine warned that his study was written to guard "against the sophistries of those who disdain to begin with faith, and are deceived by a crude and perverse love of

[10] *City of God* 14.15 (Dods' translation, as henceforth).
[11] *City of God* 14.13.

reason"; man could not penetrate beyond certain limits in conjecture "lest freedom of thought beget impiety of opinion." [12]

Augustine could not forget the necessity of humility before God's purpose as revealed in Scripture, "which has paramount authority, and to which we yield assent in all matters of which we ought not to be ignorant, and yet cannot know of ourselves." [13] Paul had laid down in First Corinthians the essential doctrine: Has not God made foolish the wisdom of this world? The Greeks seek after wisdom, and Christ crucified is to them foolishness; yet the foolishness of God is wiser than the wisdom of man.

God by His divine grace grants us that knowledge which we can only confirm by the use of reason. Writing in this frame of reference, Augustine dramatically asked in his *Confessions*, of what import is the destiny of Dido? In his study *On Christian Education* he dismissed as a trifle the study of musical theory; as superfluous, poetry and sculpture; as vain, the unharnessed "curiosity" manifested in the watching of lizards, the study of astronomy, and the like; as unnecessary to a Christian, the study of classical rhetoric, which replaced the vigor of simple sobriety by the sterility of learned obscurity. To a man who could assert "God and the soul, that is what I desire to know. Nothing more? Nothing whatever!" disinterested thought and study were not only superfluous but even pernicious.[14] The end is all that counts, and we must not dally along the way to our happy destination, the knowledge of God.

Augustine thus firmly opposed two apparently incompatible forces: the service of God as the true aim of man, and the pagan ideal of culture, possession of which was the mark of the gentleman and Roman citizen. Such a temporal good Augustine had come close to accepting in his earlier years, when he had been overproud of reason. Even when he had withdrawn to Cassiciacum to become a Christian, he had studied Virgil as well as the Bible with his friends. Later he felt that his eyes had been opened to the futility of culture; he must make men see that culture in itself was of no avail, even though he must resort to exaggerated attacks on the vanity and aimlessness of classical learning.

This preoccupation with the Divine, which rises inevitably out of Christian thought, seems to lead directly to the conclusion that faith is all, and reason naught—to justify, in sum, the worst charges which some opponents of Augustine have made. One must, however, re-

---

[12] *City of God* 10.23.   [13] *City of God* 11.3.
[14] *Soliloquies* 1.2 (7) (Starbuck); *Letter* 55.39.

member that Augustine had even pagan predecessors on his side in the attack; for Seneca and Marcus Aurelius had warned against overly deep concentration upon rational exploration of the world purely for its own sake. And one must also take Augustine whole, rather than seeking out his occasional expressions of contempt for pagan rhetoricians and pagan letters.

As Marrou has argued, Augustine broke in his heart with classical culture more completely than either Jerome or Ambrose did; in his works on Genesis he displayed far less speculative interest than did Gregory of Nyssa. Yet the fact that Augustine could thrill to the spiritual achievements of the untutored Saint Antony of Egypt does not mean that he despised the intellectual advances of earlier ages. Augustine, in truth, accepted a great deal more of pagan culture than one might assume on seeing some of his *dicta* wrenched from their context. He himself had been trained in the classical pattern. As a native of a minor African town he was less deeply learned in the old sense than many Eastern fathers, less impregnated with culture than the aristocratic Ambrose, yet he never threw off the influence of classical forms. Against pagan error he could cite pagan poets and philosophers—not as exclusively as Lactantius had done, but with no less appreciation for their abilities. Augustine saw that humanity had developed; moreover, its development was a gradual process in which the Greco-Roman world had made strides of real merit within its inevitable limits.

The study of inherited knowledge had formed Augustine's own mind, and this study he advocated for positive reasons to his Christian flock. Some of the pagan knowledge was useful in earning a livelihood. Again, men must understand the Bible. In beginning his treatise *On Christian Education* Augustine justified against possible opposition the necessity of a certain preliminary training, which included reading and much else besides. As Marrou has noted, Augustine thereby opened the door to a study which could vary, according to the temper of the times and of the individual, from the mere acquisition of one's letters to the intensive employment of all possible knowledge upon Christian problems.

Pagan education had revolved about Virgil or Homer; now Christian education was to revolve about the Bible. In either case the same methods of preliminary education and of exegesis were applicable. In fact not only the method but also much of the substance was taken over from the classical system of education, which was virtually as independent of the Church as it had been of the Caesars. Classical argumentation, sophistical oratory, even the "curiosity" of scholars about trivia appear widely in Christian learning.

The teachings of the philosophers were another motive which commended pagan knowledge to Christian study. Augustine did not forget that he himself had made his way to the Church through Neoplatonism, and he encouraged better students to go beyond the Bible and study also the Platonic philosophers. In his last days Plotinus was on his lips as well as the Psalms before his eyes. The contemplative life, which might raise men to comprehension of the eternal verity, rested (he said in his last years) on "praying and seeking and living well . . . that so far as it can be seen, that may be seen by the mind which is held fast by faith." [15]

We can never forget that Christianity arose as a coherent system at the end of ancient intellectual development and that it drew into itself much of the pagan synthesis which Stoics, Neoplatonists, and others had hammered out. At one point in the *City of God* appears a mighty paean on the achievements of the human mind, even to "the defence of errors and misapprehensions, which has illustrated the genius of heretics and philosophers." [16]

Similar theoretical justifications of Christian attention to the knowledge of the past can be found in other fourth-century Christian leaders. These men had to place other virtues beside and ahead of the pagan criteria of birth and education, but they did not on the whole discard the latter. The great Christian thinkers of the era were almost all firmly grounded in grammar and rhetoric; some even made their living by teaching pagan classics or philosophy—much to the horror of the emperor Julian, who tried to ban them from teaching subjects they could not endorse theoretically. Though Jerome might repent his love for Cicero and swear a frenzied oath never again to read worldly books, he could not wipe out of his mind classical works or liberate his pen from their echoes.

Now and again a Christian father honestly condemned pagan letters *in toto*, particularly if he were not much versed in those letters. Tertullian had already put the matter succinctly by asserting, "We have no need for curiosity after possessing Jesus Christ, nor for inquisition after enjoying the gospel." [17] Devout Christians thereafter often justified

[15] *On the Trinity* 15.27 (49) (Haddan-Shedd).   [16] 22.24.
[17] *On Prescription against Heretics* 7.

their indifference toward thought and their disinterest in learning on this basis; even worse, they at times viciously attacked the use of the human mind. Still, one must distinguish between the extreme wing of human intolerance of thought, which can assume other disguises than the Christian, and the practice of Christianity as a whole; faith and reason are two horses which men of all ages have found difficult to couple.

Taking up the sword of reason as tempered by ancient dialectic, Christian thinkers wielded it with new vigor to support their faith against each other and against pagan opponents. Lactantius, for example, had neatly argued that the Diocletianic persecutors, while relying blindly on an unproved and unprovable system handed down to them from their ancestors, made use of force rather than reason. Let the pagans (he challenged) unsheathe the weapon of their intellect; if they do, their folly and error will be apparent to old women and boys. Reasoning power has been given by God to man, and to man alone, so that he may investigate for himself and make his way to the true wisdom. The truth of Christianity, in sum, was not contradictory to reason but to the customary ideas of the world; and the Christian gained true liberty of mind through accepting God as master.

Many illustrations of the Christian appeal to reason might be given, but one of the most engaging must suffice. Dionysius, the third-century bishop of Alexandria, had to wrestle with a millenary heresy of Nepos, another Egyptian bishop. His account of the difficulty begins with a quotation from Aristotle: "Truth is dear and to be honored above all things." [18] In obedience to this precept Dionysius proceeded to the spot of the heresy, assembled the priests, teachers, and other brethren, and examined the ideas of Nepos for three days, from morning to night.

I conceived [he says] the greatest admiration for the brethren, their firmness, love of truth, facility in following an argument, and intelligence, as we propounded in order and with forbearance the questions, the difficulties raised and the points of agreement. . . . Nor, if convinced by reason, were we ashamed to change our opinions and give our assent; but conscientiously and unfeignedly and with hearts laid open to God we accepted whatever was established by the proofs and teachings of the holy Scriptures. [19]

Reason, conjoined to authority, at last convinced Nepos of his error.

[18] *Nicomachean Ethics* 1.1096a.   [19] Eusebius, *Ecclesiastical History* 7.24.8.

Augustine himself searched as relently for truth as any thinker who has ever lived. To Augustine faith must logically come first, but repeatedly his writings emphasize the value of its teammate, reason:

Far be it from us to suppose that God abhors in us that by virtue of which He has made us superior to other animals. Far be it, I say, that we should believe in such a way as to exclude the necessity either of accepting or requiring reason; since we could not even believe unless we possessed rational souls.[20]

The *City of God* is a superb testimony to the majestic power of his thought. In his elaborate argument that God is not bound by the laws of nature and that incredible events may occur, he utilized logic, examples, and critical thought; and this Christian believer was far from accepting blindly the reputed marvels of the world which pagan scientists had passed on for centuries: "For my own part, I do not wish all the marvels I have cited to be rashly accepted." Augustine distinguished those events which he knew or which could be verified by anyone from those happenings which he cited from trustworthy witnesses, and these again from others which he drew from pagan writers "without definitely affirming or denying them." [21] The Bible was an authoritative standard, but only this work was to him necessarily free from error.

When I read other authors, however eminent they may be in sanctity and learning, I do not necessarily believe a thing is true because they think so, but because they have been able to convince me, either on the authority of the canonical writers or by a probable reason which is not inconsistent with truth.[22]

When one lays down the *City of God* and thinks back to the puerile superstition of most contemporary pagans, it is easy to feel that Augustine was not far wrong in affirming that his pagan adversaries were mentally infirm, incorrigibly vain, and full of obstinacy if they did not yield to his measured attacks on their system of thought. As between the Christian bishop of Hippo and the famous imperial protector of Hellenism, Julian, the latter was far more imbued with superstition and irrationality. In Christian thought the critical power of the human mind had regained a genuine purpose; the pages of Augustine reveal not only the underlying reliance on authority which fortified

---

[20] *Letter* 120.3 (Cochrane).   [21] *City of God* 21.7.
[22] *Letter* 82.3 (To Jerome, 405; Parsons).

Christian thinking but also the tremendous advance in thought which that reliance permitted—so long as society still possessed some elements of stability.

Fortified by the previous exploration of basic Christian dogma in the debate over the Trinity, Augustine could sweep away much of the dross and inconsistency of pagan thought and the evil effects of the crude nature worship which had been imbedded in Greco-Roman thinking since primitive days. While praising the philosophers, he could see the weight of tradition which held them back and could contrast the certainty of Christian belief with the basic doubts of men who "rush hither and thither, to this side or to that, according as they are driven by the impulse of erratic opinion." [23] At the close of the sixth book of the *City of God* he opposed the complexities of ancient religious thought to the simplicity of the Christian God, the one true god. If the capacity to subsume the complicated under a general theory is a mark of intellectual advance, one assuredly must credit Christian thought with spectacular progress.

Christian View in Augustine

Augustine's thought may also be taken as a prime example of the developed Christian view of God, man, and the world in its intellectual and metaphysical aspects. To a man who put as his aim the knowledge of God there could be no doubt of the omnipotence of this force or debate on its essential goodness. Augustine swept away the hopeless wavering of the classical world between Fate and Fortune; in their place he gave man a sense of predestination which has at times had no less evil an effect.

Christianity, nevertheless, broke out of the endless cycles of ancient thought, which had posited the basic immutability of the universe. The coming of Christ marked a real break, a new order; but Christ died once for our sins and no more. From this unique event the course of human history, itself composed likewise of unique events, must run toward eventual salvation. The weary treadmill on which the hopeless Tacitus had plodded was simply abolished.

To the Christian, human history was a manifestation of the will of God; it thus had a purpose and certainty which it too often had lacked in pagan writers. Since this history was tendentious, Christian historians were not above accepting the wildest of fabrication when it suited their

[23] *City of God* 7.17.

purpose. Yet history was also important. The works written in the fourth century are often credulous; their better examples likewise contain an emphasis upon truth, an understanding of the possibility of change, an employment of the critical senses, and in many Christian (and pagan) historians a far greater emphasis upon statistics, exactness of chronology, and actual quotation of documents than in earlier ages.

Eusebius quoted faked documents and legends in his *Ecclesiastical History,* he perverted pagan facts and misinterpreted Philo and others, but he weighed carefully and reproduced earlier opinion on such subjects as the canon of the New Testament, the origin of heresies, and a host of other matters. The Christians likewise had a sense of the continuity and significance of the historical stream which led them to the production of chronological studies—from those of Africanus through Eusebius and Jerome to medieval chronicles—designed to unify the Biblical story within the frame of universal history.

Equally significant in Augustine's thought is the place of the human being as a true individual, dependent upon the grace of God and yet an agent of independent volition. Beside the treatment of predestination in the fifth book of the *City of God* Augustine was careful to place a justification of the freedom of our will: "Human wills are also causes of human actions." [24] Another treatise, *On Free Will,* he devoted entirely to this difficult position of man, who is neither independent of God nor merely His puppet.

The elaborate arguments of his great study *On the Trinity* were drawn first from Scripture and then, in the later books, from the nature and self-knowledge of the individual, whose existence as a creature of value was worked out along lines already stated in the *Soliloquies.* It is true that Augustine does not speak of man in entirely modern, secular terms, for serious search could only lead the Christian to God, as he had demonstrated in his *Confessions.* Having found oneself there, one was transformed into a changeless essence. Augustine was far from permitting unrestrained individualism; in his Fourteenth Letter he asserted that the idea of "man" was primarily in God's mind, wherefrom came the idea of each individual.

Thus far Augustine held to the main current of ancient thought, but this was only part of his rich scheme, which was always, he felt, developing and approaching closer to true doctrine. Who (protests Marrou justly) had been able before Augustine to speak with such truth of the

[24] *City of God* 5.9.

depths of the human soul? After the bishop of Hippo, and because of his penetrating analysis of essential Christian belief, the human had a new dimension and a metaphysical significance previously unimaginable. "Thou seekest the depth of the sea, what is deeper than human conscience?" [25]

It is in keeping both with Augustine's effort to fix his eyes on God and with his deep sympathy with life that he was little interested in dialectics, in mathematics, or in the physical aspects of the creation of the earth; always he came back to the human being and his soul. This universal subject, independent of class, culture, or sex, stood before his God as an individual apart from the state or other social grouping.

The position of mankind in Augustine's thought needs to be placed against the background of his era to be fully appreciated. The pagan attitude, in which the individual was well-nigh entirely dependent upon himself, had not yet disappeared, though its fruits had been bitter doubt and a troubled search for a more solid platform. Among some of the Christians at least, this footing had been achieved, and its product is naïvely displayed among some of Augustine's contemporaries. A quality marked, for instance, in the poet Prudentius is that of joyousness, of quiet happiness in divine providence; and this same quality may be observed repeatedly in the description of Christian saints and in Christian authors generally.

Such serenity must have been a source of envy to many men of the era, bound down by their secular cares. Not all could rise to the heights of belief necessary for its support—pagans like Rutilius Namatianus could not even begin to understand the attractions of the monastic life which could counterbalance the necessary secession of the monk from the world and his disregard of physical comfort. Yet Western society now had a dynamo from which it could draw energy in the parlous times to come as the barbarians sent the Empire crashing and life shrank to narrow limits; the lowliest individual could sense, if dimly, that he had an importance in the cosmic order which previously had been denied to him.

This attention to the individual and to his need for salvation had dangerous aspects. There was in the fourth century a morbid tendency to introspection and confession of human inadequacy to attain the desired goal, which linked itself all too easily to the pessimistic tenor of the

[25] *Explanations of Psalms* 76.18 (Coxe ed., 77.17).

secular world. Not all Christians were actually happy, and their psychological self-examination, though leading to a more refined analysis of human attitudes, led also in many cases to a public brooding on sins; to the influential, gloomy Ephraim of Edessa weeping was a natural function like breathing. Hand in hand with this attitude went the rise of monasticism. As the more devout Christians looked at the spiritual decay of the secular Church, engulfed by hordes of men who still lived for this world, they found it inadequate for their own salvation and turned away to the solitary life of the eremite.

Both pagan and Christian rulers fulminated against this denial of social and political obligations; and even Christian bishops cast worried glances at the ecstatic, almost inhuman, quality of the monastic search for God. Augustine, in sundry works, underlines the need for man to love his fellow men even in seeking his own salvation. In Christian thought and in Christian art the human, in ceasing to be a specimen of a Platonic ideal or a mere assemblage of atoms and in becoming a true individual, substituted for a mechanical union with his fellows a deeper, more spiritual tie. The medieval monastery is a mark both of that tie and of the significance of the individual.

A further strand of the thinking of Augustine, and of Christianity in general, was the conclusion that the physical world is not divine. Stars and planets are not gods, though the Christians felt that God set the ordered revolutions of the heavenly bodies. Astrology was sharply attacked by Augustine, lest "we be shipwrecked in the most dangerous storms of human life, cast by our free will onto the rocks of a wretched slavery." [26] The attack was delivered along lines already advanced by pagan thinkers but with new forces. Sidereal influences may bring the seasons of earth, and oysters and the tides may follow the moon; but "it does not follow that the *wills of men* are to be made subject to the position of the stars" [27] or that one may not plant a vineyard in leap year.

Augustine necessarily believed that God reveals His will to man, but he did not endorse the vehicles for that revelation which the pagans had accepted. The Christians also denied the pagan assumption that one moved from an understanding of nature to an understanding of man and then of God. As Athanasius had asserted and Augustine reiterated, the knowledge of the divine principle differed entirely from the knowl-

[26] *Letter* 55.13 (Parsons).   [27] *City of God* 5.6.

edge of nature and was to be gained in a quite independent manner.

The result was a view of nature complicated in its combination of antitheses but one which could fructify thought. Nature and humanity were alike subject to the laws of God and were in this sense on a unified plane upon which God works. Yet, while classical thought had often considered the physical world as alive, a projection of the divine, Christian nature was a thing apart from humanity, a material substance made to sustain man. To many pagans, including gnostics and Manicheans, the physical had often appeared essentially evil; to the Epicureans it was, as a natural product, imperfect and decaying; but the Christians must necessarily conceive of all creations of God as good in theory even though they might distrust the temptations of nature in practice. Christian transcendentalism, unlike that of Plotinus and essentially that of Plato, did not have to be purely ideal; and the more sober Christian thinkers found no need to deny matter and the life of the body when they accepted the myth of Genesis in place of the myth of the *Timaeus*.

Augustine relied largely on bookish knowledge about the physical world, as did the pagans and the medieval world, whose bestiaries, lapidaries, and other compendia were derived from Pliny the Elder and earlier sources. In many Christian works nature dissolved into a pattern of divine purpose, just as in contemporary art the physical became a pattern of light and shadow. Yet Augustine's essential acceptance of nature might eventually lead to the closer observation of the world about us, both in Byzantine and in Western culture, as an expression of the beneficent force of the Divine. This observation, it is now recognized, was a root of modern science and art.

Old and New in Augustine

In sum, Augustine manifested a belief in Divine order, in the existence of the human as an individual whose independence is at once deepened and weakened by Christian doctrine, in the goodness of the physical environment of man. His scheme of thought represents an essential break with the classical emphasis on culture, and at times he attacked elements of the classical system more fiercely than we today may approve. Modern freethinkers are also likely to abhor his voluntary restrictions upon the freedom of the human mind, which in practice induced him to force limitations upon the minds of heretics.

Faith, nevertheless, was only a condition for the proper use of reason. Augustine's mind was fructified by his faith to produce fruit of a beauty which no other man of the century brought forth. Augustine, far more than his pagan contemporaries Macrobius and Symmachus, represented the true drive of human development, which could have gone no further in its classical expression. Much that was old had to be swept away, but those who treasured the ancient merely because of its venerability could not use the broom.

From Augustine to Thomas Aquinas and the Renaissance, from the Christian basilicas of the fourth century to the Romanesque, Gothic, and modern views of architectural space, the path is straight. To critics who speak in classical terms the burst of intellectual activity of the fourth century must appear inexplicable, and they obfuscate it by the use of terms like "twilight," "renaissance," and so on. Once one realizes the dimensions of the intellectual change which had taken place in the preceding centuries, this flowering appears inevitable. If a poetic word must be used to describe it, "dawn" fits much better than "twilight," for by the day of Augustine Western man had taken the essential step toward the modern view of life.

The literary product of Augustine yet betrays the same curiously incomplete severance from ancient forms which has already been noted in fourth-century architecture and sculpture. In erecting their basilicas Christian builders did not scruple to use columns from ancient temples; in Augustine, too, the basic ideas were new, but the molds often were old. The product is often outwardly rough and requires sympathetic understanding. To take one tangible example, in the rhetorical style of Augustinian Latin (as in the Greek of Basil and Gregory of Nazianzus) *clausulae* or phrases based on accentual rhythm stand beside *clausulae* composed of long and short syllables in classic quantitative modes. The latter, a symbol of the old, appear most frequently in Augustine's more carefully written works, as the *City of God;* the former are a forerunner of the medieval style which can also be found in pagan orations of the fourth century.

The whole structure of Augustine's thought frequently suffered from prolixity and a willingness to detour which were born of its author's rhetorical and dialectical instruction. At other times a modern reader winces at his almost excruciating naïvity in self-expression, as in the *Confessions,* or at his vehemence in presenting Christian dogma, which at first sight seems inhuman. The bishop of Hippo, after all, lived in the fourth century, when the spirit looked forward but the forms in which the spirit was confined still derived from the past.

XVI

The Old World
of the Fourth Century

LOOKING back, we can see that Christianity best expressed an interpretation of man and the world which is the basis of modern thought. From Augustine, however, thought did not progress ever onward and upward; the Late Classical was a temporary bloom which soon withered. Not until the twelfth century were the men of Western Europe able widely to resume that intellectual advance which has impelled them forward down to the present day.

The blasted promise of the Late Classical must be the product of serious flaws in the structure of fourth-century thought. Christian doctrine had an essentially authoritarian basis, which led men to intolerance of disagreement or even at times to the rejection of rational analysis and argument as unnecessary for salvation. To put this point first, however, does not mean that it is the most significant factor, for Christian intolerance really reflects the general decline of intellectual activity. Far more important was the wide survival of classical forms and attitudes which were not at root compatible with the new view.

Any explanation of the decline of imperial civilization must also look outside the intellectual field to wider defects in the Late Empire. The barbarian pressure on the frontiers reached an unprecedented intensity in the late fourth century as the Huns drove westward. This factor was exterior and uncontrollable, but its effect was greatly intensified by the political, economic, and social deterioration within the Late Empire as measured in terms of the weakening ancient structure of life. The fourth century, to repeat an earlier observation, was Januslike. Outwardly it was an era cursed by despotism, intolerance, and decay.

Height of Imperial Absolutism

The apparent balance of the Augustan Principate between Caesar and Senate ended in the third century, and the local autonomy of the cities vanished as swiftly. To the towering figure of the emperor all men had already turned in the relative peace of the second century; now for a time they clutched this symbol as their only earthly hope. The divine appointment of the ruler, a doctrine already argued by Dio Chrysostom and others, became an accepted creed of the emperor Aurelian, who ascribed his position and success to Sol Invictus. When Christianity triumphed, it was necessary only for Constantine to replace Sol by the Christian God.

The elevation of the imperial position received full recognition in the reorganization of the state by Diocletian and Constantine, for the emperor thenceforth was admittedly absolute and took advice only from his privy council. This body solemnly "adored" him by kissing his hand on entry and departure; in outward rite as in inward thought the subject had to bend before his divinely appointed ruler and ceremonially make manifest his loyalty.

Beneath the emperor was a vast, decentralized bureaucracy, divided into military and civil sections, and descending on the latter side stepwise from the praetorian prefects to the provincial assemblies and urban councils, which acted as imperial agents. Superficially this mutually checking structure appears more complicated than that of the Principate, but a very brief study shows that the rich local variations and subtle adjustments of the earlier period had now been sacrificed to an essentially simple, brutal structure. All else had to give way to the maintenance of the all-important army. Corruption, waste of precious funds, and inefficiency were marks of the entire structure of government; the direction of this structure shifted from clique to clique, all exploiting the subjects and heaping up their own piles of gold while the Empire went to pieces.

In the struggle to maintain the unity of the Empire the rulers of the third century had had to demand, reluctantly, blindly, yet forcefully, more and more from their subjects, though production and population were declining. Inflation had resulted in coins assaying only 2 per cent silver under Gallienus; from Septimius Severus payment in kind, both for taxes and for salaries, became more common. Army units had confiscated animals, food, and other items as they moved to and fro along the great arteries of the Empire; for the rest the emperors bore ever more heavily upon the urban system of government to extort taxes from the subjects. Not until the end of the third century was Diocletian able to check the inflation, restore the currency, and establish for a time a new, though lower, plane of economic activity.

By the reign of Constantine the subjects were marshaled into one great system to maintain the government and to supply the army. Political independence had disappeared under Augustus; now, to preserve order, the subjects yielded their social and economic freedom. Town councilors and soldiers were virtually tied to their places in the third century; in the fourth the Empire had essentially to surrender its humanitarian efforts and give control of the peasantry to the large landlords. The *de facto* differentiation of the upper and lower classes, which had become marked in the Early Empire, was formulated as a distinction in law between the "more honorable" and "humbler" elements of society in the third century. Worst of all the move from one class to another became steadily more difficult as the economic structure declined.

Since change meant decay, the Empire was resolved to stop change. The Theodosian Code, a collection of fourth-century edicts in the main, contains provision after provision by which the state sought to lock men in their places and to secure from every subject his due contribution to the coffers and granaries of the Empire. "No man," said one edict to the people, "shall possess any property that is tax exempt." [1] As Cochrane wryly comments, a state which had originated (according to Cicero) with the aim of protecting property rights now made that property the basis of a system of servitudes unparalleled in history. To modern eyes the corrupt, brutal regimentation of the Late Empire appears as a horrible example of the victory of the state over the individual, and the fact that the rulers arrived at this situation in their efforts to maintain the framework of ancient civilization is the bitterest of irony.

Repression and terrorism were to last as long as the Empire endured; the more it tottered, the more evident they became. The emperors intensified the already-standard efforts of earlier Caesars to control public expression of political thought. We continue to hear of spies, arrests by night, and banishment to islands. Diocletian abolished the secret police,

[1] *Theodosian Code* 13.10.8 (383) (Pharr).

the *frumentarii;* but a new, even-more-vicious agency, the *agentes in rebus,* quickly took their place. The concept of *laesa maiestas* remained a potent tool to strike down opponents; any man of importance might dream in times of stress "of the torturer and of fetters and lodgings of darkness." [2]

Although the state continued to support arts and letters, its control, especially of education, became more extensive as the municipalities declined in initiative and resources and the upper classes withdrew from public functions. From the late third century the emperor himself sent out statues, or more often paintings, bedecked with laurel, to his colleagues and the major cities, there to be greeted in a ceremonial form with candles and incense, flowers, music, and song. The surviving statues are often colossal in size; in relief the figure of the emperor is the overwhelming focus of attention of all the other figures and so, by extension, of the spectator (see Pls. X, XII). Panegyric in prose and in verse was adulatory to an extreme degree.

The reverse of the medal is shown by such reformers of the century as the anonymous author *de rebus bellicis,* who carefully avoided assuming any ignorance on the part of the rulers or his aides or describing too bluntly the ills he wished to combat. Historians of the fourth century also walked very warily in discussing current or recent events; the emperor Theodosius has recently been shown to have had a repressive effect on the pen of Ammianus.

Credulity and barbaric brutality are evil marks of the fourth century. Astrology, magic, and poisoning were employed against the rulers or against fellow nobles on a scale unprecedented in earlier ages, and the discovery of their employment led to fearful repression by such emperors as Valens, who carried "death at the tip of his tongue." [3] The sophist Libanius, a proud partisan of ancient culture, believed in the crudest of magic, and exulted at a famine in the city where his son died; the roughly contemporary pagan farrago, the *Augustan History,* reveled in depicting the burning of adulterers, the breaking of legs and hips of deserters, and other frightful punishments. As the barbarian grew more civilized, the Romans were growing more barbarous.

The practical effects of the new view of man's significance, in truth, were not overly great. Men who have professed a reverence for human life have often been capable of peculiarly cruel actions. Constantine might prohibit branding on the face, "made in the likeness of celestial

[2] Ammianus Marcellinus 28.1.16.   [3] Ammianus Marcellinus 29.1.19.

beauty," [4] but he did not abolish branding for other parts of the body. The instigators of the Diocletianic persecution replaced the penalty of death by maiming of legs and gouging out of eyes; many a political and social law thereafter began with rhetorical praises of the ruler's mercy and serenity and then ordained the most frightful punishments for violations of its provisions. The increasing volume of moral legislation, in particular, was coupled with an inhuman treatment of those who erred.

Bookburning is more prevalent in the fourth and following centuries than in any other period of the Empire. Diocletian began with the destruction first of Manichean and alchemical, then of Christian, works; treatises on magic were always dangerous to own. In a great purge at Antioch under Valens the judges burned a great quantity of books taken from the houses of suspects, though most of the volumes were on the liberal arts and law. This act, asserts the contemporary Ammianus, caused a panic among owners of libraries throughout the East; burning their own collections to avoid accusations of magic, he and his fellows crept about in darkness. When men became orthodox Christians, they felt ever more the need of repressing dissent. The imperial ban on Porphyry's attack against Christianity, issued in 448, proclaims that "all the books that move God to wrath and that harm the soul we do not want to have come even to men's hearing." [5]

Checks on Absolutism

The horrible repression of thought, the coercion and limitation of activity by a caste system, and the inefficiency and corruption of the bureaucracy—these were ills which the subjects could counter at the moment only by the solace of resignation. In the end, however, the ideals by which the Empire had been held together were irretrievably smashed.

One ideal, that of a good life under just rulers, had had materialistic, autocratic connotations which not all elements had entirely accepted in earlier centuries. Now even the vast bulk of mankind, which had taken its bread of servitude, was sadly disillusioned by the economic decay of the imperial structure and by the vicious autocracy of the Late Empire. Some elements turned thankfully to the barbarians in the fifth

[4] *Theodosian Code* 9.40.2 (316) (Pharr).

[5] *Code of Justinian* 1.1.3 (trans. by C. A. Forbes, *Transactions of the American Philological Association* 67 [1936], 122).

century as deliverers, and others could accept the collapse of the Empire without heartfelt regret. A fugitive Greek whom Priscus interviewed among the Huns in 448 agreed that "the laws and constitution of the Romans were fair" but deplored the ruthless exaction of taxes and the unprincipled, unchecked conduct of the well-to-do. To him life with the Huns was far better.[6]

The other ideals, those of "culture" and of an eternal Rome, still cast their spells in the fourth century, but both waned rapidly thereafter save as they passed into the doctrine of the Church. The resources of classical civilization had become feeble; the political decay of the Empire, though not consciously detected, nay rather even denied in fervent apostrophes to Rome's eternity, was yet felt by men. The state control of life and thought just sketched had more distinct limits than one might suspect at first glance. These limits were provided by the army, by the aristocracy and peasantry conjoined or separately, and by the Christian hierarchy.

As the Empire became a military autocracy in the third century, the army spoke ever more independently, erecting and casting down emperors at its pleasure. A process reaching back to the time when Marius made the army professional and independent of the state had almost attained its logical end. The despoiled peasants and the civilian writers who resented the increased place of military circles in the government of the Empire draw a black picture of the military forces, a picture perhaps too black in spots. That the soldiers of the third century pillaged and looted and tore down much that earlier ages had built, one may agree; but these military forces performed one of the most herculean feats of their entire existence in beating off at last the serious external threats of the period and in restoring the unity of the Empire. Not until the fourth century did the barbarians become the backbone of the army and discipline truly wane. Then the emperors had to hearken to its voice, however misinformed, and the leaders of the army, drawn ever more from these same barbarians, played a great, though often disastrous, part in the determination of state policy.

As important, and even more independent, was the new aristocracy of the fourth century, which was drawn from the equestrian order, from the soldiery proper, and to a limited degree from the old aristocracy. The Senate itself sank virtually to the role of town council for Rome, and in the third century the old aristocracy lost access to one post after an-

[6] J. B. Bury, *History of the Later Roman Empire* 1 (London, 1889), 218–219.

other. In its place the new nobility, which was fairly stable during the Late Empire, continued to serve—or exploit—the state and lived at times in cities, but more and more it withdrew from the cramped, melancholy towns huddling behind walls to the great villas of its landed estates, where it might enjoy hunting and other sports and a freer social life, foreshadowing that of the nobles of the Middle Ages. Culturally as well as economically the cities were losing their old dominance.

The rise of these large agricultural units, independent of the cities and to a considerable extent free in practice from state control, was a major economic development of the Late Empire. Virtually self-sufficient estates had long been a characteristic of the Orient and had appeared in the West during the Roman Republic; in the Empire land appears to have become steadily more concentrated in a few hands, and to have passed frequently by confiscation or execution into the emperors' patrimony. Meanwhile, as slaves grew more difficult to get, there was a tendency to divide estates into plots of scattered strips, farmed by free tenants or slave families who paid rents in money or in kind; that part of the estate retained by the master or overseer was farmed by the tenants, who gave part of their time to the task.

In the third century parts of the imperial property moved into aggressive private hands, which could better keep the land in cultivation. When oppressed by imperial bailiffs, peasants at times threatened to flee from the imperial estates to private protectors; in other areas, where peasants had previously owned their own lands, they turned to the patronage (*patrocinium*) of local magnates for economic support or for protection against both the imperial soldiery and the barbarian invaders. Independent small landholders did not entirely disappear in the process—they remained in scattered areas throughout the Middle Ages —but the typical form of rural organization tended ever more toward what we call in medieval times the manor, a nearly self-sufficient agricultural complex dependent socially, economically, and even politically on a lord.

Theoretically the writ of the emperor still ran in estates and cities alike, and the emperors struggled to stem the current by their edicts, by asserting their sacred position, and by supporting the urban machinery. The city remained outwardly the basic form of local organization in most areas. Thus a letter of Constantine authorized the creation of a city at Orcistus in Asia Minor so that the population might no longer be afflicted "by the depredations of powerful persons." [7] So too the Caesars repeatedly issued laws against *patrocinium* over individuals or entire villages, though so frequently as to attest its persistence, and tried to protect the poor in courts.

Nevertheless the Empire was ever more based on the countryside, and imperial writ was enforced on the estates through the medium of the master. It was he who furnished imperial recruits and paid imperial taxes, but he moved independently of the lower echelons of the central bureaucracy or even controlled those echelons. At various points in the fourth century the emperors had to admit in their legislation that only provincial officials, or at times the central bureaucracy itself, could hope to deal with the great estates on anything like even terms. Whereas emperors of the second and early third centuries had often supported the peasants against their landlords or imperial bailiffs, the needs of the exchequer and the decline in population had forced the rulers by the fourth century to come to terms with the landlords; from 332 on the peasants were slowly tied by law to their land.

The peasants, in other words, were essentially serfs. Sometimes they refused to accept this lot calmly. The countryside of Africa was harassed by bands of *agonistae* or *circumcelliones,* who adopted the cloak of the Donatist heresy; in Gaul and elsewhere similar unrest was known; in the fifth century the peasants were at times to turn in relief to the invading barbarians, who might free them from the terrific social and economic pressure of the decaying imperial system.

Not always did the peasants object to the rise of the manor, for they at least gained for themselves and their descendants an inseparable tie with a piece of land from which their master could exact only those dues fixed by a law or by custom of the estate. They had, in brief, "a minimum of security, stability, of guarantee against arbitrary action." [8] Any assessment of the "statism" of the Late Empire must include the fact that the orders of the state, though more destructive of individual freedom of operation, bore directly on a far smaller proportion of the population than had the edicts of such a ruler as Trajan. Beneath the surface the aristocrats and the peasants were fashioning a network of stable, inde-

[7] *Corpus Inscriptionum Latinarum* III 7000.

[8] Ferdinand Lot, *La Fin du monde antique et le début du Moyen Age* (Paris, 1927), 131.

pendent cells which would survive the withering away of the imperial machinery and the disappearance of a money economy in the next two centuries.

Even within the cities the imperial system of repression no longer operated as efficiently as in the Early Empire. Urban riots had been more extensive in the third century than in the second, and took place in considerable numbers in the fourth, sometimes led by theatrical claques or by Christian fanatics. Though men were still exiled to islands, they occasionally contrived an escape which would scarcely have been possible in the Early Empire, when the navy held firm control over the seas. Men who went underground were not turned up by the imperial police. The dangerous Procopius, a relative of Julian, escaped the most rigorous search by the spies of Valentinian, though with considerable hardship, and finally turned up in Constantinople itself, where he raised a revolt.

Bishops and Emperors

The most open challenge to the Caesars of the fourth century was hurled by some of the followers of Christ. This fact is extraordinary, for in the first flush of joy at the end of the persecutions the Church tended to pay the deepest respect to Constantine, a veritable Christian (in spirit at least) upon the throne. The bishops accepted his hidden assertion of imperial control of Christian organization and dogma, not only because they were his subjects on the earthly plane but also because they happily beheld the utilization of the machinery of state to suppress the heretic Donatists and Arians.

When one reads the ecstatic eulogies addressed by Lactantius and Eusebius to Constantine, "the first Roman ruler to repudiate error and to acknowledge the majesty of God," [9] one can sense that the Christian Church stood in more serious danger from the friendly emperors of the fourth century than it ever had under the persecutors. "Two roots of blessing, the Roman Empire and the doctrine of Christian piety," wrote Eusebius, "sprang up together for the benefit of man." [10] Would that duality now yield to unity at the expense of Christian independence?

In the fourth century, once the emperor had become a Christian himself, the Church was perilously close to replacing in practice its ideal of

[9] Lactantius, *Divine Institutes* 1.1.

[10] *Panegyric of Constantine* 16 (*Griechische Christlichen Schriftsteller* 7, 249); trans. by Kenneth M. Setton, *Christian Attitude towards the Emperor in the Fourth Century Especially as Shown in Addresses to the Emperor* (New York, 1941), 48.

a heavenly Redeemer by the old, well-established figure of an earthly shepherd. Most bishops bent before the emperor, the vicar of God, who was irresponsible to man inasmuch as his power was divinely instituted. One bishop, Optatus of Numidia, asserted under Valentinian that "the State is not in the Church, but the Church is in the State, that is, the Roman Empire." [11] The freedom of the Christians, like that of the philosophers, remained an internal matter, not a political concept; Jesus, and then Paul, had long before defined freedom in terms of liberation from sin and of moral subjection to God.

Some thinkers, nonetheless, came to feel that internal and external independence were closely interconnected. Men of the Early Empire had inherited a tradition that the state stood above any other type of ideal, but they had turned over control of the state to the Caesars; the subjects had become "unpolitical" in their acceptance of a structure which satisfied their bodies. The theological disputants of the fourth century, on the other hand, started with an initial presupposition that the Empire was only an earthly city, which was neither all-important nor perfect. Their strife quickly shifted from a purely intellectual to a political plane, and soon nontheological grounds of complaint against the autocracy of the Empire began to enmesh themselves with doctrinal contentions.

Eusebius might prate of the divine installation of the ruler, and the emperors themselves could emphasize the eternity of the Roman state; but neither formula could permanently repress underlying tendencies in the Christian view of the relations of man and God. Constantine probably hoped, though perhaps unconsciously, to harness the new forces to the service of the political structure as the emperors of earlier centuries had made use of the strengths of the Greco-Roman synthesis, but he was to be sadly disappointed. The relations of Church and state were troubled thenceforth; religious unrest was even to help to destroy the imperial fabric.

When the Christian challenge to imperial autocracy came, it arose essentially from the problem of the source of authority for the Church in matters of faith. Could Christian leaders draw directly from God, or must they submit in all points to His earthly vicar? In the reign of Constantine himself this ticklish subject emerged first in the Donatist heresy of Africa, then in the Arian controversy. In both cases Constantine sup-

[11] *On the Donatist Schism* 3.3 (*Corpus Scriptorum Ecclesiasticorum Latinorum* 26, 74); Setton, *Christian Attitude*, 55.

ported the orthodox faction and did his utmost to coerce its opponents by threats and exile, but in both he discovered the stubbornness of the heretics. In Africa at least, heresy tended to couple itself with social disorders.

Worse was to come in the reign of his son Constantius (337–361), who was outwardly a semi-Arian; for Constantius attempted, particularly in the overweening pride of his last years, to bend the orthodox bishops to his will by blandishments and by threats. Had he succeeded in dealing with the bishops as he had with the pretenders to his throne, the development of Trinitarian thought would have suffered a rude blow, and the subservience of the Church to the state would have been essentially guaranteed.

Many Christian leaders, including the Pope, bent before Constantius, but a few refused to yield. At Alexandria Athanasius had impelled the Catholic community to address a signed, public protest to the ruler "for the salvation of his immortal soul." In the long centuries of the Empire this document is a well-nigh unique manifestation of open opposition to imperial dictates; later Athanasius addressed to his monkish adherents a vicious but anonymous attack on the ruler, the *History of the Arians*. In it the emperor was called "the enemy of Christ, leader of impiety, and as it were Antichrist himself" or again "godless, unholy, without natural affection." [12] Far bolder than Athanasius or the bulk of his supporters was the exiled bishop of Cagliari, Lucifer, who composed five open attacks on the ruler, threatening him with divine judgment and abusing him as "the filth of all the sewers," "founder of blasphemy," and so on.[13] When Constantius received one of these works, he was astounded—as well he might be—and inquired of Lucifer whether he really was the author. Even more singular is the result: upon Lucifer's acknowledgment of his authorship Constantius punished him only by shifting his place of exile. The emperors had first persecuted the Church in vain, then had accepted it with the expectation of controlling it; now they slowly discovered that exercise of that control was not always easy. To sign oneself, as Constantius did, "lord of the whole world," was to overlook a peculiar stiffness in Christian thought.[14]

In the last decades of the fourth century this suspicion of imperial authority debouched in the powerful attacks by Ambrose and John

[12] *History* 67, 45 (ed. by Opitz, *Athanasius Werke* 2.1 [Berlin, 1940]; Setton, *Christian Attitude,* 79).

[13] *On Saint Athanasius* 2.26; *On Not Agreeing with Heretics* 9 (*Corpus Scriptorum Ecclesiasticorum Latinorum* 14; Setton, *Christian Attitude,* 97).

[14] Ammianus Marcellinus 15.1.3.

Chrysostom. Various Christian communities had already treated as martyrs men executed by the imperial administration on secular grounds, and local bishops increasingly tended to protect their populace against imperial exactions and violence; now Ambrose asserted clearly the principle that Caesar was within, rather than above the Church. In matters of faith, he deduced, "the bishops are wont to judge Christian emperors, not emperors the bishops." [15]

The great bishop of Milan enunciated this stand in his struggle with the Arian mother of Valentinian II. Later he advanced to the position that the Church must reprove a ruler who failed to act for the benefit of his subjects. After a bloody massacre of the unruly residents of Thessalonica in 390 Ambrose regretfully but firmly banned the emperor Theodosius from the rites of the Church until he made penance. Before God a Caesar was only a man in Ambrose's eyes and so was bound by God's laws.

John Chrysostom, as priest at Antioch, pronounced much the same opinion: "When there is need of any good thing from above, the Emperor is wont to resort to the priest, but not the priest to the Emperor." [16] As bishop at Constantinople from 398, John at times flattered the imperial family but more often was fluently abusive in attacking the luxury of the court and the unjust actions of its Jezebel, the orthodox empress Eudoxia. Twice banished, he died in exile.

Ambrose, John Chrysostom, and other men of the era who spoke for the freedom of the Church to determine its dogma and to protect the oppressed displayed to the Empire an extraordinary example of opposition to the imperial dictation of thought and action; not even the philosophical martyrs of the Early Empire had gone so far. The new view implicit in Christian doctrine was in the last analysis incompatible with a political structure based on the old order. In this sense Christianity was able to live its life independent of the Empire. In this light, too, the Church may be called a destructive force in the decline and fall of the Empire.

Christian Intolerance

In laying down precedents for the future expounders of the independence of Christ's Church from secular control, such thinkers as Ambrose and John Chrysostom unwittingly aided in breaking the ancient bonds

---

[15] *Letters* 21.4 (Migne, *Patrologia Latina* 16, col. 1004; Setton, *Christian Attitude,* 111) (c. February 386).

[16] *Third Homily on the Statues* (*Patrologia Graeca* 49, col. 50; Setton, *Christian Attitude,* 189).

of church and state. Neither consciously would have gone so far. To John the ruler, appointed by God, was irresistible in earthly matters even though the imperial power led to pride and arrogance; the astute Ambrose, who had been trained in the public administration, maintained a respectful attitude toward the imperial office as such. No man of the fourth century could envisage a complete challenge to the imperial control of secular life, and no practical bishop could ignore the advantages of having the Caesars essentially on the side of the Church.

The orthodox leaders of the fourth century never dreamed of making a stand for general intellectual freedom, an idea which the spokesmen of the Church had occasionally enunciated in earlier centuries. Among the Christians who had argued for liberty of conscience so that they might lift their eyes to Heaven as they saw fit were Tertullian and Lactantius. The latter had asserted that "nothing is so much a matter of free will as religion" and had even announced that the Christian community would not hold anyone to it by force, "for he is unserviceable to God who is destitute of faith and devotedness." [17] While it was outside the pale, the Church did its utmost to break down the connection of civil and religious institutions, but this attitude soon vanished as the Church gained the support of secular power.

Like many other rebels against outside control, Athanasius, Ambrose, and their confreres desired liberty of action for themselves in order that they might repress those who disagreed with them. Pagans and Jews still existed in large numbers; heretics—above all the Arians—were prevalent; many orthodox Christians opposed the power of the major bishops. The Church was inclining ever more to authoritarian control within itself and was in no position to attack autocracy as a principle; the only problem which might arise was: Who was to be the ultimate autocrat?

There is little to choose, in matter of means, between Theodosius and Ambrose. By an edict of 388 the one completely forbade public discussion of religious issues, i.e., of the government's religious policy; the other packed a council at Aquileia and endured no freedom of debate as he drove it to the physically violent condemnation of two Balkan bishops charged with Arianism. Freedom of thought was a privilege only for the watchdogs within the pale. From the sheep obedience was expected; against the wolves Christianity vented a more violent intolerance on ideological grounds than had ever been manifested in the Empire. In

<hr />

[17] Lactantius, *Divine Institutes* 5.20 (Fletcher).

this respect, too, Christianity may justly be accused of hampering the potentialities of the new order of thought.

At Milan in 313 Constantine and Licinius had laid down the legal principle of general toleration for pagan and Christian alike, but from the final victory of Constantine onward the Church nibbled away at pagan rites and privileges. The curtailment of paganism was speeded up by Constantius, checked by Julian, and renewed under Gratian (375–383); the victory of the Church became obvious in the edicts of Theodosius (379–395). Pagan officials, at first tolerated, were now removed from the court. The temples were closed to sacrifice, and the state withdrew its support from pagan cults at Rome. The great temple of Sarapis at Alexandria was destroyed by a Christian mob in 391 without punishment; elsewhere the monks led the faithful against the ancient rites. Two laws of 392 consolidated earlier bans by forbidding the act of pagan sacrifice and established divination as an act of treason against the ruler. Not many years later the Romans melted down many statues of the gods to buy off Alaric's first attack of 408, and the general Stilicho burned the Sibylline oracles, to the horror of Rutilius Namatianus.

Official edicts may show the direction in which the wind was blowing, but they do not necessarily measure its intensity. Gusts of violence and intolerance blew across the Empire in the fourth century, particularly among the desperate rulers and the equally desperate lower classes; in the field of Christianity theoretical and practical factors joined to reinforce this swelling breeze. Still, some modern scholars make a great mistake in viewing the fourth century solely and simply as the scene of a mighty Kulturkampf. The interpenetration of Christian and pagan thinking was far more complex than that of mere opposition.

The imperial tradition was one of tolerance in intellectual matters, and the pagans were unwilling to fight hard for their faith, which they held more as a tradition than as a passionate belief. The emperor Julian stands as the chief representative of pagan intolerance, but this essentially dour zealot found little support, to his disgust, among his fellow pagans. As paganism became illicit, a few passionate, wrathful wails rise to our ears. Far more typical was the Roman noble Symmachus, plaintively arguing that there were many roads to the heavenly goal as he pleaded for toleration; the famous orator of Constantinople, Themistius, asserted that religious liberty was a gift of God and proved that repression could affect only the body, not the mind.

On intellectual and aristocratic levels Christians and pagans lived side by side in relative peace. At times fanatic Christian monks or minor bishops stirred up the mobs, but at other points bishops themselves are said to have protected pagan cults. Private worship of the pagan gods was not halted. Christians and pagans at Rome could join against the emperor Valentinian; Symmachus was defended by Pope Damasus against the charge of extremists that he had tortured Christian priests. Symmachus was also a friend of Ambrose, and he wrote his letters to pagans and Christians alike. His opponent, the magnanimous Pruden-tius, praised him as superior to Cicero and, in rejecting his defense of paganism, hoped that the tract of Symmachus would survive. Although those who were lukewarm pagans easily became Christians, "The idols remained rather in the hearts of the pagans, than in the niches of the temples." [18]

Pagans continued to serve the ruler long after they were officially banned. Pagan authors, though forced to be somewhat careful under Theodosius, might still write and in their works completely ignore Christianity or judiciously attack it; what they could *not* do was to ex-press political opposition or support the emperor's political opponents. An abundance of evidence indicates that men could still be devout pagans well into the fifth century and could give vent to their pagan feelings. The true repression of pagan thought, as well as of pagan worship, came slowly as the ancient pattern dissolved in the fifth century and faded away in the age of Justinian (527–565).

The same development may be found in the treatment of the Jews. Fourth-century rulers maintained the privileges of Judaism, and Chris-tian leaders upheld them in this attitude on the argument that the Jews were "witnesses of the truth," i.e., their existence proved the antiquity of the Old Testament, the coming of Christ, and other points in Christian doctrine.

Yet theological grounds required that the Jews be miserable for hav-ing killed Christ and for being an older, superseded dispensation. The preservation of privileges for the Jewish cult was accompanied first by the fierce attacks of Ambrose, Jerome, and Augustine and thereafter by a steady official diminution of the protection of Jewish life and property rights, a renewed ban on conversions, the destruction of synagogues, and the weakening of the central Jewish organization. In the fifth century the attack on the Jews became more intense in polemic, in mob riots, and in law; eventually bigotry produced the atrocious pattern of medieval

[18] Augustine, *Expositions on the Psalms* 98.2 (99.2 Coxe).

life, wherein Jews were permitted to endure a separate but legally and economically miserable life, separated from the land and driven into trade.

After the Council of Nicaea the Church had in general the support of the emperors in imposing a single doctrine upon all believers. Surviving edicts of Constantine make quite clear his repugnance to the idea that Christians could differ in belief and his willingness for a time to use imperial machinery in the hopeless effort to prevent schisms. In the last decades of the century Theodosius issued an edict bluntly ordering all Christian subjects to be orthodox on the pain of punishment by God and "by the retribution of Our own initiative, which We shall assume in accordance with the divine judgment." [19]

Early in the next century heresy was proclaimed a public crime on the grounds that it was an injury to all; but the chief principle on which the Caesars fought religious dissent was the old concept that the state was the master of its subjects. In the minds of Christian leaders there was also the certainty that only one road to salvation existed. Plato and Cicero had been unwilling in the theory of their ideal states to permit dissent, but now the shepherds of the faithful had ever more power to see to it that the flocks did tread the true path. To Augustine the city of God could not hold orthodox and heretics "indifferently without any correction," as the pagan world had held the jarring philosophers.[20] A principal landmark of this intolerance was the essay of Julius Firmicus Maternus against *The Error of Pagan Cult* (c. 346–350), which laid down clearly the duty of the rulers to save pagans from immortal destruction, even though they might resist their salvation. Repeatedly the turgid rhetoric of Firmicus returns to the idea that the pagans are sick, and the emperors must be their doctors; the Empire must be preserved from the fatal disease of polytheism.

The fight against heresy, and secondarily that against paganism and Judaism, was the main field from which a mighty theoretical basis for intolerance was added to the intellectual pattern of Western civilization. All the great Christian fathers are in greater or lesser degree responsible. Scarcely one shows any moderation in his writings against heretics; and the dismal descent of Augustine from verbal debate with heretics to the acceptance of their downright persecution is luridly lit by his letters, which were centuries later to be used as a justification for the repression of the Huguenots. Augustine, to be sure, agreed with many of his Chris-

[19] *Theodosian Code* 16.1.2 (380) (Pharr).   [20] *City of God* 18.51.

tian fellows and pagan contemporaries in disliking physical violence. The most frightful examples of intellectual distortion, appeal to the emotions, and downright cruelty came mainly from the lesser ranks of the Church; both the savage repression of Priscillianism by vengeful Gallic bishops and the brutal murder of the Alexandrian philosopher Hypatia by a Christian mob shocked pagans and Christians of the learned classes alike. In these affairs the shades of the Middle Ages loom ominously on the horizon.

Christianity opened a new view of the world and of man, which could support humanity in the ever-more-gloomy days of the Late Empire; but the new creed also ruined lives. The very forces which led to the revival of thought marked by Ammianus Marcellinus, Jerome, and Augustine produced also a suppression of serious deviation in thought. Pagans, Jews, and heretics suffered in varying degree; so too did the orthodox.

A gentle man like Synesius of Cyrene, Neoplatonic in heart, hesitated long before becoming bishop because he did not wish to give up that personal freedom of which he was so proud; in particular, he could not accept all aspects of Christian dogma on the resurrection and the end of the world, nor could he relinquish secular life. As he wrote to his brother (Epistle 105), a bishop could not be independent, but had to belong to everyone and teach what is recognized. Even more pitiful is the fate of the girl Paula, dedicated to a nunnery from her birth by her parents. Paula is the subject of a long letter by Jerome which directs her education. Psalms instead of jingles, no baby words, no gold and purple—such was the lot of the hapless waif, deprived of true childhood on the grounds of Christian piety.

In the first two centuries of the Empire neither the Caesars nor the populace had imposed a strait jacket of religious and social thought within which all must live. The very human tendency to look askance at those who departed widely from the accepted code, liberal as it was, did exist, and it can be shown most clearly in the outbreaks of anti-Semitism and in the Christian persecutions. Still, the religious freedom of the Empire had become ever more extensive as the old cults waned, and the variety of social practices was considerable, at least in the large, cosmopolitan cities.

From the third century, however, the requirements of morality became more intense. Slowly a new view of the family based on Christian belief began to supplant that of classical Roman law, as in limits on divorce. Blasphemy was forbidden. Sin and crime came to be confused in the moral indignation of imperial fulminations against adultery, rape, and other ills; the legislation of the sons of Theodosius, at the end of the fourth century, has been described as almost hysterical in its emotionalism and sentimentality.

To assert that the Church had learned intolerance in the days when Christianity was not tolerated by pagan society is to give only part of the explanation. As one looks back on the Roman Empire, two complementary conclusions may be drawn. Each is of frightful import. The individual gained a freedom for a time to think and act as he desired, but for this dubious good he paid a terrific price: he surrendered his political liberty to avoid anarchy, and he sacrificed the true bases for his system of thought.

On the other hand, when thought once more reappeared, it was grounded on a faith in the absolute. The inexorable concomitant of that faith was a limitation of the field within which thought could operate. "Das Gesetz nur kann uns Freiheit geben," said Goethe.

We may, if we wish, try to palliate this gloomy crux by arguing that faith should be strong enough to tolerate dissidence; but this is a milksop argument with which intellectuals encourage each other. Symmachus and Synesius spoke in this vein; their contemporaries led howling mobs to burn the Sarapeum or slay Priscillianists. Wide-scale toleration is only to be expected in periods in which systems of thought have gained well-nigh universal acceptance, i.e., when they have reached their apogee and are sloping down past the peak, either in society as a whole or within the governing circles. The one thing which kept the leaders of Christianity from becoming entirely despotic over men's minds was the breakdown of the state with which the Church was becoming associated.

Decline and Progress

Intolerance, in fine, was a hallmark of the fourth century. Insofar as civilization is to be measured by the complexity of interdependent relations, the Roman Empire was decaying politically, economically, and socially. At the same time it was subject to a very serious external stress from the barbarian invasions. Political intolerance was inevitable; Christianity in its turn placed distinct limits on intellectual and social freedom.

Almost as important in hampering thought were the survivals of classical forms into the fourth century. The bonds of classical style in poetry, rhetoric, historiography, and many other literary media were not easily to be broken, though they did not accord with the new views. So too in art and architecture a new spirit may be sensed in the fourth century, but the forms in which this spirit struggled for expression were those of antiquity. An accurate estimate of the extent to which this friction served as a brake is impossible, but neither the existence of this factor nor its significance can be gainsayed.

The statement of this point does not imply that the classical heritage in ideas, as distinct from that of forms, was a drawback to the formulation of thought. It was, indeed, not absolutely impossible that men of the Late Empire should form a true synthesis of old and new upon which their children might directly build. In the Eastern half of the Empire emperors and thinkers alike were able to merge Hellenic tradition, Christian faith, and imperial structure into the civilization which we call Byzantine—though one must be careful not to overestimate the originality of that civilization in reacting to its depreciation by nineteenth-century scholars.

In the West the general decay of the material base of civilization was uninterrupted, and that decay overbore the potentialities of thought displayed in the age of Augustine. Here the Empire was replaced by a congeries of loosely organized states under Germanic kings; commerce and industry almost entirely disappeared; and most men became peasants on medieval manors. This development was virtually complete, in essence, by the sixth century; but there could be no turning back to earlier patterns after the changes of the third century.

During the bleak years from 500 to 900 the ever-narrowing group of men in Western Europe who could read and write and build could do little but preserve two roots of civilization: the classical inheritance and the new views of the world and of man. Here and there a temporary flurry occurred. Now and then a man of determination and ability took a step which led a little way forward. Consecutive advance on a grand scale was impossible in this era of poor communications and poverty.

The decline and fall of ancient civilization have long exercised over modern man a dread fascination, which is heightened today by the dismal course of Western history. Yet we make a considerable mistake if we view the Empire only through dark glasses. The ancient political, economic, and intellectual structure could scarcely have proceeded much further in a direct line, and from the third century the Empire was actually paving the way for the future. To the inhabitants of the Mediterranean world who suffered the violence and misery of these centuries of outward decay such a reflection must have been cold comfort, but we may not let this sadness entirely corrupt our vision.

Politically the Empire could go no further than the absolutism set up by Diocletian and Constantine. In it the individual had lost all political rights and had become merely an obedient cog in a great machine. Despite the terrorism, however, this system came closer than any other ancient polity to solving a basic political problem of society, i.e., the organization of a large area under one government.

The old city-state ideal of organization, with its narrow loyalty and its pride in the superiority of the citizen over foreigners, was utterly incompatible with the Empire, but the Augustan Principate had still been the city of Rome writ large. By the late second century, however, an adviser could tell Commodus that "Rome is wherever the emperor may be"; [21] and the creation of an imperial citizenry was far advanced. When Constantine founded Constantinople, the Roman Empire no longer had Rome as a capital, and Italy had long since become essentially another province.

From the Late Empire the East was eventually able to turn back to a more decentralized structure while yet retaining its unity, but the West could only reduce itself to feudalism and open itself in the process to the barbarian migrations, which brought into it great groups of men untutored in Mediterranean civilization. In that dissolution the utter concentration of all political capacity in one man, aided by a corrupt, tyrannical bureaucracy, was destroyed. Later came the creation of new political units, larger than the city-states; eventually the national states commanded the patriotism of their members and formed the basis for the modern structure of thought.

These modern political units, insofar as they looked back, saw first the territorial state of the Late Empire with its bureaucracy under an absolute ruler. The Church, it must also be noted, created an administrative structure after this model, not that of the Augustan Principate. Beside the structure of the Church, which was oriented more to the hereafter, Christian leaders accepted without real reluctance the existence of secular units. The Church was not so intimately tied with the state, in its imperial form, as to fall with it; nor did medieval Christendom thereafter see that interpenetration of church and state which

21 Herodian 1.6.5.

marked Islam. The ties of local patriotism in the Middle Ages could never quite wipe out the memory of the union of large areas under a single ruler. The kings of the Western states became very weak, but they never quite vanished; about these royal houses the modern national kingdoms were to rise. Behind them continued to lurk the concept of the unity of Western civilization, one major root of which was the unity of the Roman Empire.

Economically, as one views the technological basis of ancient industry and commerce, one cannot see any possibility that this structure could have continued to expand indefinitely, or that it could have endured as political conditions worsened. The creation of agricultural units which may almost be called manors proceeded apace from the third century, though the roots of the development go much further back—the Empire was unconsciously building up social and economic organizations which were to endure its fall. These units were not as complex as the ancient cities had been. In many ways they resemble the Neolithic villages from which urban life had sprung millennia before; yet the practice of agriculture in the Middle Ages was far above that of Neolithic times in variety and rotation of crops, quality of implements, and other important aspects, and the noble life was, despite its rudeness, a thing unknown in the Neolithic Age.

In recent decades scholars have begun to see that the Late Empire was in experimentation and development of technology a period unprecedented since the fifth century B.C. Thenceforth new ways of doing things and of using nonhuman power made their way over Europe, slowly but surely during the Middle Ages and then ever more rapidly in the modern world.

The virtual disappearance of slavery had its place in this change, so too had the decline of the classical ideal of the learned gentleman of leisure which may already be sensed among the middle classes of the Empire; but we cannot overlook the concomitant breakdown of the entire structure of ancient thought. From the fourth century, man drew a greater distinction between himself and the physical world about him; this distinction eventually had a considerable effect in his manipulation of nature, as new peoples, practically unaffected by the dead weight of classical tradition and jolted by migration out of their own inherited ways, came within the orbit of civilization. Once the battle for survival had been won, the economic development of Western Europe proceeded apace under the direction of free men, who might hope to create a society in which not the few but the many could escape grinding poverty.

And finally we may draw the same conclusion in the intellectual as in the political and economic fields: the decline of the Empire was necessary for further progress. Man had thrown up a new view of himself and his environment in the Empire, had emancipated himself individually as a subject of divine guidance while yet viewing himself as grouped with his fellows and with the world in a solid bond. This emancipation might for a time be masked by the turn from the overly great individual atomization in the Roman Empire and by the economic simplification of the early Middle Ages. Still, the surplus of production, though not great, was sufficient to support the labors of those few men who consciously kept alive the vital inheritance of ideas from the ancient world. Neither books, painting, sculpture, nor even architecture entirely disappeared in the worst of the chaos following the destruction of the Empire. Through these media in part, but far more through the minds of all men, a new view of the world and the place of man in that world was preserved to fructify civilization when the chaos was over and the Mediterranean and the North could blend their ideas.

The outward decay of the West was a necessary step in its later development, for in that decay the bonds of the ancient world were snapped. The Byzantine Empire was limited in its potentialities simply because it pursued an uninterrupted pattern which was not sufficiently fertilized by new ideas; the West recoiled only to spring the farther once its energies were unleashed.

History may, after all, be a record of progress. Mankind is not necessarily an accidental collocation of atoms, tossed blindly on a sea of chance, or merely puppets whirled in great cycles eternally about the same points. If a survey of the intellectual development of the Roman Empire has a true utility, it lies in the establishment of the fact that the decline of any one system of thought does not bring an end to thought itself. Within the Empire, and unbeknownst to its governing elements, a new system arose which marked a great advance in the struggle of the human to reach his full potentialities. Man of the modern world is an individual on a far higher, far more complex plane than that of antiquity.

Our civilization may in its turn have advanced as far as its political, economic, and intellectual basis will permit. In seeking stability, modern man may well lose his political rights and his freedom of political expression; and his civilization, in being spread more widely, may grow stagnant and sterile. There is no occasion for unreasoning optimism, but there is no need for gloom. We too may hope that a new view of the nature of man will emerge in the days of our descendants, even though we are no more able to see its character than were the contemporaries of Caesar and Augustus.

BIBLIOGRAPHICAL NOTE
AND INDEX

Bibliographical Note

THE story of the preceding pages rests primarily upon the ancient sources, for upon the literary and physical evidence surviving from the Roman Empire we must always build. To aid our understanding of this evidence, however, many modern scholars have labored patiently; I am deeply indebted to their work.

To give an exhaustive bibliography of the intellectual history of the Roman Empire and related fields would require a volume larger than the present one. An easy introduction to the mass of modern studies may be found in the *Oxford Classical Dictionary* (Oxford, 1949); a fuller one, in the *Cambridge Ancient History*, vols. 9–12 (Cambridge, 1932–1939); and a yet more detailed survey, in Pauly-Wissowa-Kroll, *Real-Encyclopädie der classischen Altertumswissenschaft* (Stuttgart, 1894–). A methodical bibliography of the handbooks, tools, and major works in Roman history is conveniently presented in André Piganiol, *Histoire de Rome* (3d ed.; Paris, 1949).

The following list is intended only as a suggestion of the riches available on certain topics of immediate pertinence. In drawing it up, I have selected chiefly the most recent studies, not because these are necessarily the best but because they will suggest current opinion and earlier views; through consulting them, the student will be able to lay his hands upon the endless chain of ancient scholarship and pursue it as far as he desires. Where one work will suffice for these purposes, I have not noted parallel studies. In each category the more general works precede; in listing monographs and articles I have occasionally included earlier works of special value for my treatment.

The Greek Background

Cambridge Ancient History, vols. 3–9 (Cambridge, 1926–1932).

W. W. Tarn, *Hellenistic Civilisation* (3d ed.; London, 1951).

M. I. Rostovtzeff, *Social and Economic History of the Hellenistic World*, 3 vols. (Oxford, 1941).

Various aspects of Greek thought and of its limitations may be found in Fustel de Coulanges, *La Cité antique* (14th ed.; Paris, 1893); Eudore Derenne, *Les Procès d'impiété intentés aux philosophes à Athènes au Vme et au IVme siècles avant J.-C.* (Liège, 1930); E. R. Dodds, *The Greeks and the Irrational* (Berkeley, 1951); Benjamin Farrington, *Science and Politics in the Ancient World* (London, 1939), and his other peculiarly narrow works [see also William H. Stahl, "The Greek Heliocentric Theory and its Abandonment," *Transactions of the American Philological Association* 76 (1945), 321–332]; A. J. Festugière, *Liberté et civilisation chez les Grecs* (Paris, 1947); Hans Friedel, *Der Tyrannenmord in Gesetzgebung und Volksmeinung der Griechen* (Stuttgart, 1937); Werner Jaeger, *Paideia*, 3 vols. (New York, 1939–1944; 2d ed., vol. 1, 1945); Max Radin, "Freedom of Speech in Ancient Athens," *American Journal of Philology* 48 (1927), 215–230; John E. Sandys, *A History of Classical Scholarship* 1 (3d ed.; Cambridge, 1921), ch. 8; Bruno Snell, *The Discovery of the Mind: The Greek Origins of European Thought* (Oxford, 1953); Winifred Elberta Weter, *Encouragement of Literary Production in Greece from Homer to Alexander* (Diss., Chicago, 1936). For an example of Greek propaganda, see Lionel Pearson, "Propaganda in the Archidamian War," *Classical Philology* 31 (1936), 33–52.

Roman Republic

Cambridge Ancient History, vols. 7–9 (Cambridge, 1928–1932).

Ronald Syme, *The Roman Revolution* (Oxford, 1939).

Other political studies cannot be listed here. The political limitations on thought and action are illuminated by Maurice Besnier, "L'Interdiction du travail des mines en Italie sous la République," *Revue archéologique* 5. ser. 10 (1919), 31–50; Christoph H. Brecht, *Perduellio: Eine Studie zu ihrer begrifflichen Abgrenzung im römischen Strafrecht bis zur Ausgang der Republik* (Munich, 1938); Robert J. M. Lindsay, "Defamation and the Law under Sulla," *Classical Philology* 44 (1949), 240–243; Ernst Meyer, *Römischer Staat und Staatsgedanke* (Zürich, 1948); Eberhard Schmähling, *Die Sittenaufsicht der Censoren: Ein Beitrag zur Sittengeschichte der römischen Republik* (Stuttgart, 1938); Werner Schur, "Homo novus," *Bonner Jahrbücher* 134 (1929), 54–66.

Literary controls are discussed by Dorothy May Schullian, *External Stimuli to Literary Production in Rome, 90–27 B.C.* (Diss., Chicago, 1932); cf. Walter Allen, Jr., and Philip H. DeLacy, "The Patrons of Philodemus," *Classical Philology* 34 (1939), 59–65 (good bibliography). Tenney Frank's ideas in "Naevius and Free Speech," *American Journal of Philology* 48 (1927), 105–110, were expanded by Laura Robinson, *Freedom of Speech in the Roman Republic* (Diss., Johns Hopkins, 1940) (interestingly reviewed by A. Momigliano, *Journal of Roman Studies* 32 [1942], 120–124). See also Tenney Frank, "Status of Actors at Rome," *Classical Philology* 26 (1931), 11–20; and in rebuttal William M. Green, "The Status of Actors at Rome," *ibid.* 28 (1933), 301–304.

The aristocratic control of religion is suggested in Carl Koch, *Der römische Juppiter* (Frankfurt, 1937), perhaps exaggeratedly; Y. Béquignon, "Observations sur l'affaire des Bacchanales," *Revue archéologique* 6. ser. 17 (1941), 184–198, with bibliography of earlier studies; the classic article by Theodor Mommsen, "Der Religionsfrevel nach römischem Recht," *Gesammelte Schriften* 3 (Berlin, 1907), 389–422.

The Roman synthesis of the first century B.C. has been more fully appreciated in art than in literature. On literature see the Sather Lectures of Tenney Frank, *Life and Literature in the Roman Republic* (Berkeley, 1930); Günther Jachmann's lecture, *Die Originalität der römischen Literatur* (Leipzig, 1926), does not fully appreciate the new spirit. Bernhard Schweitzer has given a detailed analysis and dating, much needed, of *Die Bildniskunst der römischen Republik* (Leipzig, 1948); other works in the new stream are P. A. van Aken, *Nieuwe Wegen in de Romeinsche Woningbouw van Sulla tot Domitianus* (Utrecht, 1943); Christopher M. Dawson, *Romano-Campanian Mythological Landscape Painting* (New Haven, 1944); A. Zadoks-Josephus Jitta, *Ancestral Portraiture in Rome and the Art of the Last Century of the Republic* (Amsterdam, 1932).

Propaganda in the dying Republic appears incidentally in Syme and in Lily Ross Taylor, *Party Politics in the Age of Caesar* (Berkeley, 1949), etc., but, apart from monographs on Sallust's letters and the like, has had little separate study; cf. Tenney Frank, "Cicero and the Poetae Novi," *American Journal of Philology* 40 (1919), 396–415, and Otto E. Schmidt, "Flugschriften aus der Zeit des ersten Triumvirats," *Neue Jahrbücher* 7 (1901), 620–633. Jérôme Carcopino, *Les Secrets de la correspondance de Cicéron*, 2 vols. (Paris, 1947), must, I suppose, be mentioned but deserves little credit.

Another aspect of Cicero's thought is discussed in Joseph Vogt, *Ciceros Glaube an Rom* (Stuttgart, 1935); the framework of aristocratic life in Cicero's era is well presented by Wilhelm Kroll, *Die Kultur der Ciceronischen Zeit*, 2 vols. (Leipzig, 1933), and its ideal briefly described by Pierre Boyancé, "Cum dignitate otio," *Revue des études anciennes* 43 (1941), 172–191. Adam Afzelius surveys thoroughly "Die politische Bedeutung des jüngeren Catos," *Classica et Mediaevalia* 4 (1941), 100–203; cf. William M. Alexander, "Cato of Utica in the Works of Seneca Philosophus," *Transactions of the Royal Society of Canada* 3. ser. 40 (1946), 59–74.

Political and Economic History of the Early Empire

Cambridge Ancient History, vols. 10–11 (Cambridge, 1934–1936).

M. I. Rostovtzeff, *Social and Economic History of the Roman Empire* (Oxford, 1926; Italian edition, 1933).

Tenney Frank et al., *An Economic Survey of Ancient Rome,* 5 vols. and index (Baltimore, 1933–1940).

The bibliographies in these works (with the relevant articles in Pauly-Wissowa-Kroll) will lead into the many general and specialized studies. The ceremonial and ideological elevation of the imperial position is now being much studied; among the later investigations, see Andreas Alföldi's work, as "Die Ausgestaltung des monarchischen Zeremoniells am römischen Kaiserhofe," *Römische Mitteilungen* 49 (1934), 1–118; "Insignien und Tracht der römischen Kaiser," *ibid.* 50 (1935), 1–171; and more recently, "Die Geburt der kaiserlichen Bildsymbolik I," *Museum Helveticum* 7 (1950), 1–13; 8 (1951), 190–215; 9 (1952), 204–243; 10 (1953), 103–124. Among other work see also Leo Berlinger, *Beiträge zur inoffiziellen Titulatur der römischen Kaiser: Eine Untersuchung ihres ideengeschichtlichen Gehaltes und ihrer Entwicklung* (Diss., Breslau, 1935); such essays by M. P. Charlesworth as "Providentia and Aeternitas," *Harvard Theological Review* 29 (1936), 107–131; "The Virtues of a Roman Emperor: Propaganda and the Creation of Belief," *Proceedings of the British Academy* 23 (1937), 105–133 [cf. Harold Mattingly, "The Roman 'Virtues,'" *Harvard Theological Review* 30 (1937), 103–117]; and *"Pietas* and *Victoria:* The Emperor and the Citizen," *Journal of Roman Studies* 33 (1943), 1–10; Lloyd W. Daly, "Vota publica pro salute alicuius," *Transactions of the American Philological Association* 81 (1950), 164–168.

Lothar Wickert has collected material on the imperial assertion of liberty, "Der Prinzipat und die Freiheit," *Symbola Coloniensia* (Köln, 1949), 111–141. The Hellenistic background is considered by W. Schubart, "Das hellenistische Königsideal nach Inschriften und Papyri," *Archiv für Papyrusforschung* 12 (1937), 1–26, and more generally in "Das Königsbild des Hellenismus," *Die Antike* 13 (1937), 272–288; and by Mason Hammond, *City-State and World State in Greek and Roman Political Theory until Augustus* (Cambridge, Mass., 1951).

Augustus

Augustus: Studi in occasione del bimillenario Augusteo (Rome, 1938).

Anton von Premerstein, *Vom Werden und Wesen des Prinzipats* (Munich, 1937).

Early propaganda by Octavian is considered by Kenneth Scott, "The Political Propaganda of 44–30 B.C.," *Memoirs of the American Academy in Rome*

11 (1933), 7–49, and by M. P. Charlesworth, "Some Fragments of th‹ Propaganda of Mark Antony," *Classical Quarterly* 27 (1933), 172–177. T‹ efforts of Augustus to secure a favorable picture are interwoven into all his actions. Their extent may be suggested by Elizabeth M. Haight, "An 'Inspired Message' in the Augustan Poets," *American Journal of Philology* 39 (1918), 341–366 [cf. Katharine Allen, "The Fasti of Ovid and the Augustan Propaganda," *ibid.* 43 (1922), 250–266]; Henry T. Rowell, "The Forum and Funeral *Imagines* of Augustus," *Memoirs of the American Academy in Rome* 17 (1940), 131–143; and the edition of the Capitoline *Fasti* in *Inscriptiones Italicae* by Attilio Degrassi (Rome, 1947) [with Lily Ross Taylor, "The Date of the Capitoline *Fasti*," *Classical Philology* 41 (1946), 1–11; her review article *ibid.* 45 (1950), 84–95; and "New Indications of Augustan Editing in the Capitoline *Fasti*," *ibid.* 46 (1951), 73–80]. The Altar of Augustan Peace has recently been published by Giuseppe Moretti, *Ara Pacis Augustae*, 2 vols. (Rome, 1948).

The character of the Augustan Age appears best in Eduard Norden, "Vergils Aeneis im Lichte ihrer Zeit," *Neue Jahrbücher* 7 (1901), 249–282, 313–334; as seen by Livy it is discussed in Erich Burck, "Livius als augusteischer Historiker," *Die Welt als Geschichte* 1 (1935), 446–487. A descriptive treatment is to be found in the posthumous work of Richard Heinze, *Die Augusteische Kultur* (2d ed.; Leipzig, 1933); the fullest life of Augustus is that of Viktor Gardthausen, *Augustus und seine Zeit*, 2 vols. (Munich, 1891–1904).

On Virgil I have drawn the most light from the essays of W. Warde Fowler; cf. my essay on "Virgil's Acceptance of Octavian," *American Journal of Philology* (forthcoming). Of the more recent literature on Horace, cf. Stanislaus Pilch, "De Augusti laudibus apud Horatium," *Eos* 29 (1926), 51–67; Friedrich Solmsen, "Horace's First Roman Ode," *American Journal of Philology* 68 (1947), 337–352; *Horaz und die augusteische Kultur* by Walter Wili (Basel, 1948); Tadeusz Zieliński, *Horace et la société romaine du temps d'Auguste* (Paris, 1938).

The political reforms of Augustus are eternally under discussion; the latest major work to my knowledge is that of André Magdelain, *Auctoritas Principis* (Paris, 1947). See my "Perfect Democracy of the Roman Empire," *American Historical Review* 58 (1952), 1–16. Hans Volkmann discusses imperial control of the courts in *Zur Rechtssprechung im Principat des Augustus* (Munich, 1935). The latest life of Maecenas by Armand Fougnies (Brussels, 1947) is slight; J. André, *La Vie et l'oeuvre d'Asinius Pollion* (Paris, 1949) is only moderately better.

The later years of the reign are considered in their chronological aspect by Jacques Schwartz, "Recherches sur les dernières années du regne d'Auguste (4–14)," *Revue de philologie* 3. ser. 19 (1945), 21–90; much more might be done on the lines sketched above in the text. Gaston Boissier's treatment of the exile of Ovid still seems the best; different explanations are listed in Schanz-Hosius, to which may be added Rudolf C. W. Zimmermann, "Die Ursachen von Ovids Verbannung," *Rheinisches Museum* 81 (1932), 263–274. Brooks Otis, "Ovid and the Augustans," *Transactions of the American Philological Association* 69 (1938), 188–229, illuminates Ovid's relations to Augustus.

Freedom of Thought

The most direct and extensive treatment was written over a century ago by Wilhelm Adolf Schmidt, *Geschichte der Denk- und Glaubensfreiheit im ersten Jahrhundert der Kaiserherrschaft und des Christenthums* (Berlin, 1847). His judgments were affected by his Hegelian philosophy, his intense Christianity, his uncritical acceptance of Tacitus, and his reflection of the spirit of 1848; but his analysis was thoughtful. Hans Kloesel, *Libertas* (Diss., Breslau, 1935), and Ch. Wirszubski, *Libertas as a Political Idea at Rome during the Late Republic and Early Principate* (Cambridge, 1950), while considering primarily political liberty, also comment on intellectual aspects; see also the bibliography on Imperial Pagan Literature.

Liberal histories of freedom of thought, as J. B. Bury, *History of the Freedom of Thought* (London, 1913), devote little attention to the Roman Empire, and that little mainly to the effects of Christianity. On two subjects—the historical investigations of censorship and political despotism in the modern world, and the philosophical analysis of the concept of freedom—it is better to give no works than to attempt to choose a few. The nature of ancient philosophical discussion of freedom is suggested by Dom David Armand, *Fatalisme et liberté dans l'antiquité grecque* (Louvain, 1945), a survey of the later influence of Carneades' arguments against Fate; P. Ernst Bismarck, *Die Freiheit des Christen nach Paulus und die Freiheit des Weisen nach der jüngeren Stoa* (Knechtsteden, 1921); and A. J. Festugière, *Liberté et civilisation chez les Grecs* (Paris, 1947).

State Control of Public Expression

Theodor Mommsen, *Römisches Strafrecht* (Leipzig, 1899).

The basic legislation is given in *Acta Divi Augusti* 1 (Rome, 1945); the problems of imperial jurisdiction are well described by S. J. de Laet, "Où en est le problème de la juridiction impériale," *L'Antiquité classique* 14 (1945), 145–163. For its application see Ugo Brasiello, *La Repressione penale in diritto romano* (Naples, 1937); Mary V. Braginton, "Exile under the Roman Emperors," *Classical Journal* 39 (1944), 391–407 [and Ludwig M. Hartmann, *De exilio apud Romanos inde ab initio bellorum civilium usque ad Severi Alexandri principatum* (Berlin, 1887)]; Friedrich Vittinghoff, *Der*

Staatsfeind in der römischen Kaiserzeit: Untersuchungen zur damnatio memoriae (Speyer, 1936).

On statues Helmut Kruse, *Studien zur offiziellen Geltung des Kaiserbildes im römischen Reiche* (Paderborn, 1934), is incomplete; Meriwether Stuart sheds further light in "How Were Imperial Portraits Distributed throughout the Roman Empire?" *American Journal of Archaeology* 2. ser. 43 (1939), 601–617, and in his discussion on the occasions and motives of making portraits in *The Portraiture of Claudius: Preliminary Studies* (Diss., Columbia University, 1938). One example of the many analyses of the political programs displayed in imperial reliefs may be given here (cf. also Imperial Art): A. von Domaszewski, "Die Politische Bedeutung des Traiansbogens in Benevent," *Abhandlungen zur römischen Religion* (Leipzig, 1909), 25–52. The Cyrene edicts of Augustus have been most recently edited by Fernand de Visscher, *Les Édits d'Auguste découverts à Cyrène* (Louvain, 1940); a thorough study of imperial edicts to the provinces on the accession of new rulers would be useful.

State control of education is overstressed by Corrado Barbagallo, *Lo Stato e l'istruzione pubblica nell'Impero Romano* (Catania, 1911), and L. Hahn, "Ueber das Verhältnis von Staat und Schule in der römischen Kaiserzeit," *Philologus* n.f. 30 (1920), 176–191. Rudolf Herzog, "Urkunden zur Hochschulpolitik der römischen Kaiser," *Sitzungsberichte der Berliner Akademie* 1935, 967–1019, is only partly relevant. See also M. della Corte, *Iuventus* (Arpino, 1924); Clarence A. Forbes, *Neoi: A Contribution to the Study of Greek Associations* (Middletown, Conn., 1933); M. I. Rostovtzeff, *Römische Bleitesserae* (*Klio*, Beiheft 3, 1905), 61 ff.; and more generally the fine work of Henri Irénée Marrou, *Histoire de l'éducation dans l'antiquité* (2d ed.; Paris, 1950).

The influence of libraries on the preservation of literature is overstressed by Evelyn H. Clift, *Latin Pseudepigrapha: A Study in Literary Attributions* (Baltimore, 1945); the best collection of evidence on libraries remains that of C. E. Boyd, *Public Libraries and Literary Culture in Ancient Rome* (Chicago, 1915). The destruction of books is summarized by Clarence A. Forbes, "Books for the Burning," *Transactions of the American Philological Association* 67 (1936), 114–125.

Frederick H. Cramer has collected the evidence for "Expulsion of Astrologers from Ancient Rome," *Classica et Mediaevalia* 12 (1951), 9–50; see Clyde Pharr, "The Interdiction of Magic in Roman Law," *Transactions of the American Philological Association* 63 (1932), 269–295; and Jules Maurice, "La Terreur de la magie au IVe siècle," *Revue historique de droit français et étranger* 4. ser. 6 (1927), 108–120.

The basic articles on the imperial police are Otto Hirschfeld's "Die Sicherheitspolizei im römischen Kaiserreich," *Sitzungsberichte der Berliner*

Akademie 1891, 845–877; and "Die agentes in rebus," *ibid.* 1893, 421–441. See also P. K. Baillie Reynolds, "The Troops Quartered in the Castra Peregrinorum," *Journal of Roman Studies* 13 (1923), 168–189; and the rambling article by G. Lopuszanski, "La Police romaine et les chrétiens," *L'Antiquité classique* 20 (1951), 5–46.

Roman Opposition to the Emperors

Gaston Boissier, *L'Opposition sous les Césars* (3d ed.; Paris, 1892) [first century only].

Mary Roberta Irwin, "Republicanism and Freedom of Speech in Rome in the First Century" (Diss., Cornell University, 1945, unpublished).

Detailed studies of the individual emperors and of the opposition to each may be located through the *Cambridge Ancient History*. On Tiberius in particular, see G. M. Columba, "Il Processo di Cremuzio Cordo," *Atene e Roma* 4 (1901), cols. 361–382; Robert S. Rogers, *Criminal Trials and Criminal Legislation under Tiberius* (Middletown, Conn., 1935); and the studies of F. B. Marsh and E. Ciaceri.

On literary opposition, see Imperial Pagan Literature, and my "The Roman Emperor and the King of Ceylon," *Classical Philology* (forthcoming). The place of rumor in Tacitus is most recently analyzed by Leonardo Ferrero, "La Voce pubblica nel proemio degli Annali di Tacito," *Rivista di filologia* n.s. 24 (1946), 50–86. It would be useful to have a thorough analysis of the views which succeeding ages of the Empire held of the earlier history of the Republic and the Empire; for this "internal history" throws light on the development of the Empire itself.

Provinces and Cities

F. F. Abbott and A. C. Johnson, *Municipal Administration in the Roman Empire* (Princeton, 1926) [with sources].

George H. Stevenson, *Roman Provincial Administration till the Age of the Antonines* (New York, 1939).

Also valuable are the general history by M. I. Rostovtzeff (with bibliography of tremendous scope); chapters in the *Cambridge Ancient History,* vol. 11; Theodor Mommsen, *The Provinces of the Roman Empire,* 2 vols. (New York, 1887); and a host of other works drawing on the epigraphic and archeological investigations of the past 150 years. Recent bibliographies are given in *Guida allo studio della civiltà romana antica* 1, ed. Vincenzo Ussani (Naples, 1952), 329, 373–377.

For the East, see especially David Magie, *Roman Rule in Asia Minor to the End of the Third Century after Christ,* 2 vols. (Princeton, 1950); A. H. M. Jones, *The Cities of the Eastern Roman Provinces* (Oxford, 1937) and *The*

Greek City from Alexander to Justinian (Oxford, 1940); the last work of Sir William M. Ramsay, *The Social Basis of Roman Power in Asia Minor* (Aberdeen, 1941), was left woefully incomplete.

Local militia forces were discussed by Theodor Mommsen, "Die römischen Provinzialmilizien," *Gesammelte Schriften* 6 (Berlin, 1910), 145–155; and by René Cagnat, *De municipalibus et provincialibus militiis in impero Romano* (Paris, 1880).

Provincial Opposition to the Emperors

Harald Fuchs, *Der geistige Widerstand gegen Rom in der antiken Welt* (Berlin, 1938).

The Sibylline oracles are best edited by Johannes Geffcken (Leipzig, 1902); see also his *Komposition und Entstehungszeit der Oracula Sibyllina* (Leipzig, 1902). The most recent example of their significance is given by A. T. Olmstead, "The Mid-Third Century of the Christian Era," *Classical Philology* 37 (1942), 241–262, 398–420. The Oriental strain is given in Joseph Bidez and Franz Cumont, *Les Mages hellénisés: Zoroastre, Ostanès et Hystaspe d'après la tradition grecque*, 2 vols. (Paris, 1938). See also Franz Cumont, "La Fin du monde selon les mages occidentaux," *Revue de l'histoire des religions* 103 (1931), 29–96; Eva Matthews Sanford, "Contrasting Views of the Roman Empire," *American Journal of Philology* 58 (1937), 436–456; J. W. Swain, "The Theory of the Four Monarchies: Opposition History under the Roman Empire," *Classical Philology* 35 (1940), 1–21; C. Wachsmuth, "Timagenes und Trogus," *Rheinisches Museum* n.f. 46 (1891), 464–479; H. Windisch, "Die Orakel des Hystaspes," *Verhandelingen der K. Akademie van Wetenschappen* n.s. 28.3 (Amsterdam, 1929). I omit studies of the ideal of Rome apart from the fascinating collection of ancient praises of Rome ordered on the basis of ancient rhetorical theory by Wilhelm Gernentz, *Laudes Romae* (Rostock, 1918); on Jewish and Christian opposition, see below.

Professional Hellenism deserves a fuller study than Ludwig Hahn's *Rom und Romanismus im griechisch-römischen Osten* (Leipzig, 1906). Roman contempt of the Greeks and Orientals was collected by Eduard Wölfflin, "Zur Psychologie der Völker des Alterthums," *Archiv für lateinische Lexikographie und Grammatik* 7 (1892), 133–146, 333–342; Simon Davis, *Race Relations in Ancient Egypt* (New York, 1952), does not go far. We need more surveys of actual cultural interrelationships in the Early Empire on the line of A. Dain, "Les Rapports gréco-latines," *Mémorial des études latines* (Paris, 1943), 149–161; Lloyd W. Daly, "Roman Study Abroad," *American Journal of Philology* 71 (1950), 40–58; and Merle M. Odgers, "Quintilian's Use of Earlier Literature," *Classical Philology* 28 (1933), 182–188.

The Egyptian attitude is discussed in the first chapter of J. G. Winter's *Life and Letters in the Papyri* (Ann Arbor, 1933). The Acta of the Alexandrian Martyrs desperately need re-editing, which has been promised by one scholar; in the meantime one must turn to many places, including H. I. Bell, "A New Fragment of the Acta Isidori," *Archiv für Papyrusforschung* 10 (1932), 5–16; Anton von Premerstein, "Alexandrinische und Jüdaische Gesandte vor Kaiser Hadrian," *Hermes* 57 (1922), 266–316; "Zu den sogenannten Alexandrinischen Märtyrerakten," *Philologus,* Suppl. 16.2 (1923); "Das Datum des Prozesses des Isidoros in den sogenannten heidnischen Märtyrerakten," *Hermes* 67 (1932), 174–196; "Alexandrinische Geronten vor Kaiser Gaius: Ein neues Bruchstück der sogenannten Alexandrinischen Märtyrer-Akten," *Mitteilungen aus der Papyrus-sammlung der Giessener Universitätsbibliothek* 5 (1936); C. H. Roberts, "Titus and Alexandria: A New Document," *Journal of Roman Studies* 39 (1949), 79–80; Woldemar Graf Uxkull-Gyllenband, "Ein neues Bruchstück aus den sogenannten heidnischen Märtyrerakten," *Sitzungsberichte der Berliner Akademie* 1930, 664–679; Wilhelm Weber, "Eine Gerichtsverhandlung vor Kaiser Traian," *Hermes* 50 (1915), 47–92; C. B. Welles, "A Yale Fragment of the Acts of Appian," *Transactions of the American Philological Association* 67 (1936), 7–23; Ulrich Wilcken, "Zum Alexandrinischen Antisemitismus," *Abhandlungen der K. Sächsischen Gesellschaft der Wissenschaften,* phil.-hist. Kl. 27 (1909), 783–837. The major papyri are P. Ox. 33, 1089, 1242, 2177, 2264; BGU 341, 511, 588; P. Cairo 10448; P. Par. 68; P. Lond. I, p. 227 ff. P. Yale Inv. 1536; P. Fay. 217; P. Berlin 8877; P. Erlangen 5; perhaps P. Ox. 471. On Roman parallels, see F. A. Marx, "Tacitus und die Literatur des exitus illustrium virorum," *Philologus* 92 (1937), 83–103.

Imperial Coinage

Harold Mattingly *et al., Coins of the Roman Empire in the British Museum* (London, 1923–).

Harold Mattingly, E. A. Sydenham, *et al., The Roman Imperial Coinage* (Paris, 1923–).

Along with these fundamental resurveys, extensive interpretation has been achieved by Michael Grant in *From Imperium to Auctoritas: A Historical Study of Aes Coinage in the Roman Empire, 49 B.C.–A.D. 14* (Cambridge, 1946), *Roman Anniversary Issues* (Cambridge, 1950), and other speculative studies; by P. L. Strack, *Untersuchungen zur römischen Reichsprägung des zweiten Jahrhunderts,* 3 vols. (Stuttgart, 1931–1937); by C. H. V. Sutherland, *Coinage in Roman Imperial Policy, 31 B.C.–A.D. 68* (London, 1951); and by others. The control of mint policy is considered by Mattingly in his prefaces to the *British Museum Catalogues* and in *Cambridge Ancient History* 12, 713–720; and also by C. H. V. Sutherland, "The Personality of the Mints under the Julio-Claudian Emperors," *American Journal of Philology* 68 (1947), 47–63.

On coin erasures see Robert Mowat, "Martelage et Abrasion des monnaies sous l'Empire romain," *Revue numismatique* 1901, 443–471; 1902, 286–290, 464–467; Rudolf Münsterberg, "Damnatio memoriae," *Monatsblatt der numismatischen Gesellschaft in Wien* 11 (1918), 32–37; K. Regling, "Zur griechischen Münzkunde III," *Zeitschrift für Numismatik* 24 (1909), 129–144.

On Alexandrian coins Joseph Vogt, *Die Alexandrinischen Münzen* (Stuttgart, 1924), and J. G. Milne, *Catalogue of Alexandrian Coins in the Ashmolean Museum* (Oxford, 1933), are complementary. *Roman Medallions* are analyzed by J. M. C. Toynbee (New York, 1944); see also Francesco Gnecchi, *I medaglioni romani descritti ed illustrati*, 4 vols. (Milan, 1912).

Imperial Pagan Literature

Alfred and Maurice Croiset, *Histoire de la littérature grecque,* vol. 5 (Paris, 1928; corrected reprint of 2d ed.).

Martin Schanz, Carl Hosius, Gustav Krüger, *Geschichte der römischen Literatur bis zum Gesetzgebungswerk des Kaisers Justinian,* parts 1–4[1] (Munich, 1914–1935; 2d–4th eds.).

Augusto Rostagni, *Storia della letteratura latina II: L'Impero* (Turin, 1952).

The Loeb Library and the Collection des Universités de France (Budé) have serviceable translations of major pagan authors. A useful guide to texts, translations, and modern commentaries is that of Jules van Ooteghem, *Bibliotheca graeca et latina à l'usage des professeurs des humanités gréco-latines* (2d ed.; Namur, 1946); or solely on Latin, Nicolae I. Herescu, *Bibliographie de la littérature latine* (Paris, 1943).

The numerous investigations of the relations of individual authors to the emperors are noted by Henry Bardon, *Les Empereurs et les lettres latines d'Auguste à Hadrien* (Paris, 1940), and more sketchily by Claude-Odon Reure, *De scriptorum ac litteratorum hominum cum romanis imperatoribus inimicitiis* (Paris, 1891). The writings of the Julio-Claudian rulers themselves are discussed thoroughly by Enrica Malcovati, "Cultura e letteratura nella 'Domus Augusta,' " *Annali della Facoltà di Lettere, Filosophia e Magistero della R. Università di Cagliari* 11 (1941), 1–131. The *Greater Roman Historians* are the subject of the Sather Lectures by M. L. W. Laistner (Berkeley, 1947); cf. Hermann Peter, *Die geschichtliche Literatur über die römische Kaiserzeit bis Theodosius I und ihre Quellen,* 2 vols. (Leipzig, 1897).

Recent works on rhetoric include S. F. Bonner, *Roman Declamation in the Late Republic and Early Empire* (Liverpool, 1949); F. Lanfranchi, *Il Diritto nei retori romani* (Milan, 1938); E. P. Parks, *The Roman Rhetorical Schools as a Preparation for the Courts under the Early Empire* (Baltimore, 1945).

Imperial Philosophy

E. V. Arnold, *Roman Stoicism* (Cambridge, 1911).

D. R. Dudley, *History of Cynicism* (London, 1937).

Friedrich Ueberweg, *Grundriss der Geschichte der Philosophie I: Die Philosophie des Altertums,* ed. Karl Praechter (12th ed.; Berlin, 1926).

On the political attitudes of the philosophers, see for Musonius Rufus, Cora E. Lutz, "Musonius Rufus 'The Roman Socrates,'" *Yale Classical Studies* 10 (1947), 3–147. For Epictetus, my "Epictetus and the Tyrant," *Classical Philology* 44 (1949), 20–29. For Dio Chrysostom, Hans von Arnim, *Leben und Werke des Dio von Prusa* (Berlin, 1898); L. Lemarchand, *Dion de Pruse: Les oeuvres d'avant l'exil* (Paris, 1926); Vlad. Valkenberg, "La Théorie monarchique de Dion Chrysostome," *Revue des études grecques* 40 (1927), 142–162. For Seneca, Ivar A. Heikel's brief *Senecas Character und politische Thätigkeit aus seinen Schriften beleuchtet* (Helsingfors, 1886) and various essays by William H. Alexander such as "Julius Caesar in the Pages of Seneca the Philosopher," *Transactions of the Royal Society of Canada* 3. ser. 35 (1941), 15–28, and "Footnotes for a Literary Portrait of Augustus," *ibid.* 3. ser. 43 (1949), 13–34.

Seneca's political and philosophical position deserves far more attention than it has received. See generally Paul Faider, *Études sur Sénèque* (Ghent, 1921), and Concetto Marchesi, *Seneca* (Messina, 1920). The thorny question of the dates of his works is best handled by Karl Münscher, "Senecas Werke," *Philologus,* Suppl. 16.1 (1922). The Stoic base of his tragedies is explored anew by Norman H. Pratt, Jr., "The Stoic Base of Senecan Drama," *Transactions of the American Philological Association* 79 (1948), 1–11. On the *Octavia,* see R. Helm, "Die Praetexta 'Octavia,'" *Sitzungsberichte der Berliner Akademie* 1934, 283–347, with whose views I disagree; Léon Herrmann, *Octavie, tragédie prétexte* (Paris, 1924), with bibliography of earlier studies; Berthe Marti, "The *Fabulae Praetextae* and Seneca's *Octavia,*" *Transactions of the American Philological Association* 80 (1949), 427–428.

On Stoicism see also Eleuterio Elorduy, "Die Sozialphilosophie der Stoa," *Philologus,* Suppl. 28.3 (1936); Max Pohlenz, *Die Stoa: Geschichte einer geistigen Bewegung,* 2 vols. (Göttingen, 1948–1949); Margaret E. Reesor, *The Political Theory of the Old and Middle Stoa* (New York, 1951); and the bibliography on Roman Opposition.

Louis Delatte, *Les Traités de la royauté d'Ecphante, Diotogène et Sthénidas* (Liège-Paris, 1942), dates these Neopythagorean works to the second century after Christ [accepted by E. R. Goodenough, who translated the extant fragments in *Yale Classical Studies* 1 (1928)]. We badly need a sensitive survey of Neopythagorean thought to integrate the fringe studies made of its influence; see Jérôme Carcopino, *La Basilique pythagoricienne de la porte Majeure* (Paris, 1927), though the connection he asserts between the basilica and Neopythagoreanism is far from proved [cf. Jean Hubaux, "Une Epode d'Ovide," *Serta Leodensia* (Liège, 1930), 187–245]; Lucien Legrand, *Publius Nigidius Figulus: Philosophe néo-pythagoricien orphique* (Paris, 1931); Georges Méautis, *Recherches sur le pythagorisme* (Neuchâtel, 1922); A. J. Festugière, "Sur une nouvelle édition du 'de vita pythagorica' de Jamblique," *Revue des études grecques* 50 (1937), 470–494.

William R. Inge, *The Philosophy of Plotinus*, 2 vols. (3d ed.; London, 1948), and Philippus V. Pistorius, *Plotinus and Neoplatonism: An Introductory Study* (Cambridge, 1952), will lead the student into the work of Plotinus; but a full survey of the development of ancient philosophy to this point is still much to be desired. See for part of the story Willy Theiler, *Die Vorbereitung des Neuplatonismus*, in *Problemata* (Berlin, 1930).

Imperial Paganism

Franz Altheim, *A History of Roman Religion* (New York, 1938).
Martin P. Nilsson, *Geschichte der griechischen Religion 2: Die hellenistische und römische Zeit* (Munich, 1950).
Nicola Turchi, *La Religione di Roma antica* (Bologna, 1939).

Our understanding of Roman religion is still in flux, especially in its later developments. In addition to the above, Johannes Geffcken, *Der Ausgang der griechisch-römischen Heidentums* (2d ed. with supplement; Heidelberg, 1929), and A. J. Festugière, *La Révélation d'Hermès Trismégiste*, 2 vols. to date (Paris, 1944–1949), point the way; on solar syncretism, see Franz Cumont, "La Théologie solaire du paganisme romaine," *Mémoires présentés par divers savants à l'Académie des Inscriptions et Belles-Lettres* 12.2 (1909), 447–479, and M. P. Nilsson, "Sonnenkalendar und Sonnenreligion," *Archiv für Religionswissenschaft* 30 (1933), 141–173. Of the overly great literature on the Oriental cults, see Franz Cumont, *Les Religions orientales dans le paganisme romain* (3d ed.; Paris, 1928), and J. F. Toutain, *Les Cultes païens dans l'empire romain*, 3 vols. (Paris, 1908–1920). Paul Friedländer, *Documents of Dying Paganism: Textiles of Late Antiquity in Washington, New York, and Leningrad* (Berkeley, 1945), furnishes an interesting study of pagan survivals.

A simply written but profoundly thought survey of the main currents of ancient religion, which is curiously overlooked nowadays, is that of A. B. Drachmann, *Atheism in Pagan Antiquity* (London, 1922). Another thoughtful book is A. D. Nock's *Conversion: The Old and the New in Religion from Alexander the Great to Augustine of Hippo* (London, 1933).

Deification is widely treated. Lily Ross Taylor, *The Deification of the Roman Emperor* (Middletown, Conn., 1931), gives the groundwork, which is extended into later periods by various authors, noted in Julien Tondriau's "Bibliographie du culte des souverains hellénistes et romains," *Bulletin Association Guillaume Budé*, n.s. 5 (1948), 106–125. I regret that I have not seen D. M. Pippidi, *Recherches sur le culte impérial* (Paris, 1939).

George La Piana made a penetrating study on toleration toward other sects than Jews and Christians, "Foreign Groups in Rome during the First Centuries of the Empire," *Harvard Theological Review* 20 (1927), 183–403. On the Druids see Norman J. DeWitt, "The Druids and Romanization," *Transactions of the American Philological Association* 69 (1938), 319–332; and Hugh Last, "Rome and the Druids: A Note," *Journal of Roman Studies* 39 (1949), 1–5. Note also Allan S. Hoey, "Official Policy towards Oriental Cults in the Roman Army," *Transactions of the American Philological Association* 70 (1939), 456–481; Gerhard Plaumann, "Der Idioslogos," *Abhandlungen der preussischen Akademie der Wissenschaften* 1918, no. 17, section 5.

See also Franz J. Boll and Carl Bezold, *Sternglaube und Sterndeutung: Die Geschichte und das Wesen der Astrologie* (4th ed.; Leipzig, 1931); the bibliography of K. Preisendanz, "Die griechischen und lateinischen Zaubertafeln," *Archiv für Papyrusforschung* 9 (1930), 119–154; Lynn Thorndike, *A History of Magic and Experimental Science during the First Thirteen Centuries of Our Era* 1 (New York, 1923); and the works on magic listed under State Control.

Imperial Art

> Pericle Ducati, *L'Arte in Roma dalle origini al sec. VIII* (Bologna, 1939) [excellent plates].

An appendix in this work (with bibliography) superbly illuminates the development of modern views on Roman art. The pattern of the first two centuries of the Empire is the most clearly visualized, as recently in Per Gustav Hamberg, *Studies in Roman Imperial Art, with Special Reference to the State Reliefs of the Second Century* (Copenhagen, 1945); Gerhard Rodenwaldt, *Kunst um Augustus* (2d ed.; Berlin, 1943); Karl Schefold, *Orient, Hellas und Rom in der archäologischen Forschung seit 1939* (Bern, 1949).

Roman provincial art is beginning to receive detailed surveys province by province, especially in Spain, Gaul, the Rhine, Austria, and the Danube. Arnold Schober, "Zur Entstehung und Bedeutung der provinzialrömischen Kunst," *Jahreshefte des Österreichischen Archäologischen Institutes in Wien* 26 (1930), 9–52, gives a partial bibliography; of great value is the bibliographical appendix to the *Catalogo della Mostra Augustea della Romanità* (Rome, 1939).

Late Roman art is well illustrated in Richard Delbrueck, *Antike Porphyrwerke* (Berlin, 1932), and *Spätantike Kaiserporträts von Constantinus Magnus bis zum Ende des Westreichs* (Berlin, 1933). The fundamental work on its development in my judgment is that of Alois Riegl, *Spätrömische Kunstin-*

dustrie (Vienna, 1927; resetting of 1901 original). Somewhat more sober are the excellent survey by Guido Kaschnitz-Weinberg, "Spätrömische Porträts," *Die Antike* 2 (1926), 36–60; C. R. Morey, *The Mosaics of Antioch* (New York, 1938), with Glanville Downey, "Personifications of Abstract Ideas in the Antioch Mosaics," *Transactions of the American Philological Association* 69 (1938), 349–363; and essays by Rodenwaldt, as "Zur Kunstgeschichte der Jahre 220 bis 270," *Jahrbuch des Deutschen Archäologischen Instituts* 51 (1936), 82–113 [cf. Gervase Mathew, "The Character of the Gallienic Renaissance," *Journal of Roman Studies* 33 (1943), 65–70].

More radical are several works by H. P. L'Orange, *Studien zur Geschichte des spätantiken Porträts* (Oslo, 1933); *Der spätantike Bildschmuck des Konstantinsbogens,* with A. von Gerkan, 2 vols. (Berlin, 1939); *Apotheosis in Ancient Portraiture* (Oslo, 1947). The last is criticized by J. M. C. Toynbee, "Ruler-Apotheosis in Ancient Rome," *Numismatic Chronicle* 6. ser. 7 (1947), 126–149. Miss Toynbee in *The Hadrianic School: A Chapter in the History of Greek Art* (Cambridge, 1934) and in numerous reviews since sticks firmly to her concept of "Greek art in the Imperial phase"; see also G. M. A. Richter, "Who Made Roman Portrait Statues—Greeks or Romans?" *Proceedings of the American Philosophical Society* 95.2 (1951), 184–191.

Hans Lietzmann, "Das Problem der Spätantike," *Sitzungsberichte der Berliner Akademie* 1927, 343–358, reiterates the emphasis on Oriental influence raised by Stryzgowski; this influence is seen at Lepcis by, e.g., J. B. Ward Perkins, "Severan Art and Architecture at Lepcis Magna," *Journal of Roman Studies* 38 (1948), 59–80.

The latest treatment from an architectural point of view is Emerson H. Swift's *Roman Sources of Christian Art* (New York, 1951), with a good bibliography; his views are to be compared with J. B. Ward Perkins' lecture on *The Italian Element in Late Roman and Early Christian Architecture* (Oxford, 1949) and with E. B. Smith, *The Dome: A Study in the History of Ideas* (Princeton, 1950).

A glance ahead is given in Roger Hinks, *Carolingian Art* (London, 1935), and in C. R. Morey, *Medieval Art* (New York, 1942), and *Early Christian Art: An Outline of the Evolution of Style and Iconography in Sculpture and Painting from Antiquity to the Eighth Century* (Princeton, 1942).

Social History of the Roman Empire

Samuel Dill, *Roman Society from Nero to Marcus Aurelius* (2d ed.; (London, 1905).

Ludwig Friedländer, *Darstellungen aus der Sittengeschichte Roms in der Zeit von Augustus bis zum Ausgang der Antonine,* 3 vols. (9th–10th ed.; Leipzig, 1921–1923).

The most recent and thorough treatment of Roman gilds is that by Francesco M. de Robertis, *Il Diritto associativo romano dai collegi della repubblica alle corporazioni del Basso Impero* (Bari, 1938); their legal position is also discussed by P. W. Duff, *Personality in Roman Private Law* (Cambridge, 1938).

Robert von Pöhlmann, *Die Geschichte der sozialen Frage und des Sozialismus in der antiken Welt*, 2 vols. (3d ed.; Munich, 1925), does not deal adequately with the unrest of the Empire. One aspect of social trouble is surveyed by W. H. Buckler, "Labor Disputes in the Province of Asia," *Anatolian Studies presented to Sir William M. Ramsay* (Manchester, 1923), 27–50; considerable attention to the subject is indicated by Russian studies (in the *Vestnik Drevnei Istorii* and separately).

The common man remains too often ignored. The best study is Harold Mattingly's delightful *The Man in the Roman Street* (New York, 1947); a general sketch of the temporal and spiritual frame of life at a crucial point is that by A. J. Festugière and Pierre Fabre, *Le Monde gréco-romain au temps de Notre-Seigneur*, 2 vols. (Paris, 1935). The imperial escalator may be traced in the composition of the Senate, on which the latest works are Guido Barbieri, *L'Albo senatorio da Settimio Severo a Carino (193–285)* (Rome, 1952); and S. J. de Laet, *De Samenstelling van den romeinschen Senaat gedurende de eerste eeuw van het principaat* (Antwerp, 1941).

Pagan humanitarianism receives frequent incidental treatment; see especially H. Pétré, " 'Misericordia.' Histoire du mot et de l'idée du paganisme au christianisme," *Revue des études latines* 12 (1934), 376–389. Its development in law is touched on by Fritz Pringsheim, "The Legal Policy and Reforms of Hadrian," *Journal of Roman Studies* 24 (1934), 141–153. The meaning of *humanitas* in Cicero and later writers has often been reviewed, as by O. E. Nybakken, "Humanitas Romana," *Transactions of the American Philological Association* 70 (1939), 396–413. Hendrik Bolkestein, *Wohltätigkeit und Armenpflege im vorchristlichen Altertum: Ein Beitrag zum Problem "Moral und Gesellschaft"* (Utrecht, 1939), unfortunately does not consider the Empire [cf. Martin R. P. McGuire, "Epigraphical Evidence for Social Charity in the Roman West," *American Journal of Philology* 67 (1946), 129–149]. The evidence on endowments was collected by Bernhard Laum, *Stiftungen in der griechischen und römischen Antike: Ein Beitrag zur antiken Kulturgeschichte*, 2 vols. (Leipzig, 1914). See also Johannes Stelzenberger, *Die Beziehungen der frühchristlichen Sittenlehre zur Ethik der Stoa* (Munich, 1933).

On man's relation to nature see Alfred Biese, *Die Entwicklung des Naturgefühls bei den Griechen und Römern* (Kiel, 1882–1884), Henry R. Fairclough, *Love of Nature among the Greeks and Romans* (London, 1930); Sir Archibald Geikie's discursive *The Love of Nature among the Romans* (London, 1912). If I am not mistaken, more remains to be done in this area along the lines of Albin Lesky, *Thalatta: Der Weg der Griechen zum Meer* (Vienna,

1947), and Eugène de Saint-Denis, *Le Rôle de la mer dans la poésie latine* (Paris, 1935).

Individualism

Georg Misch, *A History of Autobiography in Antiquity*, 2 vols. (Cambridge, Mass., 1951).

Fritz Schulz, *Principles of Roman Law* (Oxford, 1936).

On individual portraiture, see the bibliography on Imperial Art and Jean Babelon, *Le Portrait dans l'antiquité d'après les monnaies* (Paris, 1942). Another aspect is illuminated by E. C. Evans, "Roman Descriptions of Personal Appearance in History and Biography," *Harvard Studies in Classical Philology* 46 (1935), 43–84; "The Study of Physiognomy in the Second Century A.D.," *Transactions of the American Philological Association* 72 (1941), 96–108; "A Stoic Aspect of Senecan Drama; Portraiture," *ibid.* 81 (1950), 169–184.

Ideas of afterlife are interestingly treated by Franz Cumont in *Recherches sur le symbolisme funéraire des Romains* (Paris, 1942), which beautifully parallels artistic and philosophic concepts; and the general survey of his posthumous *Lux Perpetua* (Paris, 1949). Incidental aspects are discussed by Angelo Brelich, *Aspetti della morte nelle iscrizioni sepolcrali dell'Impero Romano* (Budapest, 1937); the very thorough article by Rudolf Hirzel, "Der Selbstmord," *Archiv für Religionswissenschaft* 11 (1908), 75–104, 243–284, 417–476; A. D. Nock, "Cremation and Burial in the Roman Empire," *Harvard Theological Review* 25 (1932), 321–359 [cf. Karl Lehmann-Hartleben and the late Erling C. Olsen, *Dionysiac Sarcophagi in Baltimore* (Baltimore, 1942)]; Tadeusz Zieliński, "La Guerre à l'outretombe chez les Hébreux, les Grecs et les Romains," *Mélanges Bidez* (Brussels, 1934), 1021–1042.

Judaism

Jean Juster, *Les Juifs dans l'Empire romain: Leur condition juridique, économique et sociale*, 2 vols. (Paris, 1914).

George F. Moore, *Judaism in the First Centuries of the Christian Era: The Age of the Tannaim*, 3 vols. (Cambridge, Mass., 1927–1930).

For the position of the Jews see H. Idris Bell, *Jews and Christians in Egypt* (London, 1924), and *Juden und Griechen im römischen Alexandreia: Eine historische Skizze des alexandrinischen Antisemitismus* (Leipzig, 1927); the introduction to Herbert Box, *Philonis Alexandrini in Flaccum* (Oxford, 1939); and Simeon L. Guterman, *Religious Toleration and Persecution in Ancient Rome* (London, 1951). Moses Hadas gives an interesting collection of "Roman Allusions in Rabbinic Literature," *Philological Quarterly* 8 (1929), 369–

387 [I have not seen Nathan Wasser, *Die Stellung der Juden gegenüber den Römern nach der rabbinischen Literatur* (Diss. Zürich, 1933)].

Christianity

Fernand Cabrol, Henri Leclercq, Henri Irénée Marrou, *Dictionnaire d'archéologie chrétienne et de liturgie* (Paris, 1907–1952).

A. Fliché and V. Martin, *Histoire de l'Eglise depuis les origines jusqu'à nos jours:* J. Lebreton and J. Zeiller, *L'Eglise primitive* (Paris, 1935) and *De la fin du 2ᵉ siècle à la paix constantinienne* (1935); J. R. Palanque, G. Bardy, P. de Labriolle, *De la paix constantinienne à la mort du Theodose* (1936).

Adolf von Harnack, *Die Mission und Ausbreitung des Christentums in den ersten drei Jahrhunderten*, 2 vols. (4th ed.; Leipzig, 1924).

P. de Labriolle, *Histoire de la littérature latine chrétienne*, 2 vols. (3d ed.; Paris, 1947).

Hans Lietzmann, *History of the Early Church: The Beginnings of the Christian Church* (New York, 1937); *The Founding of the Church Universal* (1938); *The Era of the Church Fathers* (1952).

Aimé Puech, *Histoire de la littérature grecque chrétienne jusqu'à la fin du IVᵉ siècle*, 3 vols. (Paris, 1928–1930).

The above works may serve as an introduction to the tremendous mass of Church history. For the texts of Latin fathers see also Eligius Dekkers, ed., *Clavis Patrum Latinorum* (Bruges, 1951).

The intellectual relations of the Church and pagan society are suggested by Charles N. Cochrane, *Christianity and Classical Culture: A Study of Thought and Action from Augustus to Augustine* (rev. ed.; New York, 1944); Gerard L. Ellspermann, *The Attitude of the Early Christian Writers toward Pagan Literature and Learning* (Washington, 1949); M. L. W. Laistner, *Christianity and Pagan Culture in the Later Roman Empire* (Ithaca, 1951). A. Bouché-Lecercq, *L'Intolérance religieuse et la politique* (Paris, 1911), is a dated tract. Against Tertullian [Charles Guignebert, *Tertullien: Étude sur ses sentiments à l'égard de l'Empire et de la société civile* (Paris, 1901)] and Firmicus Maternus [Gilbert Heuten, trans., *De errore profanarum religionum* (Brussels, 1938)] place Basil's famous work, recently edited by Fernand Boulenger, *Aux jeunes gens sur la manière de tirer profit des lettres helléniques* (Paris, 1935). On Augustine in particular see first Henri Irénée Marrou, *Saint Augustin et la fin de la culture antique* (Paris, 1938) and his frank but just *Retractatio* (Paris, 1949); also Gustave Combès, *Saint Augustin et la culture classique* (Paris, 1927).

Pierre de Labriolle gives a general survey of *La Réaction païenne: Étude sur la polémique antichrétienne du Iᵉʳ siècle au VIᵉ siècle* (Paris, 1934). See also for the most recent edition of Celsus, Robert Bader, *Der Alethes Logos des Kelsus* (Stuttgart, 1940); and for Porphyry, Joseph Bidez, *Vie de Porphyre* (Ghent, 1913), and Amos B. Hulen, *Porphyry's Work against the Christians: An Interpretation* (*Yale Studies in Religion* 1, 1933).

The literature on the persecutions is highly polemical. Its major works, including Mommsen's article (see Roman Republic, above), may be gathered from Henri Grégoire, *Les Persecutions dans l'empire romain* (Brussels, 1951), itself highly argumentative; and the bibliographies in the *Cambridge Ancient History*. See also Giovanni Costa, *Religione e politica nell'impero Romano* (Turin, 1923). E. C. E. Owen, *Some Authentic Acts of the Early Martyrs* (Oxford, 1927), is a simple introduction in English dress.

The Third Century and Late Empire

Cambridge Ancient History, vol. 12 (Cambridge, 1939).

Maurice Besnier, *L'Empire romain de l'avénement des Sévères au concile de Nicée* (Paris, 1937), and André Piganiol, *L'Empire chrétien, 325–395* (Paris, 1947).

Ferdinand Lot, *La Fin du monde antique et le début du Moyen Age* (Paris, 1927).

Ernst Stein, *Geschichte des spätrömischen Reiches I: Vom römischen zum byzantinischen Staate, 284–476 n. Chr.* (Vienna, 1928).

On Diocletian, see William Seston, *Dioclétien et la tétrarchie* 1 (Paris, 1946); of the spate of recent works on Constantine, I adhere most closely to Norman H. Baynes, *Constantine the Great and the Christian Church* (London, 1931). See also Andreas Alföldi, *The Conversion of Constantine and Pagan Rome* (Oxford, 1948), and A. H. M. Jones, *Constantine and the Conversion of Europe* (London, 1948).

Alföldi has explored intellectual conflicts at Rome in a number of detailed but somewhat overly subtle studies, the last of which are *Die Kontorniaten: Ein verkanntes Propagandamittel der stadtrömischen heidnischen Aristokratie in ihrem Kampfe gegen das christliche Kaisertum*, 2 vols. (Budapest, 1943), and *A Conflict of Ideas in the Late Roman Empire: The Clash between the Senate and Valentinian I* (Oxford, 1952). See also John A. McGeachy, Jr., *Quintus Aurelius Symmachus and the Senatorial Aristocracy of the West* (Diss. Chicago, 1942). The history of Rome itself in the fourth century deserves a fully rounded study.

One of the best products of the gentle, sympathetic pen of Gaston Boissier was his *La Fin du paganisme: Étude sur les dernières luttes religieuses en Occident au quatrième siècle*, 2 vols. (5th ed.; Paris, 1907); on Julian, see Joseph Bidez, *La Vie de l'empereur Julien* (Paris, 1930; German translation, 1940).

For the East see the *Pro templis* of Libanius, translated by René van Loy, *Byzantion* 8 (1933), 7–39, 389–404; Vlad. Valkenberg, "Discours politiques de Thémistius dans leur rapport avec l'antiquité," *ibid.* 1 (1924), 557–580; Roger A. Pack, *Studies in Libanius and Antiochene Society under Theodosius* (Diss. University of Michigan, 1934). The unrest of the cities is recently illuminated in one aspect by Robert Browning, "The Riot of A.D. 387 in Antioch: The Role of the Theatrical Claques in the Later Empire," *Journal of Roman Studies* 42 (1952), 13–20.

For the literature of the period, apart from the general studies (see Imperial Pagan Literature, and Christianity), see the brief survey by E. Lommatzsch, "Litterarische Bewegungen in Rom im vierten und fünften Jahrhundert n. Chr.," *Zeitschrift für vergleichende Literaturgeschichte* n.f. 15 (1904), 177–192; the sometimes thin *Life and Letters in the Fourth Century* of T. R. Glover (Cambridge, 1901); and, though somewhat later, the works of Pierre Courcelle, *Histoire littéraire des grandes invasions germaniques* (Paris, 1948) and *Les Lettres grecques en Occident de Macrobe à Cassiodore* (Paris, 1943). E. A. Thompson gives a long-needed analysis of *The Historical Work of Ammianus Marcellinus* (Cambridge, 1947); see also his *Roman Reformer and Inventor* (Oxford, 1952); Aurelius Victor still remains worthy of consideration. For the art of the era see Imperial Art.

The problem of the decline and fall of the Empire is sketched by M. I. Rostovtzeff in the closing pages of his *Social and Economic History of the Roman Empire* (Oxford, 1926) and by Norman H. Baynes, "The Decline of the Roman Power in Western Europe: Some Modern Explanations," *Journal of Roman Studies* 33 (1943), 29–35. An economic explanation of Marxist nature is given by F. W. Walbank, *The Decline of the Roman Empire in the West* (London, 1946). Agricultural developments are briefly discussed (with good bibliography) by C. E. Stevens in the second chapter of *Cambridge Economic History of Europe* 1 (Cambridge, 1942). Subsequent history is developed in the works of Ferdinand Lot [including *Les Invasions germaniques: La pénétration mutuelle du monde barbare et du monde romain* (2d ed.; Paris, 1945)] *et al.;* see also *Byzantium,* ed. Norman H. Baynes and H. St. L. Moss (Oxford, 1948).

On the political interrelations of state and Christianity, Kenneth M. Setton, *Christian Attitude towards the Emperor in the Fourth Century Especially as Shown in Addresses to the Emperor* (New York, 1941), is rich in illustrative material. Erik Peterson, *Der Monotheismus als politisches Problem* (Leipzig, 1935), and F. Martroye, "La Répression de la magie et le culte des gentils au IVᵉ siècle," *Revue historique de droit français et étranger* 4. ser. 9 (1930), 669–701, are not entirely convincing. The *Theodosian Code and Novels and the Sirmondian Constitutions* have recently been translated by Clyde Pharr *et al.* (Princeton, 1952).

Index

ALL dates are A.D. unless otherwise indicated. Persons are listed under the most familiar part of their name or under their *nomen*.